Applied Statistics For Agricultural Sciences

nipa books for everyone
PAPERBACKS

NIPA® GENX ELECTRONIC RESOURCES & SOLUTIONS P. LTD.

New Delhi-110 034

www.nipaers.com
Browse, Search, Read & Buy...
Print Books
eChapters
eBooks
Publishers
Forthcoming
Subject Catalogues
New Titles
Online Resources on:
✓ Current Affairs
✓ Reasoning, Logic & Aptitude
✓ Competitive Examinations
✓ English Language Lab
✓ Writing & Pronunciation Tools
✓ Personality Development
✓ Online Programmes for Professionals
✓ Interview Preparation
Pay Using
PhonePe
Google Pay
Paytm
PayPal
UPI
CCAvenue

Applied Statistics For Agricultural Sciences

D. VENKATESAN
Department of Statistics
Annamalai University
Annamalai Nagar - 608 002,
Tamil Nadu, India

books for everyone
PAPERBACKS
NIPA® GENX ELECTRONIC RESOURCES & SOLUTIONS P. LTD.
New Delhi-110 034

books for everyone
PAPERBACKS

NIPA® GENX ELECTRONIC RESOURCES & SOLUTIONS P. LTD.

101,103, Vikas Surya Plaza, CU Block
L.S.C. Market, Pitam Pura, New Delhi-110 034
Ph : +91 11 27341616, 27341717, 27341718
E-mail: newindiapublishingagency@gmail.com
www: www.nipabooks.com

For customer assistance, please contact
Phone: + 91-11-27 34 17 17
Fax: + 91-11- 27 34 16 16
E-Mail: feedbacks@nipabooks.com

ISBN:978-81-19002-20-7

Composed and Designed by NIPA®.

Preface

The book is an introductory text, presenting some of the basic concepts and techniques of Statistical inference. It has been written primarily to suit the students and research workers in the area of agricultural sciences.

An understanding of the logic and theory of statistics is essential for the students of agriculture who are expected to know the techniques of analysing data and drawing useful conclusions. It has been the intention of the author to keep the book at a readability level appropriate for students who do not have a mathematical background.

This book can serve as comprehensive reference source of statistical techniques helpful to agricultural research workers in the interpretation of data.

The author is grateful to the authorities of Annamalai University for granting permission to publish the book.

July, 2013

D.Venkatesan

Contents

Chapter – 1

Introduction

1.1 Definition of Statistics

Statistics has been defined differently by different 'Statisticians' from time to time. These definitions emphasize precisely the meaning, scope and limitations of the subject. The reasons for such a variety definitions may be stated as follows:

i. The field of utility of statistics has been increasing steadily and

ii. The word statistics has been used to give different meanings in singular (the science of statistical methods) and plural (numerical set of data) senses.

In order to have a clear grasp of the subject, we give below some selected definitions of statistics which are grouped under two main heads: 'Statistics as numerical data' and 'Statistics as Methods'. The former one is in plural sense and the latter singular sense.

1.2 Statistics as Numerical Data

i. 'Statistics are the classified facts representing the conditions of the people in a state..... specially those facts which can be stated in numerous or in tables of numerous or in any tabular or classified arrangement' **– Webster.**

ii. 'Statistics are numerical statement of facts in any department of enquiry placed in relation to each other' **– Bowley.**

iii. 'Statistics are measurement, enumerations or estimates of natural or social phenomena, usually systematically arranged, analysed and presented as to exhibit important inter – relationships among them'
– A.M. Tuttle.

iv. 'By statistics we mean quantitative data affected to a marked exten by multiplicity of causes' **– Yule and Kendall.**

v. 'Statistics may be defined as the aggregate of facts affected to a marked extent by multiplicity of causes, numerically expressed, enumerated or estimated according to a reasonable standard of accuracy, collected in a systematic manner, for a predetermined purpose and placed in relation to each other' **– Prof. Horace Secrist.**

The last definition, (v) according to Prof. Horace Secrist is more general, comprehensive, realistic and exhaustive. Hence it may be studied in detailed form.

1. Aggregate of facts

This means that a single item, even though numerically stated cannot be termed as statistics. For example a day's production of a commodity (single number) cannot reveal anything unless such informations collected for a period and for different commodities. Therefore the aggregate of the figures of births, deaths, scales, purchase, production, profits etc., over different times, places etc., will constitute statistics.

2. Affected to a marked extent by multiplicity of causes

Numerical figures should be influenced by a large number of forces. For example (i) the phenomenon of falling sales in a business firm may be caused by a general recession in business, lack of sales promotion effort, appearance of strong competitive forces, etc., and (ii) the yield of a crop depends upon the factors like soil conditions, use of fertilizers, rainfall, methods of cultivation etc.,

Statistics helps in finding out the most potent and the most proximate cause out of the many that affect a business phenomenon. In the case of example (i) it is passive by statistical techniques to determine the factors responsible for the decline in sales.

3. Numerically expressed

This means that the facts must be numerically or quantitatively expressed. The quantitative characteristics or attributes which cannot be measured quantitatively such as intelligence, honesty etc., cannot be included in statistics unless they are quantified by assigning certain scores as quantitative measure of assessment. For example, the intelligence quotient could be regarded as statistics of attributes.

4. Enumerated or estimated according to reasonable standard of accuracy

The data pertaining to any field of enquiry can be obtained by counting or measuring or it may be estimated statistically when enumerations not feasible or involves inordinately high cost. In the case enumeration data will be exact and accurate. But the estimated values will not be exact and accurate. But the estimated values will not be as precise and accurate as the actual values. The degree of accuracy of the estimated values depends on the nature and purpose of the enquiry. However, certain rules prescribed for rounding - up etc., to achieve a fair degree of accuracy. For example, while calculating the retail prices of commodities accuracy will be aimed in terms of fractions of a rupee whereas while measuring distance between two far off places it may be in terms of metres or kilometres.

5. Collected in a systematic manner

The collection of data must be carefully and systematically done. Because the data collected in a haphazard manner will not conform to the reasonable standards of accuracy and the statistical processing, however nicely done, would not yield the desired results. Sometime they will mislead us.

6. Collected for a pre – determined purpose

The scope and purpose of inquiry should be stated clearly before actually collecting the data. The definition of various terms, units of collection and measurement also help in ensuring that the data is relevant to the purpose on hand. For example, if the purpose of enquiry is to measure the cost of living Index for the industrial workers we should select only these commodities or items which are consumed or utilised by persons belonging to this group. Thus for such an index, the collection of the data on the commodities like cars, refrigerators, high quality cosmetics etc., will be absolutely useless.

7. Comparable

The main object of collection of statistical data is to facilitate a comparative or relative study. For example the number of workers and the production of a commodity/commodities for different months constitute statistics, since they are comparable. However, the data relating to the size of the shoe of an individual and his intelligence quotient do not constitute statistics as they are not comparable. In order to make valid comparison the data should be homogeneous that is, they should relate to the same phenomenon or subject.

From the above explanations on Horace Secrist's definition, as we may conclude that:

'All statistics are numerical statements of facts but

all numerical statements of facts are not statistics.

8. Statistics as methods

Statistics has been defined as a science which provides tools for analysis and interpretation of data collected for the purpose of decision making in various fields of scientific enquiry. Hence we give below the definition of statistics used in singular sense that is statistics as statistical methods.

i. 'Statistics may be called the science of counting' **– Bowley, A.L.**

ii. 'Statistics is the science of estimates and probabilities' **– Bodding Ton.**

iii. 'Statistics is the science which deals with the methods of collecting, classifying, presenting, comparing and interpreting numerical data collected to throw some light on any sphere of enquiry' **– Selligman.**

iv. 'Statistics may be defined as the science of collection, presentation, analysis and interpretation of numerical data' **– Croxton and Cowden.**

v. 'The science and art of handling aggregate of facts- serving, enumeration, recording, classifying and otherwise systematically treating them' **– Harlow**

The first and the second definition are inadequate. The other definitions are simple, comprehensive and satisfactory.

1.3 Function of Statistics

The basic function of statistics is to simplify complexity and to present facts in such a form that they are readily understandable and comparable by human mind. The following are the important functions of the science of statistics:

i. *It Presents Facts in a Definite Form:* Any conclusions stated numerically are definite and hence more convincing than conclusions stated qualitatively. Statistics presents facts in a precise and definite form and thus helps for a proper comprehension of what is stated.

ii. *It Simplifies Mass of Figures:* Human mind is unable to assimilate a mass of complicated data at a stretch. Statistical techniques like frequency distribution, measure of central tendency, measure of dispersion, diagrammatic and graphic representations etc., make these figures intelligible, and understandable.

iii. *It Facilitates Comparison:* The various statistical methods facilitate comparison and enable useful conclusions to be drawn. Statistical devices like averages, ratios, rate, coefficients, etc., are the tools that make comparison possible between two phenomena.

iv. *It Studies Relationship:* Another function of statistics is to study relationship between two or more phenomena, for example the relationship between price and demand or supply of the commodity. It also helps in finding out association between two or more attributes, for example the association between the colour of the eyes of the father and the son.

v. *It Enlarge Individual Experience:* The proper function of statistics is to enlarge individual experience and to find solutions of various problems. It would not be an exaggeration to say that many fields of knowledge would have remained closed to mankind for ever but for the efficient and useful technique and methodology of the science of statistics.

vi. *It Help in the Formation of Policies:* Scientific analysis of statistical data constitutes the starting point in all policy making. Decisions relating to import and export of various commodities, production of particular products etc., are all based on statistics.

vii. *It Helps in Formulating and Testing Hypothesis:* Statistical techniques are more useful in formulating and testing hypothesis and to develop new theories. For example hypothesis like whether the credit squeeze is effective in checking price increases, whether students have benefited by the extra coaching, etc. can be verified by appropriate statistical tools.

viii. *It Help in Forecasting:* Plans and policies of organizations are invariably formulated well in advance of the time of their implementation. A knowledge of future trends is very helpful in framing suitable policies and plans. For example a businessman on the basis of past figures of sales can estimate how much he should produce in the coming year and then he can adjust his productive capacity in accordance with that figure.

ix. *It Measures Uncertainty:* Statistical devices help not only in ascertaining the chance of the occurrence of an event but also in finding out the total effect of any uncertain event if the consequences of various occurrences are known. For this purpose the probability estimates are employed depending on the nature of the enquiry.

1.4 Divisions of Statistics

The statistical theory can be divided into two main categories:

i. Descriptive statistics

ii. Inductive statistics

i. Descriptive statistics includes any kind of data processing which is designed to summarizes, or describe, important features of the data without going any further, that is without attempting to infer anything that foes beyond the data themselves. For example the descriptive figures or constants are mean, median, standard deviation, histogram etc.

ii. When sample descriptions are used to infer some information about the population, that is, analysis requires generalization which go beyond the data, the subject is called Inductive Statistics or Statistical Inference. This division includes two types of problems, namely estimation and tests of hypothesis.

1.5 Importance and Scope of Statistics

The importance of statistics is seen from the following points.

Statistics is the tool in the hands of mankind to translate a multitude of complex facts into simple and understandable statements of facts, without statistics the facts may remain remote from the domain of our understanding. Statistics lends precision to our ideas. It enriches and enlarges individual experience. Our knowledge of things like national income, individual production, consumption pattern or population or natural resources shall not be definite without statistics.

The scope of statistics is now so vast and ever – expanding. It is different from what it was sometime back. Formerly it was conceived as a statecraft only. But in modern times it has become a universally applicable science. The word statistics is no longer confined to such facts and figures as are required by the state for its official purposes. In modern times it pervades all departments of enquiry. In short the scope of statistics has now stretched over all those branches of human knowledge in which the grasp of the significance of large numbers is looked for. Statistics is a tool of all sciences indispensable to research and intelligent judgement and has become a recognised discipline in its own right. There is hardly any field whether it be trade, industry or commerce, economics, biology, botany, astronomy physics, chemistry, education, medicine, sociology or psychology where statistical tools are not applicable.

The importance and scope of statistics can very well be appreciated from the applications of statistics in the various fields.

i. Statistics in planning

Planning is indispensable for the best use of the nation's resources and without planning all the economic policies of the Government will be a leap in the dark. Statistics is indispensable in planning and the various decisions of the Government with regard to import, export, production etc. are all based on facts and figures. In fact statistics serves as the foundation of the super structure of planning. In India, the use of Statistics in planning was visualized long back. The National Sample Survey was primarily set up in 1950 for the collection of statistical data for planning in India.

ii. Statistics in business and management

Now-a-days the problems of the business enterprises are becoming complex and they are using more and more statistics in decision - making. So some knowledge of statistics is essential today for businessman to make a scientific analysis of the past records in order to forecast the future business conditions.

The manager and a team of management executives is imperative for the efficient handling of the various operations like sales, purchases, production, marketing, control, finance, etc., of the big business house. It is here that statistical data and the powerful statistical data and the powerful statistical tools of probability, sampling techniques. Tests of hypotheses, estimation theory and so on play an indispensable role. According Ya-Lan chou, 'Statistics is a method of decision making in the face of uncertainty on the basis of numerical data and calculated risks'. These words reflect the application of statistics in business.

The techniques of time series analysis and business forecasting enable the businessman to predict with a fair degree of accuracy the effect of a large number of variables. It is also used in business to study the trend in order to obtain the estimates of the probable demand of the goods.

The study of Index numbers of prices which are called Economic Barometers enables the businessman to have an idea about the purchasing power of money.

The study of statistical quality control, through the tools of control charts and inspection plans, is Indispensable to any business organization for ensuring that the quality of the manufactured product is in conformity wit the consumer's specifications.

Statistical methods have also been used very widely by business organisations in market and product research, investment policies, selection of personnel, inventory control, sales control and many others.

iii. Statistics in economics

Statistics is indispensable in Economics. It is almost impossible to find a problem in economics which does not require an extensive use of statistical data. Important phenomena in all branches of economics can be described, compared and correlated with the help of statistics. Statistics of production help us to adjust the supply according to demand. Statistics of consumption enable us to find out the way in which the people of different strata of society spend their incomes. How to remove poverty, unemployment, inequality of incomes etc., are the various problems that are best solved statistically.

The importance of statistics can also be seen in other disciplines (a) Physical Sciences, (b) Natural Sciences, (c) Social Sciences, (d) Biology and Medical Sciences and (e) Psychology and education.

Besides these, statistics are useful to bankers, brokers, insurance companies, social workers, chambers of commerce and the politicians.

1.6 Collection of Data

Data constitute the foundation for statistical analysis. Government, business houses and individuals collect statistical data required to carryout their activities efficiently and effectively. Similarly for any statistical enquiry, whether it is in economics, business managements or social sciences, the basic problem is to collect facts and figures relating to particular phenomenon under study.

The person who conducts the statistical enquiry hat is counts or measures the characteristic under study is known as the investigator.

The persons from whom the information is collected are known as respondents or source of information and the items on which the measurements are taken are called the statistical units.

The process of counting or enumeration or measurement together with the systematic recording of results is called the collection of statistical data.

Collected data provides the basic raw material from which analysis is made principles are formulated and conclusions are drawn. The value of statistical analysis and the validity of the conclusion will depend upon the care and accuracy with which the original figures or data have been obtained. Hence utmost care must be exercised in the collection of data.

1.7 The Preliminaries in Collecting Data

The following are the five points which the investigator should examine carefully before commencing work of collection of data.

a. Objectives and scope of the enquiry.

b. Statistical units to be used.

c. Sources of information

d. Method of data collection

e. Degree of accuracy aimed at in the final results.

(a) Every statistical inquiry is conducted for a certain object and it has its won scope. Before undertaking the work of collection of data the object of the problem at hand must be defined as clearly as possible. For example the investigator may be interested in finding out the strength of unemployed people in the country. There will be various aspects of the problems such as the unemployment either in rural or urban areas, educated or uneducated and so on. Unless the investigator is sure about the object of the inequiry, he cannot know for definite as to what facts are to be collected. If the object of the enquiry is properly determined and defined many difficulties of the collection and analysis of the data shall be automatically removed. If the object and scope of inquiry are not determined before hand, this will lead to confusion and misunderstanding and the conclusions drawn may be unreliable.

(b) The collection of statistics necessitates measurement or counting and as such it is necessary to define clearly the units or unit in which the data are to be collected and these definitions should be observed throughout the investigation. The requisites of a statistical unit are as follows:

i. it should be unambiguous

ii. it should be specific

iii. it should be stable

iv. it should be appropriate to the enquiry

v. it should be uniform

The statistical units may be broadly classified as follows:

i. *Unit of enumeration:* In any statistical enquiry, whether it is conducted by sample method or census method, unit of enumeration is the basic unit on which the observations are to be made and the unit is to be decided in advance before conducting the enquiry keeping in view the objectives of the enquiry. The unit of enumeration may be an individual, a household, a family, a firm etc.

ii. *Unit of recording:* The units of recording are the units in terms of which the data are recorded or in other words they are the units of quantification. The units of recording for quantity may be weight, say, in kilograms, quintals etc.

iii. *Units of analysis and interpretation*: The units of analysis and interpretation are those units in the form of which the statistical data are ultimately analysed and interpreted. It should be decided whether the results would be expressed in absolute or relative measurements. The units of analysis and interpretation help comparisons between different sets of data with respect to time, place or environment. Generally they are rates, ratios and percentages.

(c) Once the object and scope of the enquiry and the statistical units to be used have been laid down, the next step is to decide about the sources from which data are to be collected. Broadly speaking the sources of information may be divided into (i) primary and (ii) secondary.

If the data are collected originally by the investigator for his specific need of the particular enquiry, it is termed as primary data. The source which supplied the primary data is called the primary source.

If the investigator makes use of the data which had been earlier collected by some one else, it is termed secondary data. The source which supplied the secondary data is called secondary source.

For example census data collected by the government are primary data but the same data becomes secondary when used by others. Whether to use primary or secondary data will depend on a number of considerations, for example the purpose and scope of enquiry, the degree of accuracy desire, accuracy desired, availability of funds and time etc. Collection of primary data consists of some problems with regard to the methods of collection. Whereas the collection of secondary data has no problem because the data have already been collected under a given set of definitions of various terms and units used. It requires only the careful editing and scrutiny with respect to their reliability, suitability and adequacy.

(d) If primary data are to be collected a decision has to be taken whether (i) Census method or (ii) Sample method is to be used for data collection. A census method or enquiry implies complete enumeration of each unit of the universe or population, while a sample method relates only to a few representative items of the whole lot selected at random or deliberately. For example, if the data about the consumption pattern of the people of Chidambaram town are to be collected, an investigator has to decide as to whether heads of each family are to be contacted or whether heads of only a few families are to be contacted. In the former case, it is the census method whereas in the latter it is the sample method. Whether a particular enquiry should be of census type or sample type depends on a variety of factors such as:

i. The availability of resources, (ii) the time factor, (iii) the degree of accuracy desired and, (iv) the nature and scope in the problem. A sample method requires less time and money than a census method. In some situations such as population being infinite or very large, census methods fails. Moreover, it is not practicable if the enumeration or testing of the units (objects) is destructive, for example for testing of the breaking strength of chalk, testing the life of electric bulbs or tubes etc. In case of sample method the size of the sample and the technique of sampling like simple random sampling, stratified random sampling, systematic sampling etc. are to be decided. The detailed discussion of sampling theory is given in the next lesson.

e. The investigator has to decide about the degree of accuracy that he wants to attain in the inequiry. In may be pointed out that the absolute accuracy is seldom possible in statistical work because, (i) statistics are based on estimates, (ii) tools of measurement are not always perfect and (iii) there may be unintentional bias on the part of the investigator, enumerator or informant.

Degree of accuracy desired primarily depends upon the object and scope of enquiry. An idea about the precision aimed at is extremely helpful in deciding about the method of data collection and the size of the sample.

For example measuring the height of an individual in centimetres in material whereas measuring distance between two cities say Madras and Delhi in centimetres and metres can safely be neglected. The information gained from any previous completed sample study on the subject in the form of precision achieved for a given sample size may serve as a useful guide.

1.8 Methods of Collecting Primary Data

After going through the preliminaries discussed in the above section, we have come to the problem of obtaining or gathering the desired information or data. The collection of data refers to a purposive gathering of information relevant to the subject matter the study from the units under investigation. The method of collection of data depends mainly upon the nature, object and the scope of enquiry on one hand and the availability of resources and the time on the other. Statistical data may be classified into primary and secondary depending upon the nature of data and mode of collection.

For the specific enquiry the data gathered by actual observation, measurements and count and direct recording the course of an investigation is called primary data. This is called primary because it is collected from the very source where the information get generated.

Data which are not originally collected, rather obtained from only one or unpublished sources are known as secondary data.

The difference between the primary and the secondary data is only one of the degree of detachment with the original source. The data which is primary in the hands of one may become secondary in the hands of the other. For example, if it is desired to conduct an investigation into the working conditions of the workers of a big textile mill, the facts collected by the investigators directly from the workers themselves would be termed as primary data. But if the information is obtained from a report prepared by its trade union for its own purpose will be called secondary data. Like wise the data relating to mortality (death rates) and fertility (birth rates) in India published by the office of Registrar General of India, New Delhi are Primary whereas the same reproduced by the United Nations Organisation (U.N.O) is concerned. For this data, the office of Registrar General of India is the primary source while U.N.O is the secondary source.

The investigators must determine whether to use primary data or secondary data in an investigation. The choice between the two depends on the following considerations:

i. The nature, objective and scope of enquiry.

ii. The time and finance at the disposal of the agency.

iii. The degree of precision aimed at the status of the agency that is whether government – State government – State or Central, or private institution or an individual.

Primary data are generally used in those cases where the secondary data do not provide an adequate basis for analysis. Secondary data are increasingly used because the published statistics are now available covering diverse fields so that an investigator finds required data readily available to him in many cases.

The methods commonly used for the collection of primary data are enumerated below:

1. Direct personal investigation
2. Indirect oral interviews
3. Information from correspondents
4. Mailed questionnaire
5. Questionnaire sent through enumerators

1. This method consists in the collection of data personally by the investigator from the sources concerned. This method can take the following two ways:

   a. *Interview:* According to this method, the investigator personally observes and records the behaviour rather than ask for interrogation the person from whom the information is being sought. This is the most useful method in some marketing studies where consumer behaviour is studied. Instead of asking whether the customers prefer a particular brand of tooth-paste, it is better to observe their behaviours in well selected markets offering them an opportunity of selecting from various brands.

   b. *Observation:* Under this method the investigator personally observes and records the behaviour rather than ask for interrogation the person from whom the information is being sought. This is the most useful method in some marketing studies where consumer behaviour is studied. Instead of asking whether the customers prefer a particular brand of tooth-paste, it is better to observe their behaviours in well selected markets offering them an opportunity of selecting from various brands.

Merits and Demerits of the Method

Merits

i. This method generally ensures accuracy because of personal touch and supervision of the investigator.

ii. When the field of enquiry is small the work can be finished in much less time as compared with the questionnaire method.

iii. This method is also economical provided the field of investigation is small.

iv. When the audience is approached personally by the investigator, the response is likely to be more encouraging.

Demerits

i. This method is confined only to intensive and localized investigations. Where the field of enquiry is vast this method proves to be too expensive and time consuming.

ii. There are chances of personal prejudice and bias of the investigators as he is the sole incharge of data collection. If he is biased he can draw altogether different conclusions and thus make a misuse of statistics.

Hence we conclude that this method is suitable only where the scope of investigation is narrow and greater accuracy is desired. In cases where the scope of investigation is wide other methods should be employed.

2. The indirect oral investigation is used in case where it is not possible or desirable to approach people directly for informations or data are of complex nature or when there is unwillingness or indifference on the part of the informants. For example, if we want to get information on certain social evils like a person's addition to drinking, gambling or smoking etc, the concerned person will be reluctant to furnish correct information or he may give wrong information.

Under this method instead of directly approaching the informants, the investigator interviews several third party (friends, relatives etc.) informants who are supposed to possess information on the problem under investigation. Thus the method consists in collection of data through the enumerators appointed for this purpose. A small list of questions pertaining to the subject matter of enquiry is prepared. These questions are then put to the persons known as witnesses or informants, who are in possession of such information and their replies are recorded. All enquiry committees and commissions appointed by the government adopt this method. For example, an inequiry into communal tensions will require views of various sections of the community.

The success of this method depends mainly upon (i) the representative character of the witnesses who are interviewed and their personal knowledge about the problem under investigation, (ii) the prejudices and desires of witnesses about supplying information, (iii) the personal quality and the ability of the interviewer to draw out information form witnesses by means of appropriate questions and cross-question, (iv) the experience, sincerity and honesty of the investigator.

Merits

i. A wide area can be covered under method.

ii. Prejudices of people when approached directly can be avoided by interrogating third party informants.

iii. This method saves time, money and labour. Better results can be obtained with limited means.

Demerits

i. The information obtained by this method is not sometimes very reliable. Because it depends largely on the nature and quality of the witnesses or enumerators from whom the information is obtained.

ii. Witnesses or enumerators influenced by certain considerations may deliberately twist the results and bias the study.

3. In this method the information is not collected formally by the investigator or the enumerators. This method consists in the appointment of local agents (popularly known as correspondents) by the investigator in the different parts of the field enquiry.

Necessary instructions are given to these correspondents. The correspondents then collect the required information and transmit it to the investigator for further processing. The method is particularly adopted by newspaper agencies which require information regularly in different fields like sports, accidents, business stock and share market, politics and so on. Government agencies also use this method for the collection of information about prices of products to construct wholesale price index numbers. The agricultural statistics regarding crop estimates are gathered in our country by this method.

Merits

1. This method is quite ideal when information is needed from a vast area and where local estimates are needed on a continuing basis.
2. This method is very cheap and expeditious. The quality of data collected is also good due to long experience of local representatives.

Demerits

The data collected by this method may not be reliable because it is subjected to the bias of the local agent. Hence this techniques of data collection is suited of the purpose of investigation is to obtain rough and approximate estimates only and were a high degree accuracy is not desired.

This method of collection of primary data involves in preparing a questionnaire which will contain a number of blank tables and questions pertaining to the object under investigation with bank spaces for giving the answers. This questionnaire is then sent to the informants by post. The necessary instructions as to how this questionnaire is to be filled are also sent. The informants are also requested to return this same within a specified time. The informants after filling up this questionnaire sent it back to the investigator.

This method is widely employed by private individuals and research organisations. This method suffers mainly a problem in communication and the success of the method depends largely upon:

i. The ability with which this questionnaires are prepared.

ii. The degrees of response from the informants, and

iii. The ability and knowledge of the informants.

   i. The mailed questionnaire methods are the most economical method in terms of time, money and man power (labour) provided the respondents supply the information in time.

   ii. This method can be adopted very conveniently where the field of investigation is very vast and the informants are spread over a wide area.

   iii. Errors due to the personal biases of the investigators or enumerators are completely eliminated as the information is supplied directly by persons concerned in his own handwriting. The information so obtained is original and authentic.

Demerits

i. Where the informants are illiterate people, this method cannot be adopted.

ii. The informants may not return the questionnaire at all or may not return in time and even if they return, some returns may be inaccurately and improperly filled.

iii. This method is not flexible. In case of inadequate and incomplete answers it is difficult to obtain supplementary or incomplete answers it is difficult to obtain supplementary or correcting information. Also it is difficult to verify the accuracy of the answers given.

Hence this method can be used where the field of investigation is very vast and the investigator wants quick results at a low cost. However this method presumes that informants are literate so that they can fill up the questionnaire.

First it is desirable to make a distinction between a questionnaire and a schedule. Questionnaire is a list of questions which are answered by the respondent himself in his own handwriting while a schedule is the device of obtaining answers to the questions in a form which is filled by the interviewers or enumerators in a face to face situation with the respondents.

Under this method, a team of enumerators is selected. These enumerators are supplied with standard schedules or questionnaires to be filled up by them or by the informants. Specific training and instructions are given to them regarding the way the informations be elicited and the schedules be filled. The main difference between the mailed enquiry and this method is that whereas in the former the material is sent to the informants by post, in this case the enumerators carry these personally to the informants. The enumerators explain clearly the objectives of the survey, the definitions of the basic concepts and rules to the informants and record their responses themselves.

This method is used by big business houses, large public enterprises and research institutions like National Council of Applied Economics Research (NCAER), Federation of Indian Chambers of Commerce and Industries (FICCI) and so on. Population census all over the world is conducted by this technique.

Merits

i. This method can be adopted even in the case of illiterate informants or population.

ii. The data which are obtained by the method is more accurate and reliable. Because information given by informants can be checked on the spot by cross-examination and by supplementary questions.

iii. The problem of non-response on the part of informants is minimised as the enumerators personally obtain the information.

Demerits

i. If this method is costliest for collecting primary data because of a good deal, money should be on the maintenance and training of the enumerators.

ii. If the enumerators are negligent and are untrained, correct information cannot be collected.

iii. The success of the method also lies to great extent on the effic and wisdom with which the schedule or questionnaire equiped.

Drafting the Questionnaire

The drafting of a questionnaire is an art. Since success of a statistical investigation or quality of its results depends mainly upon tactful drafting, great care is needed in the layout of the questionnaire and the questions framed. Though drafting of a questionnaire require requires skill, wisdom, efficiency and experience, there is no hard and fast rules to be laid down for designing or framing a questionnaire, However the following are some principles or requires which may be helpful in framing questionnaire.

i. Questionnaire should be divided into two parts. The first part should contain the objective of the enquiry and the second the questions. The first part should contain the purpose of the survey and how the informants would tend to benefit from it. There should be an appeal which should assure the informants that the information rendered will be kept confidential.

ii. The size of the questionnaire should be as small as possible.

iii. Questions should be simple, clear, unambiguous and brief.

iv. As far as possible the questions should be such that they can be answered by 'Yes' or 'No' or simple numbers.

v. The questions should be arranged in a natural logical sequence.

vi. Questions should be such that they will be answered without bias.

vii. the questions in the questionnaire may be broadly classified as follows:

   a. ***Short Questions:*** In such questions possible answers are suggested by the framers of the questionnaire and the respondent is required to tick one of them. Short questions can further be subdivided into simple alternative questions and multiple choice questions.

   b. ***Open Questions:*** Open question are those in which no alternative answers are suggested and the respondents are at liberty to express their frank and independent opinions as the problem in their own words.

viii. The questionnaire should be so designed as to provide internal checks on the accuracy of the information supplied by the informants including some connected questions at least with respect to matters which are fundamental to the enquiry.

1.9 Sources of Secondary Data

Secondary data is one which is collected by some earlier agency but is used and analysed by any other for its own use. Hence the collection of secondary data does not arise.

There are various published and unpublished sources of secondary data. The published sources are:

1. Official publications of the Central, State and Local Governments.
2. Reports of Committees and Commissions.
3. Publications brought about by research workers and educational associations.
4. Trade and technical journals.
5. Report and publications of trade associations, chambers of commerce, bank etc.
6. Official publications of foreign governments or international bodies like U.N.O., O.E.E.C. etc.

1.10 Unpublished Source

All statistics are not published. Statistics of a wide range and variety can be compiled out of data taken from returns, registers and other records in the course of administrative work. A major source of statistics produced by government, private and public concerns, business associations and international organizations is based on the data drawn from the internal records. Two important types of administrative records from which data are collected are:

i. Documents prepared for purchase of registration, applications of permits, licences, loans etc.

ii. Records relating to internal activities of institutions, example: cost records, periodical profit and loss statements, balance sheet and other periodical progress reports.

Secondary data requires proper editing. Statistical material obtained from secondary sources is not always as reliable as that from the primary source. Such data should not therefore be used blindly. A careful and searching enquiry must be made as to the meaning and limitations of the secondary data.

If the secondary data satisfies the qualities such as reliability, suitability, representative and adequate, then it can be used.

1.11 Limitations of Statistics

Although statistics is indispensable to almost all sciences – social, physical and natural, and is very widely used in most of spheres of human activity, it suffers from the following limitations.

i. Statistics deals only with aggregate of facts and not with individuals.

ii. Statistics does not study qualitative phenomenon.

iii. Statistics laws are tone only on an average.

iv. Statistics is liable to be misused.

These are the chief limitations of the science of statistics. Those who use statistical methods must be aware of these limitations. Otherwise they are likely to misuse this science.

Exercise

1. Explain the meaning of statistics in (i) Singular and (ii) Plural senses
2. Discuss briefly the functions and divisions of Statistics
3. Explain the applications of statistics in Business and Management

4. What are the scope and limitations of Statistics?
5. Discuss the preliminary steps which should be taken before commencing the work of collection of data.
6. Explain the various methods of collection the data.
7. Distinguish between primary and secondary data. State the chief sources of secondary data.
8. Explain the various methods of collecting primary data.
9. What is a questionnaire? What are requisites of a good questionnaire?
10. Define a statistical unit and explain what should be the essential requirements of a good statistical unit.

❑❑❑

Chapter – 2

Classification, Tabulation and Graphical Representation

2.1 Quantitative Classification

It the data are classified on the basis of phenomenon which is capable of quantitative measurement like age, height, weight, prices, production, income expenditure, sales, profits, etc., it is termed as quantitative classification. The quantitative phenomenon under study is known as variable. For example the daily incomes of different retail shops in a town may be classified as under.

Table 2.1 : Daily earnings in rupees of 100 retail shops in a town

Daily earnings	No. of retail shops
Upto 100	7
101 - 200	22
201 - 300	31
301 - 400	25
401 – 500	9
above 500	6

In the above classification, the daily earnings of the shops are termed as variable and the number of shops in each class or group as the frequency. This classification is called grouped frequency distribution.

2.2 Variable

Any character which varies in magnitude or quality is called a variable. For example (i) the height (in centimeters) of a student, (ii) the annual, monthly or daily production of a commodity, (iii) the number of children in a family, (iv) the number of road accidents in a month, etc., are variables. The first two variables (i) and (ii) assume only isolated values or integers. Variables are usually denoted by the symbols X,Y,Z ... Hence there are two types of variables. They are (a) Continuous variable and (b) Discrete variable.

a. Continuous variable is a variable which is capable of taking all possible values in certain range.

For example (i) the age years of a person, (ii) the income in rupees of family, (iii) the weight in kilogram of student, (iv) the price in rupees of a commodity etc., are continuous variables.

b. Discrete variable is a variable which is not capable of taking all possible values in a range and thus there are gaps between one value and the other.

For example the numbers of births, deaths in a place, the number of houses in a city etc., are discrete variable.

2.3 Array

The data before it is arranged and analysed is called raw data. It is 'raw' because it is unprocessed by statistical by statistical methods.

The data array is one of the simplest ways to present data. It arranges the values from the lowest value to the highest in ascending order or from highest to the lowest in descending order.

The following tables 2.2 and 2.3 illustrate the raw data and data array in ascending order relating to the average annual Inventory Turnover in weeks for 20 large construction firms.

Table 2.2 : Raw data of Inventory Turnover in weeks for 20 construction firms

2.3	3.4	4.9	4.8	5.5
5.5	4.0	4.1	5.1	5.4
4.7	3.4	4.3	5.5	4.7
3.8	4.2	5.5	4.9	4.9

Table 2.3 : Data array of Inventory Turnover in weeks for 20 construction firms

2.0	4.0	4.7	4.9	5.5
3.4	4.1	4.7	4.9	5.5
3.4	4.2	4.8	5.1	5.5
3.8	4.3	4.9	5.4	5.5

Data arrays offer several advantages over raw data:

i. We can quickly notice the lowest and highest values in the data.

ii. We can see whether any values appear more than once in the array.

iii. We can easily divide the data into sections.

iv. We can observed the distance between succeeding values in the data.

Inspite of these advantages, sometimes a data array is not helpful. Since it lists every observation, it does not condense or compress the data. One way we can compress data is to use a frequency table of frequency distribution.

2.4 Frequency Distribution

A frequency distribution is an arrangement where a number of observations with similar or closely related values are put in separate groups, each group being n order of magnitudes in the arrangement. In short frequency distribution is an arrangement based on magnitudes.

In the words of Croxton and Cowden, "Frequency distribution is a statistical table which shows the set of all distinct values of the variable arranged in order of magnitude, either individually or in groups, with their corresponding frequencies side by side".

Thus a frequency distribution has two columns, on its left there are sizes or magnitudes or values (that is class intervals) and on its right the number of times a value or a group of value has repeated.

Table - 2.4 illustrates the frequency distribution of Inventory Turnover in weeks for 20 construction firms using the values from

Table 2.4 : Frequency distribution of inventory turnover in weeks for 20 construction firms.

Class (groups of similar values of data Points)	Frequency (number of observations in each class)
2.0 to 2.5	1
2.6 to 3.1	0
3.2 to 3.7	2
3.8 to 4.3	5
4.4 to 4.9	6
5.0 to 5.4	6

Thus a frequency distribution shows the number or observations from the data set that fall into each of the classes. An obvious advantage of the frequency distribution is that it shortens a lengthy individual series due to the fact that a short series is definitely easier to manage and process. If the number of observations is very large it is absolutely necessary to resort to grouping. Grouping may be done in two ways, depending on the nature of data.

2.4.1 Discrete frequency distribution

Discrete frequency distribution shows the number of times each value and not to a range of values, of the variable occurs in the data set. This is so in case of a discrete variable where exact measurements are possible in whole numbers. For example, the number of children in a house, the number of companies registered in a country and etc. The process of preparing this type of distribution is very simple. We have just to count the number of times a particular value of the variable is repeated which is called the frequency of that class. The counting is facilitated through the technique the technique of Tally-Marks or Tally-Bars as explained below:

In the first column we place all the possible values of the variable from the lowest to the highest. In the second column a vertical bar (1) called the Tally-mark is put against the value of the variable whenever it occurs in the data set. After a particular value has occurred four times, for the fifth occurrence we put a cross tally mark (/) and the first four tally marks like give us a block of 5. To facilitate counting, blocks of five bars are prepared and some spaces is left in between each block.

After puttering tally marks for all the values in the data set, we count the number of times each value is repeated and write it against the corresponding number (value of the variable) in the third column, entitled frequency. This type of representation of the data is called discrete or ungrouped frequency distribution. The following example gives the discrete frequency distribution of the data.

Example

In a survey of 40 families in a village, the number of children per family was recorded and the following data obtained

1	2	6	4	0	5	3	1
7	3	5	0	2	2	4	2
8	5	2	6	4	3	2	3
7	5	8	3	6	7	3	6
9	9	3	5	7	4	4	5

Construct the frequency of distribution for the above data.

Frequency Distribution of the Number of Children

No. of Children	Tally marks	Frequency (OR) Number of familires
0	11	2
1	11	2
2	~~1111~~ 1	6
3	~~1111~~ 11	7
4	~~1111~~ 1	6
5	~~1111~~	5
6	1111	4
7	1111	4
8	11	2
9	11	2
Total		40

Note

1. It is clear from the table that the number of children (variable) varied from 0 to 9. There were 2 families with no child, 7 families with 3 children each and two families with 9 children.
2. If the range of values of a variable is large, this method of representation will not condense the data. To condense the data the first step consists in classifying the data into different classes (or class intervals) by dividing the entire range of the values of the variable into a suitable number of groups called class intervals.

2.4.2 Grouped frequency distribution

Whenever the range of values of the variable is large (that is the data set consists large number of different values) for example 0 to 100 or 15 to 200 and if thc data is represented by discrete frequency distribution, the data will still remain unwidely and need further processing for condensation and statistical analysis. In these situations to condense the data the first step consists in classifying the data into different classes (or class intervals) by dividing the entire range of the values of the variable into a suitable number of groups of sub-ranges called classes and then recording the number of observations in each group (or class). This method of representation of the data is called grouped frequency distribution. To understand the contraction of the grouped frequency distribution, the following technical terms need definition and its calculations.

i. Class interval

The various groups into which the values of the variable are classified are known as class intervals or simply classes. For example, the symbol 25-35 represents a group or class which includes all the values from 25 to 35.

ii. Class limits

The two values (lowest and highest) specifying the class interval are called the class limits. The lowest value is called the lower limit and the highest value the upper limit of the class.

iii. Length or width of the class is defined as the difference between the upper and the lower limits of the class. That is

$$\text{Class mark or Mid point of a class} = \frac{\text{Lower Limit+ Upper Limit}}{2}$$

Example

Consider a class denoted as 25.50

i. The class 25-50 includes all the values in between 25 and 50

ii. The lower limit of the class is 25 and the upper limit 50.

iii. The length of the class is given by:

Length = Upper limit - Lower limit = 50-25 =25.

iv. The class mark or mid value of the class is given by

$$\text{Mid value} = \frac{\text{Lower Limit+ Upper Limit}}{2}$$

$$= (25 + 50) / 2 = 37.5$$

iii. Class frequency

The number of observations falling within a particular class interval is called is class frequency or simply frequency.

iv. Relative frequency of frequency density

It is the frequency of the class per unit of width and indicates the concentration of frequency in a class. It is given by the formula:

$$\text{Relative frequency} = \frac{\text{Class frequency}}{\text{Width of the class}}$$

v. Types of class

The classes should be clearly defined and should not lead to any ambiguity. Further they should be exhaustive and mutually exclusive (that is non-overlapping) so that any value of the variable corresponds to one and only one of the classes. In short there is one to one correspondence between the value of the variable and the class.

Generally there are three types of class intervals, namely (a) Exclusive, (b) Inclusive and (c) Open end classes.

a. Inclusive type classes

The classes of the type 15,-19, 20-29,30-49, 50-59 etc., in which both the upper and lower limits are included are called 'inclusive classes'. For instance the class interval 30-49 includes all the values from 30 to 49 both limits inclusive. The next value 50 is included in the next class 50-59 and so on. However, the fractional values between 49 and 50 cannot be accounted for in such a classification. Hence inclusive type of classification may be used for a grouped frequency distribution for discrete variable like number of accidents on the road, the number f members in a household, the number of eggs laid by a hen in a week, etc., where the variable takes only integral values. It cannot be used with advantage for the frequency distribution of continuous variable like the age, the height or the weight of a student, the amount of sales in rupees, etc. where all values (integral as well as fractional) are permissible

b. Exclusive type classes

Let us consider the distribution of heights (in inches) of a group of workers in factory into classes 65-69, 70-74 etc., each of magnitude 5 inches. This classification of inclusive type for bights is defective in the sense that it does not account for the workers with heights more than 60 inches but less than 70 inches. In a situation continuously without any gap as given below.

65 inches and more but less than 70

70 inches and more but less than 75

75 inches and more but less than 80 and so on.

In this case also class has the same length as 5 inches.

More precisely the above classes can be written as

65-70 that is $65 \leq x < 70$

70-75 that is $70 \leq x < 75$

75-80 that is $75 \leq x < 80$

....

....

Here the variable x represent the height of a worker. It is clearly seen that in the above classes the upper limit of each class are excluded from the respective classes. Such classes in which the upper limits are excluded from the respective classes and are included in the immediate next class are termed as exclusive classes'

From the above discussion it is clear that a choice between the inclusive method or exclusive method of classification will depend on the nature of the variable under study. For a data set relating to a discrete variable, the inclusive classes may be used while for a data set relating to continuous variable, the exclusive classes are to be used in the construction of the frequency distribution.

c. *Open end classes*

The class intervals of the form (i) 'Below 65' and (iii) 'Above 75 are called open end classes. The class 'Below 65' includes all the values which are less than 65 and the class 'Above 75' includes all the values which are greater than 75.

2.4.3 The construction of frequency distribution

It is difficult to lay down any hard and fast flues for constructing a frequency distribution as much depends on the nature of the given data and the object of the classification. However, the following general guidelines may be borne in mind for a good classification of the frequency data.

Step1: The nature of the variable whether it is continuous or discrete, should be determined. Because if the variable is continuous, the exclusive type of classes may be preferred and if the variable is discrete the inclusive type of classes may be preferred.

Step 2: For the sake of case in computation and comparison, the lengths of the class-intervals should be, wherever possible, be of equal width. However, in some cases, e.g., in the frequency distribution of the number of persons paying income-tax in different ranges of income or that of the number of children dying in different age-groups, it may be desirable to use unequal class-intervals due to greater concentration of observations in certain class intervals.

Step 3: The number of class-intervals should not ordinarily exceed 20 and should not be less than 5. With more than 20 classes the computations become unnecessarily tedious where as with less than 5 classes, a great deal of accuracy may be lost. The choice of number of classes basically depends upon:

a. the number of figures to be classified,

b. the magnitude of the figures,

c. the accuracy desired and

d. ease of calculation of further statistical analysis.

Step 4: The length of the class interval should generally be in multiples of 5 or 10 which would be convenient t handle and would facilitate computation. However, were the data necessitate the length of the interval of less than 5, it can be any value between 0 and 5.

Step 5: The starting point, that is the lower limit of the first class should either be zero or a multiple of 5. It may preferably be the least value of the data set.

Step 6: To ensure continuity and to get correct class interval we should adopt 'exclusive' method of classification. However, where inclusive method has been adopted it is necessary to make an adjustment to determine the correct class interval and to have continuity. The adjustment consists of finding the difference between the lower limit of the second class and the upper limit of the first class, dividing the difference by 2, sub-tracting the value so obtained from all the lower limits and adding the same value to all upper limits. That is the formula to find correction factor is given by:

$$\text{Correction factor} = \frac{(\text{Lower limit of 2nd class}) - (\text{Upper limit of the 1st class})}{2}$$

The following tables illustrate the method of adjustment or conversion of inclusive classes to exclusive classes when data are given by inclusive method.

Table 2.5 :

Monthly wages in Rupees	No. of workers
2500-2599	5
2600-2699	10
2700-2799	15
2800-2899	8
2900-2999	2

$$\text{Correction factor} = \frac{(\text{Lower limit of 2nd class}) - (\text{Upper limit of the 1st class})}{2}$$

$$= \frac{2600 - 2599}{2} = 0.5$$

Sub-tract 0.5 from the lower limits of all classes and add 0.5 to all upper limits. Then the adjusted classes or exclusive classes would be as in the following table:

Table 2.6 :

Monthly wages in Rupees	No. of workers
2499.5-2599.5	5
2599.5-2699.5	10
2699.5-2799.5	15
2799.5-2899.5	8
2899.5-2999.5	2

The length (Rs.100) and the mid values of the both type of classes are same. The following example examples make this point more clear.

Table 2.7 :

Class interval For the variable	Frequency
15-19.5	5
20-24.5	7
25-29.5	3

The correction factor = $\frac{20-\ 19.5}{2}=\frac{0.5}{2}=0.25$

After adjustment the classes will be:

Table 2.8 :

Class interval For the variable	Frequency
14.75-19.75	5
19.75-24.75	7
24.75-29.75	3

Step7: Since open-end distribution, that is either first or last of the class interval is open end class, presents problems of graphing and further analysis, the open end classes may be avoided.

The following example will illustrate the above point more clearly.

Example

The following data represent the hours spent in working by 50 workers for period of a month in a certain factory.

110	175	161	157	155	108	164	128	114	178
165	133	195	151	71	94	87	42	30	62
130	156	167	124	164	146	116	149	104	141
103	150	162	149	79	113	69	121	93	143
140	144	187	184	197	87	40	122	203	148

Construct a suitable frequency distribution.

Solution

Step 1: Since the variable, the hours spent in working by a worker is continuous, the exclusive type classes may be preferred.

Step 2: For the sake of ease in calculation we may consider the class intervals of equal width.

Step 3: If the class intervals of equal width are considered, the number of class intervals and the length of the class interval are interdependent. That is fixing the number of classes fixes the length of a class and conversely. The relationship between them is given by the formula:

$$\text{Number of class intervals} = \frac{\text{Highest value in the data} - \text{Lowest value in the data}}{\text{Length of class interval}}$$

$$\text{Length of class intervals} = \frac{\text{Highest value in the data} - \text{Lowest value in the data}}{\text{Number of class interval}}$$

Here, the highest value in the data =203

The lowest value in the data =30

Let the number of class intervals be 7. This value should be decided by the trial method or by Sturges' Rule which is given by the formula:

n = 1 + 3.322 log 10 N where n denotes the number of class intervals and N denotes the total number of observations in the data set.

$$\begin{aligned} \text{Here } N &= 50 \\ n &= 1 + 3.322 \log_{10} 50 \\ &= 1 + 3.322 \times 1.699 \\ &= 6.97 = 7 \text{ class intervals.} \end{aligned}$$

Step 4: Length of a class $= \dfrac{\text{Heigest value} - \text{Lowest value}}{\text{Number of class interval}}$

$$\frac{203-30}{6.97} = \frac{137}{6.97} = 24.8 \text{ hours} = 25 \text{ hours (Approx.)}$$

Step 5: Since the least value in the data is 30 hours, the lower limit of the first class interval is 30 hours. Hence the exclusive classes in hours are:

30-55, 55-80, 80-105, ... Using the technique of Tally-marks, the following frequency distribution table may be obtained.

Table 2.9 : Frequency distribution of the hours spent in working by 50 workers

Class interval for hours	Tally marks	Frequency (OR) No.Workers
30-55	111	3
55-80	1111	4
80-105	~~1111~~ 1	6
105-130	~~1111~~ 1111	9
130-155	~~1111~~ ~~1111~~ 11	12
155-180	~~1111~~ ~~1111~~ 1	11
180-205	~~1111~~	5
Total		50

Example

Given below are the numbers of tools produced by 100 workers in a factory

43	18	25	18	39	44	19	20	20	26
40	45	38	25	13	14	27	41	42	17
34	31	32	27	33	37	25	26	32	25
33	34	35	46	29	24	31	34	35	24
28	30	41	32	29	28	30	31	30	31
28	31	30	41	32	29	28	30	30	34
31	35	36	29	26	32	36	35	36	37
32	23	22	29	33	37	33	27	24	36
23	42	29	37	29	23	44	41	45	39
22	21	42	22	28	38	15	16	17	28

Form a frequency distribution by selecting suitable class intervals.

Solution: The number of tools produced by a worker is a variable which is discrete. Hence the inclusive type classes may be preferred. For the sake of ease in calculation we may consider the classes of equal length. The number of class interval (n) according to Sturges' Rule is:

$$n = 1 + 3.322 \log_{10} N$$

Here the total number of values, N = 100

$$n = 1 + 3.322 \log_{10} 100$$

$$= 1 + 3.322 \times 2$$

$$= 7.644 = 8 \text{ class intervals.}$$

Step 6 :

$$\text{Length of class} = \frac{\text{Highest value} - \text{Lowest value}}{\text{Number of class interval}}$$

$$= \frac{46 - 13}{7.94} = 4.3 = 5 \text{ tools approx.}$$

Since the least value in the data is 13, the lower limit of the first class is 13 tools

Frequency distribution of the number of tools produced by 100 workers in a factory.

Class interval for hours	Tally marks	Frequency (or) No.Workers
13-17	~~1111~~ 1	6
18-22	~~1111~~ 1111	9
23-27	~~1111~~ ~~1111~~ ~~1111~~ 111	18
28-32	~~1111~~ ~~1111~~ ~~1111~~ ~~1111~~ 1111	29
33-37	~~1111~~ ~~1111~~ ~~1111~~ ~~1111~~	20
38-42	~~1111~~ ~~1111~~ 11	12
43-47	~~1111~~ 1111 11	6
Total		100

2.5 Cumulative Frequency Distribution

A frequency distribution tells us how frequently a particular value of the variable (class) is occurring in a data set. However if we want to know the total number of observations which are 'less than' or greater than' a particular value of the variable (class), the frequency distribution table fails to give the information as such. This information can be obtained very conveniently from the cumulative frequency distribution.

The less than cumulative frequency (lef) corresponding to any value of a variable is the number of observations less than to that value in the data set. The less than cumulative frequency corresponding to a class is the total number of observations less than the upper limit of the class, that is the total of all the frequencies up to and including that class. (Exclusive class) Similarly the greater than cumulative frequency (g.c.f) corresponding to any value of a variable is the number of observations greater than or equal to that value in the data set. The greater than cumulative frequency corresponding to a class is the total number of observations, greater than or equal to the lower limit of the class. The construction of the cumulative frequency distributions can be explained by means of numerical illustrations.

Example

Given the following frequency distribution of daily wages in rupees of 75 workers, construct both less than and greater than cumulative frequency distributions.

Class interval For daily wages in Rs.	Number of Workers
12.5-17.5	2
17.5-22.5	22
22.5-27.5	19
27.5-32.5	14
32.5-37.5	7
37.5-42.5	5
42.5-47.5	4
47.5-52.5	2

Solution

To construct cumulative frequency distributions of both kind, the class limits of the exclusive type classes should be considered. If the classes are inclusive type, then it should be converted into exclusive classes and their limits should be taken. Conversion method is explained in Step 6 to 2.4.3.

In this problem the classes are exclusive type and hence the class limits can be taken directly and we construct the cumulative frequency distributions as follows:

Less than cumulative frequency distribution of daily wages in Rs.

Class limits	R.C.F.
12.5	0
17.5	2
22.5	24
27.5	43
32.5	57
37.5	64
42.5	69
47.5	73
53.5	75

Procedure

Since no workers wage is less than Rs. 12.5 the l.c.f. of 12.5 is 0. The less than cumulative frequency of Rs. 27.5 is obtained by summing of all the previous frequencies upto the class 22.5 - 27.5,

that is 2 + 22 + 19 =43.

Greater than cumulative frequency distribution of daily wages in Rs.

Class limits	G.C.F.
12.5	75
17.5	73
22.5	51
27.5	32
32.5	18
37.5	11
42.5	6
47.5	2
52.5	0

Procedure

Since all the the workers wages are grater than or equal to 12.5 Rs., the g.c.f. of 12.5 Rs. is 75. The greater than cumulative frequency of 17.5 Rs. Similarly the greater than cumulative frequency of 22.5 = 75-2-22 = 51 because 24 workers wages are less than 22.5 Rs. The g.c.f. of 27.5 = 75-2-22-19 = 32 and so on.

Example

Given below is the frequency distribution of the marks obtained by 90 students. Construct the cumulative frequency distribution.

Class interval for marks	Number of students
20-29	5
30-39	12
40-49	15
50-59	20
60-69	18
70-79	10
80-89	6
90-99	4

Solution

Since the class intervals of the frequency distribution are inclusive, they should be converted into exclusive classes before the construction of the cumulative frequency distributions.

Here, the correction factor is given by:

$$\text{Correction factor} = \frac{\text{Lower limit of 2nd class} - \text{Upper limit of the 1st class}}{2}$$

$$= \frac{30 - 29}{2} = 0.5$$

Subtraction 0.5 from all the lower limits and adding 0.5 to all the upper limits we get the exclusive class limits.

Less than cumulative frequency distribution of marks:

Class interval for Marks	L.C.F
19.5	0
29.5	5
39.5	17
49.5	32
59.5	52
69.5	70
79.5	80
89.5	86
99.5	90

Greater than cumulative frequency distribution of marks

Class interval for Marks	G.C.F
19.5	90
29.5	85
39.5	73
49.5	58
59.5	38
69.5	20
79.5	10
89.5	4
99.5	0

Example

Convert the following distribution into 'more than' frequency distribution.

Weekly wages Less than rupees	Number of workers
20	41
40	92
60	156
80	194
100	201

Solution

Here we are given, 'less than' cumulative frequency distribution. To obtain the 'more than' or 'greater than' cumulative frequency distribution as given in the following table.

Class interval for weekly wages in Rs.	No. of workers or frequency
0-20	41
20-40	92-41 = 51
40-60	156-92 = 64
60-80	194-156 = 38
80-100	201-194 = 7

More than cumulative frequency distribution of wages in rupees.

Class limits for wages in Rs.	G.C.F
0	201
20	160
40	109
60	45
80	7
100	0

Graphical Representation of a Frequency Distribution

2.6 Diagrammatic and Graphical Representation

One of the most convincing and appealing ways in which statistical results may be presented is through diagrams and graphs. Representation of statistical data by means of pictures, graphs and geometrical figures is called diagrammatic and graphical representations. Diagrammatic representation is used when the data relating to different times and places are given and they are independent of one another. The graphical representation is used when we have to represent the data of a frequency distribution and of a time series.

The difference between the two is that in the case of diagrammatic representation the quantities are represented by diagrams and pictures and in case of graphical representation they are represented by points which are plotted on a graph paper. A graph represents mathematical relationship between the two variables whereas a diagram does not. Finally graphs are more obvious, precise and accurate than diagrams and are quite helpful to the statistician for the study of slopes, rates of changes and estimation (interpolation and extrapolation), wherever possible.

Graphic presentation of statistical data has the following objectives.

1. Graphic presentation renders complex data simple and easily understandable by giving a picturesque view.
2. Comparisons between two or more phenomena can be made very easily with the help of graph.
3. Graphs save time and labour.
4. Graphs avoid knowledge of mathematics.

5. Graphic presentation f statistical data is helpful in interpolation, extrapolation and forecasting. With the help of them one can also determine median, quartiles and mode.

In a frequency graph the size or the value of the item is presented on the horizontal axis and the frequency or the number of items on the vertical axis. The scale of measurement has to be indicated separately on both the axis. The following types of frequency graphs are commonly used.

a. Histogram
b. Frequency polygon
c. Frequency curve
d. Ogives or cumulative frequency curves

a. Histogram

A histogram consists of bars or rectangles which are erected over the class intervals, without giving gaps between bars and such that the areas of the bars are proportional to the frequencies of the class intervals.

For equal class intervals, the heights of the rectangles will be proportional to the frequencies, while for unequal class intervals, the heights will be proportional to the relative frequencies of the classes.

The following example 4.8. illustrates the construction of the histogram.

Example

Draw histogram for the following frequency distribution of marks:

Class interval for marks	Number of students
0-10	20
10-20	31
20-30	58
30-40	42
40-50	19

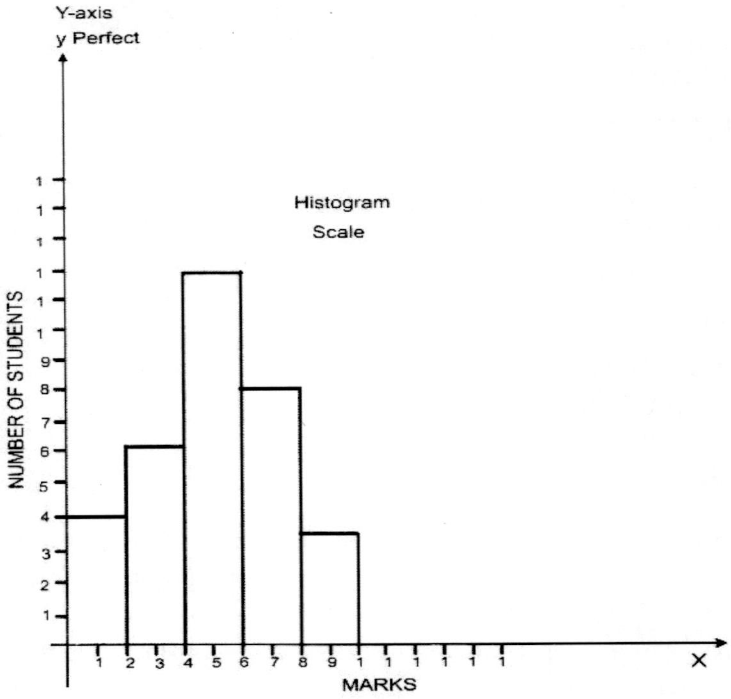

Fig. 2.1

Example

Represent the following data by means of a histogram.

Daily wages (in Rs.)	No.of workers
10-15	7
15-20	19
20-25	27
25-30	15
30-40	12
40-60	12
60-80	8

Solution

Since the class intervals are unequal, we calculate first the relative frequencies of the classes. Then the heights of the bars are proportional to the relative frequencies of the classes.

Relative frequency distribution of daily wages in rupees of workers.

Daily wages in Rs.	Frequency	Relative frequency
10-15	7	7/5 =1.4
15-20	19	19/5 = 4.8
20-25	27	27/5 = 5.4
25-30	15	15/5 = 3.0
30-40	12	12/10 = 1.2
40-60	12	12/20 = 0.6
60-80	8	8/20 = 0.4

Solution

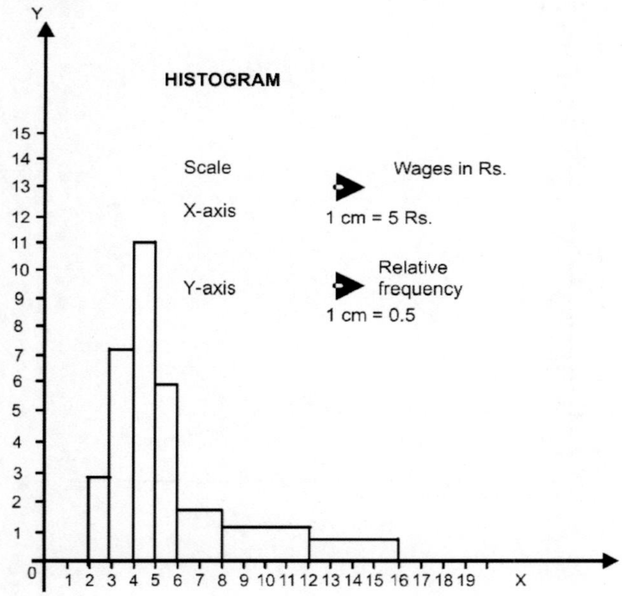

Fig. 2.2

b. Frequency polygon

Frequency polygon is another device of graphic presentation of a frequency distribution.

In case of discrete frequency distribution frequency polygon is obtained on plotting the frequencies on the vertical axis (y-axis) against the corresponding values of the variable on the horizontal axis (x-axis) and joining the points so obtained by straight lines.

In case of grouped or continuous frequency distribution the construction of frequency polygon is as follows:

This consists in plotting the frequencies of different classes (along y-axis). The points so obtained are joined by straight lines to obtain the frequency polygon. The following examples illustrate clearly the construction procedure of the frequency polygon.

Example

The following frequency distribution shows the number of accidents sustained by 100 drivers of a public utility company over a period of 5 years.

No. of accidents:	0	1	2	3	4	5
No.of drivers	34	13	28	12	7	6

Draw the frequency polygon

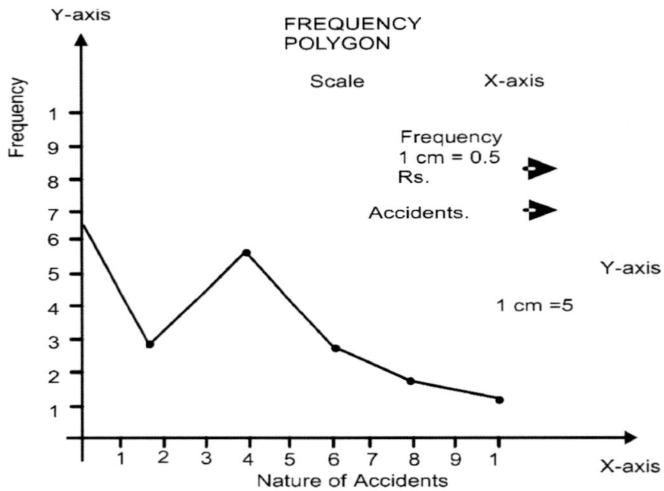

Fig. 2.3

Example

The monthly profits in rupees of 100 shops are distributed as follows:

Profits per shop	Number of shops
0-50	12
50-100	18
100-150	27
150-200	20
200-250	17
250-300	6

Draw the frequency polygon of the frequency distribution.

Solution

First we calculate the mid values of the classes of the frequency distribution

Mid value	Frequency
25	12
75	18
127	27
175	20
225	17
275	6

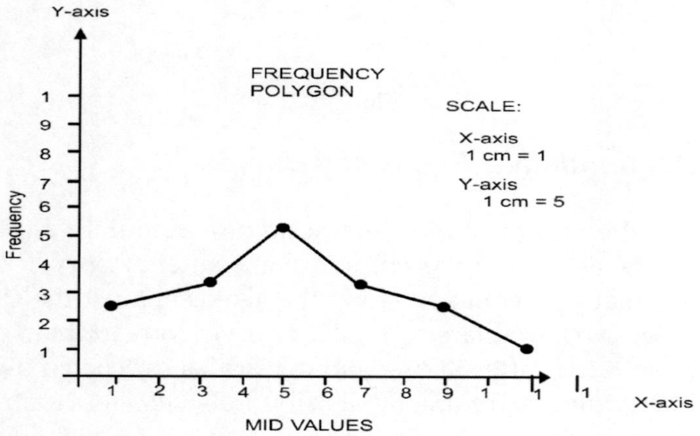

Fig. 2.4

c. Frequency curve

A frequency curve is a smooth free hand curve drawn through the vertices of a frequency polygon. The object of smoothing of the frequency polygon is to eliminate as far as possible, the random or erratic changes that might be present n the data. The area enclosed shape is smooth one and not with sharp edges.

Example

Draw a frequency curve for the following distribution of ages in years of 100 students.

Age in years	17-19	19-21	21-23	23-25	25-27
No. of students	7	23	34	21	15
Students Mid value	18	20	22	24	26
No. of students	7	23	34	21	15

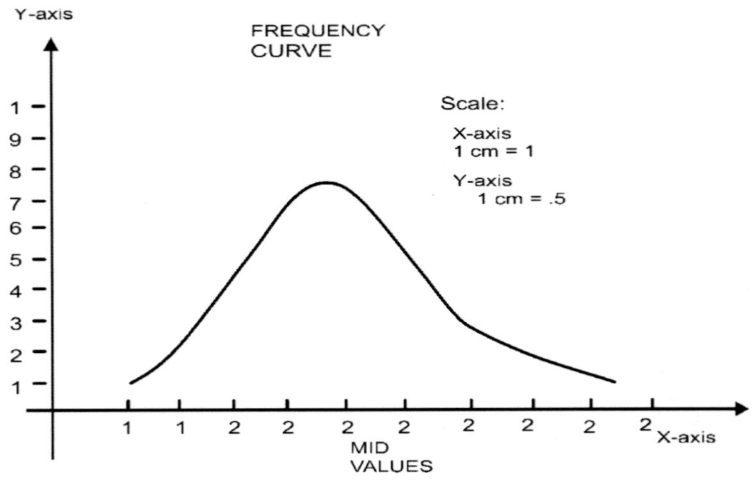

Fig. 2.5

d. Ogives or cumulative frequency curves

An ogive is the graphical representation of a cumulative frequency of a distribution and is also known as cumulative frequency curve. It consists in plotting the cumulative frequency along the Y-axis against the class limits of exclusive type classes (If the classes an inclusive, we convert than into exclusive classes) along the X-axis after taking suitable scales for each axis. Since there are two type of cumulative frequency distributions viz., 'less than' cumulative frequency distribution and 'greater than' cumulative frequency distribution, we have accordingly two types of ogives, viz.,

i. Less than ogive

ii. Greater than ogive

Less than ogive consists in plotting the less than cumulative frequencies against the class limits of the exclusive type classes. The points so obtained are joined by a smooth free hand curve to give less than ogive. The less than ogive looks like an elongated S starts from the lowest class limit on the horizontal axis (X-axis) and gradually rising upward ends at the highest class limit corresponding to the total frequency of the distribution. Obviously, it is an increasing curve, sloping upwards from left to right.

Similarly in greater than ogive, the greater than cumulative frequencies are plotted against the respective class limits of exclusive type classes. The points so obtained are joined by a smooth free hand curve to give greater than ogive. Greater than ogive is a decreasing curve and slopes downwards from left to right and has the shape of an elongated S, turned upside down.

Note

1. We may draw both the less than ogive, and greater than ogive on the same graph. If done so, they intersect at a point. The foot of the perpendicular from their point of intersection of the X-axis gives the value of median.
2. Ogives are very much used to compute graphically the value of the quantities or partition values such as median, quartiles, deciles, percentiles etc.
3. They can also be used to estimate graphically the number of proportion of observations below or above a given value of the variable or lying between certain interval of the values of the variable.
4. For drawing such a graph, instead of actual frequencies the percentage of cumulative frequencies can also be adopted. In fact, for comparing two sets of ogives, each of which is based on a different data it is essential that the percentage of cumulative frequencies instead of actual frequencies should be ploted.

Example

Draw ogives (both 'less than' and 'greater than' types) from the following distribution of wages of 500 workers of a big manufacturing concern.

Weekly wages in rupees	50-59	60-69	70-79	80-89	90-99	100-109	110 -119
No. of workers	21	62	102	150	82	53	30

Solution

Since the class intervals an inclusive, they should be converted into exclusive classes using correction factor.

$$= \frac{\text{Lower limit of the 2nd class} - \text{Upper limit of the 1st class}}{2}$$

subtract the value of the correction factor from all the lower limits and add the same to all the upper limits of the classes.

Calculation of less than and greater than cumulative frequencies

Class limits	Cumulative frequency	
	Less than	Greater than
49.5	0	500
59.5	21	479
69.5	83	417
79.5	185	315
89.5	335	165
99.5	417	83
109.5	470	30
119.5	500	0

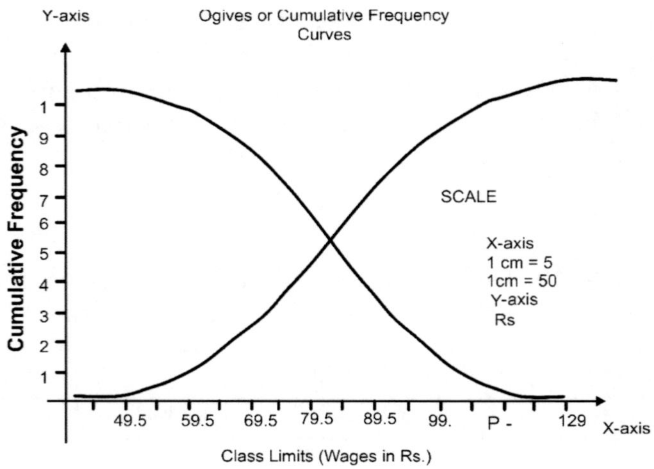

Fig. 2.6

Exercise

1. What are grouped and ungrouped frequency distribution? What are their uses?
2. What do you understand by class limits and width of the class in a frequency distribution? Mention the considerations which help you in deciding the class limits, the class width and the number of classes.
3. What are the guiding rules that one has to bear in mind while forming the frequency distribution?
4. What is graphical representation of the distribution? Discuss its utility.
5. Describe the methods of constructing the following graphs of the frequency distribution.

a. Histogram

b. Frequency polygon

c. Ogives.

6. At a newspaper office, the time required to set the entire front page in type was recorded for 50 days. The data, to the nearest tenth of a minute, are given below:

20.8	22.8	21.9	22.0	20.7
25.3	20.7	22.5	21.2	23.8
23.7	20.7	23.6	19.0	25.1
21.3	21.5	23.1	19.9	24.2
19.7	24.2	23.8	20.7	23.8
20.9	25.0	22.2	22.8	20.1
23.3	20.9	22.9	23.5	19.5
25.0	19.5	24.1	24.2	21.8
24.1	19.8	23.9	22.8	23.9
24.3	21.1	20.9	21.6	22.7

a. Arrange the data in an ascending order of array.

b. Construct a frequency distribution and a less than cumulative frequency distribution from the data using intervals of 0.8 minutes.

c. Construct a frequency polygon from the data.

d. Construct a less than ogive from the data.

7. The sales manager for a major coffee brand has a sales force of 50 persons. Each year, the sales people report to him the average retail selling price of the company's coffee within their areas during the previous 12 months. The sales manager received the following information for last year.

Average selling Price per units in Rs.	**Frequency**
0.90-0.94	2
0.95-0.99	6
1.00-1.04	9
1.05-1.09	13
1.10-1.14	10
1.15-1.19	9
1.20-1.24	3
1.25-1.29	3
Total	50

a. Construct a 'greater than' and 'less than' ogives.

b. Estimate the median f the distribution form the ogives.

8. Classify the following data by taking class-intervals such that their mid values are 17, 22,27,32 and so on (Use inclusive classes)

30	48	25	36	44	22	16	40
42	15	41	28	31	30	42	43
30	17	30	26	36	31	32	41
54	51	27	37	40	19	21	33
40	42	42	54	36	48	22	21

9. Make a frequency table having grades or wages with class-intervals of two rupees each from the following data of daily wages received by 30 laborers in a certain factory. Use exclusive classes. Daily wages in rupees are:

14	22	12	21	17	15
16	14	23	22	20	16
18	13	14	23	21	17
16	15	20	18	12	20
18	24	17	19	11	19

Also construct less than and greater than cumulative frequency distributions.

10. Prior to constructing a dam on a river, an engineer performed a seires of tests to measure the water, flow past the proposed location f the dam. The results of the testing were used to construct the following frequency distribution.

Rive flow (thousands) of gallons per minute)	**Frequency**
1001-1050	9
1101-1100	20
1151-1200	31
1201-1250	53
1251-1300	39
1301-1350	27
1351-1400	13
Total	237

Construct (a) Histogram, (b) Frequency polygon curve and (c) Ogives of the distribution.

❑❑❑

Chapter – 3

Measures of Central Tendency

3.1 Introduction

One of the most important objectives of statistical analysis is to summaries the information contained in the data which may be considered either as a population or as a sample (or sub-population). If the set of data consists of all conceivably possible (or hypothetically possible) observations of a certain phenomenon or a variable, we call it as population. If a set of data contains only a part of these observations, that is selected values of a variable, we call it as sample. Frequency distribution and graphical representation summarize to some extent. They reduce a mass of data to a more understandable form but not to a single value. The aim of this lesson is to determine descriptive measures or statistical constants which will describe the nature of the data.

The data may be a set of population measurements or sample measurements. The descriptive measures computed from the population measurements are called parameters; those computed from the sample measurements are called statistics. These descriptive measures are usually indicated by different symbols in order to denote parameter of statistic. For example the population Arithmetic mean (described below) is denoted by M or m while the sample Arithmetic mean X.

3.2 Definition of Measures of Central Tendency

The first descriptive measure is a measure of central tendency, that is a measure of the centre of the distribution. Very often the measurements of a variable will cluster around a central value or a particular value. For example, suppose that the daily wages in Rupees of 20 workers who belong to a specified grade in a factory are:

30	25	26	29	23	27	26	25	27	26
22	27	26	28	24	27	25	26	24	26

This set or group of daily wages of the workers depicts a concentration f values around a value 25 Rs. though the values in the set range from Rs.22 to Rs.30. In such a case it is possible and also meaningful to use a single value to represent the whole set of values.

Such a typical representative value of a variable which is neither the smallest not the largest in the set, usually occupies in the middle of the set of values and reveals the central tendency of the set is called as measure of central tendency or statistical average. This single value is the point of location around which individual values cluster and therefore called the measure of location.

Some important definitions of a measure of central tendency are given below.

i. 'A measure of central tendency is a typical value around which other figures congregate' **-Simpson and Kafka.**

ii. 'An average is a typical value in the sense that it is sometimes employed to represent all the individual values in a series or of a variable' **Ya-Lun-Chas**

iii. 'An average value is a single value within the range of the data that is used to represent all of the values in the series. Since an average is somewhere within the range of the data, it is sometimes called a measure of central value' **- Croxton and Cowden.**

3.3 Objectives of a Statistical Average

The main objects of determining such a measure are (i) to get one single value that describes the salient features of a mass of complex data and (ii) to facilitate comparison of two or more group of values. For example the wages in Rupees of a set of workers of a specified grade in factory may be compared with the wages of a set of workers of the same grade in factory may be compared with the wages of a sets are represented by means of a single figure. (iii) measure of central tendency is also useful in calculating various other statistical measures such as dispersion, skewness, kurtosis and various other basic characteristics of a mass of data.

3.4 Various Measures of Central Tendency

The following are the various measures of central tendency or measure of location which are commonly used in practice.

i. Arithmetic means or impel mean (A.M.)

ii. Geometric Mean (G.M.)

iii. Harmonic Mean (H.M.)

iv. Median (Me.)

v. Mode (Mo.)

The measures such as mean, median and mode are commonly used in different fields and hence their calculations are described below.

3.4.1 Arithmetic mean

The most popular and widely used measure of central tendency in business and economics is the means.

The Arithmetic Mean is defined as a figure which is obtained by dividing the sum of the values of all observations in a set by the number of items constituting the set.

In symbols, the A.M. of the N measurements $X_1, X_2, \ldots, X_N$. is given by:

$$m = \frac{X_1 + \ldots\ldots + X_N}{N}$$

$m = \frac{\Sigma X}{N}$ Where the symbol m denotes the A.M. Σ denotes the summation of N measurements of X namely $X_1, X_2, \ldots\ldots, X_N$. Calculation of A.M. of the raw data or up grouped data.

Example

The following figures represent the monthly salaries in rupees of 12 employees of a specified grade in a firm.

2130	2118	2151	2098
2062	2125	2142	2116
2145	2076	2110	2065

Find the arithmetic mean salary of a worker.

Solution

formula for mean is: $m = \frac{\Sigma X}{N}$

Here N =12

$$m = \frac{2130 + 2062 + \ldots\ldots\ldots + 2065}{12}$$

$$m = \frac{25338}{12} = 2111.50 \text{ Rs.}$$

Example

Find the A.M. of the frequency distribution of the weekly wages in rupees of 260 workers in a firm.

Table 3.1 : The frequency distribution of weekly wages of 260 workers.

Class interval for Weekly wages (Rs.)	Number of Workers or Frequency
50-60	9
60-70	39
70-80	48
80-90	60
90-100	45
100-110	37
110-120	16

Solution

Note: Here we do not know the exact values of the weekly wages in rupees of the 260 workers, but the number of values or workers (frequency) which occur in various classes. In this case there is no way to compute the exact value of the A.M. of the frequency distribution. There is however, a method for approximating or estimating the A.M. when only grouped data (frequency distribution) are available. This method is based on the assumption that the midpoint of class mark of each class in the frequency distribution is approximately equal to the A.M. of the measurements contained within that class. Hence the formula to find the mean of the frequency distribution is derived as follows:

$$m = \frac{\Sigma xf}{N} .....(2)$$

Where x denotes the mid value of the class interval, f denotes the class frequency corresponding to the mid value X and N is the total frequency of the distribution.

Table 3.2 :

Class interval for Weekly wages (Rs.)	Number of workers or frequency (f)	Mid-value of the class (x)	xf
50-60	15	55	825
60-70	39	65	2535
70-80	48	75	3600
80-90	60	85	5100
90-100	45	95	4275
100-110	37	105	3885
110-120	16	115	1840
Total	260	-	22060

$N = 260 \ \Sigma xf = 22060$

using the formula (2) the A.M. wage of the frequency distribution is:

$$m = \frac{22060}{260} = 84.8461$$

m = 84.85 Rs.

Note 1: Even if the class intervals of the frequency distribution are UNEQUAL, the formula (2) and the same procedure in the calculation are to be adopted to obtain the arithmetic mean.

Note 2: If either the first or the last class interval of the frequency distribution is an open interval then the A.M. of the frequency distribution cannot be calculated.

Example

Following is the distribution of persons in a state according to different income groups:

Table 3.3 :

Income in 1000 Rs.	No. of Persons in 1000
0-1	13
1-2	90
2-3	81
3-5	117
5-10	66
25-50	27
50-100	2
100-1000	2

calculate the mean income per head.

Solution

Formula to find the mean of the frequency distribution s given by:

$$m = \frac{\Sigma xf}{N}$$

Table 3.4 :

Income group In 1000 Rs.	Mid value X	No.of persons or Frequency (f)	xf
0-1	0.5	13	6.5
1-2	1.5	90	135.0
2-3	2.5	81	202.5
3-5	4.0	117	468.0
5-10	7.5	66	495.0
10-25	17.5	27	472.5
25.50	37.5	6	225.0
50-100	75.0	2	150.0
100-1000	550.0	2	1100.0
Total	-	404	3254.5

$N = 404\ \Sigma xf = 3254.5$

$m = \frac{324.5}{404}$ $\quad$ m = 8.056 thousands of rupees, m = Rs. 8056

3.4.2 Median

The second measure of central tendency is the median which is defined as follows:

Median of a set of N measurements of a variable is defined to be that value of the variable which divides the set into to equal parts when the values are rearranged in ascending or descending order of magnitude.

When the number of values is the set N, is odd, the middle most value - the $\frac{(N+1)}{2}$th value -in the arrangement will be the unique median of the variable. On the other hand when N is even, the mean of the (N/2) and (N/2+1) th values (that is $\frac{(N+1)}{2}$th value) will be taken as median of the variable.

Calculation of median of the raw data

The formula to find the median of the raw data is given by:

Me = the value of $\frac{(N+1)}{2}$th item, In a series of ascending order.

Example

Find the median o the measurements which represent the weights in kilograms of 10 workers in a factory.

85, 80, 91, 75, 81, 76, 95, 83, 80, 87.

Solution

Formula to find the median is:

Me = the value of $\frac{(N+1)}{2}$ the item in a series of ascending order.

First we rearrange these weights in ascending order of magnitude.

75, 76, 80, 80, 83, 85, 87, 91, 95

Here N = 10

$\frac{(N+1)}{2} = \frac{11}{2}$ = 5.5Me = The value of (5.5) th item in the series of ascending order.

= The value of 5th + 0.5 (the difference between the value of 6th and 5th item).

(Me = the arithmetic mean of 5th and 6th items in series of ascending order)

= 81 + 0.5 (83 - 81)

= 81 + 0.5 (2)

= 81 + 1.0

Me = 82 Kgs.

Calculation of median of the frequency distribution.

Since the frequency distribution does not give exact values of measurements of variable, the calculation of median of the frequency distribution consists of the following steps.

Step 1: Determine the class interval of the frequency distribution which contains the value of $\frac{(N+1)}{2}$th item. This class interval is known as median class (m.c.).

Step 2: Determine the median value from the median class using the following formula:

$$Me = l + \left[\frac{\frac{N}{2} - M}{f}\right] c$$

Where l is the lower limit of the median class; M is the less than cumulative frequency of l; f is the frequency of the median class; c is the length of the median class and N is the total frequency of the distribution.

Example

The following table give the length of life of a particular type of electric bulb in hours.

Table 3.5 :

Class interval for length of life in hours	Number of bulbs
500-700	5
700-900	11
900-1100	26
1100-1300	10
1300-1500	8

compute the median length of life of a electric bulb.

Solution

Step 1: The median class interval may be determind as follows:

Table 3.6 : Less than cumulative frequency (l.c.f) distribution of length of life.

Class Limits	L.C.F
500	0
700	5
900	16
1100	42
1300	52

$$N = 60, \frac{(N+1)}{2} = \frac{61}{2} = 30.5$$

If 60 values are hypothetically rearranged in ascending order of magnitude, 16 items of lengths are less than 900 and 42 items are less than 100.. Hence the median which is the value of 30.5 the item lies in the interval (900-1100). The median class is therefore (900-1100).

Step 2: Formula to find the median of the frequency distribution is:

$$Me = l + \left[\frac{\frac{N}{2} - M}{f}\right] c$$

1= 900, N = 60, M = 16, f = 26, and c = 200

$$Me = 900 + \left[\frac{\frac{60}{2} - 16}{26}\right] 200$$

$$900 + \frac{14 \times 200}{26} = 900 + 107.7$$

Me = 1007.7

3.4.3 Mode

The third measure of central tendency is the mode.

The mode of a set of N measurements of a variable is defined to be that value of a variable which has maximum frequency.

Example

Finds the modal score of the set of values 68, 70, 73, 71, 78, 70, 60, 70, 72, 69, 67, 70, 71, 69, 70, 74, 70 and 73 which represent the scores of 20 golf professionals.

Solution

Since the value 70 occurs often (7 times), the modal score = 70

Note1: In some cases the mode may be absent while in some cases there may be more than one mode. For example.

i. The set which consists of values 10, 13,17, 9, 21, 6 has no mode because all them are different and

ii. The set which consists of values 7, 10, 8, 15, 10, 22, 20, 26, 20, 34, 20, 6, 10 has two modes namely Mode - I = 10 and Mode - II = 20.

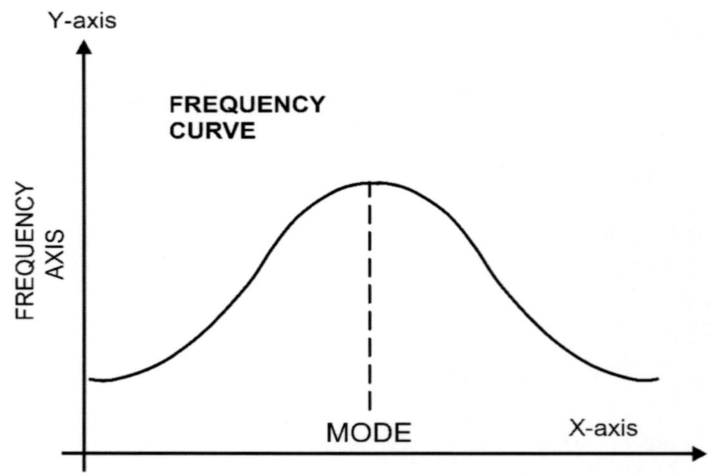

Figure 3.1 :

Note 2: Although the occurrence4 of more than one mode in a single distribution can be used in further analysis, the mode as a measure of central tendency has little significance for a bi-or tri modal distribution. In graph the mode is the value on the x - axis below the highest or maximum point on the frequency curve as can be seen from the following frequency curve.

Determination of the mode of a frequency distribution usually involves finding mathematically suitable type of frequency curve to the given grouped data and the determination of value on the x - axis below the peak of the curve. However, there are simple methods of estimating the mode of a frequency distribution. This method consists the following steps.

Step 1: Determine the modal class. Which is the class corresponding to the maximum frequency.

Step 2: Determine the value of the mode in the modal class using the formula:

$Mo = 1 + \left(\frac{f_2 X_c}{f_1 + f_2}\right)$ where l denotes the lower limit of the modal class; f_1 and f_2 are frequencies of the classes which are preceding and succeeding the modal class; and C is the length of the modal class.

Example

The following data relate to the frequency distribution of the heights in inches of 100 employees working in an office.

Table 3.7 :

	Class interval for heights in inches	No. of employees of frequency	
	Below 60	12	
	60-62	18	
	62-64	25	← f_1
Modal class →	64-66	30	← Maximum frequency
	66-68	10	← f_2
	68-70	3	

Calculate the modal height of an employee.

Solution

Since the class corresponding to maximum frequency (30) is 64-66, the modal class is 64 - 66.

Formula to find the mode is: $M_o = 1 + \left(\frac{f_2 x C}{f_1 + f_2}\right)$

$1 = 64$, $f_1 = 25$, $f_2 = 10$ and $C = 2$.

$$M_o = 1 + \left(\frac{10 \times 2}{25 + 10}\right) = 64 + 0.57$$

$M_o = 64.57$ inches.

3.5 Requisites of a Satisfactory Measure of Central Tendency

Since a measure of central tendency is a singlue value representing a group of values and since there are number of measures of central tendency, it is necessary to decide about the requirements for an ideal measure of central tendency.

Measure of central tendency is meant for condensing a set of values in one figure and therefore it is necessary that it is in the same unit in which the original data is. It is also necessary that according to Prof. Yul and Kendall, an ideal measure should possess the following characteristics.

1. It should be rigidly defined. That is the definition and the formula used to calculate the measure should be clear and unambiguous.
2. It should be based on all the observations or items in the set. The statistical average will be truly representative of the whole mass of data if it is based on all the items.
3. It should be easy to understand and compute by all.
4. It should be suitable for further mathematical treatment.

For example, if we are given the means and sizes of number of different sets, then for an ideal measure of central tendency we should be in a position to compute the mean value of the combined group. That is let m_1 Maximum frequency and m_2 be arithmetic means of two sets of sizes N_1 and N_2 respectively. The combined or pooled mean (m) of the two sets is:

$$m = \frac{m_1 N_1 + m_2 N_2}{N_1 + N_2}$$

Any measure which is not amenable for such algebraic operations will be used in limited situation.

5. It should not be unduly affected by the extreme observations.
6. It should be least affected by fluctuations of sampling.

By this we, that if we take independent random samples of the same size from a given population and calculate the same measure of central tendency, the values so obtained from different samples should but vary much from one another. The difference in the values of the measure of central tendency for different samples is attributed to the fluctuations (changes) of sampling. Hence for a measure of central tendency in which this difference is least, is considered better than those in which this difference in more.

3.6 Comparison of Mean, Median and Mode

i. The mean, median and mode are rigidly defined. All the three measures are easy to understand and calculate but the calculation of mode and median is relatively easier than that of the mean.

ii. Except the mean, the other two measures are not based on all the observations in a set.

iii. Mean alone is capable of further algebraic operations and it is least affected by the fluctuations of sampling.

Hence it is obvious that the mean may be regarded as the best measure of central tendency. In some special situations, however, the mean ceases to be the best measure of central tendency.

Two such situations are :

1. Suppose the values of a set are given in the from of a frequency distribution of which one or both of the terminal classes are not completely specified. Here the calculation of mean is not easy, because the mid values of these terminal classes cannot be determined. But in these situations the calculation of the median or mode are possible because they do not depend on the extreme values.

2. In cases where the data set consists one or two extreme values which are widely different from the majority of the values, the mean should not be used. In such cases the median or mode would be an appropriate measure of central tendency.

iv. When the population is skewed, the median is often the best measure of central tendency because it is always between the mean and the mode. The median is not as highly influenced by the frequency of occurrence of a single value as in the case of the mode, nor is it pulled by extreme values as in the c as of the mean. Hence the median s a satisfactory measure of central tendency in skewed distribution.

3.7 Empirical Relationship among Mean, Median and Mode

A distribution in which the values of mean, median and mode are equal is known as a symmetrical distribution. Conversely stated, when the values of mean median and mode are not equal the distribution is known as asymmetrical or skewed. For distributions of moderate skew ness, there is an empirical relationship between the mean, the mode and the median expressed by the equations:

Mean - Mode = 3 (Mean - Median).

This relationship equation is called Karl Pearson empirical relation.

Example

The number of telephone calls received in 245 successive one minute intervals at an exchange are shown in the following frequency distribution.

No. of calls	0	1	2	3	4	5	6	7
Frequency	14	21	25	43	51	40	39	12

Evaluate the mean, median and mode.

Note: Though the distribution of number of telephone calls is given in the form of frequency distribution the exact number of calls received in each minute is known and it is a discrete variable. Hence the values of mean, median and mode to be obtained will be exact.

Solution

Calculation of Mean.

Formula to find the mean of the frequency distributions is:

$$m = \frac{\sum xf}{N}$$

Table 3.8 :

Mid valuex	Frequencyf	Xf
0	14	0
1	21	21
3	25	50
4	43	129
5	40	200
6	39	234
7	12	84
Total	245	922

$$m = \frac{922}{245} = 3.76$$

m = 4 calls in a minute.

Calculation of median

Formula

$$Me = \text{The value of } m = \frac{N+1}{2} \text{th item in a series of ascending order.}$$

Here N = 245 $\frac{N+1}{2} = 123$

If 245 values (Number of calls) are arranged in ascending order of magnitude the value of 123th item is clearly 4. Hence the median number of calls in a minute interval is 4.

Calculation of mode

In 245 values of a set, the value 4 repeats maximum number of times (51). Therefore the mode of the frequency distribution of the number of calls is 4.

Example

The following table shows the age distribution of persons in a particular region.

Age in Years	No. of persons In thousands
Below 10	2
Below 20	5
Below 30	9
Below 40	12
Below 50	14
Below 60	15
Below 70	15.5
70 and over	0.1

i. Find the median age.

ii. Why is the median a more suitable measure of central tendency than the mean in this case.

Solution

i. The calculation of median of the frequency distribution is as follows:

Determine the median class:

Here N = 15.6

$$\frac{N+1}{2} = \frac{16.6}{2} = 8.3$$

Less than cumulative frequency distribution is:

	Class Limits	LCF	
	10	2	
Median class	20	5	8.3th item
	30	9	
	40	11	
	50	14	
	60	15	
	70	15.5	

The value of 8.3th item lies in the interval 20 -30 which is called the median class. Datermine the median in the median class.

formula: $Me = 1 + \left(\frac{\frac{N}{2} - M}{f}\right)c \quad 1 = 20, \quad N = 15.6, \quad M = 5, \quad f = 4, \quad c = 10.$

$$Me = 20 + \left(\frac{\frac{15.6}{2} - 5}{4}\right)10$$

$$= 20 + \frac{2.8 \times 10}{4} = 20 + 7.0 \qquad Me = 27$$

Hence median age is 27 years.

ii. Since the last class interval viz., 70 and over is open end class, the A.M. cannot be computed. hence in this case median is a more suitable measure of central tendency than A.M.

Exercise

1. What is meant by 'Measure of central tendency'? What are various measures of central tendency? Describe their calculations.
2. Explain clearly the requirements of a satisfactory measure of central tendency.

3. Compare the merits and demerits of the mean, median and mode.
4. State any two situations where the A.M. will be a poor representative.
5. Find the mean, median and mode of the following frequency distribution of the number of members in 75 families.

Number of Members	Number of Families
1	2
2	4
3	15
4	27
5	11
6	8
7	5
8	3

6. Calculate the mean, median and mode of the frequency distribution give below:

Tensile strength of items processed	No. of items
60-63	4
63-68	14
69-89	59
69-72	33
72-75	8
75-78	2

7. Calculate the median and mode from the data given below:

Wages in Rupees	No. of Workers
Above 30	520
Above 40	470
Above 50	399
Above 60	210
Above 70	105
Above 80	45
Above 90	7

❑❑❑

Chapter – 4

Measures of Dispersion

4.1 Introduction and Measuring

A measure of central tendency exhibits only one of the important characteristics of distribution, namely they typical representative figure to the whole set of its values. This measure alone will not adequately describe a set of observation unless all the observations are alike. Moreover one cannot understand completely about the data set with a measure of central tendency. Because in real practical situation there may exits a number of sets of observations (or different distributions) whose measures of central tendency are same but they may differ individually from each other in a number of ways. In particular two sets of values have the same mean but whilst one set of data is grouped close to the mean the other one is more spread out. The following examples will illustrate this view point clearly.

1. Let us consider the following three sets of data A, B and C of seven items each.

Set Name	Seven observation of set							Total	Mean
A	20	20	20	20	20	20	20	140	20
B	20	16	25	18	19	22	20	140	20
C	5	13	19	20	20	27	36	140	20

In the set A, there is no variation in the values. The set B has less variation whereas in the set C the variation among the values is more, even though all the three sets A, B and C have the same size 7 and the same mean 20.

2. A good practical example is of two investment proposals with the same initial investments and differing cash inflows as below:

Project A		Project B	
Possible in flow In Rs.	**Probability**	**Possible in flow In Rs.**	**Probability**
4000	0.2	7000	0.2
8000	06	8000	0.6
12000	0.2	9000	0.2

The Arithmetic mean in both the cases is same as Rs.8000/- but the inflow of project B are less dispersed about the mean. With the information of mean inflows alone, one would be indifferent whether A or B is undertaken.

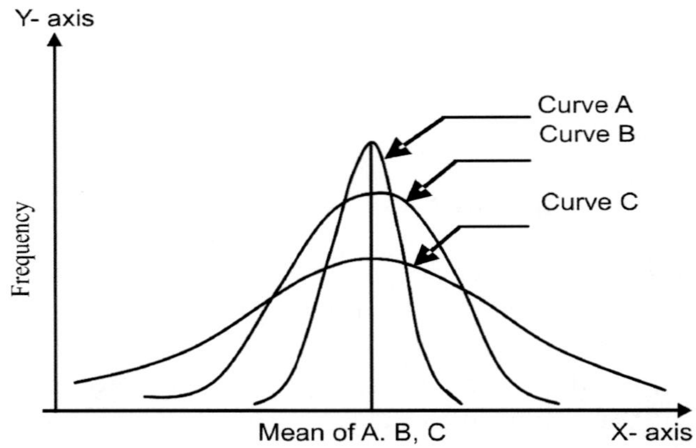

Figure 4.1

3. The same point may also be seen graphically, sing three frequency distributions with the same measure of central tendency.

All the three frequency curves A, B and C in figure 6.1. have the same mean but Curve A has less spread (or variability) than the curve B, and curve B has less variability than curve C. If we measure only mean of these three distributions, we will miss an important difference among the three curves. Likewise for any data, the mean, the median and the mode tell us only part of what we desire to know about the characteristics of the data. Hence to know more about the pattern of data, we must also must measure its dispersion – its spread or variability.

Definition

Dispersion is a measure of the extend to which the individual items or observations vary from their measure of central tendency in a set. The following are some definitions of dispersion given by different statisticians from time to time.

i. "Dispersion is the measure of the variation of the items". – **A.L. Bowley.**

ii. "Dispersion is a measure of the extent to which the individual items vary **- L.R. Connor.**

iii. "The degree to which numerical data kind to spread about an average value is called the variation or dispersion of the data". **- Spiegel.**

4.2 The Characteristics for an Ideal Measure of Dispersion

The requisites for an ideal measure of dispersion are the same as those for an ideal measure of central tendency. They are as follows:

1. The measure should be rigidly defined.
2. It should be based on all the observations in a set.
3. It should be easy to understand and calculate by all.
4. It should be capable of further algebric operations.
5. It should not be unduely affected by extreme observations (largest or smallest observations) in a set.
6. It should be least affected by fluctuations of sampling.

4.3 Absolute and Relative Measures of Dispersion

Measure of dispersion may be either absolute or relative. Absolute measures of dispersion are expressed in the same statistical unit in which the original data are given such as rupees, kilograms, centimetres, etc., They are useful only for assessing the absolute magnitude of variability in a distribution. These measures may also be used to compare the variation in two distributions provided the variables in two distributions are expressed in different units of the same size. If two sets of data are expressed in different units such as inches of heights of students versus centimetres of height of another set of students, the absolute measures of dispersions cannot be used to compare the variability in the two sets. In such cases measures of relative dispersion should be used.

A relative measure of dispersion is the ratio of a measure of absolute dispersion to an arithmetic mean or a particular fixed value. It is called a coefficient of dispersion, because "coefficient" means a pure number that is independent of the unit of measurement. Hence for comparing the variability of the two distributions, we compute the relative measures of dispersion instead of absolute measures of dispersion. Even if the unit is the same in two distributions but the size magnitudes differ, a relative measure is generally employed for comparison purpose.

4.4. Various Measures of Dispersion

The various measures of dispersion are:

1. Range
2. Quartile deviation
3. Mean deviation
4. Standard deviation

1. Range

The range is the simplest measure of dispersion. It is defined as the difference between the largest and the smallest values of the variable or a data set. Symbolically,

Range (R) = L - S where L = largest item and

S = smallest item.

Clearly the range takes no account of those values in between the largest and the smallest values in a set.

The relative measure corresponding to range, called the coefficient or range is obtained by applying the following formula:

$$\text{Coefficient of Range} = \frac{L-S}{L+S}$$

If the averages of the two distributions are the same, comparison of the ranges indicates that the distribution with the smaller range has less dispersion and the average of that distribution is more typical of the group.

Example

The following are the prices of shares of AB Co. Ltd from Monday to Saturday:

Table 4.1 :

Day	Monday	Tuesday	Wednesday	Thursday	Friday	Saturday
Prices in Rs.	300	310	208	260	320	350

Calculate range and its coefficient.

Solution

Range = L – S

Here L = 350 and S = 260

Range = 350 – 260 = Rs. 90

$$\text{Coefficient of Range} = \frac{L-S}{L+S} = \frac{350-260}{350+260} = 0.147$$

The range of the grouped data or the frequency distribution is obtained as follows:

The range is equal to the difference between the upper limit (or mid value) of he last class interval and the lower limit (or mid value) of the first class interval in the frequency distribution.

Though the range is simple to calculate, it is a very poor measure of dispersion. Because it depends on the two extreme values of the variable which are the least reliable. However it has more use in quality control where it is assumed that the distribution is normal.

2. Quartile deviation

The quartile deviation or semi interquartile range is a measure of the distribution based on quartiles of the distribution. Thus we first define quartiles and their computations for raw as well as grouped data.

Definition of quartiles

The values which divide the data set into a number of equal parts are called the quartiles or partition values. Some important partition values are median, quartiles, deciles and percentiles. Quartiles are those values which divide the total frequency into four equal parts. Deciles and percentiles divide the total frequency into ten and one hundred equal parts respectively.

The values which divide the given data into four equal parts are known as quartiles and they are usually denoted by the symbols Q_1, Q_2, Q_3 is ascending order of magnitude. Q1, known as the lower or first quartiles is the value in the set that exceeds ¼ (25%) of the measurements and is less than the remaining ¾ (75%) of the measurements. Incidentally Q_2, the second quartiles coincides with median and has an equal number of observations above it and below it (that is Q_2- bisects the data). The upper quartile or the third quartile (Q_3) is a value that exceeds ¾ (75%) of the measurements and is less than the remaining ¼ (25%) of the measurements in the set.

Calculation of quartiles Q_1, Q_2 and Q_3 of raw data:

Formula to find the quartiles are:

Q1 = the value of (1/4) $(N+1)^{th}$ item in a series of ascending order.

Q2 = the value of (2/4) $(N+1)^{th}$ item in a series of ascending order.

Q3 = the value of (3/4) $(N+1)^{th}$ item in a series of ascending order.

Where N denotes total number of values in the set.

Example

From the following data, calculate the values of the quartiles.

Months:	1	2	3	4	5	6	7	8	9	10	11	12
Sales in 1000 Rs.	78	90	80	88	80	88	82	86	85	82	84	86

Solution

Here N = 12

(1/4) (N+1) = 13/4 = 3.25

(2/4) (N+1) = 26/4 = 6.50

(3/4) (N+1) = 39/4 = 9.75

Rearrange the sales in ascending order of magnitude:

78, 80, 80,82,82,84,85,86,86,88,88,90

Q1 = the of (1/4) $(N+1)^{th}$ item

= the value of 3.25^{th} item

= 80 + 0.25 (82-80)

= 80 + 0.25 (2)

Q1 = 80 + 0.5 = 80.5 thousands of Rs.

Q2 = the of (2/4) $(N+1)^{th}$ item

= the value of 6.50^{th} item

= 84 + 0.5 (85-84)

= 84 + 0.5 (1)

Q2 = 84 + 0.5 = 84.5 thousands of Rs.

Q3 = the of (3/4) $(N+1)^{th}$ item

= the value of 9.75^{th} item

= 80 + 0.75 (88-86)

= 80 + 0.75 (2)

Q3 = 80 + 1.50 = 87.50 thousands of Rs.

Calculation of quartiles of frequency distribution:

The calculation of quartiles of the frequency distribution is similar to the calculation of median of the distribution. They also consist tow steps:

Step – (i): Determine the quartile classes.

The first quartile class is a class which contains the value of (1/4) $(N+1)^{th}$ item.

The second quartile class is a class which contains the value of (21/4) (N+1) = (1/2) $(N+1)^{th}$ item; (that is median class)

The third quartile class is a class which contains the value of (3/4) $(N+1)^{th}$ item.

Step – (ii): determine the exact values of the first, second and third quartiles (Q_1, Q_2, Q_3).

Formula to find quartiles are:

$$Q_1 = 1_1 + \left[\frac{\frac{N}{4} - m_1}{f_1}\right] C_1$$

$$Q_2 = 1_2 + \left[\frac{\frac{N}{4} - m_2}{f_2}\right] C_2$$

$$Q_3 = 1_3 + \left[\frac{\frac{3N}{4} - m_3}{f_3}\right] C_3$$

Where 1_1, 1_2 and 1_3 are lower limits of the first, second and third quartile classes; m_1, m_2 and m_3 are less than cumulative frequencies of the lower limits of the I, II and III quartile classes, 1_1, 1_2 and 1_3 respectively; f_1, f_2 and f_3 are frequencies of the I, II, and III quartile classes; C_1, C_2 and C_3 are the lengths of the I, II and III quartile classes and N is the total frequency of the distribution.

Example

The following table gives the frequency distribution of 250 workers of a factory according to their weekly wages in Rupees.

Table 4.2 :

Class interval for weekly wages (Rs.)	Number of workers
30-32	2
32-34	9
34-36	25
36-38	30
38-40	49
40-42	62
42-44	39
44-46	20
46-48	11
48-50	3
Total	250

Step – (i): Calculation of quartile classes:

Here N = 250

(1/4) (N+1) = 251/4 = 3.25

(2/4) (N+1) = 502/4 = 6.50

(3/4) (N+1) = 753/4 = 9.75

The quartile classes are obtained, using the following the less than cumulative frequency distribution.

Less than cumulative frequency distribution

Table 4.3 :

	Class limits	l.c.f	
	30	0	
	32	2	
	34	11	
	36	36	62.75
	38	66	
Q_2 Class	40	115	125.50
	42	177	
Q_3 Class	44	216	188.25
	46	236	
	48	247	
	50	250	

It is clear from the less than cumulative frequency distribution that if the 250 measure or values are arranged in ascending order, the first 36 measurements are less than Rs. 36 and the first 66 lies between Rs. 36 and Rs. 38. Therefore the I quartiles (Q_1 Class) is 36 -38. Similarly the II quartile class (Q_2) is Rs. 40-42 and IIIrd quartile class (Q_3 class) is Rs. 42-44.

Step-(ii): Calculation of the values of the quartiles

Q_1, Q_2 and Q_3.

$$Q1 = 1_1 + \frac{N/4 - m_1}{f_1} \quad C_1$$

$$Q2 = 1_2 + \frac{N/2 - m_2}{f_2} \quad C_2$$

$$Q3 = 1_3 + \frac{N/4 - m_3}{f_3} \quad C_3 \quad C_2$$

$$1_1 = 36 \quad m_1 = f_1 = 30 \quad C_1 = 2$$

$$1_2 = 40 \quad m_2 = f_2 = 62 \quad C_2 = 2$$

$$1_3 = 42 \quad m_3 = f_3 = 39 \quad C_2 = 2$$

$$Q_1 = 36 + \frac{250/4 - 36}{36} \quad 2$$

$$= 36 + 1.76$$

$$Q_1 = 37.36 \text{ Rs.}$$

$$Q_2 = 40 + \frac{250/4 - 115}{62} \quad 2$$

$$= 40 + 0.323$$

$$Q_2 = 40.323 \text{ Rs.}$$

$$Q_3 = 42 + \frac{3 \times 250/4 - 177}{39} \quad 2$$

$$= 40 + 0.538$$

$$Q_3 = 40.323 \text{ Rs.}$$

Definition

Quartile deviation or semi – interquartile deviation is defined as the half of the difference between the upper and the lower quartiles of the set of measurements.

If Q_1 and Q_3 are respectively the lower and the upper quartiles of the distribution, the quartile deviation (QD) is given by:

$$QD = \frac{Q_3 - Q_1}{2}$$

Quartile deviation is an absolute measure of distribution. The relative measure of dispersion corresponding to the quartile deviation in the coefficient of quartile deviation (CQD) and is given by the formula:

$$CQD = \frac{Q_3 - Q_1}{Q_3 + Q_1}$$

Example

Evaluate an appropriate absolute and relative measures of dispersion for the following data:

Table 4.4 :

Income in Rs	Number of persons
Less than 50	54
50 – 70	100
70 – 90	140
90 – 110	300
110 – 130	230
130 – 150	125
Above 150	51
Total	1000

Solution

Since the frequency distribution contains open end intervals the only measure of dispersion that we can compute is the quartile deviation

Calculation of the lower and the upper quartiles (Q_1 and Q_3).

Here N = 1000

$$\frac{N+1}{4} = \frac{1001}{4} = 250.25$$

$$\frac{3(N+1)}{4} = \frac{3 \times 10001}{4} = 750.75$$

Less than cumulative frequency distribution of income.

Table 4.5 :

Class limits		l.c.f	
Least Value			
	50	50	
Q1	70	154	
Class	90	294	250.25
Q3	110	594	750.25
Class	130	824	
	150	949	
Highest value		1000	

I quartile class is 70 – 90

III quartile class is 110 – 130

$$Q_1 = l_1 + \left(\frac{N/4 - m_1}{f_1}\right) c_1$$

$l_1 = 70 \quad m_1 = 154 \quad f_1 = 140 \quad C_1 = 20$

$$Q1 = 70 + \frac{1000/4 - 154}{140} 20$$

$$= 70 + 13.741$$

$$Q_1 = 83.714 \text{ Rs.}$$

$$Q_3 = l_3 + \frac{3N/4 - m_3}{f_3} C_3$$

$1_3 = 110, \quad m_3 = 594, \quad f_3 = 230, \quad C_3 = 20$

$$Q_3 = 110 + \frac{3 \times 1000/4 - 594}{230} 20$$

$$Q_3 = 123.565 \text{ Rs.}$$

Quartile deviation is given by

$$\text{Q.D.} = \frac{Q_3 - Q_1}{2}$$

$$= \frac{123.565 - 83.714}{2}$$

$$= 39.851/2 = 19.9255$$

Q.D. = 19.93 Rs.

Coefficient of quartile deviation is given by

$$\text{C.Q.D.} = \frac{Q_3 - Q_1}{Q_3 + Q_1}$$

$$\frac{123.565 - 83.714}{123.565 + 83.714} = \frac{39.851}{207.279} = 0.192$$

CQD = 0.192

3. Mean deviation

Definition

The mean deviation (M.D.) is defined as the arithmetic mean of the numerical deviations of the individual values from the measure of central tendency of the data. The measure of central tendency is either mean or median. It is also known as the average deviation. If the measure of central tendency is mean (or median), then we get the mean deviation about the mean (or median). Calculation of mean deviation of the raw data:

Formulae to find the mean deviation about the mean and about the median are respectively given by:

$$\text{MD (about mean)} = \frac{\sum |(X - m)|}{N}$$

$$\text{MD (about median)} = \frac{\sum |(x - me)|}{N}$$

Where m and me are respectively the mean and median of the N values of X. The symbol $|(X - m)|$ read as mode (X-m), is the modulus value or numerical value of the deviation of x from m, ignoring plus and minus signs.

Coefficient of mean deviation (CMD) is the relative measure of dispersion corresponding to mean deviation and it is given by the formula.

$$\text{CDM} = \frac{\text{MD(about the mean)}}{\text{Mean}}$$

Example

From the following data of the weight of 9 persons calculate mean deviations and its coefficient about Mean Median.

Weight in 1bs. 80,85,90,92,98,105,120,105,125.

Solution

Calculation of mean and MD (about mean) weight of a person.

$$m = \frac{\sum X}{N}$$

m = 900/9 = 100 lbs.

The table below gives the calculation of mean and median deviation.

Table 4.6 :

	Weight in 1bs-X	Numerical deviation from mean |X-m|	Numerical deviation from median |X-me|
	80	20	18
	85	15	13
	90	10	8
	92	8	6
	98	2	0
	105	5	7
	120	20	22
	105	5	7
	125	25	27
Total	900	110	108

Formula to find MD (about mean) is :

$$\text{Mean deviation about mean} = \frac{\sum|X-m|}{N} = \frac{110}{9}$$

MD (about mean) = 12.22 1bs

Coefficient of mean deviation is:

$$\text{CMD} = \frac{\text{MD(about the mean)}}{\text{Mean}}$$

$$\text{CMD} = \frac{12.22}{100} = 0.1222$$

Calculation of median and mean deviation about median weight of a person:

Formulae to find median is:

Me = the value of $\frac{N + 1}{2}$th item in a series of ascending

Rearranging the weights in ascending order we have:

80,85,90,92,98,105,120,125

$$N = 9$$

$$\frac{N + 1}{2} = 10/2 = 5$$

Me = the value of 5th item

Me = 98

Formula to find MD (about median) is:

$$\text{MD (about median)} = \frac{\sum|X - me|}{N}$$

$$= 108/9 = 12$$

MD (about median) = 12 1bs

Coefficient of mean deviation is :

$$\text{CMD} = \frac{\text{MD(about the mean)}}{\text{Mean}} = 12/98$$

CDM = 0.122

Calculation of mean deviation of frequency distribution.

Formulae to find the mean deviations of the frequency distribution about mean and median are:

$$\text{MD (about mean)} \frac{\sum|X - m|f}{N}$$

$$\text{MD (about median)} \frac{\sum|X - Me|f}{N}$$

Where x denotes the mid value of the class interval, f denotes the frequency of the class corresponding to the mid X, m and Me are respectively the mean and median of the frequency distribution: and N is the total frequency of the distribution.

Example

Calculate the mean deviation from the mean and also from the median for the following frequency distribution of marks of 50 students in a class. Find out their coefficients.

Table 4.7 :

Class interval for marks	0-10	10-20	20-30	30-40	40-50
Number of students	5	8	15	16	6

Solution

Calculation of mean and mean deviation of marks.

The formula to find the MD (about mean) of the frequency distribution is:

$$\text{MD (about mean)} = \frac{\sum |X - m| f}{N}$$

The formula to find the mean of the frequency distribution is:

$$m = \frac{\sum Xf}{N}$$

Table 4.8 :

Mid Value X	Frequency Y	Xf	|X-m|	X-m f	|X-Me|	|X-Me|f
5	5	25	22	110	23	115
15	8	120	12	96	13	104
25	15	375	2	30	3	45
35	16	560	8	128	7	112
45	6	270	18	108	17	102
Total	50	1350	-	472	-	478

Here N = 50, S Xf = 1350, S | X-m | f = 472

$$m = \frac{1350}{50} = 27$$

m = 27 marks

MD (about mean) = 472/50 = 9.44 marks

Coefficient of mean deviation is:

$$CMD = \frac{\text{MD (about median)}}{\text{Mean}}$$

$$= 9.44/27$$

CDM = 0.35

Calculation of median and mean deviation about median.

$$\text{Here } N = 50 \; \frac{N+1}{2} = \frac{51}{2} = 25.5$$

Less than cumulative frequency distribution of marks

Table 4.9

	Class limits	l.c.f	
	0	0	
	10	5	
	20	13	
Median Class	30	28	25.5
	40	44	
	50	50	

Median Class is 20-30

$$Me = 1 + \left(\frac{\frac{N}{2} - m}{f} \right) C$$

1 = 20, m = 13, f = 15, c = 10

$$Me = 20 + \left(\frac{\frac{50}{2} - 13}{15} \right) 10$$

$$= 20 + 120 / 15$$

Me = 28

$$\text{MD (about median)} = \frac{\sum |X - Me| f}{N}$$

From the above table 4.8

S |X - Me| f = 478

MD (above median) = 478/50

= 9.56 marks

Coefficient of mean deviation is :

$$\text{CMD} = \frac{\text{MD (about median)}}{\text{Mean}}$$

= 9.56/28 = 0.34

CDM = 0.34

Note: The same procedure is to be followed to calculate mean deviation if the classes are unequal.

4. Standard deviation

The most important and widely used measure of dispersion is standard deviation, the measure was first suggested by Karl Pearson in 1983.

Definition

Standard deviation (SD) is defined as the positive square root of the arithmetic mean of the squared deviations of the measurements or observations of a set from their arithmetic mean. It is usually denoted by the Greek alphabets (small sigma). It is also called as root mean squared deviation. The square of the standard deviation is known as variance.

Calculation of the standard deviation of the raw data:

The formula to find the SD of the raw data is:

$$\sigma = \sqrt{\frac{\Sigma(X-m)^2}{N}}$$ where m is the arithmetic mean of the N values of X.

$$\text{Variance} = \sigma^2 = \frac{\Sigma(X-m)^2}{N}$$

For easy calculation the formula may be simplified as follows:

$$\sigma^2 = \sqrt{\frac{\Sigma X^2}{N} - m^2}$$

Coefficient of variation (CV).

The coefficient of variation is a relative measure of dispersion corresponding to the standard deviation of a set of measurements. It is given by the formula:

$$CV = \frac{\text{Standard Deviation}}{\text{Mean}} \times 100$$

That is CV = σ/m X 100

Example

Prices in rupees of shares of a company on the different days in a month were found to be 66, 69, 70, 69, 71, 63, 64 and 68. Find the standard deviation and its coefficient of the share prices.

Solution

Formula to find the standard deviation of the raw data is:

$$s = \sqrt{\frac{\sum X^2}{N} - m^2}$$

$$m = \frac{\sum X}{N}$$

$$m = \frac{675}{10}\ 67.5$$

$$m^2 = (67.5)^2$$

$$= 4556.25$$

$$\Sigma X^2 = 45633$$

$$\sigma = \sqrt{\frac{45633}{10} - 4556.25}$$

$$= \sqrt{4563.3 - 4556.25}$$

$$= \sqrt{7.05}$$

$$\sigma = 2.6552$$

Table 4.10 :

Share Price X	X^2
66	4356
65	4225
69	4761
70	4900
69	4761
71	5041
70	4900
63	3969
64	4096
64	4096
68	4624
675	45633

Coefficient of variation is given by:

$$CV = \left(\frac{\sigma}{m}\right)\times 100$$

$$= \frac{2.6552}{67.5}\times 100$$

$$CV = 3.9336\%$$

Calculation of the standard deviation of the frequency distribution.

The formula to find the standard deviation of the frequency distribution is:

$$\sigma = \sqrt{\frac{\Sigma(X - m)^2 f}{N}}$$

The corresponding simplified formula is:

$$\sigma = \sqrt{\left[\left(\frac{\Sigma X^2 f}{N}\right) - m^2\right]}$$

where X denotes the mid value of the class interval.

f denotes the frequency of the class

Corresponding to mid X

N denotes the total frequency of the distribution,

m denotes the arithmetic mean of distribution and is given by the formula

$$m = \frac{\Sigma X f}{N}$$

Example

Calculate standard deviation and its coefficient for the following distribution of net profits earned by a group of companies.

Table 4.11

Profit (1000 Rs.)	Number of companies
20-30	30
30-40	58
40-50	62
50-60	85
60-70	112
70-80	70
80-90	57
90-100	26
Total	500

Solution

Formula to find the standard deviation of the frequency distribution is

$$s = \sqrt{\left(\frac{\Sigma X^2 f}{N}\right) - m^2}$$

$$m = \frac{\sum Xf}{N}$$

Table 4.12 :

Mid value X	Frequency f	Xf	x^2f
25	30	750	18750
35	58	2030	71050
45	62	2790	125550
55	85	4675	468000
65	112	7200	393750
75	70	5250	393750
85	57	4845	411825
95	26	2470	234650
Total	500	30090	1980700

N = 500

$\Sigma Xf = 30090$

$\Sigma X^2f = 1980700$

m = 30090/500

m = 60.18 thousands of rupees

$$\sigma = \sqrt{\left(\frac{1980700}{500}\right) - (60.18)^2}$$

$$= \sqrt{3961.4 - 3621.6324}$$

$$= \sqrt{339.77}$$

σ = 18.43 thousands of rupees

The coefficient of variation is given by

CV = s / m X 100

$$= \frac{18.43}{60.18} \times 100$$

CV = 30.63 %

Note : Even if the class intervals are unequal in a frequency distribution the same formula and the same procedure are to be adopted to calculate the standard deviation.

Standard Deviation of the Combined Sets

Just as it possible to compute combined arithmetic mean of two or more sets of measurements, similarly we can also calculate the combined standard deviation of two or more than two sets.

If m_1 and m_2 are the arithmetic means σ_1 and σ_2 are standard deviations; and N_1 and N_1 are the sizes of the two sets of data, then the standard deviation (σ) of the combined sets of size $N = N_1 + N_2$ is given by the formula:

$$\sigma = \sqrt{\frac{\sigma_1^2 N_1 + \sigma_2^2 N_2 + d_1^2 N_1 + d_2^2 N_2}{N_1 + N_2}}$$

where the combined mean, $m = \dfrac{m_1 N_1 + m_2 N_2}{N_1 + N_2}$

and d_1 and d_2 are given by

$d_1 = m - m_1$

and $d_2 = m - m_2$

Example

The means of two groups of sizes 20 and 30 are respectively 65 and 73 and the standard deviations are 5 and 7. Compute the standard deviation of the combined group of size 50 obtained by combining the two groups.

Solution

Combined mean is given by the formula:

Group I	**Group II**
$N_1 = 20$	$N_2 = 30$
$m_1 = 65$	$m_2 = 73$
$\sigma_1 = 5$	$\sigma_2 = 7$
${}_1\sigma^2 = 25$	${}_2\sigma^2 = 49$

$$m = \frac{m_1 N_1 + m_2 N_2}{N_1 + N_2}$$

$$= \frac{65 \times 20 + 73 \times 30}{20 + 30}$$

$$= \frac{1300 + 2190}{50}$$

$m = 69.8$

$d_1 = 69.8 - 65 = 4.8$

$d_1^2 = 69.8 - 73 = -3.2$

$d_2^2 = (-3.2)^2 = 10.24$

Combined standard deviation is:

$$\sigma = \sqrt{\frac{\sigma_1^2 N_1 + \sigma_2^2 N_2 + d_1^2 N_1 + d_2^2 N_2}{N_1 + N_2}}$$

$$= \sqrt{\frac{25 \times 20 + 49 \times 30 + 23.04 \times 20 + 10.24 \times 30}{20 + 30}}$$

$$= \sqrt{\frac{2738.0}{50}} = \sqrt{54.76} = \sigma = 7.4$$

Example

From the following table of marks obtained by A and B in 10 tests of 100 marks each, find out who is more intelligent and who is more consistent.

A:	25	50	45	30	70	42	36	48	34	60
B:	10	70	50	20	95	55	42	60	48	80

Solution

In order to find out the more intelligent student between A and B will calculate the mean marks and for finding out the more consistent student we will compare the coefficient of variations for two sets of marks.

Calculation of mean and standard deviation. Formulate to find the mean and standard deviation for the sets of data are:

$$m = \frac{\sum X}{N}$$

$$\sigma = \sqrt{\frac{\sum x^2}{N} - m^2}$$

The coefficient of variation is given by the formula.

$CV = (\sigma/m)100$

Table 4.13 :

Standard A		Standard B	
Test mark X	X^2	Test markY	Y^2
25	625	10	100
50	2500	70	4900
45	2025	50	2500
30	900	20	400
70	4900	95	9025
42	1764	55	3025
36	1296	42	1764
48	2304	60	3600
34	1156	48	2304
60	3600	80	6400
440	21070	530	34018

Student A: m = 440/10 = 44 marks

$$\sigma = \sqrt{\left(\frac{21070}{10}\right) - (44)^2}$$

$$= \sqrt{2107 - 1936} = \sqrt{171}$$

$$\sigma = 13.0767 \text{ marks}$$

$$CV = \frac{13.0767}{42} \times 100 \quad CV = 29.72\%$$

Student B: m = 530/10 = 53 marks

$$\sigma = \sqrt{\left(\frac{3401.8}{10}\right) - 53} \qquad = \sqrt{3401.8 - 28.09} - \sqrt{592.8}$$

$$= 24.3475 \text{ Marks}$$

$$CV = \frac{24.3475}{53} = 45.92\%$$

Since mean mark obtained by student B is higher, he may be regarded as more intelligent student. However, student A is more consistent (lesser variation) because coefficient of variation is much less in case of student A than student B.

Example

An analysis of the monthly wages paid to workers in two firms, A and B, belonging to the same industry, gave the following result.

	Firm A	Firm B
Number of wages earners	550	650
Mean monthly wages Rs.	50	45
Standard deviation of the distribution of wages Rs.	90	120

Answer the following questions with propar justifications:

a. Which firm A or B pays out larger amount as monthly wages?

b. In which firm, A or B is there greater variability in individual wages?What are the measures of (i) Mean monthly wages and (ii) standard deviation of individual wages of all workers in the two firms taken together?

Solution

a. In order to find out which firm A or B pays larger amount as monthly wages, we compare the total wage bills of firm A and firm B.

Firm A:

Total Wage Bill = 550X 50 = Rs. 27500

Firm B:

Total Wage Bill = 650X 45 = Rs. 29250

Hence firm B plays larger amount as monthly wages

b. To determine the firm in which there is greater variability in individual wages, we shall compare the coefficient of variation.

Firm A:

$$CM = \sigma/m \text{ X } 100 = \frac{90}{50} \times 100 = 18.97 \text{ percent}$$

Firm B:

$$CM = \sigma/m \text{ X } 100 = \frac{120}{45} \times 100 = 24.34 \text{ percent}$$

There is greater variability in individual wages in firm B.

c. Combined mean (m) and standard deviation (s) when all workers in two firms taken together:

$$m = \frac{m_1 XN_1 + m_2 XN_2}{N_1 + N_2}$$

$$= \frac{50 \times 550 + 45 \times 650}{550 + 650}$$

$$= \frac{27500 + 29250}{1200}$$

$$m = 47.29 \text{ Rs.}$$

$$\sigma = \sqrt{\frac{\sigma_1^2 N_1 + \sigma_2^2 N_2 + d_1^2 N_1 + d_2^2 N_2}{N_1 + N_2}}$$

$$d_1 = m\text{-}m_1$$

$$= 47.29 - 50$$

$$d_1 = -2.71$$

$$d_2 = m\text{-}m_2$$

$$= 47.29 - 45$$

$$= 2.29$$

$$\sigma = \sqrt{\frac{90 \times 550 + 120 \times 650 + 550(-2.71)^2 + 650(2.29)^2}{550 + 650}}$$

$$= \sqrt{\frac{49500 + 78000 + 4039.235 + 3408.665}{1200}}$$

$$= \sqrt{112.457}$$

$$\sigma = 10.605 \text{ Rs.}$$

4.5 Skewness

4.5.1 Introduction

In the previous two chapters we have discussed measures of central tendency and variability. However, they do not reveal the entire story. There are tow other comparable characteristics called skewness and kurtosis that help us to understand a distribution. Two distributions may have the same mean and standard deviation but may differ widely in their overall appearance as can be seen from the following:

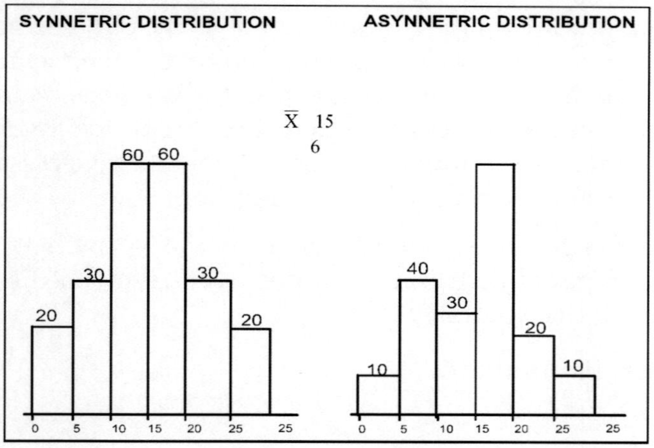

In both these distributions the value of mean and standard deviation is the same (X = 15, α=5). But it does not imply that the distributions are alike in nature. The distribution on the left-hand side is a symmetrical one whereas the distribution on the right-hand side is asymmetrical or skewed. Measures of skewness help us to distinguish between different types of distributions.

4.5.2 Skewness defined

Some definitions of skewness are as follows:

(1) "When a series is not symmetrical it is said to be asymmetrical of skewed". ***-Croxton & Cowden***

(2) "Skewness refers to the asymmetry or lack of symmetry in the shape of a frequency distribution." ***-Morris Hamburg***

(3) "Measures of skewness tell us the direction and the extent of skewness. In symmetrical distribution the mean, median and mode are identical. The more the mean oves away from the mode, the larger the asymmetry of skewness. ***-Simpson & Kafka***

(4) "A distribution is said to be 'skewed' when the mean and the median fall at different potions in the distribution, and the balance (or centre of gravity) is shifted to one side or the other – to left or right. ***-Garrett***

The analysis of above definition shows that the term 'skewness' refers to lack of symeetry, i.e., when a distribution is not symmetrical (or is asymmetrical) it is called skewed distribution. Any measure of skewness indicated the difference between the manner in which items are distributed in a particular distribution compared with a symmetrical (or normal) distribution. If, for example, skewness is positive, the frequencies in the distribution are spread out over a greater range of values on the high-value end of the curve (the right-hand side) than they are on the low value end. If the curve is normal, spread will be the same on both sides of the centre point and the mean, median and mode will all have the same value. The concept of skewness gains importance from the fact the statistical theory is often based upon the assumption of the normal distribution. A measure of skewness is, therefore, necessary in order to guard against the consequences of this assumption.

The concept of skewness will be clear from the following three diagrams showing a symmetrical distribution, a positively skewed distribution and negatively skewed distribution.

(a) Symmetrical distribution

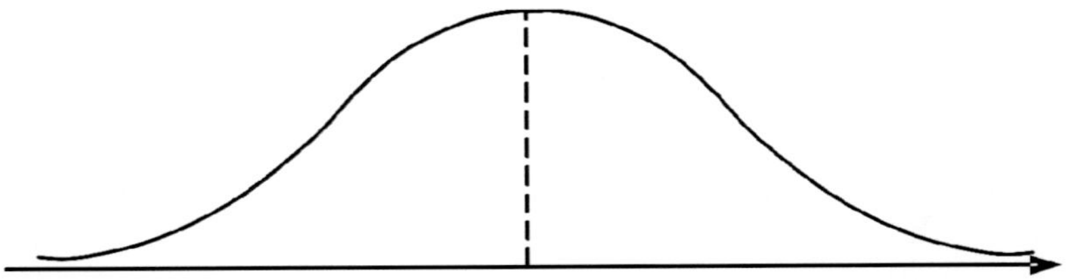

$\overline{X}$=MED = MODE

It is clear form the above diagram that in a symmetrical distribution the values of mean, median and mode coincide. The spread of the frequencies is the same on both sides of the centre point of the curve.

(b) Positively skewed distribution

A distribution which is not symmetrical is called a skewed distribution and such a distribution could either could either be positively skewed or negatively skewed as would be clear from the following diagram:

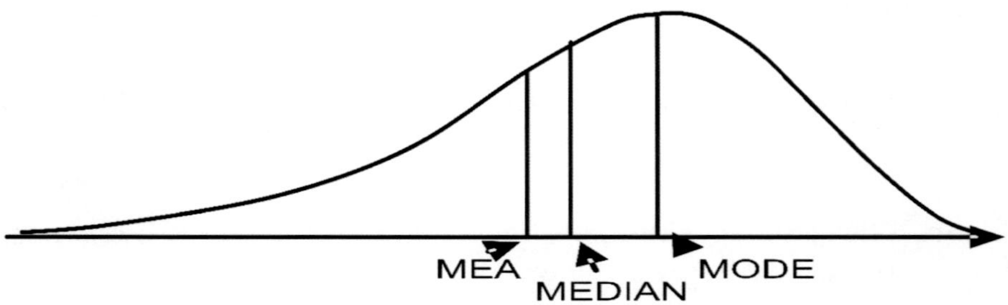

(c) Negatively skewed distribution

In the positively skewed distribution the value of the mean is maximum and that of mode least – the median lies in between the two. In a negatively skewed distribution the value of mode is maximum and that of mean least-the median lies in between the two. In the positively skewed distribution the frequencies are spread out over a greater range of values on the high-value end of the curve (the right-hand side) than they are on the low – value end. In the negatively skewed distribution the position is reversed, i.e., the excess tail is on the left-hand side

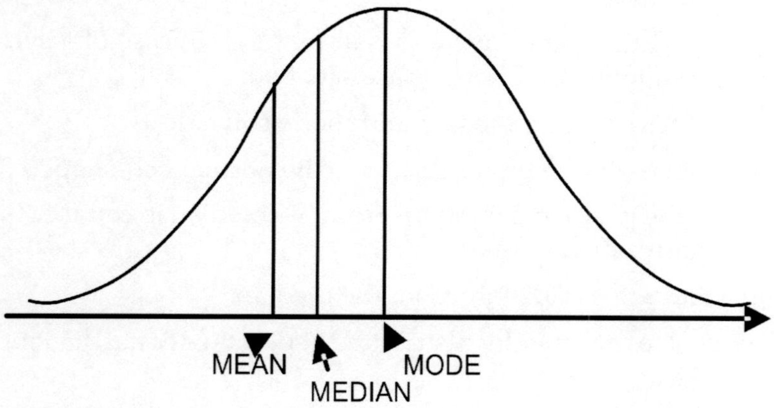

It should be noted that in moderately symmetrical distribution the interval between the mean and the median is approximately one-third of the interval between the mean and the mode. It is this relationship which provides a means of measuring the degree of skewness.

Difference between Dispersion and Skewness

Dispersion is concerned with the amount of variation rather than with its direction. Skewness tells us about the direction of the variation or the departure from symmetry. In fact, measures of skewness are dependent upon amount of distribution.

It may be noted that although skewness is an important characteristic for defining the precise pattern of a distribution, it is rarely calculated in business and economic series. Variation is by far the most important characteristic of a distribution.

4.5.3 Tests of skewness

In order to ascertain whether a distribution is skewed or not, the following tests may be applied. Skewness is present if:

(i) The values of mean, median and mode do not coincide.

(ii) When the data are plotted on a graph they do not give the normal bell-shaped form, i.e., when cut along a vertical line through the centre the two halves are not equal.

(iii) The sum of the positive deviations from the median is not equal to the sum of the negative deviations.

(iv) Quartiles are not equidistant from the median.

(v) Frequencies are not equally distributed at points of equal deviation from the mode.

Conversely state, when skewness is absent, i.e., in case of a symmetrical distribution, the following conditions are satisfied:

(i) The values of mean, median and mode coincide.

(ii) Data when plotted on a graph give the normal bell-shaped form.

(iii) Sum of the positive deviations from the median is equal to the sum of the negative deviations.

(iv) Quartiles are equidistant from the median.

(v) Frequencies are equally distributed at points of equal deviations, from the mode.

4.5.4 Measures of skewness

Measures of skewness tell us the direction and extent of asymmetry in a series, and permit us to compare two or more series with regard to these. They may either be absolute or relative.

Absolute measures of skewness

Skewness can be measured in absolute terms by taking the difference between mean and mode. Symbolically,

Absolute Sk* = $\overline{X}$ – Mode.

If the value of mean is greater than mode skewness will be positive i.e., we shall get a plus sign in the above formula. Conversely, if the value of mode is grater then mean, we shall get a minus sign meaning thereby that the distribution is negatively skewed.

The reason why the difference between mean and mode can be used to measure skewness is that in a symmetrical distribution the values of mean, median and mode are alike, but the mean moves away from the mode when the observations are asymmetrical. Consequently, the distance between the mean and the mode could be used to measure skewness-the grater this distance, whether positive of negative, the more asymmetrical the distribution. However, such a measure is unsatisfactory on two counts:

(i) It would be expressed in the unit of value of the distribution and could, therefore, not be compared with another comparable series expressed in different units.

(ii) Distribution vary greatly and the difference between, say, the Mean and Mode in absolute terms might be considerable in one series and small in another, although the frequency curves of two distributions were similarly skewed.

If the absolute difference were expressed in relation to some measure of the spread of values in their respective distribution, the measure would be relative and can be used directly for comparison. This leads us to the discussion of the relative measures of skewness.

Relative measures of skewness

There are four important measures of relative skewness, namely,

1. The Karl Pearson's coefficient of skewness.

   *When skewness is based on quartiles, absolute skewness is given by the formula absolute Sk = $Q_2 + Q_{1\text{-}2}$ Median.

2. The Bowler's coefficient of skewness.
3. The Kelly's coefficient of skewness.
4. Measure of skewness based on moments.

The measures of skewness should mainly be used for making comparison between two or more distributions. As a description of one distribution alone, the interpretation of a measure of measure of skewness is necessarily vague as "slight skewness', or 'moderate skewness.

Requisites of good measure of skewness

A good measure of skewness should have three properties. It should

1. be a pure number in the sense that its value should be independent of the units of the series and also of the degree of variation in the series,
2. have a zero value, when the distribution is symmetrical, and
3. have some meaningful scale of measure so that we could easily interpret the measured value.

Karl pearson's coefficient of skewness

This method of measuring skewness, also known a Pearsonian Coefficient of Skewness, was suggested by Karl Pearson (1857 – 1936), a great British Biometrician and Statistician. It is based upon the difference between mean and mode. This difference is divided by standard deviation to give a relative measure. The formula thus becomes:

$$Sk_p = \frac{\text{Mean} - \text{Mode}}{\text{Standard Deviation}} \qquad \text{(i)}$$

Sk_p = Karl Pearson's coefficient of skewness.

There is no limit to this measure in theory and this is a slight drawback. But in practice the value given by this formula is rarely very high and usually lies between ± 1.

When a distribution is symmetrical, the values of mean, median and mode coincide and, therefore, the coefficient of skewness will be zero. When a distribution is positively skewed, the coefficient of skewness shall have plus sign and when it is negatively skewed, the coefficient of skewness numerical value, say, 0.8 or 0.2, etc. Thus this formula gives both the direction as well as the extent of skewness.

The above method of measuring skewness cannot be used where mode is ill defined. However, in moderately skewed distribution the averages have the following relationship:

Mode =3 Median -2 Mean

Around 1890, the British Mathematician Karl Pearson (1857 – 1936) began to publish work that has come to be regarded as the beginning of modern statistics, and, therefore, if this value of mode is substituted in the above formula we arrive at another formula for finding out skewness,

$$sk_p = \frac{\left[\overline{X} - \left(3\text{Med} - 2\overline{X}\right)\right]}{\sigma} = \frac{\overline{X} - 3\text{Med} + 2\overline{X})]}{\sigma} = \frac{3(\overline{X} - \text{Med.})}{\sigma} \qquad \text{(ii)}$$

Theoretically, the value of this coefficient varies between ± 3 ; however, in practice it is rare that the coefficient of skewness obtained by the above method exceeds ± 1.

Bowley's coefficient of skewness

An alternative measure of skewness has been proposed by late Professor Bowley. Bowley's measure is based on quartiles. In a symmetrical distribution first and third quartiles are equidistant from the median as can seen from the following diagram.

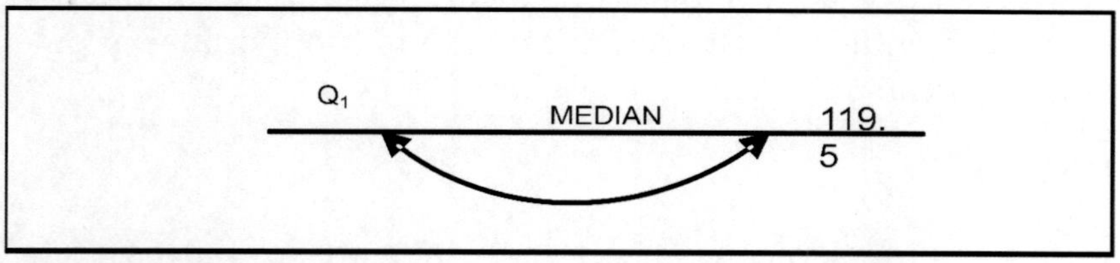

In an asymmetrical distribution the third quartile is the same distance over the median as the first quartile is below it i.e.,

Q_3 – Med. = Med.-Q_1 or $Q_3 + Q_1$ -2 Med. = 0

If this distribution is positively skewed the top 25 per cent of the values will tend to be father from median than the bottom 25 per cent, i.e., Q_2 will be farther from median than Q_1 is from median and the reverse for negative skewness. Hence a possible measure is

$$Sk_B = \frac{(Q_3 - \text{Med}) - (\text{Med.} - Q_1)}{(Q_3 - \text{Med.}) + (\text{Med.} - Q_1)} \text{ or } \frac{(Q_3 + Q_1 - 2\text{Med})}{Q_3 + Q_1}$$

Sk_B = Bowley's coefficient of skewness

It must be remembered that the results obtained by these two measures are not to be compared with one another. Especially, the numerical values are not related to one another since the Bowley's measure. Because of its computational basis, is limited to values between -1 and ± 1, while Pearson's measure has no such limits.

Not only do the numerical values obtained from these two formula bear no necessary relationship to one another but, on rare occasions, with unusually shaped distribution, it is possible for them to emerge with opposite signs.

Kelly's coefficient of skewness

Bowley's measure discussed above neglects the two extreme quarters of the data. It would be better for a measure to cover the entire data especially because in measuring skewness, we are often interested in the more extreme items. Bowley's measure can be extended by taking any two deciles equidistant from the median or any two percentiles equidistant form the median. Kelly has suggested the following formula for measuring skewness upon the 10th and the 90th percentiles (or the first and ninth deciles)

$$Sk_{\overline{K}} = \frac{P_{10} + P_{90} - 2\text{Med.}}{P_{90} + P_{10}} \text{ also Sk } = \frac{D_1 + D_9 - 2\text{Med}}{D_9 + D_1}$$

$Sk_{\overline{K}}$ = Kelley's coefficient of Skewness.

This measure of skewness has one theoretical attraction if skewness is to be based on percentiles. However, this method is not popular in practice and generally Karl Pearson's method is used.

4.6 Kurtosis

Kurtosis in Greek means "bulginess". In statistics kurtosis refers to the degree of flatness or peakedness in the region about the mode of a frequency curve. The degree of kurtosis of distribution is measured relative to the peakedness of normal curve. In other words, measured of kurtosis tell us the extent to which a distribution is more peaked of flat-topped than the normal curve.* If a curve is more peaked than the normal curve, it is called 'leptokurtic'. In such a case items are more closely bunched around the mode. On the other hand if a curve is more flat-topped than the normal curve, it is called 'platykutic'. The normal curve itself is known as 'mesokurtic'. The condition of peakedness or flat-toppedness itself as kurtosis of excess. The concept of kurtosis is rarely used in elementary statistical analysis.

The following diagram illustrates the shape of three different curves mentioned above:

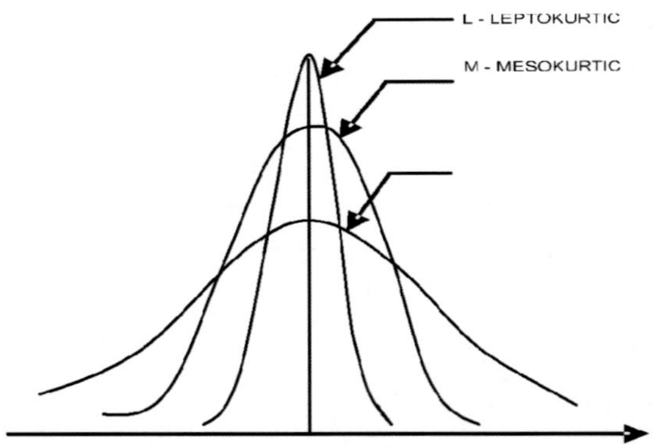

The above diagram clearly shows that these curves differ widely with regard to convexity, an attribute which Karl Pearson referred to as 'kurtosis'. Curve M is a normal one and is called 'mesopkurtic'. Curve L is more peaked than M and is called 'leptokurtic'. A leptokurtic curve has narrower central portion and higher tails than does the normal curve. Curve p is less peaked (or more flat-topped) than curve M and is called 'platykurtic'. As may be seen from the diagram, such a curve has broader central and lower tails.

A famous British Statistician William S. Gosset ("Student") has very humorously pointed out the nature of these curves in the sentence, "Platykurtic curves, like the platypus, are squat with short tails: leptokurtic curves are high with long tails like the kangaroos noted for lepping".

4.6.1 Measures of kurtosis

The most important measure of kurtosis is the value of the coefficient β_2. It is defined as :

$$\beta_2 = \frac{\mu_4}{\mu_2^2} \text{ where } \mu_4 = 4^{th} \text{ moment and } \mu_2 = 2^{nd} \text{ moment}$$

The greater the value of $\beta_{2,}$ the more peaked the distribution.

For a normal curve, the value of $\sigma y_2 = 3$. When the value of β_2- is greater than 3, the curve is more peaked than the normal curve, i.e., leptokurtic. When the value of β_2 is less than 3 the curve is less peaked than the normal curve, i.e., platykurtic. The normal curve and other curves with $\beta_2 = 3$ are called mesokurtic.

Sometimes γ_2 the derivative of β_2, is used as measure of kurtosis. γ_2 is defined as

$$\gamma_2 = \beta_2 - 3$$

For a normal distribution $\gamma_2 = 0$. If γ_2 is positive, the curve is leptokurtic and if γ_2 is negative, the curve is platykurtic.

Exercise

1. What is dispersion? What are various measures of dispersion?
2. What is meant by relative measure of dispersion? Describe its uses.
3. Define mean deviation. How does it differ from standard deviation?
4. What is standard deviation? Explain its important properties? What is variance?
5. Calculate median and mean deviation for the following frequency distribution:

Age in Years	No. of persons
1-5	7
6-10	10
11-15	16
16-20	32
21-25	24
26-30	18
31-35	10
36-40	5
41-45	1

6. The mean of two sample sizes 50 and 100 respectively are 54.1 and 50.3 and the standard deviations are 8 and 7. find the mean and standard deviation of the sample size of 150 obtained by combining the two samples

7. Following data represents the lifes of two models of refrigerators A and B.

Life (No. of years)	Refrigerator	
	Model A	Model B
0-2	5	2
2-4	16	7
4-6	13	12
6-8	7	19
8-10	5	9
10-12	4	1

Find the mean life of each mode. Which model has greater uniform it? Also obtain mode for both models.

8. Calculate the coefficient of quartile deviation and coefficient of variation from the following data:

Size	06	09	12	15	18
Frequency	7	12	19	10	2

9. Calculate the appropriate measure of dispersion from the following data

Wages in Rs.	Below 35	35-37	38-40	41-43	Over 43
Earners	14	60	95	24	7

10. Two brands of tyres are tested with the following results

Life 1000 of miles:	20-25	25-30	30-35	35-40	40-45	45-50
Brand A:	8	15	12	18	13	9
Brand B:	6	20	32	30	12	0

11. Find the mean days S.D. of confinement after delivery in the following series.

Days of confinement	5	6	7	8	9
No. of patients	18	14	9	3	1

❑❑❑

Chapter – 5

Probability

In day-to-day life, one comes across many statements which create doubt about certain happenings and one may want to determine the chance of occurrence of a particular happening, e.g., if one desires to know the chance of rain based on some metrological observations. In the case of coin tossing, one wants to know what will be the chance of winning if a person always stakes for head in a fixed number of tossing. There can be innumerable such queries which one would like to make and meanwhile evaluate mathematically the chance of the occurrence of such possibilities. This invoked the need of probability theory. The theory of probability came in existence when problems of games were referred to mathematicians like Karl Pearson, Laplace and others. Complicated applications involving advanced theory of probability and axionmatic approach of probability are not dealt within this book.

The definition of probability, on the basis of observational phenomenon, needs some basic ideas on random experiments, sample space and event etc. These are explained and followed by an explanation of probability theory.

5.1 Random Experiment

If an experiment or trial can be repeated any number of times similar conditions and it is possible to enumerate the total number of outcomes, but individual outcome is not predictable, such an experiment is called a *random experiment*. For instance, if a fair coin is tossed three times, it is possible to enumerate all the possible eight sequences of head (H) and tail (T). But it is not possible to predict which sequence will occur at any occasion. This is one example of a random experiment. Many more can be thought of.

5.2 Sample Space

Each conceivable outcome of random experiment under consideration is said to be a *sample point.* The totality of all conceivable sample point is called a sample space. Sample space of a trail conducted by three tossing of a coin is, *HHH, HHT, HTH, HTT, THH, THT, TTH, TTT.*

In the above experiment it is simple to note that anyone sequence of H and / or T is a sample point whereas all the possible eight sample points constitute the sample space.

5.3 Event

Any subset of the sample space is an *event.* In other words, the set of sample points which satisfy certain requirement(s) is called an event.
For example, in the event, that are exactly two heads in three tossings of a coin, it would consist of three points *HTH, HHT* and *THH*..

Complementary Event: The *complement* of an event A, means non-occurrence of A and is denoted by $\overline{A}$ or A^c, $\overline{A}$ contains those points of the sample space which do not belong to A.

Elementary Event: An event having only one sample point is called an *elementary event* or *simple event.*

Mutually Exclusive Events: Tow events E_1 and E_2 are said to be mutually exclusive if the occurrence of E_1 precludes the occurrence of E_2 and vice versa. In other words if there is no sample point in E_1 which is common to the sample points in E_2, i.e., $E_1 \cap E_2 = \phi$, the events E_1 and E_2 are said to be *mutually exclusive.* For example, if we flip a fair coin, the coin will display either head or tail. Hence, the two events that the coin displays head E_1 and tail E_2 are mutually exclusive.

Independent Events: Two events E_1 and E_2 are said to be *independent* if the occurrence of E1 has no bearing on the occurrence of E_2 i.e., the knowledge that the event E_1 has occurred gives no information about the occurrence of the event E_2. Formally, two events E_1 and E_2 are independent if and only if.

$$P(E_1 \cap E_2) = P(E_1)\,P(E_2) \tag{5.1}$$

The intersection, $(E_1 \cap E_2)$, between two events E_1 and E_2 is known as joint event.

5.4 Mathematical or Classical Definition of Probability

This definition of probability is credited to Laplace. If there are *N* mutually exclusive and equally likely outcomes of random experiment, and out of these *N* outcomes, only n are favourable to an attribute i.e. *N* sample points constitute an event *E* under consideration, the probability of the event *E* is

$$P(E) = \frac{n}{N} \tag{5.2}$$

In the trail of tossing a coin three times, N=8 and for the event E that there are exactly two heads, n = 3. It means that there are only three points favourable to E. Thus, the probability of event E is 3/8. Similarly if for the event E_1 is there are atleast two heads, n = 4. The probability of the event E_1 is 4/8 i.e. ½.

The above definition of probability is widely used, but it cannot be applied under the following situations:

(i) If it is not possible to enumerate all the possible outcomes for an experiment.

(ii) If the sample points (outcomes) are not mutually independent.

(iii) If the total number of outcomes is infinite.

(iv) If each and every outcome is not equally likely.

It is clear that the above drawbacks of a classical approach restrict its use in practical problems. Some of the drawbacks of a classical probability are removed in another definition given below.

5.5 Statistical Definition of Probability

If out of a large number of trials, only *n* of them are conducted and out of these *n* outcomes under each trial, only *k* outcomes under each trial, only *k* outcomes are favourable to an event *E*, then the probability of *E* is,

$$P(E) = \lim_{n\to\infty}\left(\frac{k}{n}\right) \tag{5.3}$$

The above definition of probability involves a concept which has a long term consequence. The approach was initiated by von Mises. Moreover *n* is not equal to infinity. Thus, in this case, the probability is the limit of relative frequency. Whether such a limit always exists, is not definite. Hence statistical definition of probability is also not very sound. The probability calculated by conducting an actual experiment is called a *posterior probability,* whereas the probability specified by logic or based on some prior information is called a *priori probability.*

Basic Properties of Probability

(1) The probability of an event E lies between 0 and 1. i.e., $0 \le P(E) \le 1$. If an event is certain not to occur, its probability is zero and if it is certain to occur, its probability is one.

(2) The assignment of probability to each outcomes of an experiment is a rule to assign a non-negative number such that the sum of these numbers to all possible outcomes 'Ω' is unity, i.e. $P(\Omega) = 1$.

(3) Any two equivalent events will be assigned the same probability.

(4) If two events E_1 and E_2 are mutually exclusive, the probability of occurrence of either E_1 or E_2 i.e., of $(E_1 \cup E_2)$ is given as the sum of the individual probabilities, symbolically,

$$P(E_1 \cup E_2) = P(E_1) + P(E_2) \qquad (5.4)$$

This property of probability is known as *general additive property of probability or addition law.* This theorem may be extended to any number of mutually exclusive events. If E_1 E_2, ... E_x are k mutually exclusive events, the probability.

$$P(E_1 \cup E_2 \cup \ldots \cup E_k) = P(E_1) + P(E_2) + \ldots + P(E_k) \qquad (5.5)$$

Example

If we draw a card from a pack, what is the probability that the card is either ace or a king? The events that the card drawn is either an ace or a king are mutually exclusive. Let the event of the ace and card drawn be denoted by E_1 and the king card drawn be denoted by E_2. A pack consisting of 52 cards will have 4 aces and 4 kings, hence.

$$P(E_1) = \frac{4}{52} \text{ and } P(E_2) = \frac{4}{52}$$

$$P(E_1 \cup E_2) = P(E_1) + P(E2) = \frac{4}{52} + \frac{4}{52} = \frac{2}{13}$$

Readers will come across many other problems in which the additive property will be used.

Consider the case where two events, E_1 and E_2 are not mutually exclusive. The probability of the event that either E_1 or E_2 or both occur is given as,

$$P(E_1 \cup E_2) = P(E_1) + P(E_2) - P(E_1 \cap E_2) \qquad (5.6)$$

The events $(E_1 \cup E_2)$ consists of those points which are common to E_1 and E_2. In $\{P(E_1) + P(E_2)\}$, the probability $P(E_1 \cap E_2)$ has been included twice while in $(E_1 \cup E_2)$, $(E_1 \cap E_2)$ has occurred only once. Hence for finding out $P(E_1 \cup E_2)$, the probability $P(E_1 \cap E_2)$ has been subtracted once from $P(E_1) + P(E_2)$.

In the like manner, the formula for probability of the union of three mutually nonexclusive events E_1, E_2, and E_3 is,

$$P(E_1 \cup E_2 \cup E_3) = P(E_1) + P(E_2) + P(E_3) - P(E_1 \cap E_2) - P(E_1 \cap E_3) - P(E_2 \cap E_3) + P(E_1 \cap E_2 \cap E_3) \quad (5.7)$$

By induction, formula (5.7) can be extended to any number of mutually nonexclusive events.

Example

A die is thrown twice. The probability that the sum of the spots on the die at two throws is divisible by 2 or 3 can be calculated in the following manner. Let the events, be that the sum of the sports on the die is divisible by 2, denoted by E_1 and the sum if divisible by 3 is denoted by E_2 and are given bellow.

E_1	(1.1), (4.2),	(1.3), (4,4),	(1.5), (4.6),	(2.2), (5.1),	(2.4), (5.3),	(3.3), (5.5)	(4.2), (6.2)	(5.1), (6.4)	(6.6) (6.6)
E_2	(1.2), (5.4),	(1.5), (6.3),	(2.1), (6.6).	(2.4),	(3.3),	(3.6),	(4.2),	(4.5),	(5.1)

The point common the the events E_1 and E_2 are,

$E_1 \cap E_2$: (1,5), (2,4), (3,3), (4,2), (5,1), (6,6)

Total number of pairs of sports = 36,

Obviously the events E_1 and E_2 are not mutually exclusive. Hene the probability of the event $(E_1 \cup E_2)$ i.e., the sum of the spots is divisible by 2 or 3 is,

$$P(E_1 \cup E_2) = P(E_1) + P(E_2) - P(E_1 \cap E_2)$$

$$\text{where } P(E_1) = \frac{18}{36} = \frac{1}{2}, P(E_2) = \frac{12}{36} = \frac{1}{3}; P(E_1 \cap E_2) = \frac{6}{36} = \frac{1}{6}$$

$$\text{Thus, } P(E_1 \cap E_2) = \frac{1}{2} + \frac{1}{3} - \frac{1}{6} = \frac{2}{3} = 0.667$$

(5) Two events E_1 and E_2 defined over a sample space Ω are said to be independent if and only if,

$$P(E_1 \cap E_2) = P(E_1)\,P(E_2)$$

The above rule may be extended to any number of events. Let $E_1, E_2 \ldots, E_k$ be k events defined over the sample space Ω, the events. E_1's (i=1,2,…,k) are said to be independent if and only if.

$$P(E_1 \cap E_{2 \cap} \ldots {}_{\cap} E_k) = P(E_1\text{-})\,P(E_2) \ldots P(E_k) \quad (5.8)$$

Or $$P\left(\bigcap_{i=1}^{k} E_i\right) = \prod_{i=1}^{k} P(E_1) \qquad (5.8.1)$$

The above rule is known as Multiplicative law of probability.

Example

A bag contains 8 white balls and 4 red balls. One ball is drawn from the bag and it is replaced after noting its colour. In the second draw again one ball is drawn and its colour is noted. The probability of the event that both the balls drawn are of different colours can be found out as follows:

Let the events that the ball at first draw is of white colour and at the second draw is of red colour be denoted by E_1 and E_2 respectively.

Total number of ways in which a ball can be drawn = $\binom{12}{1} = 12$

Number of ways in which a white ball can be drawn = $\binom{8}{1} = 8$

Number of ways in which a red ball can be drawn = $\binom{4}{1} = 4$

Hence, $P(E_1) = \frac{8}{12} = \frac{2}{3}$

$P(E_2) = \frac{4}{12} = \frac{1}{3}$

Since the events E_1 and E_2 are independent.

$P(E_1 \cap E_2) = P(E_1)P(E_2)$

$= \frac{2}{3} \times \frac{1}{2} = \frac{2}{9} = 0.22$

Now, consider the situation when a unit selected is not replaced. In this case, the number of points in the sample are reduced by the number of units selected. Hence the total number of sample points at each subsequent draw would change. The probability at any draw can be calculated as per the rules discussed so far. Now we consider an example for this situation.

Example

Consider again the example 5.3 with the modification that the ball selected at the first draw is not replaced. We calculate the probability of the event E that the two balls selected at two successive draws are of different colours. The balls can be selected in two easy.

Case (i) if the ball at the first draw, white and at the second draw, red is represented by the event A.

As in example 5.3, $P(E) = \frac{2}{3}$

At the time of the second draw, total number of balls in the bag is 11 and the number of red balls is 4. The prob. of selection of red ball = $\binom{4}{1} / \binom{11}{1} = \frac{4}{11}$.

Thus, the prob. of the event A

$$P(A)\frac{2}{3} \times \frac{4}{11} = \frac{8}{33}$$

Case (ii) If the ball drawn at the first draw, red and at the second draw, white is represented by the event B.

Prob. of a red ball selected at first draw

$$= \binom{4}{1} / \binom{12}{1} = \frac{4}{12} = \frac{1}{3}.$$

Prob. of a white ball selected at second draw

$$= \binom{8}{1} / \binom{11}{1} = \frac{8}{11}.$$

Prob. of the event $B = \frac{1}{3} \times \frac{8}{11} = \frac{8}{33}$

Since the two cases are mutually exclusive, their probabilities will be added.

Thus, P(E) = P(A) + P(B)

$$= \frac{8}{33} + \frac{8}{33} = \frac{16}{33} = 0.485$$

Example

A sheet containing 10 riddles is given to three graduate students of three different subjects. It is considered that a mathematics' student can solve 60% riddles, a Physics' student can solve 40% riddles and that of economics 30% riddles. The probability of an event 'E' that a riddle chosen from the sheet will be solved by all the three students is calculable as given below.

Prob. of solving the riddle by a Math. student = 0.6

Prob. of solving the riddle by a Physics' student = 0.4

Prob. of solving the riddle by an Economics' student = 0.3

Solving of a riddle by a student is independent of solving the riddle by the other student.

Hence the probability,

$P(E) = 0.6 \times 0.4 \times 0.3 = 0.072$

Example 5.6 : A stockist has 20 items in a lot. Out of which, 12 are non-defective and 8 defective. A customer selects 3 items from the lot.

(i) What is the probability that all the three items are non-defective.

(ii) What is the probability that out of these three items, two are non-defective and one is defective.

The probability in the two cases is calculable in the following manner.

Case (i) Let the event, that all the three items are non-defective, be denoted by E_1.

There are 12 non-defective items and out of them 3 can be selected in $\binom{12}{3}$ ways

Total number of ways in which 3 items can be selected are $\binom{20}{3}$.

Hence the probability.

$$P(E_1) = \binom{12}{3} / \binom{20}{3} = \frac{12 \times 11 \times 10}{20 \times 19 \times 10} = 0.193$$

Case (ii) Let the event, that two items are non-defective and one is defective, be denoted by E_2.

Two non-defective items out of 12 non-defective items can be selected in $\binom{12}{2}$ ways and one item out of 8 defective items can be selected in $\binom{8}{1}$ ways.

Thus the total number of favourable ways to $E_2 = \binom{12}{2}\binom{8}{1}$

The probability, $P(E_2) = \binom{12}{2}\binom{8}{1} / \binom{20}{3} = \dfrac{12 \times 11 \times 8 \times 3}{20 \times 19 \times 18} = 0.463$

Example 5.7 : A fair die is thrown twice. The probability that the sum of spots at two throws is more than nine can be calculated in the manner given below.

The sum of spots being more than nine means that it can be 10,11 or 12. Let the three events be denoted by E_1 E_2 and E_3, respectively.

In two throws, total number of sample points = 36

The sample points in E_2 are: (4,6), (5,5), (6,4)

The sample points in E_2 are: (5,6) (6,5)

The sample point in E_3 is: (6,6)

Let the event that sum of spots at two throws is more than nine is denoted by E.

The event E_1, E_2 and E_3 are mutually exclusive. Hence the probability.

$$P(E) = P(E_1) + (P(E_2) + P(E_3)$$

$$= \frac{3}{36} + \frac{2}{36} + \frac{1}{36} = \frac{1}{6}$$

Example

There are three radio stations A,B and C which can be received in a city of 2000 families. The following information is available on the basis of a survey.

(a) 1200 families listen to radio station A.

(b) 1100 families listen to radio station B.

(c) 800 families listen to radio station C.

(d) 865 families listen to the radio stations A and B.

(e) 450 families listen to the radio stations A and C.

(f) 400 families listen to the radio stations B and C.

(g) 100 families listen to the radio stations A, B and C.

The probability that a family selected at random listens at least to one ratio station can be calculated as follows. We first define the events.

A family listens to radio station A = E_1

A family listens to radio station B = E_2

A family listens to radio station C = E_3

We can defined the events that a family listens to any two radio stations by $E_1 \cap E_2$, $E_1 \cap E_3$ and $E_2 \cap E_3$. The event that a family listens to all the three stations is given by $E_1 \cap E_2 \cap E_3$. The event that a family listens to at least one radio station is equivalent to $E_1 \cup E_2 \cup E_3$. The probability of the event $E_1 \cup E_2 \cup E_3$ is obtained by formula (5.7).

Total number of families = 2000

Number of favourable ways to different events are from data in (a) to (g).

Hence the probability,

$$P(E_1 \cup E_2 \cup E_3) = P(E_1) + P(E_2) + P(E_3) - P(E_1 \cap E_2)$$
$$- P(E_1 \cap E_3) - P(E_2 \cap E_3) + (P(E_1 \cap E_2 \cap E_3)$$

$$= \frac{1200}{2000} + \frac{1100}{2000} + \frac{800}{2000} - \frac{865}{2000} - \frac{450}{2000} - \frac{400}{2000} + \frac{100}{2000} = \frac{1485}{2000} = 0.742$$

There is around 74% chance that a family selected at random listens to one or more radio stations.

5.6 Conditional Probability

In many situations we have the information about the occurrence of an event. A and are required to find out the probability of the occurrence of another event B. This is denoted By P(B/A). For example, if we know that a card drawn from a pack is black and we want to calculate the probability that it is the ace of spade.

Let us take the problem of throwing a fair die twice. Suppose, the same number of spots do not appear in both the throws and we are required to find out the probability that the sum of the number of spots in both the throws is six.

Let us consider a biometrical problem. A patient comes to a doctor with his family history that his elders suffered from high blood pressure. He wants to know the probability of the event that he will also suffers from high blood pressure.

Now we consider an industrial problem. There are two lots of certain finished parts, lot A and lot B. Each lot has some defective parts. If we flip a coin and it turns up with its head upside we select lot A and if it turns with tail up, we select the lot B. We are interested to know the probability of the event, that a part selected from the lot obtained in this manner is defective.

Any number of examples in various disciplines can be cited. The readers themselves can think of problems relevant to the conditional probability pertaining to their own sphere of activity.

Definition: Let A and B be two events. The *conditional probability* of event B, if an event A has occurred, is defined by the relation,

$$P(B / A) = \frac{P(B \cap A)}{P(A)} \quad \text{if} \quad P(A) > 0 \tag{5.9}$$

In case when P(A) = 0, P(B) (A) is not defined because $P(B \cap A) = 0$ and P(B/A) = 0/0 which is an indeterminate quantity.

The conditional probability concept can be extended to the case where B_1, $B_{2,} ......$ B_k is a sequence of mutually exclusive events given that an event A has occurred. The probability of the event $\overset{k}{\underset{i=1}{\cup}} B_i$, if the event A has occurred is,

$$P\left(\overset{k}{\underset{i=1}{\cup}} B_1 / A\right) = \frac{P\left(\overset{k}{\underset{i=1}{\cup}} B_1 \cap A\right)}{P(A)} = \frac{\sum_{i=1}^{k} P(B_i \cap A)}{P(A)} \tag{5.10}$$

$$\text{if } P(A) > 0 \tag{5.10.1}$$

Example

If a card drawn from a pack of cars is black, represented by the event A, the probability of the event B that the card drawn is ace of spade, can be calculated by formula (5.9).

The number of cards in the pack = 52.

Out of 52 cards, the number of black cards = 26

Prob. of drawing a black card i.e. P(A) = 26/52 = ½

Out of 26 black cards, only one is an ace of spade.

The event $B \cap A$ contains only one point and thus,

$$P = (B \cap A) = 1/52$$

Now the probability,

$$P(B / A) = \frac{P(B \cap B)}{P(A)} = \frac{1/52}{1/2} = \frac{1}{26}$$

Example

An experiment is conducted by throwing a fair die twice. Suppose the event that the same number of spots do not turn up in two throws is denoted by A, and the event that the sum of spots in two throws is 6, is denoted by B.

The probability of the event (B/A) can be worked out as follows:

There can be in all 36 pairs of spots which are:

1,1	1,2	1,3	1,4	1,5	1,6
2,1	2,2	2,3	2,4	2,5	2,6
3,1	3,2	3,3	3,4	3,5	3,6
4,1	4,2	4,3	4,4	4,5	4,6
5,1	5,2	5,3	5,4	5,5	5,6
6,1	6,2'	6,3	6,4	6,5	6,6

Out of these 36 pairs, 30 are favourable to the event A. It means that in A, the pairs (1,1) (2,2), (3,3), (4,4), (5,5) and (6,6) are excluded.

$$P(A) = 30/36 = 5/6$$

The points favourable to event B are:

(1,5), (2,4), (4,2) and (5,1)

Hence the probability,

$$P(B \cap A) = 4/36$$

Thus, the required probability,

$$P(B / A) = \frac{4 / 36}{30 / 46} = \frac{4}{30} = 0.133$$

Example

The information at hand reveals that 10% of the patients feel they suffer from tuberculosis (T.B.) and are really suffering from it, 30% feel that they suffer from T.B. but they don't suffer from this disease, 25% don't feel it but are suffering from T.B. The remaining 25% neither feel nor suffer from T.B. Then the probability of the four events.

E_1 : A person who has T.B. and feels the suffers from T.B.

E_2 : The person who has T.B. and does not feel it.

E_3 : The person who feels that he has T.B. and does suffer from T.B.

E_4: A person who feels that he has T.B. and has T.B.

Is calculated in the manner given below.

Let us defined the events as follows:

The person who feels that he has T.B.:A

The person who suffers from T.B. :B

The complementary events to A and B are denoted by $\overline{A}$ and $\overline{B}$ respectively. Now,

$A \cap B$: The person who feels he suffers from T.B. and does suffer from its.

Thus, $P(A \cap B) = 0.10$

Similarly,

$P(A \cap \overline{B}) = 0.30$, $P(\overline{A} \cap B) = 0.25$ and $P(\overline{A} \cap \overline{B}) = 0.35$

we can write,

$$P(A) = P(A \cap B) + P(A \cap \overline{B}) = 0.10 + 0.30 = 0.40$$
$$P(B) = P(A \cap B) + P(A \cap B) = 0.10 + 0.25 = 0.35$$
$$P(\overline{A}) = P(\overline{A} \cap B) + P(\overline{A} \cap \overline{B}) = 0.25 + 0.35 = 0.60$$
$$P(\overline{B}) = P(A \cap \overline{B}) + P(\overline{A} \cap \overline{B}) = 0.30 + 0.35 = 0.65$$

Now the probabilities of the events E_1, E_2, E_3 and E_4 are given below straight way.

(i) $$P(E_1) = P(B / A) = \frac{P(B \cap A)}{P(A)} = \frac{0.10}{0.40} = \frac{1}{4} = 0.25$$

(ii) $$P(E_2) = P(B / \overline{A}) = \frac{P(B \cap \overline{A})}{P(A)} = \frac{0.25}{0.60} = \frac{5}{12} = 0.417$$

(iii) $$P(E_3) = P(A / \overline{B}) = \frac{P(A \cap \overline{B})}{P(B)} = \frac{0.30}{0.65} = \frac{6}{13} = 0.462$$

(iv) $$P(E_4) = P(A / B) = \frac{P(A \cap B)}{P(B)} = \frac{0.10}{0.35} = \frac{2}{7} = 0.286$$

Example

There are two lots of a manufactured item. Lot one contains 40 pieces whereas lot two contains 5- pieces. It is known that the former lot contains 25 per cent defective pieces and the later one 10 per cent. We flip a coin and select a piece from lot one if it turns with head up otherwise we select piece from lot two. The probability of the event that the selected piece will be defective is calculable in the following manner. Define the events as follows.

The piece is selected from lot 1:A

The selection piece is defective : B

Since the probability of turning head up = ½, we have

$$P(A) = \frac{1}{2} \text{ and } P(\overline{A}) = \frac{1}{2}$$

Lot 1 has 10 defective and 30 non-defective pieces.

Lot 2 has 5 defective and 45 non-defective pieces.

Given that,

$$P(B / A) = \frac{1}{4} \text{ and } P(B / \overline{A}) = \frac{1}{10}$$

From relation (5,9) we have,

$$P(A \cap B) = P(B / A)\ P(A) = \frac{1}{4}.\frac{1}{2} = \frac{1}{8}$$

$$P(\overline{A} \cap B) = P(B / \overline{A})\ P(\overline{A}) = \frac{1}{10}.\frac{1}{2} = \frac{1}{20}$$

The probability that the selected piece is defective

$$= P(A \cap B) + P(\overline{A} \cap B)$$

$$= \frac{1}{8} + \frac{1}{20} = \frac{7}{40} = 0.175$$

5.7 Bayes' Probabilities

The principle given by Thomas Bayes in 1763 was reprinted in *Biometrika* (1958). His contention was that in absence of any idea about the prior probability of an event occurring, out of all possible events, one may assume that all the values of the probabilities are equal. Then on the basis of the experimental results (out comes), one modifies his equally likely probabilities giving the posteriori probabilities. Briefly, assuming certain apriori probabilities, the posteriori probabilities are obtained. That is way Bayes probabilities are also called posteriori probabilities.

Suppose $E_1, E_2, \ldots E_k$ are k mutually exclusive events defined in B (a collection of events) each being a subset of the sample space Ω such that $\bigcup_{i=1}^{x} E_i = \Omega$ and $P(E_i) > 0$ for i = 1,2,3, …., k. Then for some arbitrary event B, which is associated with E_i's such that $P(B) > 0$, we can find out the probabilities

$P(B/E_1), P(B/E_2), \ldots P(B/E_k)$

In Bayes' approach we want to find out the posterior probability of an event E_1 given that B has occurred, ie., $P(E_i/B)$.

By formula (5,9), we know

$$P(E_i / B) = \frac{P(E_i \cap B)}{P(B)} \tag{5.11}$$

We know B is also a set in Ω and hence $B \cap \Omega = B$ or in the other form,

$$B = B \cap (E_1 \cup E_2 \cup \ldots \cup E_k)$$

Since $\bigcup_{i=1}^{k} E_1 = \Omega$ and E_i's are disjoint.

Or $= B = (B \cap E_1) \cup (B \cap E_2) \cup . \cup (B \cap E_k)$

Thus $P(B) = \sum_{i=1}^{k} P(B \cap E_i)$ (5.12)

From (5.11), $P(B \cap E_i) = P(E_i/B)\, P(B)$ (5.13)

From (5.9),

$$P(B \cap E_i) = P(B/E_i)\, P(E_i) \tag{5.14}$$

Putting the value of $P(B \cap E_i)$ from (5.15) and P(B) from (5.15) in (5.11) we obtain,

$$P(B) = \sum_{i=1}^{k} P(B / E_i) P(E_i) \tag{5.15}$$

Substituting the value of $P(B \cap E_i)$ from (5.14) and P(B) from (5.15) in (5.11) we obtain.

$$P(E_i / B) = \frac{P(B / E_i) P(E_i)}{\sum_{i=1}^{k} \Sigma\, P(B / E_i) P(E_i)} \tag{5.16}$$

Formula (5.16) is known as Bayes' formula. It is used to obtain the posteriori probability of $E\text{-}_{i\text{-}}$ when the event B has occurred. To elucidate the theoretical concepts further, we give two examples.

Example

On the basis of certain information it is known that the judgement given by a judge is correct in 90 per cent of the cases. Also let us suppose that 40 per cent of the criminals produced before the court are actually innocent. The probability of the event that an innocent person produced before the court has been declared innocent, can be worked out in the following manner.

Let the event that the person is innocent = I

The event that the judge declares him innocent = J.

We have to evaluate P(I / J).

Given that,

$P(I)$	=	0.40 and	$P(\bar{I})$	=	0.60
$P(J / I)$	=	0.90 and	$P(\bar{J} / \bar{I})$	=	0.90
$P(J / \bar{I})$	=	0.10 and	$P(\bar{J} / I)$	=	0.10

Using formula (5.16) we get,

$$P(I / J) = \frac{P(J / I)\ P\ (I)}{P(J / I)P(I) + P(J / I)P(I)}$$

$$= \frac{(0.90)\ (0.40)}{(0.90)(0.40) + (0.10)(0.60)} = 0.857$$

Example

In city there are three stores each having 20 pieces of an item. Let these stores be denoted by S_1, S_2 and S_3. The stores, S_1, S_2 and S_3 have 10%, 20% and 30% defective items, respectively. A customer first chooses a store randomly and then selects an item randomly from the store. The probability of an event that the selected item is defective can be calculated as follows: let E_{-I} denote the event that the store S_i (I = 1,2,3) is selected. Then,

$$P(E_i) = 1/3$$

Let B denote the event that a selected item is defective. Given that 10i% items in store I are defective where I = 1,2,3. Hence.

$$P(B / E_i) = \frac{10i}{100} = \frac{i}{10}$$

Now using formula (5.15), the probability of a selected item being defective is,

$$\sum_{x=0}^{2} \frac{e^{-28}(2.8)^x}{x!}$$

If we find that the item selected is defective, the probability that it has come from store S_2 is,

$$P(E_2 / B) = \frac{P(B / E_2)P(E_2)}{\sum_{i=1}^{3} P(B / E_i)P(E_i)} = \frac{\frac{2}{10} \times \frac{1}{3}}{1/5} = \frac{1}{3}$$

Similarly $P(E_i / B) = \frac{1}{6}$ and $P\ (E_2 / B) = \frac{1}{2}$

Exercise

1. Define probability and conditional probability?
2. What is the probability of picking a card that was red or black?
3. A bag contains 30 balls numbered from 1 to 30. One ball is drawn at random. Find the probability that the number of the ball drawn will be a multiple of (a) 5 or 7 and (b) 3 or 7.
4. A problem in Statistics is given to five students A,B,C,D, and E. Their chance of solving of problem are 1/2, 1/3, 1/4, 1/5 and 1/6. What is the probability that the problem will be solved?
5. A bag contains 5 white and 3 black balls. Two balls are drawn at random one after another without replacement. Find the probability that both balls drawn are black.
6. Explain Bayes' theorem and its importance.

❑❑❑

Chapter – 6

Probability Distributions

It has been a general notion that if an experiment is conducted under identical conditions, values so obtained would be similar. But the experiences of people have dispelled this belief. Observations are always taken about a factor or character under study, which can take different values, and the factor or character is termed as variable.

Hence, we have a set of outcomes (sample points) of a random experiment. A rule that assigns a real number to each outcome (sample points) is called *random variable*. The rule is nothing about a function of the variable, say, X, that assigns a unique value to each sample point of the sample space.

From the above discussion it is clear that there is a value for each outcome, which it takes with certain probability. Hence a list of values of a random variable together with their corresponding probabilities of occurrence, is termed as *probability distribution.* As a tradition, probability distribution is used to denote the probability mass or probability density, of either a discontinuous or a continuous variable. The definitions of random variable and certain operations on random variable are explained in the following.

6.1 Random Variable (r.v)

A random variable X is a real valued function, $X(x)$, of the elements of the sample space Ω where x is an element of the sample space. It should be noted that the range of the random variable will be a set of real number.

Generally, a random variable is denoted by capital letters like X, Y, Z, U,V..., whereas the values of the random variable are denoted by the corresponding small letters like x, y, z, u,v, ...

Illustration (i) If we flip a coin and denote the head by 1 and tail by 0, then the random variable X takes only two values 1 and 0. symbolically, the random variable.

$X(x) = \{x: x = (1,0) \in \Omega\}$

Where $\in$ is a connotation for 'belongs to'.

Illustration (ii) If we measure the height of people, the random variable,

$X(x) = \{x: x \text{ is any real positive number}\}$

Random variables are of two types (i) Discrete random variable and (ii) Continuous random variable.

Discrete Random Variable : A random variable X, which can take only a finite number of values in an interval of the domain, is called discrete random variable. A few examples are: (i) If we throw two dice at a time and note the sum of spots which turn up on the upper face, the discrete r.v.,

$$X(x) = \{x: x = (x_1+x_2) = 2, 3...., 12)$$

Where x_1 is the number of spots on the upper face of one die and x_2 is the number of spots on the other die. (ii) The random variable denoting the number of students in a class is.

$$X(x) = \{x: x \text{ is any positive integer}\}$$

Continuous Random Variable: A random variable X, which can take any value in the domain, or when its range 'R' is an interval or the union of intervals on the real line, is called a continuous random variable.

Note that the probability of any single x, a value of X, is zero, i.e.

$$P(X = x) = 0$$

Example (i). The height of students in India lies between 3 and 6 feet. The continuous r.v

$$X(x) = \{ x : 3 \leq x \leq 6\}$$

6.2 Distribution Function

The distribution of a random variable X is a function $F_x(x)$ for a real value x which is the probability of the event $(X \leq x)$, i.e.

$$F_x(x) = P(X \leq x)$$

It is evident from the expression that the distribution function is the probability that X take a value in the interval $(-\infty, x)$.

Discrete Probability Distribution : If a random variable is discrete, its distribution will also be discrete, except in some exceptional situations. For a discrete random variable X, the distribution function or cumulative distribution is given by P(x) and is same as given by (6,1) i.e.

$$P(x) = P(X \leq x)$$

Discrete Probability Function : The probability function is the probability of a discrete random variable X, which takes the value x and is denoted by p(x) i.e.

$$P(x) = P(X = x)$$

The probability function always possesses the following properties

(i) $p(x) \geq 0$ for all x in sample space Ω

(ii) $\sum_{\text{all } x} p(x) = 1$

Mathematical Expectation : The expected value of a random variable X is given as.

$$E(X) = \sum_{\text{all } x} x.\, p(x)$$

E(X) is also known as theoretical average value. In general, the expected value of a function H(X) of a discrete random variable X is given as,

$$E\{H(X)\} = \sum_{\text{all } x} H(x)\, p(x)$$

Some Results on Expectation : If X and Y are two variates defined over the same sample space and if E(x) and E(Y) exist, then

$$E(X + Y) = E(X) + E(Y)$$

Also if X and Y are independent, then

$$E(XY) = E(X)\, E(Y)$$

Consider a variable X and a constant C. The expected values of X in relation to C are as follows:

$$E(C) = C$$

$$E(CX) = CE(X)$$

$$E(X+C) = E(X) + C$$

If X and Y are two variables and C_1 and C_2 are any constants, then

$$E(C_1X + C_2Y) = C_1E(X) + C_2E(Y)$$

If $X \leq Y$, then

$E(X) \leq E(Y)$

(The operations given from (6.8) to (6.12) are also true for functions of X and Y.)

6.3 Moments

The rth moment of a random variable X is defined as the expected value of X^r where r is an integer i.e. r = 1, 2.... The rth moment $E(X^r)$, about the origin (Zero), is known as the rth *moment* and is generally denotd by μ. Thus,

$$\mu'_r = E(X^r)$$

Similarly the rth moment of a random variable X about the mean m of a frequency distribution is given by the formula,

$$\mu_r = E\{X - \mu)^r\}$$

where μ_r is symbolically known as the rth *central moment* of a random variable X.

The first raw moment (about origin) is the mean of the distribution i.e.

$$E(X) = \sum_{\text{all } x} x\, p(x) = \frac{1}{N} \sum_{\text{all } x} x = \mu$$

Where p(x) = 1/N for all x, and the first central moment about mean is zero, i.e.,

$$E(X - \mu) = \sum_{\text{all } x} (x - \mu)\, p(x)$$

$$= \frac{1}{N} \sum_{\text{all } x} (X - \mu) = \frac{1}{N} \sum_{\text{all } x} x - \mu = \mu - \mu = 0$$

Also $\quad E(X) - E(\mu) = 0$ or $\mu'_1 = \mu$

The second raw moment,

$$\mu'_2 = E(X^2) = \sum_{\text{all } x} x^2\, p(x)$$

The third raw moment,

$$\mu'_3 = E(X^3) = \sum_{\text{all } x} x^3\, p(x)$$

and so on.

The second central moment is

$$\mu_2 = E\{X - \mu)^2\}$$

$$= E\{(X^2 - 2\mu X + \mu^2)\}$$

$= E\{(X)^2 - 2\mu E(X) + \mu^2\}$

$= \mu'_2 - 2\mu.\ \mu'_1 + \mu'^2$

$= \mu'_2 - \mu'^2_2$ Since $\mu'_1 = \mu$.

The second central moment is also known as the variance.

Similarly,

$\mu_3 = E\{X - \mu)^3\} = E(X^3 - 3\mu X^2 + 3\mu^2 X - \mu^3)$

$= E(X^3) - 3\mu E(X^2) + 3\mu^2 E(X) - \mu^2$

Using the relation (6.16.1), we get

$\mu_3 = \mu'_3 - 3\mu'_2\mu'_1 + 3\mu'^3_1 = \mu'^3_1 = \mu'_3 - 3\mu'_2\mu'_1 + 2\mu'^3_1$

In the same manner, we can get,

$\mu_4 = \mu'_4 - 4\mu'_3\mu'_1 + 6\mu'_2\mu'^2_1 - 3\mu'^4_1$

Now it will not be difficult for the readers to derive the relationship between the central moments and raw moments of any order.

The probability function or probability density function of any random variable, generally involves one or two parameters, particularly the mean and variance. But, still the importance and need for higher moments cannot be ruled out. The third and fourth moments are extremely useful for determining the shape of a frequency curve.

Sometimes the moments about an arbitrary constant a are found out. In that case, the rth moment about a is.

$\mu^a_r = E\{(X - a)^r\}$

The first moment about 'a' is,

$\mu^a_1 = E(X - a) = E(X) - E(a) = \mu_1 - a$

The second moment about 'a' is,

$\mu^a_2 = E\{(X - a)^2\} = E(X^2 - 2aX + a^2)$

$= E(X^2) - 2aE(X) + E(a^2)$

$= \mu'_2 - 2a\,\mu'_1 + a^2$

Similarly,

$\mu^a_3 = \mu'_3 - 3a\,\mu'_2 + 3a^2\mu'_1 - a^3$

and $\mu^a_4 = \mu'_4 - 4a\,\mu'_3 + 6a^2\mu'_2 - 4a^3\mu'_1 + a^4$

in general,

$$\mu_q^r = \mu'_r - \binom{r}{1} a\mu'_{r-1} + \binom{r}{2} a^2 \mu'_{r-2} - \dots + (-1)^r a^r$$

Using these relation we can find out the moments about the mean o. Utilizing further the relationships between raw moments and central moments, the later can be obtained.

Factorial Moments : In case of a discrete random variable X, which takes values at unit intervals, the rth factorial moment is given as,

$$\mu_r = E\{X(X\text{-}1)(X\text{-}1)(X\text{-}2)\dots(X-r+1)\} = \sum_i (X_i)_r\, p(x_r)$$

where $(X_i)_r = X_i(X_i\text{-}1)(X_i - 2)\dots(X_i - r + 1)$.

For example, if we throw a die, the possible outcomes will be 1, 2, 3, 4, 5 and 6 which are at unit intervals. Hence, a in this case,

$$\mu'_1 = \sum_i X_i p(x) = \frac{1}{6}(1+2+\dots+6) = \frac{21}{6}$$

$$\mu'_2 = \sum_i X_i (X_i - 1)\, p(x)$$

$$= \frac{1}{6}\{1 \times 0 + 2 \times 1 + 3 \times 2 + 4 \times 3 + 5 \times 4 + 6 \times 5\}$$

$$= \frac{1}{6}\{0 + 2 + 6 + 12 + 20 + 30\} = \frac{70}{6}$$

Similarly,

$$\mu'_3 = \sum_1 X_1 (X_i - 1)(X_i - 2)\, p(x) = \frac{210}{6}$$

and so on.

6.4 Moment Generating Function (M.G.F.)

From the discussion of moments, it is apparent that moments play an important role in the characterization of various distribution. Hence, to know the distribution, we need to find out the moments. For this, the moment generating function is a good device. The moment generating function is a special form of mathematical good device. The moment generating function is a special form of mathematical expectation and is very useful in deriving the moments of a probability distribution.

Definition if X is random variable, then the expected value of e^{tx} is known as the moment generating function, provided the expected value exists for every value of t in an interval, - h < t<h where h is some positive real value. The moment generating function which is denoted as $m_x(t)$ for a discrete random variable is

$$m_x(t) = E(e^{tx}) \sum_{\text{all } x} e^{t(x)} p_x(x)$$

$$= \sum_{\text{all } x}\left(1 + tx + \frac{t^2x^2}{2!} + \frac{t^3x^3}{3!} + \ldots\right)p_x(x)$$

$$= 1 + t\mu'_1 + \frac{t^2}{2!}\mu'_2 + \frac{t^3}{3!}\mu'_3 \ldots = \sum_{r=0}^{\infty}\frac{t^r}{r!}\mu'_r$$

The convergence of the above sum is assumed here. In the above expression, the rth raw moment is the coefficient of $\frac{t^r}{r!}$ in the above expanded sum.

The main use of the moment generating function is that, if it exists, it can uniquely determine the distribution. But many distribution functions are known for which the moment generating functions do not exist.

The moment generating function is also useful for finding out the moments of a distribution. The technique for it is to differentiate the moment generating function with respect to (w.r.t) t once, twice, thrice, ... and put t = 0 in the first, second and third... derivatives to obtain the first, second, third,... moments. From the resulting expression we get 1st, 2nd, 3rd, ... raw moments about the origin. The central moments are obtained by using the relationship between raw moments and central moments.

Characteristic Function (C.F.)

The moment generating function does not exist or every distribution. Hence another function, which always exists for all the distributions, is known as characteristic function. It is the expected value of e^{itx}, where $i = \sqrt{-1}$ and t is a real valued continuous variable. Let the characteristic function of a random variable X be denoted by $\phi_x(t)$, then

$$\phi_x(t) = E(e^{itx})$$

For a discrete variable X having the probability function p(x), the characteristic function

$$\phi_x(t) = \sum_{\text{all } x} e^{itx}\, p(x)$$

and for a continuous variable X having density function f(x), such that $a < X \leq b$, the characteristic function,

$$\phi_x(t) = \int_a^b e^{itx} f(x)\, dx$$

it is easy to prove that $\phi_x(0) = 1$.

Here are two important theorems without proof.

Uniqueness Theorem : Two distribution functions are identical if their characteristic functions are identical.

Inversion Theorem : Let *F* be a distribution function and $\phi_x(t)$ be its characteristic function. If a and b are any two points on a real line such that a < b, then we have,

$$F(b) - F(a) = \lim_{T\to\infty} \frac{1}{2\pi} \int_{-T}^{T} \frac{e^{-iat} - e^{-ibt}}{it} \phi_x(t)dt$$

6.5 Cumulants

The idea of cumulants was given by Thieles. Just like moments, cumulants are equally important as descriptive constants of a distribution to specify it. If the rth μ'_r moment of a random variable X exists, then from Maclaurin's theorem the characteristic function $\phi_x(t)$, in the neighbourhood of t = 0, can be expanded as follows:

$$\phi(t) = \sum_{j=1}^{r} \frac{(it)^j}{j!} \mu_j + 0(t^r)$$

If expression is feasible, we can also expand $\log_e \phi(t)$ as

$$\log_e \phi(t) = \sum_{j=1}^{r} \frac{(it)^j}{j!} k_j + 0(t^r)$$

The quantity k_j is called the j-th cumulant of the distribution function F. The r-th cumulant k_r is the coefficient of $(it)^r/r!$ in the expansion of $\log_e \phi(t)$, whereas , the r-th raw moment is the coefficient of $(it)^r/r!$ in the expansion of $\phi(t)$. The following relations between raw moments and cumulants are evident.

$$\mu_1 = k_1$$

$$\mu'_2 = k_2 + k_1^2$$

$$\mu'_3 = k_2 + 3k_2 k_1 + k_1^3$$

6.6 Binomial Distribution

It is one of the most popular discrete distributions. The origin of binomial distribution lies in Bernoulli's trials. A Bernoulli's trial is an experiment having only two possible outcomes, that is success or failure. In other words, there results of the trial are always dichotomous. For example, if we flip a coin, it will show either head or tail on the upper face. The sex of an expected baby will either be male of female (excluding exceptions). A manufactured item will either be defective or non-defective. A person will either be healthy or sick.

Since a Bernoulli's trial has been considered, certain conditions for the application of binomial distribution are obvious. For clarity, (i) the probability of a success (or failure) remains same in each trial, (ii) trials must be independent, (iii) number of trials must be finite, (iv) the sum of probabilities of success and failure is one, (v) the probability of success vis-à-vis failure is not very low. A dichotomous variable X, which has the probability function.

$$P_x(x) = \binom{n}{x} p^x q^{n-x} \quad \text{for } x = 1, 2, \ldots n$$

$$= 0 \text{ otherwise}$$

is said to have binomial distribution. In the binomial function n = number of trials; p = probability of a success; q = probability of a failure and $p_x(x)$ = probability of getting exactly x successes in n trials.

The distribution given by $P_x(x)$ is called binomial distribution since it is the (x +1)th term in the binomial expansion of $(q+p)^n$

Properties of Binomial Distribution

(1) Binomial distribution has two parameters, n and p (or q)

(2) The mean of the binomial distribution is np and variance is npq.

(3) The moment generating function is $(q + pe^t)^n$.

(4) The characteristic function is $(q + pe^{it})^n$.

(5) Binomial distribution tends to normal distribution as n increases. The normal approximation is correct enough if the mean np is greater than 15 for $p = 1/2$.

Example

Consider a simple trial of tossing a perfectly round and balanced coin. Six times. Then the probability of getting (i) E_1: exactly three heads, (ii) E_2: at least three heads and (iii) E_3: not more than two heads, can be calculated by binomial distribution as follows:

Solution: For the given example, n =6, p =q = 1/2

(i) $$P(E_1) = \binom{6}{3}\left(\frac{1}{2}\right)^3\left(\frac{1}{2}\right)^{6-3} = \frac{6!}{3!(6-3)!}.\frac{1}{2^6} = \frac{5}{16}$$

(ii) $$P(E_2) = \sum_{x=3}^{6} px(x)$$

$$= \binom{6}{3}\left(\frac{1}{2}\right)^3\left(\frac{1}{2}\right)^{6-3} + \binom{6}{4}\left(\frac{1}{2}\right)^4\left(\frac{1}{2}\right)^{6-4}$$

$$+ \binom{6}{5}\left(\frac{1}{2}\right)^5\left(\frac{1}{2}\right)^{6-5} + \binom{6}{6}\left(\frac{1}{2}\right)^6$$

$$= \frac{1}{2^6} - \left\{\binom{6}{3} + \binom{6}{4} + \binom{6}{5} + \binom{6}{6}\right\}$$

$$= \frac{1}{64}\left\{\frac{6\times5\times4}{3\times2\times1} + \frac{6\times5}{2\times1} + 6 + 1\right\} = 21/32$$

(iii) $$P(E_3) = \sum_{x=0}^{2} px(x)$$

$$= \binom{6}{0}\left(\frac{1}{2}\right)^0\left(\frac{1}{2}\right)^6 + \binom{6}{1}\left(\frac{1}{2}\right)\left(\frac{1}{2}\right)^{6-1} + \binom{6}{6}\left(\frac{1}{2}\right)^2\left(\frac{1}{2}\right)^{6-2}$$

$$= \frac{1}{2^6} - \left\{\binom{6}{0} + \binom{6}{1} + \binom{6}{2}\right\} = \frac{11}{32}$$

Theorem

If r_1 and r_2 are two independent binomial variate whose parameters are (n_1, p) and (n_2, p) respectively, the distribution of $(r_1 + r_2)$ is also binomial.

Proof. The characteristic function of $(r_1 + r_2)$ is

$$\phi\,(r_1 + r_2)\,(t) = E\left\{e^{it(r_1+r_2)}\right\} = E\left(e^{itr_1}\right)\,E\left(e^{itr_2}\right)$$

(since r_1 and r_2 are independent)

$$= (q + pe^{it})^{n_1} \left(q + pe^{it}\right)^{n_2} = \left(q + pe^{it}\right)^{n_1+n_2}$$

The right hand expression is the characteristic function of a binomial variate whose parameters are $(n_1 + n_2)$ and p. Hence by the uniqueness theorem, the distribution of $(r_1 + r_2)$ is also binomial. This theorem may be extended to may finite number of binomial variates.

6.7 Bernoulli's Theorem

If the number of successes of *n* trials is *r*, and the probability of a success is *p*, then the probability that the difference of r/n from p is greater than or equal to an infinitesimal small quantity ε, tends to zero as n tends infinity. Symbolically,

$$\lim_{n\to\infty} P\left(\left|\frac{r}{n} - p\right| \geq \varepsilon\right) = 0 \tag{6.3}$$

In other words, if a trial is repeated a large number of times under the same conditions, the sample proportion of successes, $\overline{X}_n$ ($\overline{X}_n$ = r/n) in n Bernoullian trials converges in probability to p, the probability fo a success, i.e. $X_n \xrightarrow{P} p$.

This is also known as the *Weak Law of Large Numbers* (WLLN).

Example

Let the probability of an item, to be defective, produced by a factory be. 0.10. A sample of 10 items has been inspected. Then the probability of an event E that the sample has two defective items is,

$$P(E) = \binom{10}{2}(.1)^2(.9)^{10-2} = \frac{10\times9}{2\times1}\,\frac{1}{10^2}\left(\frac{9}{10}\right)^8 = \frac{1}{2}\left(\frac{9}{10}\right)^9$$

6.8 Relation between the Probabilities of X and (X+1) Successes in Binomial Distribution

We know,

$$p(X = x) = \binom{n}{x} p^x q^{n-x} = \frac{n!}{x!(n-x)!} p^x q^{n-x}$$

$$\text{and } p(X = x+1) = \binom{n}{x+1} p^{x+1} q^{n-x-1}$$

$$= \frac{n!}{(x+1)!(n-x-1)} p^x q^{n-x}. \frac{p}{q}$$

$$= \frac{n!\,(n-x)}{x!(n-x)!\,(x+1)} p^x q^{n-x}. \frac{p}{q}$$

$$= p(X=x). \frac{n-x}{x+1}.\frac{p}{q}$$

The above relation helps in calculating the term by term probabilities.

6.9 Poisson Distribution

Before we know the distribution, it becomes necessary to understand what is a Poisson random variable. A variable which can take only one discrete value in an internal of time, howsoever small, is known as Poisson variable. Some of the well known examples of Poisson variable are:

(i) number of mistakes in a typed page;

(ii) number of cars parked at a place in an hour, say between 10:00 a.m. and 11:00 a.m.;

(iii) number of defects in the insulation of a fifty metre length of wire;

(iv) number of suicides in a certain period in a city or town etc.

If we consider a Poisson's process for a unit length of interval (time, length, space etc.), the number of occurrences are a random variable which follow Poisson distribution. It has been named after its inventor, Simeon D. Poisson, a French probabilist of nineteenth century. It is one of the most important discrete distributions. Poisson distribution is a classical approximation to binomial distribution, in which case n, the number of trials, is comparatively large and p, the probability of an occurrence, is small.

Let X be the number of occurrences in a Poisson process and m be the actual. Average number of occurrences of an event in an unit length of interval, the probability function for Poisson distribution is,

$$P_x(x) = \frac{e^{-\mu}\mu^x}{x!} \text{for } x = 0, 1, 2, \ldots.$$

$$= 0 \text{ otherwise.}$$

If we consider the length of interval as d instead of unit length, the average number of occurrences in d length of interval is md. Thus, the probability function in this situation is

$$P_x(x) = \frac{e^{-\mu d}(\mu d)^x}{x!} \text{ for } x = 0, 1, 2, \ldots$$

$$= 0 \text{ other wise.}$$

Properties of Poisson Distribution

1. Poisson distribution has mean m and its variance is also μ. It is the only distribution known so far, of which the mean and variance are equal.
2. Poisson distribution possesses only one parameter (μ)
3. The moment generating function of a Poisson variate or equivalently the Poisson distribution is $e^{\mu(e^R-1)}$.
4. The characteristic function f Poisson distribution is $e^{\mu(e^R-1)}$.

Theorem

If a number of independent Poisson random variables $r_1, r_2, \ldots r_k$ (where k is an integer) are distributed with mean $\mu_1, \mu_2, \ldots \mu_k$ respectively, then their sum $(r_1 + r_2 + \ldots r_k)$ has also Poisson distribution with mean $(\mu_1, \mu_2, \ldots \mu_k)$

Proof

The characteristic function of $(r_1 + r_2 + \ldots r_k)$ is,

$$\phi_{r_1+r_2+\ldots r_k}(t) = E\left\{e^{it(r_1+r_2+\ldots+r_k)}\right\}$$

$$E\left(e^{itr_1}\right)E\left(e^{itr_2}\right)\ldots E\left(e^{itr_k}\right)$$

since all r_i' s are independent

$$= e^{\mu_1(e^{it}-1)}e^{\mu_2(e^{it}-1)}\ldots e^{\mu_k(e^{it}-1)}$$

$$= e^{(\mu_1+\mu_2-\ldots\ldots\mu_k)(e^{it}-1)}$$

The right-hand expression is the characteristic function for a Poisson variate whose mean is $(\mu_1 + \mu_2 + \ldots. + \mu_k)$. Hence, by uniqueness theorem, the variable $(r_1 + r_2 + \ldots + r_k)$ has Poisson distribution whose mean is $(\mu_1 + \mu_2 + \ldots + \mu_k)$.

Note :

(1) It has been said that for Poisson variate the number of trials n is large and the probability of the so called success is small. Now the question arises what value of n is to be considered as large and what value of p as small. There is no hard-and-fast rule for this, but as a tradition if $n \geq 20$, it may be taken as large and p=0.05 may be taken as small. Otherwise, the discrete variable with only two possibilities is generally taken to follow binomial distribution.

(2) The value of e-μ should either be seen from the table III or may be calculated with the help of logarithm.

Example

Suppose at a particular place, the average number of cars parked per hour is 3. Under Poisson's model, the probability of 5 cars parked in a particular hour can be calculated as under.

$$P(x=5) = \frac{e^{-3}3^5}{5!}$$

Knowing that $e^{-3} = 0.050$, the probability,

$$P(x = 5) = \frac{0.050 \times 3^5}{5!} = 0.101$$

Example

The number of mistakes counted in one hundred typed pages of a typist revealed that he made 2.8 mistakes on an average per page. The probability, that in a page types by him, (i) there is no mistake (ii) there are two or less mistakes, can be calculated as under,

Given that $\mu = 2.8$

(i) The probability, $P(x = 0) + \frac{e^{-28}(2.8)^0}{0!}$

From Table III, $e^{-2.8} = 0.061$, the probability

$P(x = 0)\ e^{-2.8} = 0.061$

(ii) The probability, $P(X \leq 2) = \sum_{x=0}^{2} \frac{e^{-28}(2.8)^x}{x!}$

$$= e\text{-}2.8 \left\{ \frac{(2.8)^0}{0!} + \frac{(2.8)^1}{1!} + \frac{(2.8)^2}{2!} \right\}$$

From Table III, $e^{-2.8} = 0.061$, the probability,

$P(X \leq 2) = 0.061\ (1 + 2.8 + 3.92) = 0.471$

Example

It is known that the average number of suicides per week in Delhi is 1.5. Let X be the number of suicides which occur in a month. The probability, that there will five or more suicides in a month, is obtained in the following manner. The distribution of X will be a Poisson distribution. In this problem.

$d = 4$, $\mu = 1.5$ and hence

$\mu d = 1.5 \times 4 = 6$

The probability that there are five or more suicides in a month can be calculated with the help of (6.45). Thus, the probability,

$$P(X \geq 5) = \sum_{x=5}^{\infty} \frac{e^{-6}(6)^x}{x!}$$

It is difficult to evaluate $P(X \geq 5)$ from the above expression. But we can easily calculate $P(X \leq 4)$ and then to find $P(X \geq 5)$, we use the relation,

$P(X \geq 5) = 1 - P(X \geq 4)$

Again,

$$P(X \leq 4) = \sum_{x=0}^{4} \frac{e^{-6}(6)^x}{x!}$$

From Table III, $e^{-6} = 0.002$, the probability

$$P(X \leq 4) = e^{-6} \left(\frac{6^0}{0!} + \frac{6}{1!} + \frac{6^2}{2!} + \frac{6^3}{3!} + \frac{6^4}{4!} \right)$$

$= 0.002\ (1 + 6 + 18 + 36 + 54)$

$= 0.230$

Now, the probability,

$P(X \geq 5) = 1 - 0.230 = 0.77$

Example

The number of calls arriving on in internal switchboard of an office is 90 per hour. The probability of 1 to 3 calls in a minute on the board is calculable as follows. Let X denote the number of calls per minute. Obviously, X will follow Poisson distribution.

Average number of calls per minute, $\mu = \frac{90}{60} = 1.5.$

Now the probability,

$$\sum_{x=1}^{3} Px(x) = \sum_{x=1}^{3} \frac{e^{-15}(1.5)^x}{x!}$$

From Table III $e^{-15} = 0.223$, the probability,

$$\begin{aligned}\sum_{x=1}^{3} Px(x) &= e^{-15}\left\{\frac{1.5}{1!}+\frac{(1.5)^2}{2!}+\frac{(1.5)^3}{3!}\right\} \\ &= 0.223\,(1.5 + 1.125 + 0.562) \\ &= 0.711\end{aligned}$$

Example

It is known that the number of breaks in a coil of 100 metres insulated electric wire, on an average, is two. Let X denote the number of breaks in a 100 metres insulated wire. The independence of these breaks in non-overlapping intervals is assumed. Then the probability of exactly 4 breaks in 100 metres wire will be,

$$P(X = 4) = \frac{e^{-2}(2)^4}{4!} \text{ since } \mu = 2.$$

From Table III $e^{-2} = 0.135$

$$P(X = 4) = \frac{0.135 \times 16}{24} = 0.09$$

6.10 For Poisson Variate X, Relationship Between the Probabilities, P(X=x) And P(X = x+1)

We know that for a Poisson random variable X having the mean μ, the probability,

$$P(X = x) = \frac{e^{-\mu}\mu^x}{x!}$$

and $$P(X = x+1) = \frac{e^{-\mu}\,\mu^{x+1}}{(x+1)!}$$

$$= \frac{e^{-\mu}\,\mu^{x}}{x!} \quad \frac{\mu}{(x+1)}$$

Example

If a Poisson random variable X is such that P(X=1) = P(X =2), then the probability P(X =3) can be found out as under. Then

$$P(X=2) = P(X=1) \,.\, \frac{\mu}{2}$$

Since P(X =1) = P(X =2)

$$\frac{\mu}{2} = 1 \text{ or } \mu = 2$$

$$\text{Hence, } P(X=3) = \frac{e^{-2}\,.2^{3}}{3!}$$

$$P(X=3) = \frac{0.135 \times 8}{6} = 0.180$$

6.11 Normal Distribution

Normal distribution is the most popular and commonly used distribution. It was discovered by De Moivre in 1733, about twenty years after Bernoulli gave binomial distribution. A random variable X is said to follow normal distribution, if and only if, its probability density function (p.d.f) is

$$f_x(x) = \frac{1}{\sigma\sqrt{2\pi}} e^{-\frac{1}{2\sigma^2}(x-\mu)^2}$$

where x is the real value of X, i.e., $-\infty < X < \infty$.

The variable X is said to be distributed normally with mean μ and variance σ^2, i.e. $X \sim N(\mu, \sigma^2)$.

The density function given by above has two parameters, namely μ and σ. Here μ can take any real value in the range $-\infty$ to ∞, where σ is any positive real value, i.e. $\sigma > 0$.

Since the probability can never be negative,

$f_x(x) \geq 0$ for all x.

In case, $\mu = 0$, $\sigma = 1$, the density function for X is

$$fx(x) = \frac{1}{\sqrt{2\pi}} e^{-\frac{1}{2}x^2}$$

where $-\infty < X < \infty$. Nationally, $X \sim N(0, 1)$.

In this situation the variable X is called the *standardized normal variate and the distirbuition* is called the *standardized normal distribution.*

Properties of Normal Distribution

1. If we plot the curve for the values of the standard normal variate X and the corresponding probabilities, it is of the shape given in Fig. 6.1.

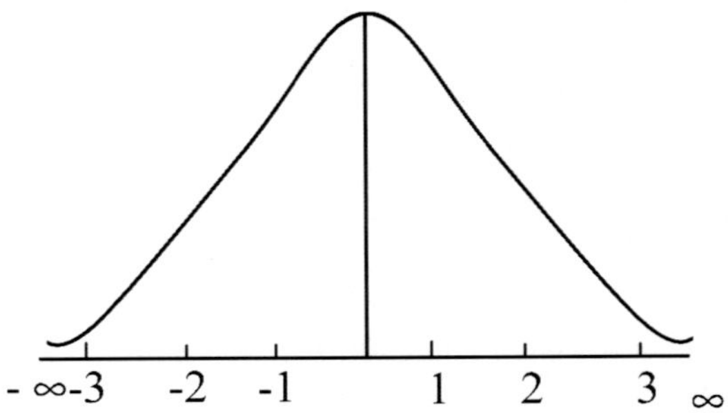

Fig.6.1 : Standard Normal Curve.

The curve is bell-shaped and symmetrical about the vertical line at x = 0. For the random variable $X \sim N(\mu, 6^2)$, the curve is symmetrical about the mean μ. Symmetry implies $f_x(x) = f_x(-x)$.

2. The vertical line at x = 0 cuts the curve at its highest point i.e. *fx*(x) at x =0 is maximum. The value of *fx*(x) decreases as the value of x is other than zero (or the mean μ).

3. The area under the normal curve within the limits $-\infty$ to ∞ is unity

i.e. $$\frac{1}{\sigma\sqrt{2\pi}} \int_{-\infty}^{\infty} e^{-\frac{2}{2\sigma^2}(x-\mu)^2} dx = 1$$

If $\mu = 0$, $\sigma = 1$, then

$$\frac{1}{\sqrt{2p}} \int_{-\infty}^{\infty} e^{-\frac{1}{2}x^2} = 1$$

4. On either side of the mean μ, the frequency decreases more rapidly within the range $(\mu \pm \sigma)$ and gets slower and slower as it goes away from the mean. The frequencies are extremely small beyond the distance of $\pm 3\sigma$. As a matter of fact 99.73 per cent units of the population lie within the range $\mu \pm 3\sigma$.

5. Theoretically the curve never touches the X – axis.
6. As the value of σ increases, the curve becomes more and more flat and vice versa.
7. The moment generating function of the general normal distribution is,

$$m_x(t) = e^{(\mu t + \frac{1}{2}\sigma^2 t^2)}$$

8. All central moments of odd order are zero.
9. The characteristic function of the general normal distribution is

$$\phi_x(t) = e^{(\mu t + \frac{1}{2}\sigma^2 t^2)}$$

Normal distribution is most widely used in statistics despite the fact that theoretically a population hardly follows the exact normal distribution. This is due to various reasons which are as follows:

(i) Conveniences is a strong support for its use in statistics. Extensive tables have been prepared and provided for ordinates and area under the normal curve. This has facilitated the job of the scientist immensely.

(ii) If the variable does not follow normal distribution, it can be made to follow after making a suitable transformation like square root, arcsine, logarithm etc.

(iii) The most important and convincing reason is that whatever be the original distribution, the distribution of sample mean can, in most of the cases, be approximated to normal distribution, when the sample size is sufficiently increased.

Standard Normal Deviate For a random variable $X \sim N(\mu, \sigma^2)$, the location and shape of the normal curve depends on μ and σ where μ and σ can take any value within their range. Hence, no master table for the area under the curve can be prepared. This difficulty is very well overcome by consideration of a variable Z where $Z = (X - \mu)/\sigma$. The variable Z is always distributed with mean zero and variance unity, i.e., $Z \sim N(0,1)$.

In this way, whatever be the parameters of the normal distribution whose parameters area 0 and 1. Hence, only one table for area or ordinates of the normal curve is sufficient. Remember that normal curve is a symmetric curve and the area on either side of the ordinate at the origin is 0.5, since the tota area under the curve is unity. The area as a matter of fact gives the probability for a event that Z takes certain values. These probabilities (areas) can always be found with the help of Table IV given in the appendix B.

For better under standing, consider the following situations.

(i) $P(Z \leq Z_0) = 0.5 - A$.

If Z_0 is a negative real value where A is the area between ordinates at x =0 x = Z_0. See (Fig.6.2).

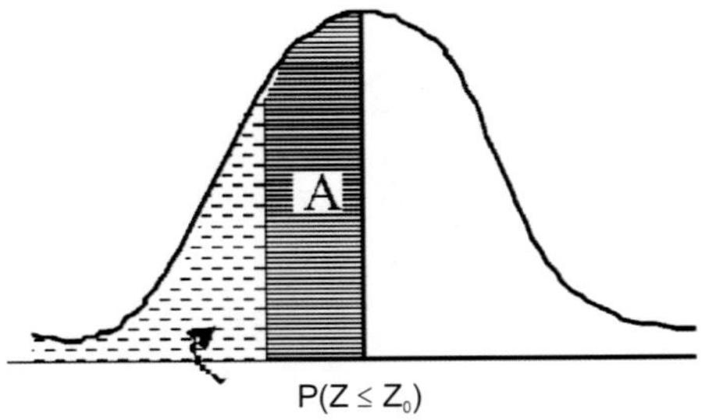

Fig.6.2

(ii) If Z_0 is a positive real number, then

$P(Z \leq Z_0) = 0.5 + A$.

Where A is the area between the ordinates at x = 0 and x = Z_0. (Fig.6.3).

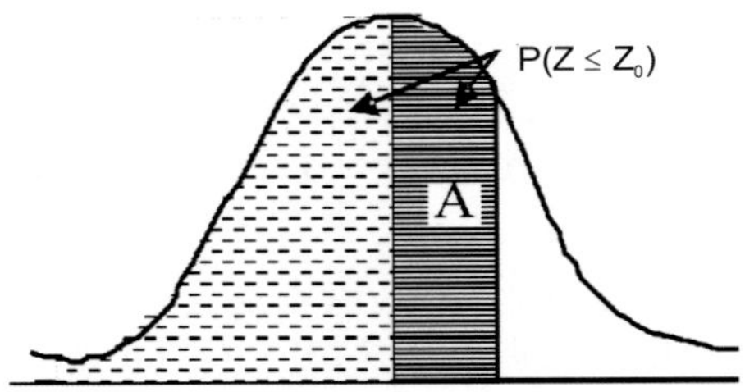

Fig.6.3

(iii) $P(Z_1 \leq Z \leq Z_2) = A_1 +$

(iv) A_2.

If Z_1 is negative and Z_2 is positive where A_1 is the area between ordinates at, x =0 and x = Z_1 and A_2 is the area between the ordinates at x =0 and x = Z_2 (Fig. 6.4).

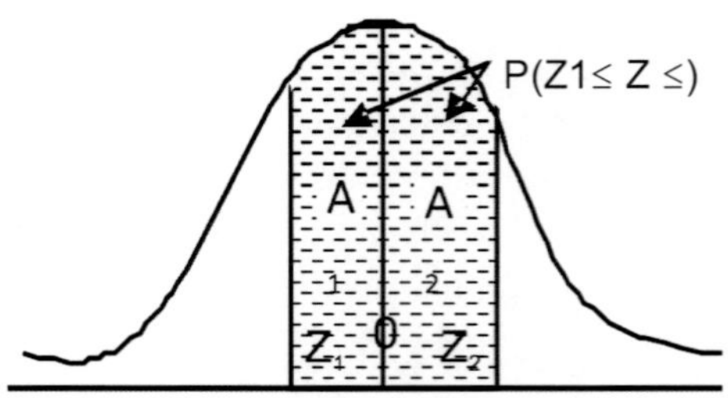

Fig. 6.4

If Z_1 and Z_2 are both positive, the probability

$P(Z_1 \leq Z \leq Z_2) = A_2 - A_1$ (Fig. 6.5).

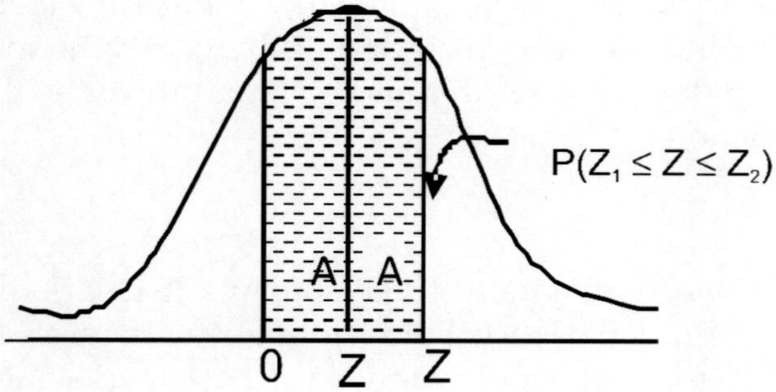

Fig. 6.5

In case Z_1 and Z_2 are negative, the areas A_2 and A_1 will be to the left of the oridinate at the point zero.

(v) $P(Z \geq Z_0) = 0.5 - A.$

If Z_0 is a positive real number, where A is as explained earlier (Fig.6.6).

(vi) $P(Z \geq Z_0) = 0.5 + A,$

if Z_0 is a negative real number, where A is as explained earlier (Fig.6.7).

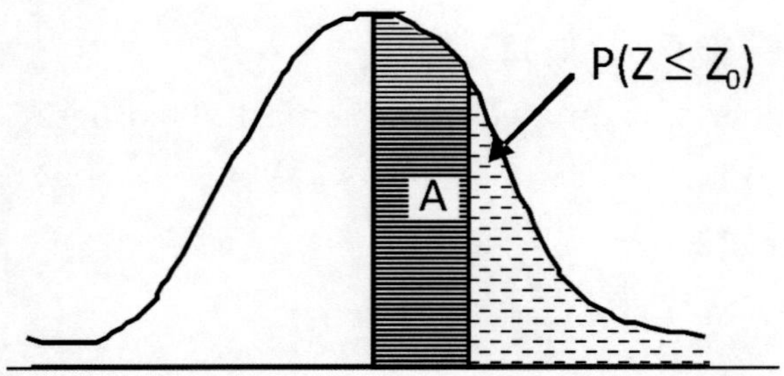

Fig. 6.6

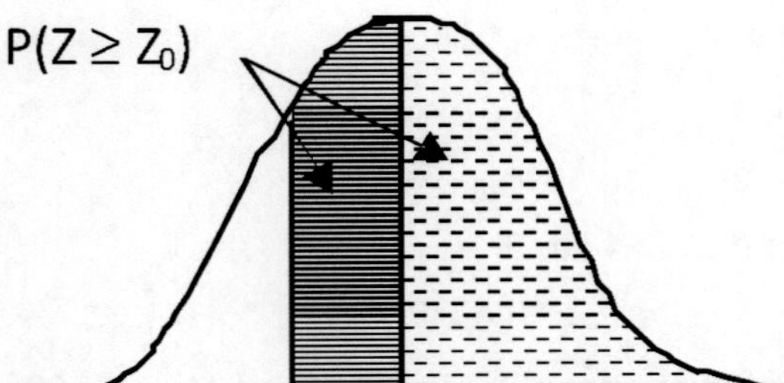

Fig. 6.7

From the above description of probabilities, one can easily understand the approach of finding the required area under the standard normal curve. Wherever the values of X are not given for standard normal variable, they should be standardized by the transformation $(X-\mu)/\sigma$. In case we are interested in finding out the number of individuals or units lying in some specified interval, we should find out the required area and then multiply it by the total number of units of population.

Example

In a competitive examination of 5000 students, the marks of the examinees in statistics were found to be distributed normally with mean 45 and standard deviation 14. Then the number of examinees whose marks out of 100 were: (i) less than 30, (ii) between 30 and 70, (iii) between 60 and 80, (iv) more than 60, (v) more than 40, can be found out in the manner described above with the help of Table IV.

Give that, $\mu = 45$, $\sigma = 14$ and N = 5000.

(i) $X = 30, Z = \dfrac{30-45}{14} = -1.07$

(ii) Using Fig. 6.5, the required area $A_1 = 0.5 - A$

From Table IV, A = 0.3577

$A_1 = 0.5 - 0.3577 = 0.1423$

The number of examinees having marks 30 or less

$= 5000 \times 0.1423$

$= 711.5 = 712$

similarly,

(iii) $Z_1 = \dfrac{30-45}{14} = 1.07$

and $Z_2 = \dfrac{30-45}{14} = 1.79$

Using Fig. 6.7 and consulting Table 6.4.

$A_1 = 0.3577$ and $A_2 = 0.4633$

Thus, the required area $= 0.4938 - 0.3577 = 0.1361$

The number of students securing marks between 60 and 80

$= 5000 \times 0.1361 = 680.5 = 680$

(iv) $Z_0 = \frac{60-45}{14} = 1.07$

Using Fig. 6.9 and from Table IV,

$A_1 = 0.3577$

Hence the required area = 0.5 – 0.3577 = 0.1423

The number of examinees having marks more than

60 = 5000 × 0.1423 = 711.5 = 712

(v) $Z_0 = \frac{40-45}{14} = 0.36$

Using Fig. 6.7 and from Table 6.4,

$A_1 = 0.1406$

Hence the required area = 0.5 + 0.1406 = 0.6406

The number of examinees have marks more than 40

= 500 × 0.6406 = 3203

Besides the most widely used normal distribution, there are numerous other continuous distributions.

Exercise

1. Define Binomial distribution and state its mean and variance?
2. Find the Binomial distribution whose mean is 6 and variance is 4.
3. A coin is tossed six times. What is the probability of getting four or more heads?
4. Define Poisson distribution and state its mean.
5. Define Normal distribution.
6. State the properties of Normal distribution.
7. In Normal distribution, 7% of the items are under 35 and 79% are under 63. What is the mean and standard deviation of the distribution?

❑❑❑

Chapter – 7

Sampling and Sampling Distribution

7.1 Meaning of Sampling

Before we consider sampling theory, we first define the terms population and sample.

The word 'population' or 'universe' in statistics is used to refer to any collection of individuals or of their attributes or of results of operations which can be numerically specified. For example the assemblage of heights of all the individuals in the population is called a population of heights. Similarly we may consider the population of weights, wages, yields of grain; prices of wheat, mileages of automobile tyres, etc. a population containing a finite number of individuals or members is called a finite population. For instance the population f ages of the workers in a factory constitute a finite population of ages. A population with infinite number of members is known as infinite population. For example the population of pressures of temperatures at various points in the atmosphere is an infinite population.

A part or small section selected from the population is called a sample and the process of such selected from the population is called a sample and the process of such selection is called sampling. The number of units in the sample is known as the sample a small quantity of any item before purchasing. They decide from this small quantity the characteristics (quality and taste of the items) of the whole r complete items, Similarly in statistics the theory of sampling is a tool to get as much information as possible about the population from which the sample has been drawn. When sample descriptions are used to inter some information about the population, the subject is called inductive statistics of statistical in statistical inference.

It has been pointed out in the previous lesson that the primary data may be obtained by following either the census method or the sample method. The census method or complete enumeration deals with the investigation of the entire population whereas the sample method or partial enumeration deals with the part of universe which is considered as representative of the whole.

7.2 Census Method

In a census enumeration or the complete enumeration survey method, information is collected for each and every unit of the population. A unit may be household, field, factory, shop or any other similar unit in any specified geographical area to be covered under study. The aggregate of all the units under consideration is related to the living conditions of textile workers, the population consists of all the workers in various textile mills in India. The method of obtaining information from each and every unity belonging to the population is defined as complete enumeration or census inequiry. For example to find the find the average wage or worker working in sugar industry in India, wage figures would be obtained from each and every worker (Population unity), working in the sugar industry and by dividing the sum of the wages which all these workers receive by the total number of workers working in sugar industry. Generally more material, time, personnel and effort required for carrying out a complete enumeration are found to be large.

Merits of Census Method

i. This is an extensive study. Because in a census enumeration, information can be obtained from each and every item and many facts relating to the problem may also be brought out. For example population census gathers information not only in the number, it also collects information on age, martial stats, employment, education, sources of income, etc.

ii. The results are to be more representative, accurate and reliable.

Demerits

i. The census method would require a large number of enumerators and other staff involving a good deal of time, energy and expenditure.

ii. The census method is useless in case the results are urgently required.

iii. If the population is infinite or the evaluation process destroys the population unit, the census method cannot be adopted.

7.3 Sample Method

In many statistical enquires it may not be necessary to obtain the information from each and every unit of the population. A few units selected from the population in accordance with some specified procedure constitute a sample and the procedure of obtaining information on the units constituting the sample is referred as sample survey.

In a sample enumeration, the inquiry is based on a few units, representative of the whole which can warrant a reliable estimate of the characteristics of the population. For example suppose it is desired to carry out an inquiry into the spending habits of students in a university hostel. According to the census method, each and every student will be approached while in the sampling method a few students as representatives will be selected by the specific rule and the spending habits of only these students will be investigated.

The primary objective of sample inquiry is to obtain maximum information about the characteristics of the population with minimum of cost, time and effort and also to set out the limits of accuracy of such estimates.

7.4 Merits of the Sample Method

The sample method has a number of distinct advantages over the complete enumeration method.

1. Sample enumeration requires comparatively much less time because data on relatively fewer items has to be collected and processed.
2. The sample method is much more economical than a complete census.
3. The organisation and administration of a sample survey is relatively much convenient than census survey. Because it requires less personnel staff and the field of enquiry is also limited.
4. Although the sampling technique involves certain inaccuracies owing to sampling errors, the result obtained is generally more reliable than the obtained from a complete count. There are several reasons for it. (i) it is always possible to determine the extent of sampling errors, (ii) The non-sampling errors such as due to measuring and recording observations inaccuracy or incompleteness of information, location of units, non-response or incomplete response, bias of the investigators etc., are of a more serious nature in a complete census. In a sample survey these errors can be effectively controlled and minimised, by (a) employing highly qualified, skilled and trained personnel, (b) imparting sufficient training to the investigators for conducting the enquiry (c) better supervision and (d) using move sophisticated

equipment and statistical techniques for the processing and analysis of the relatively limited data.

5. Sampling method is the only method that can be used in certain cases. When the investigation entails destruction of material (unit of the population), for example the strength of a bullet, the life of a lamp, the breaking strength of chalks manufactured in a factory, sampling is the only practical way of assessing the quality of the whole lot. Also if the population is too large or infinite or spread over a large geographical area, it is difficult to collect information about each unit and there is no alternative but to resort to sampling. For example a study relating to fish in a tank can be studied by sample method only.
6. Since the sampling techniques save time and money, it is possible to collect more detailed information from the selected unit of the population n a sample survey.
7. The sample method is often used to judge the accuracy of the information obtained on a census basis.

Prof. R.A. Fisher sums up the advantages of sampling techniques over complete census in just four words: speed, economy, adaptability and scientific approach. A properly designed and carefully executed sampling plan yields good results.

7.5 Methods of Sampling

The various methods of sampling can be classified into two broad heads-Random sampling and non-random sampling.

7.5.1 Random sampling

Random sampling is also referred to as probability sampling. Because if the sampling process is random, the laws of probability can be applied. Here the term random sample is not used to describe the data in the sample but the process employed to select the sample members. Hence randomness is a property of the sampling procedure instead of an individual sample.

Probability sampling provides a scientific method of drawing samples from the population according to some laws of chance in which each unit in the universe has some definite pre-assigned probability of being selected in the sample.

7.5.2 Random sampling methods

Random sampling method can be further divided into the following.

a. Simple or unrestricted random sampling; and

b. Restricted random sampling

    i. Stratified sampling

    ii. Systematic sampling

    iii. Cluster sampling

a. Simple random sampling is a technique which consists in selecting the individuals from the population in such a way that each individual of the population has the same chance of being selected. The sample so drawn is called the random sample.

A random sample may be collected by (i) Lottery method and (ii) use of table of random numbers.

i. Lottery method

The simplest method of drawing a random sample is the lottery method. Under this method, all units of the universe are numbered or named on separate slips of paper of identical size, shape and colour to avoid the human bias. These slips are then folded like paper rolls and mixed up in a container or box. The slips in a box is a kind of miniature of the population for sampling purposes. A slip is drawn from the box. This will give the first number to be included in the sample. After noting the number or name from the slip, the slip should be returned to box before the second slip, is drawn. This procedure must be repeated till we get the required number of units in the sample.

For example let us suppose that we want to draw a random sample of 15 individuals from a population of 100 individuals. We assign the numbers 1 to 100 , one number to each individual of population and prepare 100 identical slips bearing the numbers from 1 to 100. These slips are then placed in a drum and mixed thoroughly finally a sample of 15 slips is drawn out one by one. The individual bearing the number of these selected slips will constitute the random sample. This method is very popular in lottery draws where a decision about prizes is to be made.

ii. Table of random numbers

The lottery method becomes very difficult to use as the size of population increases. An alternative method of random selection is that of using the table of random numbers which have been so constructed that each of the digits 0, 1, 2, ... , 9 appears with approximately the same frequency and independently of each other. If we have to select a sample from a population of size (N = 99) then the numbers can be combined two by two to give pairs form 00 to 99. Similarly N = 999 or N = 9999 and so no, then combining the digits three by three or four and so on, we get the numbers from 000 to 999 or 0000 to 9999 and so on.

Since each of the digits 0, 1, 2, ..., 9 occurs with approximately the same frequency and independently of each other, so does each of die pairs 000 to 9999 and so on.

The method of drawing a random sample comprises the following steps:

i. Identify N units in the population with numbers 1 to N.

ii. Select at random any page of the random number table and pick up the number in any row, column or diagonal at random.

iii. The population units corresponding to the numbers selected in step (ii) constitute the random sample.

Several standard table of random numbers are available, among which the following may be specially mentioned as they have been tested for randomness.

1. Tippett's (1922) random number tables consisting of 41,600 random digits group into 10,400 sets of four-digited random numbers.
2. Fisher and Yates (1938) table of random numbers with 15,000 random digits arranged into 1,500 sets of ten digited random numbers.
3. Table of random numbers (The ISI series, Calcutta) by C.R. Rao. Mitra and Mathai.

Tippett's table of random numbers is most popularly used in practice. The first forty sets from Tippett's table have been reproduced below for illustrating their use in the selection of random samples.

Table 7.1 : Random Numbers

2952	6641	3992	9992	7669	5911	3170	5624
4167	9523	1545	1396	7203	5356	1300	2693
2370	7483	3408	2762	3563	1089	6913	7691
0560	5246	1112	6107	6008	8125	4233	8776
2754	9143	1405	9025	7002	6111	8816	6446

Example

Draw a random sample (Without replacement) of 10 students from a class of 85 students.

Solution

First we identify the 85 students of the class with numbers from 01 to 85. Starting with the first number in the above random number Table-3.1 and moving row wise, we pick out one by one the two digital numbers less than or equal to 85, till 10 numbers out of 85 are obtained. In this process the numbers over 85 are discarded and the repeated number if any are taken only once.

The numbers grouped in two (row wise) are:

29	52	66	41	39	92	97	92	79	79
59	11	31	70	56	24	41	And	So	on

Ignoring the numbers greater than 85, we obtain for our purpose ten random numbers namely:

29	52	66	41	39
79	59	11	31	70

The students corresponding to these random numbers constitute the desired random sample of size 10.

b. Restricted random sampling includes (i) stratified, (ii) Systematic (iii) cluster sampling.

   i. This method of sampling is used when the population is composed of heterogeneous units. The method consists in classifying the population units into a certain number of groups each group consists of homogeneous values called strata (plural) and then selecting random samples independently from each group or stratum (singular).

The division of the population into strata (termed stratification) is usually done in such a way that.

i. There is greater homogeneity within the each stratum and as marked a difference as possible between the strata.

ii. There is no over-lapping in various strata.

For example, if it is desired to study the wage levels of workers in an industry, it would be better to classify all workers into skilled and unskilled, clerical and non-clerical, sex wise categories and then select random sample from each class or group in proportion to the size of that group in the population. The combined sample so obtained will represent better the characteristics of the population as a whole.

There are two main objects of stratification (i) to increase the accuracy of efficiency of the overall population estimates and (ii) to ensure that the sat divisions of the population, which are themselves of interest, are adequately represented.

Merits

1. This method ensures better representation of the characteristics of population in the sample.
2. In simple random sampling the results at times may be most non-random because certain portions of the population are completely left. This cannot happen under stratified sampling.
3. This method is most effective in dealing with highly skewed population such as income data or retail sales.

ii. A systematic sample is obtained by selecting one unit at random and then selecting additional units at evenly spaced intervals until the sample has been formed. This method is commonly used in those cases where a complete list of the population from which sample has to be drawn is available. The list may be prepared in alphabetical, geographical, numerical or some other order. The units or items are serially numbered.

Let us suppose that N sampling units in the population are arranged in some systematic order and serially numbered from 1 to N. Let us suppose that the size of the sample is n. Let K=N/n which is usually called the sample interval.

Systematic sampling consists in selecting any unit at random from the first k units numbered form 1 to k and then selecting every k th unit in succession subsequently.

For example suppose a complete list of all the 100 students in some serial order in a class is available and we want to take a sample of 10.The required sample can be obtained if every 10th student in the list is taken. The first student between 1 and 10 will be chosen at random. Suppose it comes to 4. We will then take every 14th, 24th, 34th, 44th, 54th, 64th, 74th 84th and the 94th student. This will make a sample f 10.

Merits

1. It is operationally more convenient than simple random sampling.
2. It will give quite accurate results if the lists are arranged wholly at random.
3. It requires little time and money.

Demerits

If there are periodic features associated with the sampling interval the results obtained will be biased. Systematic sampling can be used safely only when one is sure that thee are no periodic features associated with sampling interval.

iii. In the method of cluster sample the total population is divided, depending on problem under study into some recognisable sub-groups which are termed as clusters and a simple random sample of this clusters is drawn. We then observe, measure and interview each and every unit in the selected clusters.

For example, if we are interested in obtaining the income or opinion data in a city, the whole city may be divided into N different blocks, called clusters and a simple random sample of n blocks is drawn. The individuals in the selected blocks determine the cluster sample.

This method will adopted if the following conditions are satisfied.

i. Clusters should be as small as possible consistent with the cost and limitations of the survey, and

ii. The number of sampling units in each cluster should be approximately same.

The cluster sampling is not be recommended if we are sampling areas in city where there are private residential houses, business and industrial complexes, apartment buildings etc., with widely varying number of persons or households.

7.5.3 Non-random sampling method

Non-random sampling methods are:

i. Judgement sampling and

ii. Quota sampling

i. ***In Judgement Sampling:*** The sample is selected with definite purpose in view and the choice of the sampling units depends entirely on the discretionand judgement of the investigator. This method suffers from drawbacks of favouritism and nepotism depending upon the beliefs and prejudices of the investigator. It does not give a representative sample of the population.

For example if the sample of 10 students is be selected from a class of sixty for analysing the spending habits of students, the investigator would select 10 students who, in his opinion are representative of the class.

This sampling method is seldom used and cannot be recommended for general use since it is often biased due to element of subjectiveness on the part of the investigator.

ii. ***Quota sampling.*** Quota sampling is a restricted type of purposive or judgement sampling. This consists in specifying quotas of the samples from these strata by judgement sampling. The basic objectives is to make the best use of stratification without incurring. high costs which may be involved in any probabilistic method of sampling. Sample quotas may be fixed according to some specified characteristics such as income group, sex, occupation, political or religious affiliations, etc.

For example, in a radio listening survey the interviewers may be told to interview 500 people living in a certain area and that out of every 100 persons interviewed 60 are to be housewives, 25 farmers and 15 boys under the age of 15. Within these quotas the interviewers is free to select the people interviewed.

Quota sampling is often used in public opinion studies. It occasionally provides satisfactory results.

7.6 Sampling and Non-sampling Errors

The errors involved in the collection, processing, and analysis of data maybe classified under the following two heads.

i. Sampling errors

Sampling errors have their origin in sampling and arise due to the fact that only a part of the population (that is sample) has been used to estimate population characteristics and draw inferences about population. As such the sampling errors are absent in a complete enumerations survey.

ii. Non-sampling errors

The non-sampling errors primarily arise at the stages of observations, approximation and processing of the data and are thus present in both the complete enumeration and sample survey.

7.7 Classification of Data

The data collected in any statistical investigation, known as raw data, are so voluminous and huge that they are unwidely and incomprehensible. Therefore after the data have been collected and edited, they must be analysed so that their salient points can be brought out clearly. As a rule the fist step in the analysis is to classify and tabulate the information collected. If the secondary data have been employed, we rearrange those into new groups and tabulate the new arrangement, classification is the first step in tabulation, for in general, items must be brought together before the data can be displayed in a tabular form.

The process of arranging the data into groups or classes according to resemblances and similarities is technically called classification. According to secrist 'classification in the process of arranging data into sequences and groups according to their common characteristics, or separating them into different but related parts.

It will be clear from the above definition that the process of grouping the given data into homogeneous classes is called classification. By homogeneous classes we mean that all the items comprising the aggregates are of one type only. They possess a characteristic in common. For example retail business may be classified according to turnover, school boys according to their heights, shares quoted in a stock exchange according to dividends paid. The characteristics in these cases are turnover, height and dividends respectively, that is these constitute the link or basis of comparison between all the items within each group. As an another illustration in the data relating to socio-economic enquiry the family budget data relating to socio-economic enquiry the family budget data relating to nature, quality and quantity of the commodities consumed by the group of people together with expenditure on different items of comparison may be classified under the following heads: (i) food, (ii) clothing, (iii) fuel and lighting (iv) house rent (v) miscellaneous.

7.8 Sampling and Its Uses

Sampling in statistics is as common and important as salt in the food. The origin of sampling is as our civilisation. The use of sampling in day-to-day life has been illustrated through certain examples. In homes, ladies take out one or two rice grains (any other food item) from the cooking pan and test so that they are able to decide whether the food in the pan is fully cooked or not. In medical sciences a few drops of blood are taken and tested microscopically or chemically to know whether the blood contains some abnormalities or not. Whatever is observed in the few drops is true for the blood of the whole body. In a bulb manufacturing factory, one tests the life of few bulbs and comes to a conclusion about the average life of bulbs in the whole lot. In the grain market, a person takes a handful of grain, judges its quality and decides about the quality of grain in the heap on the basis of this handful of grain. All these examples clearly reveal that sampling has been an age old practice.

Nowadays, sampling methods are extensively used in socio-economic surveys to know the living condition, cost of living index etc. of a class of people. In biological studies, experiments are conducted on some units (persons, animals or plants) and inferences are drawn about the breed or variety to which the units belong. In the industries, sampling procedures are predominantly used for quality control.

7.9 Definitions

From the discussion so far, it is apparent that in sampling process we have to consider a complete set of objects or things known as population and a fraction of population selected in any manner is known as a *sample*. It will be appropriate to define and discuss these terms adequately.

Population In statistics, the term 'population' is used in an altogether different sense form its literary sense. Population may consist of the animates or inanimate. In literature, population omens there number of inhabitants in a well-defined area. But in statistics, *"It is the totality of persons,* objects, items or anything conceivable pertaining to certain characteristics".

As per statistical by Kendall and Backland (1975), the population is defined as, "*In statistical usage,* the term population is applied to any finite or infinite collection of individuals." For example, the population of students in a University. It means anybody who is enrolled in a University belongs to this population. The number of plants in a field, persons suffering from cancer, workers in textile industry, persons in army services in India, are some other examples of population in statistical sense.

From the definition it is evident that population can be finite as well as infinite. Obviously, the finite population consists of individuals or items which are finite in number, An infinite population is one which either possesses the infinite property through some limiting process or is non-enumerable. The population of all real numbers between 0 and 1,the population of all integers are examples of infinite population. In case of random sampling with replacement (discussed later), any population is always infinite. Without going too deep in the matter, we may say that a population consisting of a large number of units or items may be deemed to possess the properties of an infinite population.

From the above discussion it is evident that every population consists of individuals or items which are known as *sampling units.* The formal definition of sampling unit is given below.

Sampling Unit The population may be regarded as consisting of units which are to be used for the purpose of sampling. Each unit is regarded as individual and indivisible when the selection is made. Such a unit is known as a sampling unit. A sampling unit may be specified on some natural basis or any other criterion fixed for it. The criteria for it depend on the purpose of the survey and the sampling scheme to be followed. A person, an animal, a household, an orchard, a factory or a village are few examples of sampling units.

Sample A finite part of population or a subset of a set of sampling units, selected by some process, usually by deliberate selection with the object of investigating the properties of the parent population or set, is called a sample. For example, if we select five students from a class of forty students, five selected students constitute a sample. We select fifty bulbs to test the life of bulbs, from a lot of bulbs manufactured by a factory in a week. Fifty selected bulbs constitute a sample.

Sampling is a device which makes one able to draw inferences about the whole population simply by observing or measuring a few of the sampling units. However, this crates many doubts like (a) whether the conclusions drawn on the basis of sample observations really hold good for the whole population or the whole mass? (b) would the results not be unreliable? Such questions always surface in the mind of applied scientists. But the fact remains that the sampling has served the purpose of all the scientists to a great extent. Many arguments can be put forth in its support. A few of them are as given below.

(1) It is difficult to handle a population which usually consists of a large number of units.

(2) Too much time is required to study the whole population and often the study becomes outdated by the time it is complete.

(3) Finances required to cover the whole population can hardly be made available.

(4) In a study where individuals are killed or perished under observation, studying the population serves no purpose. To clarify this point further we give an example. If all the battery cells of a manufacturing concern are put to life testing, nothing will be left for use.

(5) In case, the population is infinite or consists of uncountable number of units, its study is impossible.

Some people also think that complete enumeration yields better results than the sampling studies. However, this is not correct because complete enumeration (census studies) adds many errors which are reduced or eliminated by sampling. Hence, in many cases sample studies yield better results than population studies. The reliability of results depends more on the quality of the sample. If the sample is a true representative of the population, the results obtained from it are very near to the true value. In the view of mathematicians, a 'random sample' can always be deemed as a true representative of the population. To a great extent it is correct. But the moment one starts identifying various sampling units belonging too a population, one resorts to thinking of various sampling schemes. The use of a particular type of sampling schemes depends on: (i) type of population, (ii) information available about sampling units, (iii) object of the study, (iv) availability of resources like sampling frame, time, money and trained personnel, and (v) last but not the least, the knowledge and experience of the person selecting the sample.

Errors in Surveys In nay survey two types of errors are likely to occur (i) sampling errors (ii) non-sampling errors.

Sampling Errors: The errors which are introduced due to errors in selection of a sample or the discrepancies between population parameters and estimates which are derived from a random sample. This discrepancy generally decreases as the sample size is quite rapid but gradually the decrease in error becomes negligible with increasing sample size. Hence a sample of optimum size must be obtained for a study. In this way one can minimize the error or keep the error as small all we-please and at the same time minimizing the cost of the survey. To determine the optimum sample size, a tolerable amount of error is prefixed and the smallest sample size is determined to help keep the error within tolerable limit.

Non-sampling Error: An error in sample estimates cannot be attributed to sampling fluctuations. It is experienced that the studies based on complete enumeration do not yield similar results in repeated enumerations. Such a discrepancy occurs due to many errors which are termed as non-sampling errors. Various sources of many which may be visualized are.

(i) Observational error or response error: if the observations are taken repeatedly on the same unit, the observed values generally fifer or otherwise even the same respondent is asked the same question repeatedly, his response may differ.

(ii) Lack of preciseness of definition also adds to the non-sampling errors. For example, in judging the loss of crop due to a disease like wilt or rust, will be subject to error due to definitions of what we call severely diseased, moderately diseased and a low intensity of disease. Moreover this measure of intensity will vary from person to person depending on the maturity, qualifications and training , the person has.

(iii) Errors are also introduced in editing and tabulation of data. Since the population data are large, the chances of errors in complete enumeration are more compared to a sample data.

Some better ways of minimising the sampling errors are the choice of an appropriate sampling scheme, selecting a sample of optimum size and the use of standard techniques of estimation. Whereas the non-sampling errors can be minimized through superior management of survey or investigation, employing befitting personnel and by using modern computational aids.

Here we define a few more terms which will be used often in this chapter and elsewhere.

Parameter Any population constant is called a parameter. For example, population mean (μ) and population variance (σ) etc. are parameters. To obtain a parameter value, the observations are taken on each and every unit of the population and a value of a constant pertaining to a characteristic is calculated from those observations. This constant value is termed as parameter. Such constant measure(s) of a population characterise a population.

Estimator An estimator is a rule or method of estimating a population parameter. It is generally expressed as a function of sample variates. An estimator is itself a random variable.

Estimate A particular value of an estimator obtained from a set of values of a random sample is known as estimate. As an explanation, generally few units are selected from a population and then observations are taken on these selected units. The constant for a characteristic is calculated from these sample observations. The constant, so obtained, is known as an estimate and stands for a population parameter. For example mean x is an estimate of population mean μ and sample variance s^2 is an estimate of population variance σ^2.

Statistics : A statistic is a function of observable random variables and does not involve any unknown parameter. All the more, the function itself is a random variable. But a statistic is not necessarily an estimator of some population parameter. For example, $\frac{I}{n} \sum_i X_I$ (I =1,2,...n) is a statistic, student-t, i.e. $\sqrt{n}$ (X-μ) /s is a statistic etc.

Selection with Replacement (Swr) : In this case, a unit is selected from a population with a known probability and the unit is returned to the population before the next selection is made (after recording its characteristic (s)). Thus, in this method at each selection, the population size remains constant and the probability at each selection or draw remains the same. Under this sampling plan, a unit has chances of being selected more than once. For example, a card is randomly drawn from a pack of cards and placed back in the pack, after noting its face value, before the next card is drawn of from an urn containing balls of different colours a ball is drawn, its colour is noted and kept back in the urn before another ball is drawn. Such a sampling method is known as sampling with replacement. There are N" possible samples of size *n* from a population of N units in case of sampling with replacement.

Sampling without Replacement (swer) In this selection procedure, if a unit from a population of size N is selected, it is not returned to the population. Thus, for any subsequent selection, the population size is reduced by one. Obviously, at the time of the first selection, the population size is N and the probability of a unit being selected randomly is I /N ; for the second d unit to be randomly selected, the population size is (N-1) and the probability of selection of any one of the remaining sampling unit is I / (N-2) and so on.

If we consider the limiting case that N is very large $\rightarrow \varpi$, the probabilities $\frac{1}{N}, \frac{1}{N-1}, \frac{1}{N-2}, \ldots\ldots,$ become constant and in the limiting situation, the selection procedures with replacement and without replacement become equivalent. Whereas in the case of small populations, the values $\frac{1}{N}, \frac{1}{N-1}, \frac{1}{N-2}, \ldots\ldots, \frac{1}{N-n+1}$ differ considerably. The sampling from small and large populations is generally expressed as sampling from finite and infinite populations respectively. There are $\binom{N}{n}$ possible samples, in case of sampling without replacement.

Size of a Sample : The size of a sample is the number of sampling units which are selected from a population by a random method. The problem that arises is how to decide what should actually be the number of sampling units to be selected from a population. As a matter of fact, the sample size depends on a number of consideration which are as follows:

(1) The purpose for which the sample is drawn.

(2) The type of population from which the sample is to drawn. That is, if the sampling units constituting the population are highly variable, then a large sample is required and conversely, if the population comprises of less variable units, then a small sample is good enough. For a perfectly homogeneous population, a single unit is sufficient to get the correct results for the whole population. For example, the blood of a person is perfectly homogeneous and hence a drop of blood taken for investigation gives the true picture of blood constitution in the body.

(3) Availability of technical people or equipment needed.

(4) Resources allotted for the study in terms of time and money.

(5) Precision required: If we want to detect very minute differences, most probably a large sample will be required and vice-versa. The mathematical formulation for determining sample size is as below.

$$d = u_R \frac{\hat{s}_x}{\sqrt{n}}$$

or

$$n = \frac{(u_R \hat{s}_x)^2}{d^2}$$

where d is the precision required to the differences to the extent of d; u_R —the number of standard deviations necessary for the required level of reliability R, which is generally in terms of probability. The value of u_{R}-- is obtained from the table of the probability distribution which the data follow. For example, if the data are selected from a normal distribution, then for a 95 per cent level of confidence $u_R = 1.96$ and $\hat{s}_x$ – – the standard deviation of x. Its value is substituted from experience or is based on the information obtained from some earlier study.

From (7.1.1) it is evident that if *d* is i.e. greater precision is required, we will to select a large sample. Also, if $\hat{s}_x$ is large, *n* is to be large. Moreover, as the level of reliability increases, *n* also increases.

7.10 Sampling Methods

In the selection of a sample, always the effort is to make the sample a true representative of the population. A large number of schemes have been worked out to achieve this objective. In general, we do probability sampling which is free from human bias. But in some situations, judgemert sampling or purposive sampling is preferred to probability sampling. For example, if we want a sample of persons who are suffering from cancer, we have to select cancer patients who happen to come to the hospital (s). But, in general, probability sampling errors and avoid human bias.

Probability sampling scheme leads to two types of samples (i) Unrestricted random samples (ii) Restricted random samples.

7.11 Unrestricted Random Sampling

If from a population, selection of sampling units is done in such a manner that each and every unit in the population has the same probability (chance) of being selected, such a probability sampling plan is called random sampling. Suppose there are N sampling units in a population, the probability of selection of any unit is 1/N.

Simple Random Sampling (srs) : In this type of sampling, *n* units from a population of N units are selected, without replacement, in such a way that the probability of selection of any one sample, out of $\binom{N}{n}$ possible samples is same i.e. $1/\binom{N}{n}$. In practice, the units are drawn one by one from the population numbered from 0 to (N-1). This process gives an equal chance of being selected to all units not previously selected. A random number table is always helpful in selecting a simple random sample.

Method of Selection : A random sample may be selected either by drawing the chits or by the use of random members. The *chit method* is a random method but is subject to many human biases as people can identify chits in many ways. The Roulette wheel is another device for drawing numbers randomly. It is more prevalent in lotteries. But the best of all is the use of random numbers given by Fisher and Yates—known as Fisher and Yates random numbers. The random number table is also given by Tippett's random number table. But Fisher and Yates' random number tables are more popular. Which random number tables one uses, does not matter in an y way. For selecting a random sample from a population fo size N, each sampling unit is numbered from 0 to (N-10). If N is a two-digit figure, the units can be numbered as 00,01.02,..up to the maximum of 98. In case N is a three-digit figure, the units can be numbered as 000,001,002,... up to the maximum of 998 and so on. In this way, the list of serially numbered sampling units is a map showing the position of sampling units with identification marks. Once the sampling frame is ready, a sample of size n can be selected in the following manner. Let N be a d-digit number. Make use of a d-digit random number table. Now read numbers one by one from the random number table, If this observed number, say K, is less than or equal to (N-1), then select k-th unit. If the observed number is equal to N, select the unit at serial number 00. In case, k is greater than N, (K>N), divide K by N and get the remainder 'R'. Now the R-th unit is selected. This process continues till n sampling units are selected.

The sample may be selected with replacement or without replacement. In the case of sampling with replacement, a number occurring more than once is accepted. A unit is repeated as many times as a random number occurs. But in the case of sampling without replacement, if a random number directly or by way of a remainder occurs more than once is omitted at any subsequent stage. In the above selection procedure numbering of units from 00 onwards an making use of remainders have an advantage, as no random number is being wasted during the selection procedure. This saves time and labour.

To explain the selection procedure further consider an example where a population consists of 18 units and a sample of size 5 is be selected from this population.

Since 18 is a two-digit figure, units are numbered as 00,01,...17. Five random numbers are obtained from a two digit random number table.

They are as given below:

65, 43, 62, 54, 46.

On dividing 65 by 18, the remainder is 11. Similarly dividing 43,62,54 and 46 by 18, the respective remainders are 7,8,0 and 10. Hence, select units of serial numbers, 11,07,08,00 and 10 and these selected units constitute the sample.

7.12 Estimation of Population Parameters

Let $X_1, X_2, \ldots X_n$ be a random sample of size n from a population of N units and $x_1, x_2, \ldots, x_n$ be the corresponding observed values. The values of the known parameter(s) should be estimated from the set of these sample observations. These estimates are often single valued which are known as point estimates. Also, many times an interval is to be estimated in which the parameter is expected to lie with a certain level of confidence. Here we will not pursue the estimation theory and hence the formulae for sample mean, sample variance, etc, are given directly.

Some properties of estimates are also discussed in this chapter. Formulae are presented in terms of x_i (I =1,1,..,n), the actual observed value corresponding to x_i.

Formulae for mean and Variance Let $U_1, U_2, .., U_n$ be N population units. A random sample of *n* units is selected. Suppose the observations on the sampled units are $x_1, x_2, \ldots x_n$. The sample mean,

$$\overline{x} = \frac{x_1 + x_2 + \ldots + x_n}{n}$$

$$= \frac{1}{n} \sum_i x_i$$

for i= 1,2,.., n.

The sample variance,

$$S^2 = \frac{1}{(n-1)} \sum_i (x_i - \overline{x})^2$$

$$= \frac{1}{(n-1)} \left\{ \sum x_1^2 - n\overline{x}^2 \right\}$$

$$= \frac{1}{(n-1)} \left\{ \sum_1 x_1^2 - \left(\sum_i x_1 \right)^{2/n} \right\}$$

Let the population mean be μ and variance be σ^2. is an estimated value of μ and σ^2 is an estimated value σ^2. Formulae for μ and σ^2 are given by (3.8) and (4.8).

Now, we define a special term σ^2, which is slightly different from σ^2 and is given as,

$$S^2 = \frac{1}{(n-1)}\sum_{1}(X_i - \mu)^2$$

$$= \frac{1}{(n-1)}\left\{\sum_{1} X_i^2 - N\mu)^2\right\}$$

where I = 1,2,….,N.

=

7.13 Properties of Estimates

Unbiasedness : As estimate is said to be unbiased if its expected value is equal to its parameter value. For example, if $\overline{x}$ is an estimate of μ, $\overline{x}$ will be an unbiased estimate if and only if,

$$E(\overline{x}) = m$$

The expectation may well be understood with this example. If from a population, we take all possible samples of size *n* and take the mean fall samples, the mean of the estimates is known as the expected value. If can theoretically be proved that $\overline{x}$ is an unbiased estimate of μ. In formula (7.3) for s^2, the divisor is (*n*-1) instead of *n*. The reason for this is that using the divisor (*n*-1) makes s^2 an unbiased estimate of s^2,,.i,e.

$$E(s^2) = s^2$$

Mathematical proofs are avoided in this book. Hence, the above conjecture of unbiasedness will be shown through an example.

Example

A population of five units has the observations.

7, 6, 8, 4, 10

Random samples of three units are drawn such that no unit is repeated in a sample and the order of selection does not matter. Out of the 5 units, there can be 10 samples each consisting of 3 units.

Possible samples, their means and variances are given in the following table.

Sample Nos.	1	2	3	4	5
Observations	7,6,8	7,6,4	7,6,10	7,8,4	7,8,10
$\overline{x}$	7	17/3	23/3	19/3	25/3
s2	1	7/3	13/3	13/3	7/3
	6	7	8	9	10
	7,4,10	6,8,4	6,8,10	6,4,10	8,4,10
	7	6	8	20/3	22/2
	9	4	4	28/3	28/3

$$\text{Mean of } \overline{x},\ s = \frac{1}{10}\left(7 + \frac{17}{3} + \frac{23}{3} + \frac{19}{3} + \frac{25}{3} + 7 + 6 + 8 + \frac{20}{3} + \frac{22}{3}\right)$$

$$= \frac{210}{30} = 7$$

Similarly, mean of S^2 s = $\frac{50}{10}$ = 50

Population mean $\mu = \frac{35}{5} = 7$

And variance

$$S^2 = \frac{1}{4}\{(7-7)^2 + (6-7)^2 + (8-7)^2 + (4-7)^2 + (10-7)^2\}$$

$$= \frac{20}{4} = 5.0$$

The above calculations verify the statement that the sample mean is an unbiased estimate of population mean whereas, s^2 is an unbiased estimate of S^2.

Simple Consistency : The notion of consistency is mainly concened with infinite population. If T_n is an estimator of a parameter θ where T_n is based on a random sample $X_1, X_2, \ldots, X_n$ such that $T_n = t_n(x_1, x_2, .. x_n)$ then the sequence $\{T_n\}$ is said to be a consistent estimator of θ if for every $\varepsilon > 0$, the following condition holds:

$$\lim_{n\to\infty} p\{\theta - \varepsilon < T_n < \theta + \varepsilon\} = 1$$

$$= 0$$

Mean Squared Error : If $T_n = t_n(x_1, x_2, \ldots x_n)$ be an estimator of a parameter θ, then $E\{(T_n - \theta)^2\}$ is said to be the mean-squared error of the estimator T_n. The sequence of estimators $\{T_n\}$ is said to be a mean squared error consistent if the following condition holds

$$\lim_{n\to\infty} E\left\{(T_n - \theta)^2\right\} = 0$$

Note : When the observed values $x_1, x_2, \ldots x_n$ are substituted in the estimator, we get the estimated value.

Standard Error (S.E) Standard deviation has been disused in Chapter 4 as a measure of variability. Another measure is standard error, which is the standard deviation of the sampling distribution of an estimator. The idea is that if we draw a number of repeated samples of fixed size n from a population having a mean μ and variance σ^2. Each sample mean, say $\overline{x}$, will have a different value. Here $\overline{x}$ itself is a random variable and hence it has a distribution. The standard deviation of $\overline{x}$ is called *standard error*. It has been proved that the standard error '$\sigma_{\overline{x}}$' of the mean $\overline{x}$ based on a sample of size n is,

$$\sigma_{\overline{x}} = \frac{\sigma}{\sqrt{n}}$$

From formula (7.9), it is obvious that the larger the sample size, the smaller the standard error and vice-versa. The advantage of considering standard error instead of a standard deviation is that this measure is not influenced by the extreme values present in a population under consideration. Moreover, it upholds all the virtues of standard deviation.

In practice we avoid studying or surveying the whole population. The process of drawing repeated simples is still more cumbersome. Hence, in reality neither we use σ to calculate the standard error of $\overline{x}$ nor we take more than one sample. As a matter of fact, what we do is, that we select only one sample, find its standard deviation s and use the following formula to find out the standard error of $\overline{x}$ i.e.

$$S.E.(\overline{x}) = \frac{s}{\sqrt{n}}$$

Standard error is commonly used in testing of hypothesis and interval estimation. Many distributions, which are originally not normally distributed, have been taken as normal by considering the distribution of mean for a large *n* . This theorem has been stated below.

7.14 Restricted Sampling

Stratified Random Sampling In the introductory part under the heading 'sampling methods', it has been mentioned that a sample is good, if it is a true representative of the population. The moment one starts identifying various sampling units, one is able to think of various sampling schemes. Stratified sampling is one of them. In this type of sampling plan, the whole population is divided into a number of homogeneous groups or *strata* on the basis of certain characteristic(s) of the sampling units. For example, a city is divided into groups according to wards. If the sampling units is a household, then the households may be divided into homogeneous groups according to the income per family. In an opinion survey, persons may be divided into homogeneous group according to their qualifications, age, sex, size of family etc. Each homogeneous group is known as *stratum.* From each stratum a random sample of required size is selected.

It is apparent from the preceding para that in this type of sampling plan, we need information about each and every sampling unit. If such prior information can be made available, stratified sampling proves to very good. But generally such minute detail about each and every unit of a population is not available. Hence, the strata are based on some broad basis, e.g. different zones in a regional survey, nearby areas in a district serve as strata for estimation purposes. In short stratifies sampling is suitable only when the population is known to have heterogeneity with regard to some factors and those factors are used for stratification. All the more, stratified sampling have the following advantages.

1. If the admissible error is given, we need a small sample resulting into a cut in the expenditure.
2. In the case where the cost of the survey is fixed, there is reduction in error.
3. It helps in determining the estimates for various groups, zones etc. i.e. for each stratum separately.
4. Stratified sampling is convenient from the organization point of view. Linguistic zones are often formed and each zone serves as a stratum.
5. Sometimes various sampling schemes may be used to draw samples from different strata. But this creates problems in getting the overall estimates. Besides the above-mentioned advantages, many problems remain to be solved are:
   (i) What should be the criterion for stratification ?
   (ii) How many strata can be formed ?
   (iii) How does one find the points of demarcation between the strata?

(iv) What should the sample size for each stratum be?

(v) What should the method of sampling be for each stratum ?

(vi) How does one get the estimates from each stratum and how does one pool them to get the population estimates ?

All the above points are dealt with briefly in this chapter taking them one by one.

Stratification and Estimation

(i) The variable or criterion for stratification depends on the purpose of the survey and the information available. As already indicated, strata are formed on the basis of administrative zones, socio-economic conditions or any other factor found suitable. Strata should be formed in such a way that they ae as homogeneous as possible, especially in respect of the characteristic, factor or variable, which is likely to influence the results of the survey.

(ii) We should from as many strata as required so that they are homogeneous; in fact, the more the number of strata the better the result. Some formulation has also been done to decide the number of strata. But keeping in view the requirements of this book, they have been kept out.

(iii) Points of demarcation of the strata should be clearcut so that not two strata overlap each other. For mathematical formulae, the readers are advised to read an advance book on sampling theory.

(iv) The problem of deciding the sample size for each stratum is known as the allocation problem. We know that the size of the sample directly influences the estimates. Hence, a sample of optimum size has to be chosen. Only formulae for optimum sample size are given in the following discussion.

(v) Centrally, a random sample is drawn from each stratum. Any other sampling scheme, like selection of units with probability proportional to size (pps), may be adopted if the situation demands it.

(vi) Various formulae for mean and variance are given ahead, considering that a simple random sample is selected from each stratum.

First we have to clarify the notations which will commonly be used in all the formulae.

Population size $\rightarrow$ N units

Total number of strata $\rightarrow$ K

Size of the *j*th stratum → N*j* for j =1,1,...,K

Such that $\sum_j N_j = N$

Sample size = *n*

Sample size in *j*th stratum $= n_j$

Such that $\sum_j n_j = n$

Suppose x_{ij} denotes *j*th observation belonging to *j*th stratum.

We give formulae for means and variances.

The mean of the *j*th stratum is, $\overline{X}_j = \frac{1}{N_j}\sum_{i=1}^{N_j} x_{ij}$

And its estimated mean, $\overline{X}_j = \frac{1}{n_j}\sum_{i=1}^{N_j} x_{ij}$

Variance for the *j*th stratum, $S_j^2 = \frac{1}{N_j - 1}\sum_{i=1}^{N_j}(x_{ij} - \overline{X}_j)^2$

*j*th stratum sample variance, $S_j^2 = \frac{1}{n_j - 1}\sum_{i=1}^{N_j}(x_{ij} - \overline{X}_j)^2$

Suppose μ is the population mean. An unbiased estimate of μ under stratified sampling is,

$$\overline{x}_{st} = \frac{1}{N}\sum_{j=1}^{k} N_j\ \overline{x}_j$$

variance of stratified sample mean $\overline{x}_{st}$ is,

$$V(\overline{x}_{st}) = \frac{1}{N^2}\sum_{j=1}^{k} N_j(N_j - n_j)\frac{S_J^2}{n_j}$$

$$= \sum_{j=1}^{k} \frac{N_j^2}{N^2}\left(1 - \frac{n_j}{N_j}\right)\frac{S_j^2}{n_j}$$

putting $N_j/N = W_j$, we obtain

$$V(\bar{x}_{st}) = \sum_{j=1}^{k} W_j^2 \left(1 - \frac{n_j}{N_j}\right) \frac{S_j^2}{n_j}$$

If the sampling fraction nj /Nj for each stratum is negligible, then

$$V(\bar{x}_{st}) = \sum_{j=1}^{k} \frac{W_j^2 \; S_j^2}{n_j}$$

Replacing S_j^2 by its estimate S_j^2, we get the estimate of $V(\bar{x}_{st})$, sayv $(\bar{x}_{st})$.

Thus,

$$V(\bar{x}_{st}) = \sum_{j=1}^{k} \frac{W_j^2 \; S_j^2}{n_j}$$

Mean and Variance for Proportions in Stratified Sampling

As in the case of simple random sampling, there are only two classes say c_1 and c_2. A unit under study fals in either of the classes. If it belongs to c_1; it receives the coded value 1 and if it belongs to the other class it receives the value 0. Let the number of units belonging to c_1 in the *j*th stratum be *Mj* and in the sample size n_j from *j*th stratum, the number of units belonging to c_1 be m_j. Denoting the proportion of units in c1 for the population, the jth stratum and sample from the jth stratum by P, P_j and p_j respectively, various formulae for means and variance are as follows:

$$P_j = \frac{M_j}{N_j} \text{ and } p_j = \frac{m_j}{n_j}$$

and

$$P = \sum_j \frac{N_j}{N} P_j = \sum_j W_j P_j$$

For j =1, 2,…., k.

The estimated proportion p_{st} under stratified sampling for the units belonging to c_1 is

$$P_{st} = \frac{1}{N} \sum_j W_j \; p_j$$

and variance of p_{st} is,

$$V(p_{st}) = \frac{1}{N^2}\sum_j \frac{N_j^2(N_j - n_j)}{(N_j - 1)} \frac{p_j Q_i}{n_j}$$

Where $Q_i = (1-P_j)$.

n_j reveals that one must choose a large nj, if,

(i) n is large.

(ii) Sj is large, i.e., stratum is more heterogeneous.

(iii) Cj is small

The result was first given by Tchuprow (1923) which became popular only when Neyman in 1934 independently derived it. That is why such an allocation is known as *Neyman allocation*. On using the optimum value of *nj* and putting it in the variance of $\overline{x}_{st}$ under Neyman's allocation is given as,

$$V_{Ney}(\overline{x}_{st}) = \frac{1}{n}\left(\Sigma_j W_j S_j \sqrt{c_j}\right)\left(\Sigma_j \frac{W_j S_j}{\sqrt{c_j}}\right) - \frac{1}{N}\Sigma_j W_j S_j^2$$

In case c_1 is the same for all the units, i.e. say $c_j = c$, the variance

$$V_{Ney}(\overline{x}_{st}) = \frac{1}{n}\left(\Sigma_j W_j S_j\right)^2 - \frac{1}{N}\Sigma_j W_j S_j^2$$

Case 1: When the cost of the survey is fixed. In this situation we obtain the value of nj for each stratum so that $V(\overline{x}_{st})$ is minimum. Since c and c_0 are fixed quantities, we take $c_1 = c - c_0$. Therefore, we get,

$$c_1 = \Sigma_j c_j n_j$$

Now, substituting the optimum value of n_j, we obtain the optimum sample size n in terms of V_u as follows,

$$c_1 = \Sigma c_j n \frac{(W_j S_j / \sqrt{c_j})}{\Sigma_j (W_j S_j / \sqrt{c_j})}$$

or

$$n_{opt} = c_1 \frac{\Sigma_j (W_j S_j / \sqrt{c_j})}{\Sigma (W_j S_j / \sqrt{c_j})}$$

Case 2: If the variance $V(\overline{x}_{st})$ is fixed, and its value is V_0, then substituting the optimum value of nj , we obtain the optimum sample size n in terms of V_0 as follows:

$$n_{opt} = \frac{\left(\Sigma_j W_j S_j / \sqrt{c_j}\right)\left(\Sigma_j W_j S_j / \sqrt{c_j}\right)}{V_0 + \frac{1}{N}\Sigma_j W_j S_j^2}$$

From the usage point of view, stratified sampling may be considered next to simple random sampling. The reasons for this are: increased precision, administrative convenience and many other reasons discussed in the running matter. It can easily be seen that variance of man under random sampling is greater than the variance under proportional allocation is stratified sampling. Whereas out of the three, the variance of mean under Neyman allocation is minimum. These results can be written as

$$V_{ran} \geq V_{prop} \geq V_{ney}$$

At lot of research work has been done on stratified sampling and for further details, readers are advised to study an advanced book on the theory of sampling.

7.15 Systematic Sampling

Often we have to obtain the information from cards or registers which are in serial order. Sometimes we might need the sample of trees from a forest or houses in a city. In such a case, a sampling plan known as *systematic sampling* often works better than the simple random sampling. In order to draw a systematic sampling often works better than the simple random sampling. In order to draw a systematic sample of size n, divide the population into n equal parts. Supposing each part to consist of k units, draw a random number from a to k. Let the selected number bej. Then select j, (J+K), (J +2k), …, $(j + \overline{n-1}k)$ - th units. This constitutes a systematic sample of size n. For example, if there are 100 units in a population serially numbered from 1 to 100 and we want to draw a sample of 5 units. Draw a random number from 1 to 20 since k=20 and let the selected number be 7, i.e. j=7. then select units in serial numbers 7, 27, 47, 67 and 87. These units constitute a systematic sample of 5 units. Further details will be given later.

Systematic sample has some advantages as well as disadvantages. Some of the advantages are:

(1) The method of selection is very simple and is not very expensive.

(2) The sample is evenly distributed over the whole population and hence all contiguous parts of the population are represented in the sample.

(3) It has an advantages over other sampling plans because it has organising control of field work.

The disadvantages are:

(1) If the variation in units is periodic i.e. the units at regular intervals are correlated, then the sample becomes highly biased. For example, if the houses are in blocks and if a corner house is selected are random then all other houses selected in the sample will be corner ones and this definitely gives a biased sample.

(2) No single reliable formula for estimating standard error of sample mean is available. A formula is good enough, if the population is of the type it has been assumed to be. This is, of course, a great draw-back.

7.16 Methods of Selection

Linear Systematic Sampling Though this selection procedure has already been given in the general discussion briefly, we will discuss it is detail now. Suppose a population consists of N units and from this a systematic sample of n units is to be selected. Also, assume that N is a multiple of n, i.e., let N-nk. The procedure is to select a random number, say j, such that $1 \leq j \leq$ and then select the jth and every subsequent j+k, j+2k, …, $(j+\overline{n-1}k)$ -th positional units. This sampling plan is known as linear systematic sampling. But the situation that N is a multiple of n does not always hold. In this situation it is just possible that we get a sample of (n-1) units instead of n. for example, if N=13 and n=4, then k has to be taken as 4. Now select a random number from 1 to 4, say it is 3. Then, the remaining three units to be selected are at positions 7,11,15. There is no unit in the population at serial number 15. hence, we can select only a sample of size 3 in this situation. To cope with this situation, a sampling plan known as circular systematic sampling is used.

Circular Systematic Sampling This is applied when N [1] nk. This type of sampling was first used by D.B. Lahri (1952) in national sample surveys. Here we take N/n as k by rounding of N/n to the nearest integer. Select a random number from 1 to N. let this number be m. Now select every 9m + jk)-th unit when m=jk < N and select every (m + jk – N)-th unit when m + jk > putting j = 1,2, 3, … till n units are selected. By this method we always get a sample of size n. suppose for the example given in the previous section with N=13n=4 and k=3, the random ly selected num ber from 1 to 13 is 8 and later the 11th, 1st, 4th and 7th units are selected. When N=nk, the linear and circular systematic plans become identical. For example, if N-12, n = 4, k = 3 and the selected unit from 1 to 3 is 3 and from 1 to 12 is either of the numbers 3, 6, 9 and 12, then, under both the sampling schemes, the selected units will be those bearing serial numbers 3, 6, 9 and 12. Also, if the selected number from 1 to 3 is and from 1 to 12 is any one of the 2,5,8 or 11, the selected units will be those bearing the serial numbers 2,5 8 and 11. This example shows the equivalence between two selection plans.

Mean and Variance of systematic Sampling : Let the observations on selected units be x_1, x_2,…,. Then the sample mean $\overline{x}_{sy}$ of the systematic sample is

$$\overline{x}_{xy} = \frac{1}{n}\,\Sigma_i x_i$$

for I = 1,2,…, n and variance of $\overline{x}_{xy}$ when N = nk is

$$v(\overline{x}_{xy}) = \frac{N-1}{N}S^2 - \frac{k(n-1)}{N}S^2 wsy$$

As we have noticed that for every random number selected from 1 to k, a separate systematic sample will be obtained. Let x_{ij} represent the ith observation in the jth systematic sample which is obtained when a random number j = 1,2,…k is selected. Thus, the variance between systematic samples is,

$$S^2 = \frac{1}{N-1}\,\Sigma_j\,\Sigma_i (x_{ij} - \mu)^2$$

for j = 1,2,…k; and i = 1,2,….n.

Also, $\frac{N-1}{N}S^2 = \sigma^2$

And the variance S^2_{wsy} within the systematic sample is,

$$S^2_{WSY} = \frac{1}{K(n-1)}\Sigma_j\,\Sigma_i (X_{ij} - \overline{x}_j)^2$$

and $\frac{k(n-1)}{N}S^2_{WSY} = \frac{1}{N}\Sigma_j\,\Sigma_i \left(x_{ij} - \overline{x}_j\right)^2 = \sigma^2_w$

Thus, reduces to,

$$V(\overline{x}_{sy}) = (\sigma^2 - \sigma^2_w)$$

σ^2, the population variance is a constant quantity and σ^2_w is the variance within the systematic sample which is being subtracted from σ^2 to get $V(\overline{X}_{sy})$. Hence, the greater the heterogeneity among units within the sample, the better it is. We would like to remind readers that if the units at equal intervals are more alike, then the systematic sample is not a good sampling scheme.

Another point that may strike the mind is that systematic sampling in some sense resembles stratified sampling where k units form a stratum. But it differs widely in the sense that no independent sample is selected from each of the k units, which may be considered a stratum of contiguous units. Other argument are trivial to think of. Hence systematic sampling can be used when no cyclic trend is evident.

7.17 Cluster Sampling

In the discussion so far we have been considering the smallest well-identifiable unit of the population known as elementary unit. The observations have been taken on these elementary units. But in some cases it is not possible to take a sample of these elementary units. Even if it is possible it is very costly, time consuming, less precise and inconspicuous. Various reasons, that cause problems is the selection of a sample of elementary units, are elucidated below:

(i) The sampling frame may not be available or may be too costly in terms of money, time and labour. For example, a list of fields and their owners in a state, a list of households in a big city etc.

(ii) The elementary units are situated for apart from one another and if selected it consumes a lot of time and money to survey them. If we select farmers in a state, the selected farmers will generally be at long distances. This, of course, increases the cost of the survey.

(iii) The elementary units may not be well identifiable and easily locatable. For instance, the population consisting of shepherds, the animals of a particular species in the forests of a country etc. In general, the migratory elementary units of a population are not easily identifiable and locatable.

Thus, to cope with the above problems, in sampling of elementary units, a sampling plan known as *cluster sampling* or area sampling yields satisfactory results. In cluster sampling, groups of elementary units are formed generally on location, class or area basis. When the whole of area constituting the population is divided into small area segments are being sampled, then it is called area sampling, otherwise cluster sampling. The clusters or segments are called the *primary units*. For example, cluster may be consisting of all households in a ward and hence there are as many clusters as the number of wards in a city. In area sampling it is easy to select a village as a whole rather than the individual farms of a district. Hence, all the farms in a village may be thought of as a cluster. Certain precautions should necessarily be taken for cluster sampling which are as given below.

(i) Each elementary unit should belong to one and only one cluster, area of segment.

(ii) The clusters constituting the population should include each and every elementary unit belonging to the population.

(iii) All clusters should be distinct, meaning that there should neither be overlapping nor omission of units.

Generally a simple random sample of clusters is selected from a population. Here we have considered the case when all clusters consist of unequal numbers of elementary units. First we define various notations and then give the formulae for various estimates.

Number of clusters = N

Number of elementary units in the jth cluster = M_j

Number of elementary units in the population, M= $\Sigma_j M_j$ where j=1,2,...N.

Sample size = n

Number of elementary units in the sample= $\Sigma_j M_j$ Where j = 1,2,...., n.

Let x_{ij} denote the ith observation in the jth cluster,

Thus, the mean of jth cluster,

$$\overline{x}_j = \frac{1}{M_j} \Sigma_j x_{ij}$$

for j = 1,2,..., N and i = 1,2,..., Mi and population mean,

$$\overline{x}_c = \Sigma_j \Sigma_i x_{ij} / \Sigma_i M_j$$

$$= \frac{1}{M} \Sigma_j M_j \overline{x}_j$$

Where M = $\Sigma_j M_j$ for j = 1,2,..., N.

An estimate $\overline{x}_c$ of population mean $\overline{x}_c$ which is unbiased but not consistent is given as,

$$\overline{x}_c = \frac{1}{n} \Sigma_j M_j \overline{x}_j / \overline{M}$$

Where $\overline{M} = \frac{M}{N}$

Let S_b^2 and S_w^2 denote the variance between and within clusters respectively. Now the population variance,

$$\sigma^2 = \frac{1}{NM-1}\Sigma_j\,\Sigma_i(x_{ij}-\overline{x}_c)^2$$

$$S_b^2 = \frac{1}{NM-1}\Sigma_j\left(\overline{x}_j-\overline{x}_c\right)^2$$

and

$$S_w^2 = \frac{1}{N(M-1)}\Sigma_j\,\Sigma_i\left(x_{ij}-\overline{x}_c\right)^2$$

An unbiased estimate of the variance of $\overline{x}_c$ is given as,

$$v(\overline{x}_c) = \frac{N-n}{Nn}S_b^2$$

Where $S_b^2 = \dfrac{1}{n-1}\,\Sigma_j\left(M_j\,\overline{x}_j-\overline{x}_c\right)^2;\ j=1,2,\ldots n.$

Also, an estimate of S_w^2 is,

$$S_w^2 = \frac{1}{n(M-1)}\Sigma_j\,\Sigma_i\left(x_{ij}-\overline{x}_j\right)^2$$

Where j = 1,2,...n, and I = 1,2..., Mj.

An intuition of a statistician came true when the variation within the cluster was proved less than the variation between clusters, i.e. $S_w^w \leq S_b^2$ because the units within a cluster are more homogeneous that the units in different clusters.

Efficiency : *The information* of sampling design is equal to the inverse of its variance and the *efficiency* of a sampling design, as compared to the other one, is the ratio of the invert of their variances. If the variance of two sampling designs are V_1 and V_2 respectively, then the efficiency of sampling design -1 as compared to sampling design-2 is,

$$E_{12} = \frac{1/V_1}{1/V_2} = \frac{V_2}{V_1}$$

Using the above approach, the efficiency of cluster sampling as compared to random sampling is,

$$E = \frac{\dfrac{NM-nM}{NM}\,\dfrac{S^2}{nM}}{\dfrac{N-n}{N}\,\dfrac{S_b^2}{n}}$$

$$= \frac{S^2}{M\,S_b^2}$$

Likewise, we can find them efficiency of a design as compared to any other design. Moreover, from (7.65.1) it is apparent that the efficiency of cluster sampling increases as the cluster size decreases. Hence one should take clusters of as small size as possible, provided the set norms are not vitiated. Another point of as small size as possible, provided the set norms are not vitiated. Another point worth nothing is that, in most respects, cluster sampling resembles stratified sampling. The silent difference is that in stratified sampling all the sampling units are each stratum (cluster) whereas sampling all the sampling units are included. In large scale surveys, cluster sampling is often helpful and efficient.

7.18 Multistage Sampling

As already pointed out, a survey has certain limitations, mainly budget and time. Hence to survey too many elementary units is often not possible. In stratified sampling, a sample of optimum size is drawn from each strartum. In cluster sampling, a sample of clusters is selected in which each and every elementary unit of the selected clusters has to be studied. This is also costly in terms of time and money. In case the selected units (clusters) are homogenous, i.e., the elements of the selected units give same response, it is advisable not to study the whole cluster or unit as it increases the cost and time of the survey. Hence if the cluster is homogeneous and basically each unit in the population is divisible into a number of smaller units or elements, a new sampling scheme known as multistage sampling or sub-sampling is extremely helpful. When large scale surveys on district, state or national level are to be conducted, it is one of the most suitable sampling plan. For example if the government or some other agency wants to collect information about the tax payer house-holds in a city, it is better to select a sample of various mohallas (wards) or localities before selecting a sample of households from these selected localities. In this way, the localities are *first stage units* and households are *second stage units.* Such a sampling procedure on the whole is known as *two-stage sampling.* Again if survey is conducted to estimate the crop production of a district, it is preferable to select villages as *first stage units,* sample of farms in selected villages as second stage units, and select a sample of plots from each selected farms as third stage unit. In this case, the selection procedure is known as selected farms as three-stage sampling. Selection procedure may be extended to any number of stages. Hence the sampling in various stages in general is known as multistage sampling.

7.19 Sampling Distribution

Statistic

A statistic is a function of one or more random variables not involving any unknown parameter, e.g.

$\Sigma_i X_i / n$, i.e., $\overline{X}$, $\Sigma_i (X_i - \overline{X})^2 / (n-1)$, i.e., s^2, s and $\overline{X} / s$ etc. Moreover, a statistic itself is a random variable and follows some distribution.

Generally, we draw a random sample from a population and calculate its mean, range, median, variance and standard deviation. We know that there are $\binom{N}{n}$ possible samples of size n from a population of N units. One way is to draw all possible samples and then calculated for each sample, the mean $\overline{X}$, S.D.s., etc. And find their frequency distribution. But this is possible only for small populations. Another approach is to draw a large number of samples and collect information on the sample distribution of various statistics. The studies from this approach have become easier with the help of electronic computers. But this technique is not always feasible because of the cost and ambiguity of results involved with it. Moreover, it is not an exact approach as we are concerned with the theoretical sampling distribution of various statistics.

Definition : *Sampling distribution* describes the way in which a statistic or a function of statistics, which is /are the function(s) of the random variables X_1, X_2, ..., X_n will vary from one sample to another sample of the same size. Such sampling distribution have given a fillip to the number of test statistics for hypotheses testing.[1] Hence, some important sampling distributions are discussed in this chapter.

Standard Error(SE): Standard error is the standard deviation of the sampling distribution.

7.20 Student's t-Distribution

If a random sample $X_1, X_2, \ldots X_n$ of size n, with observed values $(x_1, x_2, \ldots x_n$ is drawn from a normal population having mean μ and S.D. σ. The mean 'x is distributed normally with mean μ and S.D. $\sigma/\sqrt{n}$ i.e., '$x \sim N(\mu, \sigma / \sqrt{n})$.

Also the variable, Z where,

$$Z = \frac{\overline{x} - \mu}{\sigma / \sqrt{n}}$$

is a normal variate with mean 0 and standard deviation 1, i.e., Z~N (0,1).

In practice, the standard deviation is not known and in such a situation the only alternative left is to, use s, the sample estimate of standard deviation. Thus the variate $\sqrt{n}\,(\bar{x} - \mu)/s$ is approximately normal provided n is sufficiently large. If n is not sufficiently large, the variate $\sqrt{n}\,(\bar{x} - \mu)/s$ is distributed as t and hence.

$$t = \frac{\bar{x} - \mu}{s/\sqrt{n}}$$

Where

$$s^2 = \frac{1}{n-1}\Sigma_i(x_i - \bar{x})^2$$

t is a widely used variable and the distribution of t is called student's t-distribution. This distribution was discovered by W.S. Gosset in 1908. The statistician Gosset is better known by the pseudonym 'student' and hence t-distribution is called student's t-distribution. He derived the distribution of $\bar{x}/s_{\bar{x}}$ (where $s_{\bar{x}} = s/\sqrt{n}$) to find an exact test of a mean by making use of estimated standard deviation s, based on a random sample of size n. R.A fisher in 1925 published that t-distribution can also be applied to the test of regression coefficient and other practical problems. Here, we give the density function and properties of t-distribution without derivation. The readers interested in the derivation should consult a book on mathematical statistics. The density function of variable t with k=n-1 degrees of freedom is,

$$f_k(t) = \frac{1}{\sqrt{k}.B\left(\frac{1}{2}, \frac{k}{2}\right)} \frac{1}{\left(1 + \frac{t^2}{k}\right)^{\frac{k+1}{2}}} - \infty < t < \infty$$

Where

$$B\left(\frac{1}{2}, \frac{k}{2}\right) = \frac{(\Gamma 1/2)(\Gamma / k/2)}{\Gamma\left(\frac{k+1}{2}\right)} = \frac{\sqrt{\pi}\Gamma k/2}{\Gamma\left(\frac{k+1}{2}\right)}$$

Therefore,

$$f_k(t) = \frac{\Gamma(k+1)/2}{\sqrt{k\pi}\;\Gamma k/2}\left(1 + \frac{t^2}{k}\right)^{\frac{-(k+1)}{2}}$$

Properties of t-Distribution

(1) t -distribution is a unimodal distribution.

(2) The probability distribution curve is symmetrical about the line t=0.

(3) It is a bell-shaped curve just like a normal curve with its tails a little higher above the abscissa than the normal curve. Its spread increases as degrees of freedom 'K' decreases. This means that for the same value of t-variate and x, the normal variate, the area beyond t is larger than the area beyond x.

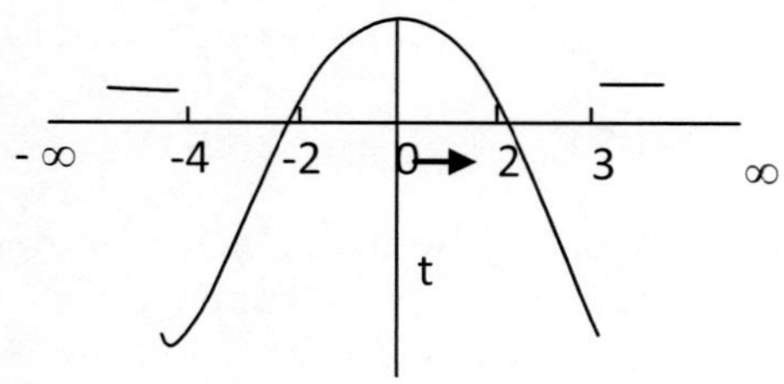

Fig 7.1 : t - distribution curve

(4) t-distribution has only one parameter k, the degrees of freedom equal to (n-1).

(5) The constant of t-distribution are as follows:

(Mean) $\mu = 0$ for $k \geq 2$.

(Variance) $\sigma^2 = \frac{k}{k-2}$ for $k \geq 3$

Skewness $(\alpha_3) = 0$ for k>, 4

Kurtosis $(\alpha_4) = \frac{3(k-2)}{(k-4)}$ for k >, 5

(6) The area under t-distribution curve for t<t' is determined by the equation.

$$F_k(t) = p(t < t') = \int_{-\infty}^{t'} f(t)\ dt$$

Student and other readers need not integrate actually for the area as the table of area under the curve for different values of t are available and vice-versa.

Equation (8.4) is given to acquaint the reader with the know-how of getting the area if t is given and the value of t area is given.

(7) t-distribution tends to normal distribution as k increase. For practical purpose, t is taken as equivalent to the normal distribution provided $k \geq 30$.

(8) Moment generating function for t-distribution does not exist.

t-distribution has tremendous utility in testing of hypothesis about one population mean or about equality of two population means when standard deviation is not known. Other uses of t-distribution will be known to the readers in the chapters ahead. t-distribution table has been provided in appendix.

7.21 Chi-Square Distribution

So far, we have been discussing the distribution of mean obtained from all possible samples, or a large number of samples drawn from a normal population, distributed with mean m and variance σ^2 / n. Now we are interested in knowing the distribution, of sample variances s^2 of these samples. Consider a random sample $X_1, X_2 \ldots, X_n$ of size n. let the observations of this sample be denoted by $x_1, x_2, \ldots, x_n$. We know that the variance.

$$s^2 = \frac{1}{n-1} \Sigma_i (x_i - \overline{x})^2 \text{ for } i = 1, 2, \ldots\ldots\ldots n,$$

or

$$\Sigma_i (x_i - \overline{x})^2 = (n-1)s^2 - ks^2$$

where k = (n-1)

A quantity ks^2/σ^2, which is a pure number, is defined as x^2_k. Now we will give the distribution of the random variable x^2_k which was first discovered by Helmert in 1876 and later independently given by Karl Pearson in 1900. Another way to understand chi-square is: if $x_1, x_2 .. x_n$ are n independent normal variant's with mean zero and variance unity, the sum of squares of these variates is distributed as chi-square with n d.f. The Chi-square distribution was discovered mainly as chi-square with n d.f. The chi-square distribution was discovered mainly as a measure of goodness of fit in case of frequency distribution, i.e., whether the observed frequencies follow a postulated distribution or not. The probability density function (p.d.f) of x^2-variate is,

$$f_k(x^2) = \frac{1}{2^{k/2}\Gamma(k/2)}(x^2)^{\frac{1}{2}k-1} e^{-\frac{1}{2}x^2}$$

Properties of Chi-square Distribution

(1) The whole chi-square distribution curve lies in the first quadrant since the range of x^2 is from 0 to ∞.

(2) From the density function given by (8.6), it is evident that x^2-distribution has only one parameter k, the degrees of freedom for x^2.

Thus, the shape of the probability density curve mainly depends on the parameter k. The shape of the curves for four different degrees of freedom say, k=2, k=7, k=12, k=20 are given below.

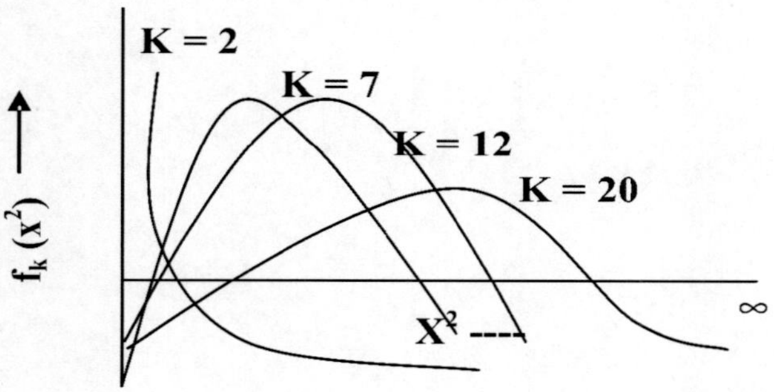

Fig 7.2 : Chi-square Distribution Curves

(3) Chi- square distribution curve is highly positive skewed.

(4) It is an unimodal curve and its mode is at the point, x^2 = (k-1).

(5) The shape of the curve varies immensely specially when k is small. For k = 1 and 2, it is just like a hyperbola.

(6) Chi-square distribution is completely defined by one parameter 'k', which is known as the degrees of freedom of chi-square distribution.

(7) The constants for chi-square distribution are as follows:

(Mean) $\mu = k$

(Variance) $\sigma^2 = 2k$

(Skewness) $\alpha_1 = 2\left(\frac{2}{k}\right)^{\frac{1}{2}}$

(8) The moment generating function for chi-square distribution is,

$$\varphi_x{}^2 = (1-2t)^{-k/2}$$

(9) r-th raw moment of chi-square distribution is,

$$\mu_r^{'} = \frac{2^r \Gamma\left(\frac{k}{2}+r\right)}{\Gamma k/2}$$

Putting r = 1, $\mu_1^{'} = \dfrac{2^2 \Gamma\left(\frac{k}{2}+1\right)}{\Gamma k/2} = K$

r = 2, $\mu_2^{'} = \dfrac{2^2 \Gamma\left(\frac{k}{2}+2\right)}{\Gamma k/2} = 4\left(\frac{k}{2}+1\right)\left(\frac{k}{2}\right) = k(k+2)$

Again,

$\mu_2 = \mu'_2 - (\mu'_1)^2$

$= K(K+2) - k^2 = 2k$

and so on,

(10) It can be shown that for large degrees of freedom say, $k \geq 100$, the variable $\left(\sqrt{2x^2} - \sqrt{2k-1}\right)$ is distributed normally with mean 0 and variance 1.

(11) If x_1^2 and x_2^2 are two independent chi-square with degrees of freedom k_1 and k_2 respectively, their sum (x_1^2 + x_2^2) will be distributed as chi-square with (k_1+k_2) d.f. This additive property of independent chi-square, holds good for any number of chi-squares, i.e if there are m independent chi-squares with k_1, k_2, ..., k_m d.f. respectively, the sum $\Sigma_i x_1^2 (i = 1,2,.......,m)$ will be distributed as chi-square with $\sum_i k_i$ d.f.

7.22 Fisher's z-Distribution

Sir Ronald A. Fisher defined a statistic z which is based upon the ratio of two-sample variances. Suppose s_1^2 and s_2^2 are two variances of random samples of sizes n_1 and n_2 respectively, drawn from two normal populations.

The statistic z is defined as,

$$z = \frac{1}{2}\log_e\left(\frac{s_1^2}{s_2^2}\right)$$

or $\quad z = \log_e s_1 - \log_e s_2$

Or $\quad e^{2z} = s_1^2 / s_2^2$

Putting $\left(\frac{s_1^2}{s_2^2}\right)$ = F, we get $\quad e^{2z} = F$

The letter F is the first of Fisher's name as a mark of respect. Z-distribution is of the form,

$$y = \frac{e^{k_1 z}}{\left(k_2 + k_1 e^{2z}\right)^{(k_1+k_2)/2}}$$

Where c is a constant, $k_1 = (n_1 - 1)$ and $k_2 = (n_2 - 1)$.

Properties of Z-Distribution

(1) z-distribution is symmetrical about the point z=0.

(2) z-distribution is a family of distribution in which each one exists for a pair of degrees of freedom k_1 and k_2.

Here the readers are acquainted with Fisher's z-distribution as it is closely associated with F-distribution given below.

F-Distribution

From (8.7.3) it is evident that the ratio of two independent sample variances is denoted as F. Now we will consider the distribution of the ratio of two-sample variances in another manner and based on this new approach, the distribution of F is given. The distribution of F was worked out by G.W. Shedecor.

Consider two normal populations $N(\mu_1, \sigma^2{}_1)$ and $N(\mu_2, \sigma^2{}_2)$. An independent sample of size n_1 is drawn from a population $N(\mu_1, \sigma^2{}_1)$ and of size n_2 from a population $N(\mu_2, \sigma^2{}_2)$. Let the sample variances be $s_1{}^2$ and $s_2{}^2$ respectively. From the chi-square distribution theory we know $k_1\, s^2{}_1/\sigma^2{}_1$ is distributed as chi-square with $k\text{--}_I$ d.f.., i.e.

$$\frac{k_1 s_1^2}{\sigma_1^2} \sim x_1^2$$

Where x_1^2 has d.f. $k_1 = (n_1 - 1)$

Similarly,

$$\frac{K_2S_2^2}{\sigma_{2^2}} \sim \Psi_2^2$$

When x_2^2 has df $k_2 = (n_2 - 1)$

From (8,9) and (8,10) we can write that,

$$\frac{s_1^2 / \sigma_2^2}{s_2^2 / \sigma_2^2} = \frac{x_1^2 / k_1}{x_2^2 / k_2}$$

$F_{k_1,.k_2}$

k_1 and k_2 are called the degrees of freedom of F. Dividing s_u^2 (u = 1, 2) by its corresponding population variance standardizes the sample variance, in the sense that on the average both the numerator and denominator approach 1. Now we may be interested in testing the hypothesis that both the normal populations have the same variance, i.e. $\sigma_1^2 = \sigma_2^2$. Under this hypothesis.

$$\frac{s_1^2}{s_2^2} = F_{k_1.k_2}$$

As a norm, the greater sample variance is taken as the numerator.

It is apparent that the ratio of two independent chi-squares is distributed as F and reveals that under the hypothesis $\sigma_1^2 = \sigma_2^2$, the ratio of two independent sample variances is distributed as f. The probability density function of F-distribution is,

$$_{k_1,k_2}(F) = \frac{(k_1 / k_2)^{k_1/2}}{B\left(\frac{k_1}{2}, \frac{k_2}{2}\right)} \frac{F^{k_1/2-1}}{\left(1 + \frac{k_1}{k_2}F\right)(k_1 + k_2)/2} ; 0 \leq F < \infty$$

Obviously, F is always a positive number and the F-distribution curve wholly lies in the first quadrant. There are two parameters of F-distribution namely, k_1 and k_2. Hence the shape of F-distribution curve depends on k_1 and k_2. For two pairs of degrees of freedom (k_1, k_2), the shape of the F-distribution are shown in Fig. 7.3.

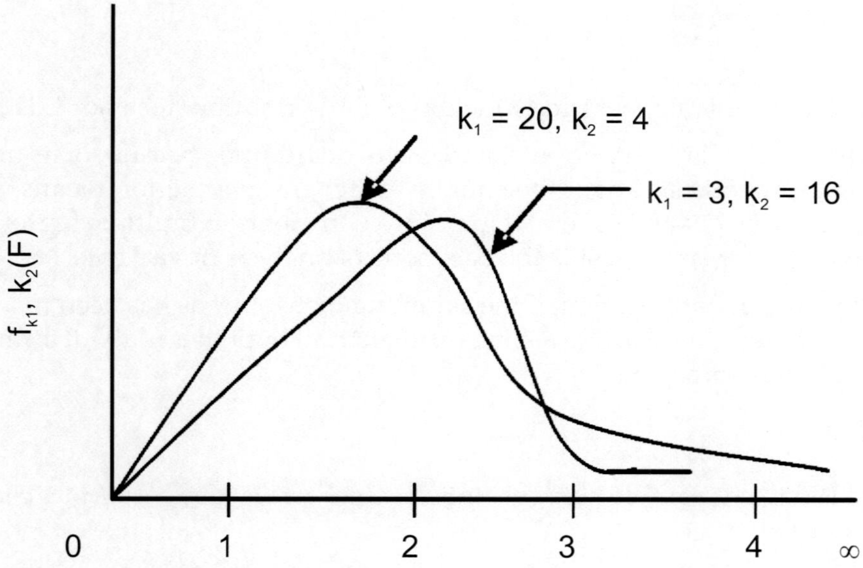

Fig. 7.3 : F-distribution Curves

Properties of F-Distribution

1. F-distribution curve extends on abscissa from 0 to ∞.
2. It is an unimodal curve and its mode lies on the point

$$F = \frac{k_2(k_1 - 2)}{k_1(k_2 + 2)}$$

Which is always less than unity.

3. F-distribution curve is a positive skew curve. Generally the F-distribution curve is highly positive skewed when k_2 is small.
4. The constants of F-distribution are,

(mean) $\mu = \dfrac{k_2}{k_2 - 2}$ for $k_2 \geq 3$.

(Variance) $\sigma^2 = \dfrac{2k_2^2 (k_1 + k_2 - 2)}{k_1(k_2 - 2)(k_2 - 4)}$ for $k_2 \geq 5$.

5. There exists a very useful relation for interchange of degrees of freedom k_1 and k_2, i.e.

$$F_{1-\alpha}(k_1,k_2) = \frac{1}{F\alpha(k_2,k_1)}$$

6. The moment generating function of F-distribution does not exist.

F-distribution is a very popular and useful distribution because of its utility in testing of hypothesis about the equality of several population means. Two population variances and several regression coefficients in multiple regression etc. As a matter of fact, F-test is the backbone of analysis of variance.

Wide use and application of the sampling distributions has been made in different chapters ahead while testing different null hypotheses about a variety of population parameters.

Exercise

1. What is is sample survey? In what respects is it superior to a census survey?
2. What is a simple random sample? Mention the various methods of drawing a random sample.
3. Describe the procedure of Startified random sampling.
4. What are the advantages of stratified sampling?
5. Explain systematic sampling and state the circumstances when it is optimum.
6. Discuss the advantages and disadvantages of systematic sampling.
7. Explain cluster sampling and multistage sampling.

❑❑❑

Chapter – 8

Tests of Significance Testing Hypothesis about Population Mean

8.1 Statistical Hypotheses

In attempting to reach decisions about the populations, it is useful to make assumptions or guesses about the populations involved. When the assumption or statement about a phenomenon occurring under certain conditions is formulated as proposition it is called a *scientific hypotesis.* We can construct criteria by which a scientific hypothesis may be 'the yield of a new paddy variety will be 3500 kg per hectare'. In statistical language it may be stated as 'the random variable (yield of paddy) is distributed normally with mean 3500 kg/ha'. Such a statement or proposition about the probability distribution of a random variable is called the *statistical hypothesis.*

When a hypothesis specifies all the parameters of a probability distribution, it is known as *simple hypothesis.* For example the hypothesis 'the random variable X is distributed normally with mean $\mu = 0$, and standard deviation $\sigma = 1$' is a simple hypothesis. The hypothesis specifies all the parameters of the probability distribution, it is known as *composite hypothesis.* For example, the hypothesis 'the random variable X is distributed normally with $\mu=0$' is a composite hypothesis. In this case only one parameter (μ) of the normal distribution is specified. Similarly, the hypothesis 'the random variable X is distributed normally with $\sigma = 1$' is a composite hypothesis.

The null hypothesis may be stated as follows: 'there is no difference between the effects of two treatments' or equivalently 'the effects of two treatments are same'; there is no association between two attributes' or equivalently 'the two attributes are independent'; and so on. The original hypothesis is then stated as an alternative to the null hypothesis. Hence the original hypothesis is called the *alternate hypothesis.*

The null hypothesis is usually denoted by H_0 and the alternative hypothesis is denoted by H_1.

8.2 Statistical Test

Once the hypothesis is formulated we have to make a decision on it. A statistical procedure by which we decide to accept or reject a statistical hypothesis is called testing of hypothesis.

To make a decision the hypothesis with certainty we would have to examine the entire population. In many problems the populations are very large. Hence the decision is made on the basis of sample data. From sample data, the statistic is computed and the parameter is estimated through that statistic. The difference between the parameter and the statistic is known as the sampling error. Based on the sampling error the sampling distributions are derived. The observed results are then compared with the results expected on the basis of the sampling distribution. If the difference is significant the null hypothesis is rejected; otherwise it is accepted. The process of deciding whether to accept or reject the null hypothesis is known as *testing of hypotheis.*

The test procedure and can be explained by an example. Consider the hypothesis on the average paddy variety a gives more yield than variety B'. Symbolically, the hypothesis is $\mu_1 > \mu_2$. By definition it is the alternative hypothesis to the null hypothesis $\mu_1 = \mu_2$. From the sample data on paddy variety a and b we can compute the mean yields. Suppose the mean yield for paddy variety is A is $\overline{x}_1$ and that of variety B is $\overline{x}_{2.}$ We know that the difference $(\overline{x}_1 - \overline{x}_2)$ is a statistic which estimates the parameter $(\mu_1 - \mu_2)$. This statistic may follow a normal distribution or a t-distribution depending on the sample size. We can compute the standard error of this statistic by methods discussed under sampling distributions. We then compare the difference between the statistic and parameter with the standard error of the statistic by methods discussed under sampling distributions. We then compare the difference between the statistic and parameter with the standard error of the statistic. The difference between the statistic and parameter is given by $(\overline{x}_1 - \overline{x}_2) - (\mu_1 - \mu_2)$. Since $\mu_1 - \mu_2 = 0$ under null hypothesis, the different will reduce to the value $(\overline{x}_1 - \overline{x}_2)$. Suppose this value is more than two times the standard error, that is, $(\overline{x}_1 - \overline{x}_2) > 2SE$ of $(\overline{x}_1 - \overline{x}_2)$. We can then say, with 95 percent confidence, that the value $(\overline{x}_1 - \overline{x}_2)$ differs significantly from 0. This means that $\overline{x}_1 > \overline{x}_2$ and hence $\mu_1 > \mu_2$. In this case the null hypothesis is rejected and the hypothesis that $\mu_1 > \mu_2$ is accepted.

On the other hand, if the value $(\overline{x}_1 - \overline{x}_2) > 2SE$ of $(\overline{x}_1 - \overline{x}_2)$, we can say that the value $(\overline{x}_1 - \overline{x}_2)$ does not differ significantly from 0. In that case we accept the null hypothesis and reject the original hypothesis.

For understanding the process of hypothesis testing, knowledge of some more fundamental concepts is required. These concepts are explained in the following sections.

8.3 Decision Errors

By performing a test we make a decision on the hypothesis by accepting or rejecting the null hypothesis, H_0. In the process we may make a correct decision on H_0 or commit one of two kinds of errors. We may reject H_0 when in fact it is true. This error in decision is known as *Type I error*. We may accept H_0 when in fact it is not true. It is known as *Type II error*.

For example, consider the mean yields μ_1 and μ_2 of two varieties of paddy. If the entire population is covered it could have been found that $\mu_1 = \mu_2$. In that case the null hypothesis $H_0 : \mu_1 = \mu_2$ is true. Based on sample data we may reject H_0 and claim that there is a significant difference between the yields of the two paddy varieties. Here the error committed is type I. If in the population $\mu_1 > \mu_2$, the $H_0 : \mu_1 = \mu_2$ is false. Suppose we accept H_0 based on sample data. In this case we have committed type II error.

The relationship between type I and type II errors is that one increases the other will decrease. Hence both errors cannot be controlled simultaneously. It is customary to control type I error and increase the sample so that type II error is minimised as far as possible.

The probability of type I error is denoted by α (read 'alpha) and the probability of type II error of denoted by b (read beta). The correct decision of rejecting the null hypothesis when it is false is known as the power of the test. The probability of the power is given by $1 - \beta$.

8.4 Critical Region

The testing of statistical hypothesis involves the choice of a region on the sampling distribution of statistic. If the statistic falls within this region, the null hypothesis is rejected. Other wise it is accepted. This region is called the critical region. The concept of critical region is explained below.

Let our null hypothesis be H_0: $\mu_1 = \mu_2$ and its alternative be $H_1 : \mu_1 \neq \mu_2$. Suppose H_0 is true. Based on the sample data, it may be observed that the statistic $(\overline{x}_1 - \overline{x}_2)$ follows a normal distribution given by

$$Z = \frac{(\overline{x}_1 - \overline{x}_2) - (\mu_1 - \mu_2)}{SE(\overline{x}_1 - \overline{x}_2)}$$

we know that 95 percent values of the statistic from repeated samples will fall in the range $(\overline{x}_1 - \overline{x}_2) \pm 1.96$ times SE $(\overline{x}_1 - \overline{x}_2)$. In other words, this range is 95 percent confidence limits for the parameter $(\mu_1 > \mu_2)$. This range can be represented by diagram as in Figure 10.1

The value ± 1.96 is the critical value of Z. The area beyond the critical value (shaded area) is known as the critical region of rejection. The remaining area is known as the region of acceptance. If the statistic falls in the critical region, we reject the null hypothesis; if it falls in the region of acceptance we accept the null hypothesis. In other words, if the calculated value of test statistic (Z, t, x^2, etc.) is ore that the critical value in magnitude we reject H_0 and otherwise we accept H_0. The critical values of different distributions (Z, t, x^2, etc.) are available from statistical tables.

8.5 Level of Significance

The probability that the statistic will fall critical region is $\frac{\alpha}{2} + \frac{\alpha}{2} = \alpha$. This a is nothing but the probability of committing type I error as level of significance. Conventionally, the level of significance is taken as 5 percent (0.05) or 1 percent (0.01).

8.6 One and Two-Tailed Tests

The nature of the original hypothesis determines the nature of the alternative hypothesis H_1. If the original hypothesis states that two groups will differ with respect to means, then H_1 is that $\mu_1 \neq \mu_2$ or $(\mu_1 > \mu_2)$. Here the direction of the differences is not known. But if the hypothesis predicts, the direction of the differences as one group will have larger mean that the other, then H_1 may be either $\mu_1 < \mu_2$ or $\mu_1 > \mu_2$. For example, suppose we want to compare the mean yield of a new paddy variety (μ_1) with that of an old variety (μ_2). Unless the new variety is more promising that the old one, we are not going to accept the new variety based on yield performance. In this case our H_1 is $\mu_1 > \mu_2$. On the other hand, if both the varieties are new our interest will be to choose the best of the two. Here our H_1 is $\mu_1 \neq \mu_2$.

In case the direction of the difference is known, the critical region will be on one end of the sampling distribution. Hence the test is known as one-tailed test. If the direction of the difference is not known, the critical region will be on either end of the sampling distribution. Therefore, the test is known as two-tailed test.

8.7 Degrees of Freedom

The number of degrees of freedom is the number of observation that are free to vary after certain restriction have been placed on the data. If there are n observations in the sample, for each restriction imposed upon the original observations the number of freedom is reduced by one.

8.8 Test Statistic

The sampling distribution of a statistic such as Z, t and x^2 are known as the *test criterion or test statistics.* The test statistic measures the extent to which the sample departs from the null hypothesis in some relevant aspect. The theoretical value of the test statistic is the critical value. If the value of the test statistic based on the sample data exceeds its theoretical value, it is said to be significant. When the test statistic is significant we reject the null hypothesis, and accept the alternative hypothesis. We accept the null hypothesis when the test statistic is not significant.

The choice of the test statistic depends on the nature of the variable, the statistic involved and the sample size. For example, foresting the equality of means we will use the test statistic Z if the sample size is large or t if the sample size is small. We will use the test statistic F for testing the equality of two variances, and X^2 for comparing the frequencies. We may use non-parametric tests in case of measurements based on nominal and ordinal scales.

8.9 Steps in Testing of Hypothesis

The process of testing a hypothesis involves many steps. A summary of the steps is presented below :

1. Formulation of null and alternative hypothesis,
2. Specification of the level of significance,
3. Selection of test statistic and its computation,
4. Finding out the critical value from tables using the level of significance, sampling distribution and its degrees of freedom,
5. Determination of the significance of the test statistic,
6. Decision about the null hypothesis based on the significance of test statistic,
7. Writing the conclusion in such a way that it answers the question on hand.

Introduction

The design of an experiment is just like construction of a house. Based on the basic requirements, cost, etc., different house plans may be drawn up. We may choose one which has potential advantages compared to others. Similarly, an experiment is designed based on the objectives, availability of experimental material, cost of the experiment, etc. In order to test hypothesis with acceptable degree of precision, we should have carefully designed experiments.

Modern concepts of experimental design are due primarily to R.A. Fisher. He developed them in the planning of agricultural field experiments. They are now used in many fields of science.

Basic Concepts

The choice of treatments, the method of assigning treatments of experimental units and arrangement of experimental units in various patterns to suit the requirement of particular problems, are combined known as the design of experiment.

Through experiments, the method of assigning treatment t experiment.

The problem is exactly the same as in section 11.1 but the sample size is small. Due to practical difficulties we can not take large samples in some investigations. We have already seen that when the sample size is small, the ratio $\frac{\bar{x}-\mu}{s/\sqrt{n}}$ will follow a t distribution and not the standard normal distribution. Hence the test statistic is given as

$$t = \frac{\bar{x}-\mu_0}{\frac{s}{\sqrt{n}}}$$

This test statistic follows a t distribution with n-1 degrees of freedom. To get the critical value of t we have to refer the table for t distribution against n-1 degrees of freedom (d.f.) and the specific level of significance. Comparing the calculated value of t with the critical value, we can accept or reject the null hypothesis as explained in section 11.1.

For using t-test, the variables involved must be continuous. Also, the population from which the samples are drawn must be normal.

Example

Based on field experiments, a new variety of greengram is expected to give an yield of 12 quintals per hectare. The variety was tested on 10 randomly selected farmers fields. They yields (quintal/hectare) were recorded as 14.3, 12.6, 13.7, 10.9, 13.7, 12.0, 11.4, 12.0, 12.6 and 13.1. Do the results conform the expectation?

H_0 : The average yield of the new variety of greengram is 12q/ha.

H_1 : The average yield is not 12 q/ha

Symbolically, H_o: = 12 and $H_1 : \mu \neq 12$. Here we have two-tailed test.

Let $\alpha = 0.05$.

The test statistics is $t = \frac{\bar{x} - \mu}{s / \sqrt{n}}$. The necessary computations are as follows:

$$\Sigma x = 14.3 + 12.6 + \ldots. + 13.1 = 126.3$$

$$\Sigma x^2 = 14.3^2 + 12.6^2 + \ldots\ldots + 13.1^2 = 1605.77$$

$$\bar{x} = \frac{\Sigma x}{n} = \frac{126.3}{10} = 12.63$$

$$\frac{(\Sigma x)^2}{n} = \frac{(126.3)^2}{10} = 1595.169$$

$$\text{Sum of squares} = SS = \Sigma x^2 - \frac{(\Sigma x)^2}{n}$$

$$= 1605.77 - 1595.169$$

$$= 10.601$$

$$\text{Standard deviation} = s = \sqrt{\frac{SS}{n-1}} = \sqrt{\frac{10.601}{9}}$$

$$= \sqrt{1.177889} = 1.0853$$

$$SE(\bar{x}) = \frac{s}{\sqrt{n}} = \frac{1.0853}{\sqrt{10}} = \frac{1.0853}{3.1623}$$

$$= 0.3432$$

Now,

$$t = \frac{12.63 - 12.00}{0.3432} = \frac{0.63}{0.3432}$$

$$= 1.836$$

For (n-1) = (10-1) = 9 d.f. and $\alpha = 0.05$ the critical value of t is 2.262. Since the calculated value of t is less than the critical value, t is not significant. Hence we accept the null hypothesis. We conclude that the new variety of greengram will give an average yield of 12 quintals per hectare.

8.10 Comparing Two Population Means Independent Samples with Equal Variances

The problem is similar to that in section 11.3. But, as the sample sizes are small, we use the test statistic

$$t = \frac{\overline{x}_1 - \overline{x}_2}{\sqrt{s^2\left(\frac{1}{n_1} + \frac{1}{n_2}\right)}}$$

Where, s^2 is the pooled variance and is given by

$$S^2 = \frac{SS_1 + SS_2}{n_1 + n_2 - 2}$$

Here, SS_1 and SS_2 are the sums of squares for first and second samples, respectively. The test statistic t follows a t distribution with $n_1 + n_2 - 2$ degrees of freedom.

This test statistics is used under certain assumptions in addition to the assumptions made for single sample case. First, the samples should be independent.

Secondly, the variances of the two populations from which the samples are drawn should be homogeneous (equal). The homogeneity of two variances can be tested by using F-test discussed in Section 11.9.

If the above assumptions fail, this test statistic can not be used. The remedies are available in case of failure of these assumptions. They are discussed in Sections 11.5 and 11.6.

Example

In order to compare the effectiveness of two sources of nitrogen, namely, ammonium chloride and urea, on grain yield of paddy, an experiment was conducted. The results on the grain yield of paddy (kg/plot) under the two treatments are given below.

Ammonium chloride: 13.4, 10.9, 11.2, 11.8, 14.0, 15.3, 14.2, 12.6, 17.0, 16.2, 16.5, 15.7.

Urea: 12.0, 11.7. 10.7. 11.2, 14.8, 14.4, 13.9, 13.7, 16.9, 16.0, 15.6, 16.0

Assess which source of nitrogen is better for paddy.

H_0 : The effects of the two sources of nitrogen on paddy yield are same.

H_1: The effects of the two sources of nitrogen on paddy yield are not same.

Symbolically, $H_0 : \mu_1 = \mu_2$; $H_1 : \mu_1 \neq \mu_2$. a= 0.05

Ammonium Chloride	Urea
$n_1 = 12$	$n_2 = 12$
$\Sigma x_1 = 168.8$	$\Sigma x_2 = 166.9$
$\Sigma x_1^2 = 2423.72$	$\Sigma x_2^2 = 2369.09$
$x_1 = 14.07$	$x_2 = 13.61$
$SS_1 = 2423.72 - \frac{(168.8)^2}{12}$	$SS_1 = 2423.72 - \frac{(166.9)^2}{12}$
$= 49.2667$	$= 47.7892$
$s_1^2 = \frac{SS_1}{n_1 - 1} = \frac{49.2667}{11}$	$s_2^2 = \frac{SS2}{n_2 - 1} = \frac{47.7892}{11}$
$= 4.4788$	$= 4.3445$
$F = \frac{s_1^2}{s_2^2} = \frac{4.4788}{4.3445} = 1.031$	

For (11, 11) d.f. and $\alpha = 0.05$ the critical value of F is 2.82. here F is not significant. Therefore, the variances are equal. We have,

$$S^2 = \frac{SS_1 + SS_2}{n_1 + n_2 - 2} = \frac{49.2667 + 47.7892}{12 + 12 - 2} = \frac{97.0559}{22}$$

$$t = \frac{14.07 - 13.91}{\sqrt{\frac{97.0559}{22}\left(\frac{1}{12} + \frac{1}{12}\right)}} = \frac{0.16}{\sqrt{0.735272}} = \frac{0.16}{0.8575}$$

$$= 0.1865$$

The critical value of t for 22 d.f at $\alpha = 0.05$ is 2.074. Since t is not significant we accept the null hypothesis. We conclude that both the sources of nitrogen have similar effect on the grain yield of paddy.

8.11 Comparison of Two Population Means Independent Samples with Unequal Variances

In section 11.4, we had pooled the variances of the two samples to get a common variance, s^2. This can be done, if and only if, the population variances are homogeneous (equal). It is possible that the variances of the sampled populations are not equal. In such situations we can not apply the method explained in section 11.4. If a significant difference is found between s_1^2 and s_2^2, which are the estimators of population variances, then a special procedure is required. There are various ways of coping with the difficulty.

When the samples have unequal variances and equal number of observations ($n_1 = n_2$), the test statistic is the same, that is,

$$t = \frac{\bar{x}_1 - \bar{x}_2}{\sqrt{s^2\left(\frac{1}{n_1} + \frac{1}{n_2}\right)}}$$

However, the degrees of freedom is altered to compensate the heterogeneity of variances. The degrees of freedom associated with this t is ½ $(n_1 + n_2) - 1$.

When the samples have unequal variances and unequal number of observations ($n_1 \neq n_2$), the test statistic is

$$t = \frac{\bar{x}_1 - \bar{x}_2}{\sqrt{\frac{s_1^2}{n_1} + \frac{s_2^2}{n_2}}}$$

This statistics follows neither the t-distribution nor the normal distribution. It follows what is known as Behrens – Fisher d – distribution. The Behrens – Fisher test is laborious one. An alternative simple method has been suggested by Cochran and Cox. In this method the critical value of t is altered as

$$t_w = \frac{t_1\left(\frac{s_1^2}{n_1}\right) + t_2\left(\frac{s_2^2}{n_2}\right)}{\frac{s_1^2}{n_i} + \frac{s_2^2}{n_2}}$$

Where, t_1 is the critical value for n_1 d.f. at a specified level of significance, t_2 is the critical value for n_2-1 d.f at the same level of significance.

Example

The summary of the result of yield trial on onion with two methods of propagation is given below. Determine whether the methods differ with regard to onion yield. The onion yield is given in kg/plot.

Method I	Method II
$n_1 = 12$	$n_2 = 12$
$\bar{x}_1 = 25.25$	$\bar{x}_2 = 28.83$
$SS_1 = 186.25$	$SS_2 = 737.6667$
$s_1^2 = 16.9318$	$s_2^2 = 67.0606$

H_0 : The two propagation methods do not differ with regard to onion yield.

H_1: The two propagation methods differ with regard to onion yield.

$\alpha = 0.05$.

$$F = \frac{s_2^2}{s_1^2} = \frac{67.0606}{16.9317} = 3.961$$

for (11,11) degrees of freedom and $\alpha = 0.05$, the critical value of F is 2.82. Here the variances are not equal. Hence.

$$t = \frac{\bar{x}_1 - \bar{x}_2}{\sqrt{s^2\left(\frac{1}{n^2} + \frac{1}{n^2}\right)}} = \frac{25.25 - 28.83}{\sqrt{\left(\frac{186.25 + 737.6667}{12 + 12 - 2}\right)\left(\frac{1}{12} + \frac{1}{12}\right)}}$$

$$= \frac{3.58}{6.9994} = \frac{3.58}{2.6456} = 1.353$$

$$\text{For}\left(\frac{n_1 + n_2}{2}\right) - 1 = \left(\frac{12 + 12}{2}\right) = 1 = 1\ \text{ld.f. and}$$

$\alpha = 0.05$, the critical value of t is 2.201. Since t is not significant, we conclude that the two propagation methods do not differ with regard to onion yield.

8.12 Comparison of Two Population Means Correlated Samples

In this section we consider the test procedure familiarly known as paired t-test for comparing the population means when the samples are not independent.

In independent sampling, two groups of experimental units are selected at random. One treatment is applied to first group and another treatment to the second group. For this, experimental units must be homogeneous. Only then a difference in responses between the two groups can be attributed to the differences in treatments. The heterogeneity of experimental units will cause a large variability in the responses. Consequently, the real differences in treatment effects would be obscured.

In practice it may not be possible to get required number of homogeneous experimental units. In field experiments, for example, plots which are similar in all characteristics may not be available. Similarly, in animal experiments it may not be possible to get animals of same breed, sex and age.

As a compromise, the experimental units may be paired on the basis of certain characteristics like soil texture, micro –nutrient content in the soil, etc. Each pair may be considered as a block. Thus units in different pairs may not be similar. Within a block one treatment is applied to one unit and the second treatment is applied to another unit at random. The response will result in two samples.

Consider a specific examples of the study on the residual effect of nitrogen on yield of paddy. In the first crop, a uniform level of nitrogen may be applied on all the plots. In the second crop, each plot is divided into two equal parts. In one half of the plot the nitrogen application will be continued; and in the second half nitrogen will not be applied. The paddy yields from these plots will result in two correlated samples. As another example, consider the comparison of two preparations of a virus in producing number of lesions on tobacco leaves. One preparation may be applied on one half of a leaf and the other preparation on the other half of the same leaf. Such experiment will result in two correlated samples.

In some other situations two observations may be taken on the same experimental unit. For example, the soil properties before and after the application of industrial effluents on number of plots may be observed. In feeding experiments, the weights of animals may be taken before and after the experiment. Taking observations on the same experimental unit before and after a treatment will result in paired observations. This is known as self-pairing.

Comparison of two such samples is known as paired comparison. The structure of the paired observations will be as follows:

Pair	Treatment A	Treatment B	Difference A-B = d
1	x_1	Y_1	x_1-y_1 =d_1
2	x_2	Y_2	x_2-y_2 =d_2
3	x_3	Y_3	X_3-y_3 =d_3
.	.	.	.
.	.	.	.
.	.	.	.
n	x_n	y_n	x_n-y_n=d_n

Since the paired observations will result in correlated samples, the usual estimates of the standard error of the difference between two means are not applicable. Treating the differences as observations the standard deviation is calculated as

$$s = \sqrt{\Sigma d^2 - \frac{(\Sigma d)^2}{n}}$$

The standard error of the mean difference, $\overline{d}$, is computed as

$$SE(\overline{d}) = s / \sqrt{n}$$

Where, n is the number of pairs.

Under paired observations the null hypothesis will be $H_o : \mu_1 - \mu_2 = \overline{D} = 0$, and the alternative hypothesis will be $H_1 : \overline{D} \neq 0$ (or $\overline{D} > 0$ or $\overline{D} < 0$). The appropriate test statistic will be

$$t = \frac{\overline{d}}{\frac{s}{\sqrt{n}}}$$

This t follows t-distribution with n – 1 degrees of freedom.

The above test procedure is known as paired t-test. The assumption of equality of variances is not required in case of paired t-test. This is an advantage of this test compared to two sample t-test.

It may be remembered that pairing is effective only when there is positive correlation between the two samples. Further, pairing is effective when natural pairs or self-pairs are considered. By pairing an appreciable reduction in variability can be anticipated. An arbitrary paring may fail to achieve a reduction in variance. Hence artificial pairing may lead to wrong conclusions.

The effectiveness of pairing may be determined by comparing the estimate of variance form paired and independent samples. Let the variance for the paired sample be s^2 (d) and the pooled variance of the independent samples be s^2. If $s^2(d) < 2s^2$, then pairing is said to be effective. It is only a rough test of the effectiveness of pairing.

It is possible that we can have two sets of paired observations. For example, the grain yield of paddy from first two tillers may constitute a pair. When we consider two different varieties and observe such pairs of observation we will get two sets. For such cases the test statistic is

$$t = \frac{\overline{d}_1 - \overline{d}_2}{\sqrt{s^2\left(\frac{1}{n_1} + \frac{1}{n_2}\right)}}$$

Where,

$$s^2 = \frac{SS_1 + SS_2}{n_1 + n_2 - 2}$$

n_1 = number of pairs in the first set,

n_2 = number of pairs in the second set,

This t follows a t-distribution with $n_1 + n_2 - 2$ degrees of freedom. It may be noted that this test statistic is similar to that given in section 11.4.

Example

In an experiment on sorghum the plots were divided into two equal parts each. One half of each plot received soil treatment A and the other half received soil treatment B. Each plot was planted with sorghum. The results are presented in Table 11.1. Test whether the sorghum yield is same in both the treatments.

Table 8.1 : Sorghum yield (kg.plot) under two soil treatments

	Soil treatment		
Plot No.	**A**	**B**	**d = A-B**
1	26.3	28.0	-1.7
2	24.2	25.7	-1.5
3	23.1	22.9	0.2
4	21.6	22.4	-0.8
5	24.5	25.2	-0.7
6	23.3	25.4	-2.1
7	21.8	23.0	-1.2
8	22.9	23.4	-0.5
9	25.7	25.5	0.2
10	24.1	24.8	-0.7
11	25.8	25.6	0.2
12	26.1	25.7	0.4

H_o : The average yield of sorghum will be same under the two soil treatments.

H_1 : The average yield of sorghum will not be the same under the two soil treatments.

Symbolically, $H_0 : \overline{D} = 0; H_1 \overline{D} \neq 0.$

Let $\alpha = 0.05$

The basic calculations required are shown below.

First find out the differences, d, between the pairs of observations, as shown in Table 11.1. Then we have.

$$\Sigma d = -8.2; Sd^2 = 13.14; \bar{d} = -0.68$$

$$s^2 = \Sigma d^2 - \frac{(\Sigma d)^2}{n} / n-1$$

$$= \left[13.14 - \frac{(-8.2)^2}{12}\right] / 11 = 0.685155$$

$$s = \sqrt{0.685155} = 0.8277$$

$$t = \frac{\bar{d}}{\frac{s}{\sqrt{n}}} = \frac{0.68}{\frac{0.8277}{\sqrt{12}}} = -2.846$$

$$|t| = 2.846.$$

For 11 d.f. and α = 0.05 the critical value of t is 2.201. Here t is significant and hence we reject the null hypothesis. We conclude that soil treatment B increases the sorghum yield significantly.

8.13 Testing the Significance of an Observed Correlation Coefficient

Given a random sample from a bivariate Normal population and we are interested in testing the hypothesis that the correlation coefficient of the population is zero. i.e., the variables in the population are uncorrelated; we have to apply the following test:

$$t = \frac{r}{\sqrt{1-r^2}} \times \sqrt{n-2}$$

Here t is based on (n-2) degrees of freedom.

If the calculated value of t exceeds $t_{0.05}$ for (n-2). d.f., we say that the value of r is significant of 5% level. If $t < t_{0.05}$ the data are consistent with the hypothesis of an uncorrelated population.

Example A random sample of 27 pairs of observations from a normal population gives a correlation coefficient of 0.42. Is it likely that the variables in the population are uncorrelated?

Let us take the hypothesis that there is no significant difference in the sample correlation and correlation in the population. Applying t-test:

$$t = \frac{r}{\sqrt{1-r^2}} \times \sqrt{n-2}$$

Here r = 0.42, n=27

$$t = \frac{0.42}{\sqrt{1-0.42^2}} \times \sqrt{27-2}$$

$$= \frac{0.42}{0.908} \times 5 = 2.31$$

$$v = n - 2 = 27 - 2 = 25$$

For v = 25, $t_{0.05}$ = 1.708. The calculated value of t is more than the table value. The hypothesis is rejected. Hence it is likely that the variables in the population are uncorrelated.

Tests of Significance of Attributes

The various tests of significance for attributes are discussed under the following

(i) Tests for Number of Successes.

(ii) Tests for Proportion of Successes.

(iii) Tests for Difference between Proportions.

The test Statistic for testing the significance is given by

Test Statistic = (Statistic-parameter)/SE of the test statistic.

Tests for Number of Successes

The sampling distribution of the number of successes follows a binomial probability distribution. Hence its standard error is given by the formula:

S.E. of no. of successes = $\sqrt{npq}$

Where n = size of sample

p = probability of success in each trial.

q = (1 – p), i.e., probability of failure.

Example: A coin was tosses 400 times and the head turned up 216 times. Test the hypothesis that the coin is unbiased.

Let us take the hypothesis that the coin is unbiased. On the basis of this hypothesis the probability of getting head or tail would be equal. Hence in 400 throws of a coin we should except 200 heads and 200 tails.

Observed number of heads = 216

Difference between observed number of heads and expected number of heads = 216 – 200 = 16.

S.E. of no. of successes = $\sqrt{npq}$

$$\text{S.E.} = \sqrt{400 \times \frac{1}{2} \times \frac{1}{2}} = 10$$

$$\frac{\text{Difference}}{\text{S.E.}} = \frac{16}{10} = 1.6$$

The difference between observed and expected number of heads is less than 1.96 SE (5% Level of Significance). Hence our hypothesis is true and we conclude that the coin is unbiased.

Test for Proportion of Successes

Instead of recording the number of successes in each sample, we might record the proportion successes. That is $\frac{1}{n}$ of the number of successes in each sample. As this would amount to dividing all figures of the record by n, the mean proportion of successes must be p, and the standard deviation of the proportion of successes $\sqrt{\frac{pq}{n}}$. Thus we have the following formula:

$$\text{S.E.}_{p} = \sqrt{\frac{pq}{n}}$$

Example: 500 apples are taken at random from a large basket and 50 are found to be bad. Estimate the proportion of bad apples in the basket and assign limits within which the percentage most probably lies.

The proportion of bad apples in the given samples = $\frac{50}{500} = 0.1$

Hence p = 0.1 and q = 0.9

$$\text{S.E.} = \sqrt{\frac{pq}{n}} = \sqrt{\frac{0.1 \times 0.9}{500}} = \sqrt{\frac{0.09}{500}} = 0.13$$

The limits within which percentage of bad apples lies

$$\left[p \pm 3\sqrt{\frac{pq}{n}}\right] \times 100$$

$= [0.1 \ \pm 3\ (0.013)]100$

$= [0.1 \ \pm 3\ (0.039)]100$

$= 6.1$ and 13.9

Thus the percentage of bad apples in the consignment almost certainly lies between 6.1 and 13.9.

Test for Difference between Proportions

If two samples are drawn from different populations, we may be interested in finding out whether the difference between the proportion of successes is significant or not. In such a case we take the hypothesis that the difference between p_1, i.e., the proportion of successes in one sample, and p_2. i.e., the proportion of successes in another sample is due to fluctuations of random sampling.

The standard error of the difference between proportions is calculated by applying the following formula:

$$S.E.(p_1 - p_2) = \sqrt{pq\left(\frac{1}{n_1} + \frac{1}{n_2}\right)}$$

where p = the pooled estimate of the actual proportion in the population. The value of p is obtained as follows:

$$p = \frac{n_1 p_1 + n_2 + p_2}{n_1 + n_2} \text{ or } p = \frac{x_1 + x_2}{n_1 + n_2}$$

where x_1 and x_2 stand for the number of occurrence in the two samples of sizes n_1 and n_2 respectively.

If $\frac{p_1 - p_2}{S.E.}$ is less than 1.96 S.E. (5% level of significance), the difference is regarded as due to random sampling variation, i.e. as not significant.

Example: In a random sample of 1,000 persons from town. A, 400 are found to be consumers of wheat. In a sample of 800 from town, B, 400 are found to be consumers of wheat. Do these data reveal a significant between town A and town B, so far as the proportion of wheat consumers is concerned?

Let us set up the hypothesis that the two towns do not differ so far as proportion of wheat consumers is concerned, i.e., $H_0: p_1 = p_2$ against $H_a: p_1 \neq p_2$.

Computing the standard error of the difference of proportions

$$S.E.(p_1 - p_2) = \sqrt{pq\left(\frac{1}{n_1} + \frac{1}{n_2}\right)}$$

$$n_1 = 1000,\ p_1 = \frac{400}{1000} = 0.4;\ n_2 = 800,\ p_2 = \frac{400}{800} = 0.5;$$

$$p = \frac{(1000\times0.4) = (800\times0.5)}{1000+800} = \frac{400+400}{1800}$$

or simply $p = \frac{x_1 + x_2}{n_1 + n_2} = \frac{400+400}{1000+800} = \frac{4}{9}$

$$q = 1 - \frac{4}{9} = \frac{5}{9}$$

$$p_1 - p_2 = 0.4 - 0.5 = -0.1^1$$

$$\frac{\text{Difference}}{\text{S.E.}} = \frac{0.1}{0.024} = 4.17$$

$$S.E.(p_1 - p_2) = \sqrt{\frac{4}{5}\times\frac{5}{9}\left(\frac{1}{1000} + \frac{1}{800}\right)} = \sqrt{\frac{20}{80}\times\frac{9}{4000}} = 0.024$$

Since the difference is more than 2.58 S.E. (1% level of significance). It could not have arisen due to fluctuations of sampling. Hence the data reveal a significant difference between town A and town B so far as the proportion of wheat consumers is concerned.

Large Sample Tests

(i) **Test for Mean :** We may be interested in testing whether the population mean is equal to a specified value. To test the hypothesis we use the sample data. A random sample of large size n, is taken. The test statistic is given by Z= Diff / SE.

Example The mean height of the plant obtained from a random sample of size 100 is 64 inches. The standard deviation of the distribution of height of the population is known to be 3 inches. Test the statement that the mean height of the population is 67 inches at 5% level of significance. Also set up 99% limits of the mean height of the population.

Let us take the hypothesis that there is no significant difference between the sample mean and the population mean.

$$S.E.\bar{x} = \frac{\sigma}{\sqrt{n}} = \frac{3}{\sqrt{100}} = 0.3$$

$$Z = \frac{\text{Diff.}}{\text{S.E.}} = \frac{67-64}{0.3} = 10$$

Since the difference is more than 1.96 S.E. (5% level) the hypothesis is rejected. Hence the mean height of the population could not be 67 inches.

99% probable limits of the mean height of the population

$$= \bar{x} \pm 2.58 \text{ S.E.}$$

$$= 64 \pm 2.58(.3)$$

$$= 64 \pm 0.774 = 63.2 \text{ to } 64.8$$

(ii) Testing the equality two population means : A common situation in agricultural research is to compare two treatments. The treatments may be varieties, fertilizers and so on. In such problem our interest is to test whether the mean of one population is equal to the mean of a second population. The test statistics for testing this hypothesis

$$\text{Test Statistics} = Z = \frac{\text{Difference}}{\text{S.E}}$$

Where $S.E.(\bar{X}_1 - \bar{X}_2) = \sqrt{\frac{\sigma_1^2}{n_1} + \frac{\sigma_2^2}{n_2}}$

Example A breeder claims that the number of grains per panicle in a new variety of paddy compared to that of an old variety. To verify his claim a random sample of 100 plants each has a means 150 and 155 with Standard deviation 50 and 60 were selected from the experimental fields. Can it be concluded that two varieties differ significantly at 1% level of significance in equality.

Let us take the hypothesis that there is no significant difference in the mean number of grains of two varieties of paddy.

$$S.E.(\bar{X}_1 - \bar{X}_2) = \sqrt{\frac{\sigma_1^2}{n_1} + \frac{\sigma_2^2}{n_2}}$$

$$S.E.(\bar{X}_1 - \bar{X}_2) = \sqrt{\frac{(50)^2}{100} + \frac{(60)^2}{100}} = \sqrt{25+36} = 7.81$$

$$Z = \frac{\text{Diff.}}{\text{S.E.}} = \frac{155-150}{7.81} = 0.645$$

Since the difference is less than 2.58 S.E. (1% level of significance), the hypothesis is accepted. Hence there is no significant difference in the mean number of grains of the two varieties of paddy.

(iii) **Testing the difference between two Standard Deviations :** In case of two large random sample, each drawn from a normally distributed population, the S.E. of the difference between the standard deviations is given by:

$$\text{S.E.}(\sigma_1 - \sigma_2) = \sqrt{\frac{\sigma_1^2}{2n_1} + \frac{\sigma_2^2}{2n_2}}$$

Where population standard deviations are not known

$$\text{S.E.}(S_1 - S_2) = \sqrt{\frac{S_1^2}{2n_1} + \frac{S_2^2}{2n_2}}$$

Example : In a sample of 1000 the mean is 17.5 and the S.D 2.5. In another sample of 800 the mean is 18 and S.D 2.7. Assuming that the samples are independent discuss whether the two samples can have come from a population which have the same S.D.

Let us take the hypothesis that there is no significant difference in the standard deviation of the two samples

$$\text{S.E.}(\sigma_1 - \sigma_2) = \sqrt{\frac{\sigma_1^2}{2n_1} + \frac{\sigma_2^2}{2n_2}}$$

$\sigma_1 = 2.5, n_1 = 1000, \sigma_2 = 2.7, n_2 = 800$

$$\text{S.E.}(\sigma_1 - \sigma_2) = \sqrt{\frac{(2.5)^2}{2000} + \frac{(2.7)^2}{1600}} = \sqrt{\frac{6.25}{2000} + \frac{7.29}{1600}}$$

$$\text{S.E.}(\sigma_1 - \sigma_2) = \sqrt{0.003012 + 0.00456} = 0.0876$$

$$Z = \frac{\text{Diff.}}{\text{S.E.}} = \frac{2.7-2.5}{0.0876} = \frac{.2}{0.876} = 2.283$$

Since the difference is more than 1.92 S.E. at 5% level of significance the hypothesis rejected. Hence the two samples have not come from a population which has the same standard deviation.

8.14 Comparison of Two Population Variances

In agricultural experiments the performance of a treatment is assessed not only by its mean but also by its variability. The treatment with more variability may not be preferred. Hence, it is of interest to us to compare the variability of two populations. Moreover, under t test the assumption of equality of variances has to be tested.

For the purposes of comparing the variability of two populations the null hypothesis, H_0: $\sigma_1^2 / \sigma_2^2 = 1$ is tested against the alternative hypothesis, $H_1 : \sigma_1^2 / \sigma_2^2 > 1$. In testing the equality of variances, the greater variance is always placed in the numerator and the smaller variance is placed in the denominator. For testing this hypothesis we take random samples from the populations under study. The two samples must be independent and the populations from which the samples are drawn must be normal. From the random sample of size n_1 representing a normal population with variance σ_1^2, we compute the variance s_1^2. Similarly we compute the variance s_2^2 for the random sample of size n_2 drawn from the second normal population with variance, σ_2^2. We then use the test statistic

$$F = \frac{s_1^2}{s_2^2}$$

In the above formula s_1^2 is the greater variance and s_2^2 is the smaller variance. This F follows F distribution with $n_1 - 1$ and $n_2 - 1$ degrees of freedom.

Example

For a random sample representing one normal population, we have n_1=11, and s_1^2 = 21.87. For another random sample representing the second normal population, we have n_2 = 8 and s_2^2 = 15.36. For testing the equality of variances we have.

$$F = \frac{s_1^2}{s_2^2} = \frac{21.87}{15.36} = 1.424$$

For 10 and 7 df. and α = 0.05 the critical value of F is 3.14. Here F is not significant. We conclude that the variances are equal (homogeneous).

Exercise

1. What are steps involved in testing procedure?
2. For a random sample of 10 persons, fed on diet A, the increased weight in Kg.

   For a period of three months were; 10, 6, 16, 17, 13, 8, 14, 15, 9.

   For another random sample of 12 persons, fed on diet B, the increase in the same period were; 7, 13, 22, 15, 12, 14, 18, 21, 23, 10, 17. Test whether the Diets A and B differ significantly as regards their effect on increase in weight.
3. Define F test and its importance?
4. Two random sample samples were drawn from two Normal populations and their values are

   A : 66 67 75 76 82 84 88 90 92

   B : 64 66 74 78 82 85 87 92 93 95 97

   Test whether the two populations have the same variance at the 5% level.

❑❑❑

Chapter – 9

Chi-Square and Association of Attributes

We have seen the procedures of testing hypothesis about population parameters in chapter 11. Frequently our interest is to test whether a set of observed values are in agreement with those which would occur if some specified hypothesis were true. The χ^2 statistic provides a measure of agreement between such observed and expected frequencies.

The χ^2 distribution has a number of applications in testing of hypotheses. It is used to test, (1) the independence of attributes, (2) the goodness of fit, (3) the homogeneity of variances, (4) the homogeneity of correlation coefficients, and (5) the linkage in genetic problems. For applying χ^2 test procedure we have to use only the actual observed frequencies and not the percentages or ratios. Further, the samples should be independent and the observations within a sample should be non-overlapping. The expected frequency in each category should be more than 5. The number of observations should be large, say, more than 50.

In χ^2 test the alternative hypothesis, H_1 predicts the direction. Hence we always use one-tailed test. Accordingly, χ^2 tables are given for one-tailed region only.

9.1 Expected Frequencies

The calculation of expected frequencies is crucial in χ^2 test. The expected frequencies may be derived from a theoretical distribution or from scientific principles or from empirical data. The methods of computing the expected frequencies are explained in the subsequent sections.

Theoretically, the distribution of χ^2 is a continuous distribution which approximates normal distribution. The entries in the χ^2 table are the values generated on the basis of this continuous distribution. On the other hand, the computed χ^2 is a discrete variable because the observed frequencies from which χ^2 statistic is computed are integer values or discrete. This can be explained with an example. Consider a 2 × 2 contingency table whose cell frequencies are a = 10, b = 15, c=25 and d = 10. the calculated χ^2 value for this data is 5.97. If we change the values as a = 11, b = 14, c = 24, d = 11, the value of χ^2 will be 3.66. We can get a χ^2 value in between 3.66 and 5.97, if the observed frequencies are a = 10.5, b = 14.5, c = 24.5 and d = 10.5 But it is impossible to have such fractional frequencies. Hence, the calculated χ^2 can not take values in between 3.66 and 5.97. Thus, the χ^2 values 3.66 and 5.97 obviously form and secrete distribution.

Although the observed frequencies are not continuous, it is assumed that the observed frequencies are not far from normal. On this assumption only the χ^2 analysis is carried out. This assumption fails when some or all of the observed frequencies are very small. Conventionally, the condition is that the expected frequency of any category should not be less than. 5. Later research findings showed that the χ^2 test is accurate enough if the smallest expected frequency is at least 1. However, we will use the conventional number 5 for our discussions. The effect of discontinuity of observed frequencies is small if the expected frequency of a category is atleast 5. In that case the computed distribution of χ^2 values will closely approximate a continuous distribution.

The closeness of the actual and theoretical distributions of χ^2 is satisfactory if the degrees of freedom is large. Even when the degrees of freedom is 1, the approximation is good if the sample size is large. In any case the smallest expected frequency should be at least 5.

Since the actual distribution of χ^2 is only an approximation to the theoretical χ^2 distribution, our conclusions are not really taking place exactly at the level of significance specified by us. Hence we shall tend to reject the null hypothesis with a probability greater than the specified by us. Hence we shall tend to reject the null hypothesis with a probability greater than the specified level of significance. Subsequently, our conclusions will be wrong. This will be more so when the expected frequency is less than 5 for an category in which case the χ^2 value is inflacted.

To overcome the difficulty of lack of approximation in a given situation, we employ any one of the following methods. First, we may eliminate the categories with very low expected frequencies from the null hypothesis and the subsequent analysis. Second, we may combine two or more neighbouring categories meaningfully so as to result in all values being large enough to proceed with the analysis. When such combinations are made there will be a corresponding decrease in the degrees of freedom. If *k* categories are combined *k-1* degrees of freedom will be lost. Third, we can employ Yates correction for continuity in case of 2×2 contingency table. In case of 2×2 contingency table the method of combining neighbouring χ^2 with o degrees of freedom which is meaningless. Fourth, we may use likelihood-ratio method when the sample size is not sufficiently large. Fifth, we may use Fisher's exact probability method.

9.2 Testing of Independence of Attributes in Contingency Table

At times we may consider two characteristics or attributes simultaneously. Our interest will be to test the association between these two attributes. For example an entomologist may be interested to know the effectiveness of different concentrations of a chemical in killing the insects. In this case the concentrations of the chemical form one attribute. The state of insects 'killed' and 'not killed' forms another attribute. The results of this experiment can be arranged in the form of a contingency table. The association between these two attributes may be tested using x^2 statistic.

In a contingency table if each attribute is divided into two classes it is known as 2 x 2 contingency table. When one attribute is divided into two classes and another into r or c the resultant contingency table is knows as r x 2 or 2 x c contingency table. Here, r denotes the number of rows and c the number of columns. In a similar way we can get r x c contingency table. For such data, the statistical hypothesis under tests is that the two attributes are independent of one another. To test this hypothesis we use the test statistic.

$$x^2 = \Sigma \frac{(O-E)^2}{E}$$

Where , O = Observed frequency, and

E = Expected frequency.

This x^2 follows x^2 distribution with (r-1) (c-1) degrees of freedom. The degrees of freedom in case of 2 x 2 contingency table (9-1) is (2-1) = 1.

The computation of expected frequency in such problems can be explained with the help of 2 x 2 contingency table. Consider the 2 x 2 contingency table (Table 9.1) with cell frequencies a, b, c, and d.

Table 9.1 : The 2 x 2 contingency table

	Category		
Group	**I**	**II**	**Total**
1	a	b	$a + b = r_1$
2	c	d	$c + d = r_2$
Total	$a + c = c_1$	$B + d = c_2$	n

Suppose that we select a unit a random from n units. The probability that it belongs to category I is $\left(\frac{c_1}{n}\right)$ the probability that it belongs to group 1 is $\left(\frac{r_1}{n}\right)$. If the unit belongs to category I, it may or may not belong to group 1. Hence these two events are independent. By the multiplicative law of probability, the probability that the selected unit belongs simultaneously to category I and group 1 is given by $\frac{c_1}{n}\frac{r_1}{n}$. This probability corresponds to the first cell with observed frequency a. The cell frequency is then got by multiplying the probability by the total number of observations. Symbolically,

$$\left(\frac{c_1}{n}\frac{r_1}{n}\right).n = \frac{c_1.r_1}{n} \text{ Winamp3.LNK}$$

This is expected frequency for the first cell. In the similar way we can get the expected frequencies corresponding to *b,c* and d as $\frac{c_2.r_1}{n}, \frac{c_1.r_2}{n}$ and $\frac{c_2.r_2}{n}$ respectively. These values are nothing but the product of the corresponding row and column totals divided by the total number of observations. This method is applied for all r × c contingency tables to get the expected frequencies.

For a 2 × 2 contingency table of the type given in Table 9.1, it can be shown that the c^2 formula will reduce to the form

$$\chi^2 = \frac{(ab - bc)^2 \;.\; n}{c_1 c_2 r_1 r_2}$$

The computation of χ^2 will be simpler with this formula.

Example

In a survey a random sample of 198 farms were classified into three classes according to tenure status as owned, rented and mixed. They were also classified according to the level of the soil fertility as highly fertile, moderately fertile and low fertile farms. The results are given in Table 9.2.

Table 9.2 : Classification of farms by tenure status and fertility level.

Soil fertility	Tenure status			Total No.(%)
	Owned No.(%)	Rented No.(%)	Mixed No.(%)	
High	40(64.5)	12(19.4)	10(16.1)	2(100.0)
Moderate	22(47.9)	10(21.7)	14(30.4)	46(100.0)
Low	22(24.4)	26(28.7)	42(46.7)	90(100.0)
Total	84(42.4)	48(24.3)	66(33.3)	198(100.0)

Does tenure status depend on soil fertility?

The null hypothesis is that the tenure status does not depend on soil fertility, and the alternative hypothesis is that the tenure status depends on soil fertility. The level of significance can be taken as $\alpha = 0.05$.

Table 9.2a : Computation of χ^2

O	E	O-E	$(O - E)^2$	$(O - E)^2/E$
40	26.3	13.7	187.69	7.136
22	19.5	2.5	6.25	0.321
22	38.2	-16.2	262.44	6.870
12	15.0	-3.0	9.00	0.600
10	20.7	-10.7	114.49	5.531
14	15.3	-1.3	1.69	0.110
42	30.0	12.0	144.00	4.800
198	198.0	0	x^2=26.307	

Thus, the calculated $\chi^2 = 26.307$. For $\alpha = 0.05$ and (3-1) (3-1) = 4 d.f., the critical value of χ^2 is 9.488. Since χ^2 is significant, we reject the null hypothesis. The conclusion is that the tenure status depends on soil fertility. Based on the percentages, the trend can easily be assessed. The trend indicates that if the fertility of the soil is high own farming is more, if the fertility is moderate own farming reduces and if the fertility is low own farming reduces further. The interpretation can also be written by comparing the individual percentages with the overall percentages.

Example

In order to determine the possible effect of a chemical treatment on the rate of germination of cotton seeds a pot culture experiment was conducted. One hundred and forty chemically treated seeds and 160 untreated seeds were sown. The results are given in table 9.3

Table 9.3 : Chemical treatment and germination of cotton seeds.

	Germinated		Not Germinated		Total	
	No	(%)	No.	(%)	No.	(%)
Chemically treated	118	(84.3)	22	(15.7)	140	100
Untreated	120	(75.0)	40	(25.0)	160	100
Total	238	(79.3)	62	(20.7)	300	(100)

Does the chemical treatment improve the germination rate of cotton seeds?

H_O: The chemical treatment does not improve the germination rate of cotton seeds (or, the chemical treatment and germination of cotton seed are independent).

H_1: The chemical improves the germination rate of cotton seeds.

$\alpha : 0.01$

It can be verified that $\chi^2 = \Sigma \frac{(0-E)^2}{E} = 3.927$, by taking three decimals for expected frequencies. By using the χ^2 formula for 2 × 2 contingency table also the same value is obtained.

$$\chi^2 = \frac{(ab-bc)^2 . n}{c_1 . c_2 . r_1 . r_2}$$

$$= = \frac{[(118)(40)-(120)(22)]}{(238)(62)(140)(160)}$$

$$= \frac{(4720-2640)^2 . (300)}{330534400}$$

$$= \frac{(2080)^2 (300)}{330534400} = \frac{(4326400)(300)}{330534400} = 3.927$$

For 1 d.f. and $\alpha = 0.01$, the critical value of χ^2 is 6.635. Here we accept the null hypothesis. It may be concluded that the chemical treatment will not improve the germination rate of cotton seeds significantly.

9.3 Association of Attributes

As pointed out earlier, Statistics deals with quantitative phenomenon only. However, the quantitative character may arise in any of the following two ways:

1. In the first place, we may measure the actual magnitude or size of some phenomenon. For example, we may measure the height of

students of class, their weight, etc. similarly, we may study the wage structure of the workers of a particular factory, the amount of rainfall in a year. The characteristic of this type of phenomena is that they can be quantitatively measured. Data regarding such phenomena are known as statistics of variables. The various statistical techniques like measures of central tendency, dispersion, correlation which have been discussed in earlier pages deal such variables.

2. In the second place, there are certain phenomena like blindness, deafness, etc., which are not capable of direct quantitative measurement. In such cases the quantitative character ari8ses only indirectly in the process of counting. For example, we can determine out of 1,000 persons, how many are blind and how many are not blind but we cannot precisely measure blindness. Such phenomena, where direct quantitative measurement is not possible, i.e., where we can study only the presence or absence of a particular characteristic, are called statistics of attributes.

9.4 Difference between Correlation and Association

The tool of correlation is used top measure the degree of relationship between two such phenomena as are capable of direct quantitative measurement. On the other hand, the method of association of attributes is employed to measure the degree of relationship between two phenomena whose size we cannot measure and where we connote only determine the presence or absence of a particular attribute.

While dealing with statistics of attributes we have to classify the data. The classification is done on the basis of presence or absence of particular attribute or characteristic. When we are studying only one attribute, two classes are formed-one possessing that attribute and another not possessing it. For example, when we are studying the attribute employment two classes shall be formed: those who are employed and those who not employed. When two attributes are studied, four classes shall. If besides employment, we study the sex-wise distribution, and four classes shall be formed: number of males employed, number of females employed, number of male unemployed and number of females unemployed.

It should be noted that in some cases while classifying the attributes no clear-cut definition of an attribute and line of demarcation be between classes can be drawn. For example, when the attribute 'employment' is being studied the data are classified into 'employed' and 'Unemployed'. But there can be further category of those people who are partially employed (i.e., part - time). Also there may be some persons who are employed before the survey but on the data of survey they are employed. So we cannot treat them as employed and also as unemployed because there is some difference between those persons who have not got any job, and thos4e who have got some job but were retrenched after some time. Hence, it is absolutely essential to all down clear-cut definition of the various attributes under study. This is often a difficult task. Hence, this limitation must be kept in mind while studying association between attributes.

9.5 Notation and Terminology

For the sake of simplicity and convenience it is imperative to use certain symbols to represent different classes and their frequencies. It is customary to use capital letters A and K to represent the presence of the attributes and the Greek letter 'α' (alpha) and 'β' (beta) to represent absence of the attributes. Thus 'α'=not A and 'β'=not B. For example, if A represents males then 'α' would represent females. Similarly, if B represents literates that β would denote illiterates. The combination of the different attributes id denoted by (AB), (Aβ), (aB) and (α β). Thus in the example. (AB) would mean number of literate males and (α β) illiterate females. The number of observation in different classes is called 'class frequency'. Thus if the number of literate males is 50, the frequency of class (AB) is 50. Class frequencies are denoted by enclosing class notation in brackets like (AB), (α β), etc. Thus,

(A) Denotes number of individuals possessing attribute A.

(AB) denotes the number of individuals possessing attributes A and B.

(α β) denotes number of individuals possessing attributes a and B.

Any letter or combination of letters like A, AB, α β, etc., by means of which we specify the characters of the members of a classes, may be termed class symbol.

Class Frequencies : The number of observations assigned to any class is termed for the sake of brevity the frequency of the class or the 'class frequency'. Class frequencies are denoted by enclosing the corresponding class symbols in brackets. Thus (B) denotes the number of B's i.e., objects possessing attribute B. (Aβ) the number of Aβ's, i.e., objects possessing attribute A but not B, and soon for any number of attributes.

Order of Classes and class Frequencies : The order of a class depends upon the number of attributes specified. A class having one attribute is known as the class of the first order, a class having two attributes as class of the second order, and so on. The total number of observations denoted by the symbol N is called the frequency of the zero order since n o attributes are specified. Thus we have:

N	frequency of the zero order	
(A)	(B)	Frequencies of the second order
(α)	(β)	
(AB)	(αB)	Frequencies of the second order
(Aβ)	($\alpha\beta$)	

Number of Frequencies : In a study of n attributes the total number of class frequencies is given by 3^n.

(i) For one attribute, the frequencies are $3^1 = 3$.

(ii) For two attributes, total frequencies are $3^2 = 9$. They are in the order 1+4+4=9.

Any class frequency can always be expressed in terms of class frequencies of higher order since the total number of observation must be equal to the number of A added to the number of α's, i.e.,

$$N=(A) + (\alpha)$$

Similarly, the number of A's is equal to the number of A's which are B's added top the number of A's which are β's i.e.,

$$(A) = (AB) + (A\beta)$$

Similarly, $$(\alpha) = (\alpha B) + (\alpha\beta).$$

Ultimate Class frequencies : It is clear from above that every class frequency can be expressed interims of the frequencies of the highest order, i.e., of order n. Any frequency can be analysed into highest frequencies, and the process need stop only when we have reached the frequencies of the highest order. For example, with two attributes

$$\left.\begin{array}{l}(A) = (AB) + (A\beta) \\ (\alpha) = (\alpha B) + (\alpha\beta).\end{array}\right\} \quad \text{Ultimate class frequencies}$$

The classes specified by n attributes, i.e., those of the highest order, are termed the ultimate class-frequencies. A given data can be completely specified if only the ultimate class frequencies given.

The total number of classes of ultimate order is determined by the formula 2^n when n stands for the number of attributes studied. If two attribute are studied then the number of classed of ultimate order shall be $2^2 = 4$. In case three attributes are studied then there would be $2^3 = 8$ classes of the ultimate order.

The frequencies of the positive, negative and ultimate classes can be known from the following table which is known as the nine square table (since nine squares are formed).

	A	α	Total
B	(AB)	(αβ)	β
β	(Aβ)	(αβ)	(β)
Total	(A)	(α)	N

From this table certain relationships can be described:

$$(A) = (AB)+(A\beta); (\alpha) = (\alpha B)+(\alpha\beta)$$

$$(B) = (AB)+(\alpha B); (\beta) = (A\beta) + (\alpha\beta)$$

$$N = (A) + (\alpha) \text{ Or } N = (B) +(\beta)$$

Or

$$N = (AB) + (A\beta) + (\alpha B) + (\alpha\beta)$$

From these relationships if we known any of the ultimate class frequencies and any other there values, we can find out the frequencies of the remaining classes.

Example

From the following data find out the missing frequencies:

$$(AB) = 100, (A) = 300, (N)= 1{,}000, (B) = 600$$

Solution

Putting these values in the nine-square table:

	A	α	Total
B	(AB) 100	(αβ) 500	(B) 600
β	(Aβ) 200	(αβ) 200	(β) 400
Total	(A) 300	(α) 700	N 1,000

The missing frequencies are (Aβ), (αB), (αβ),(α) and (β),

$$(A\beta) = (A) - (AB) = 300\text{-}100=200$$

$$(\alpha) = N - (A) =1000 - 300 =700$$

$$(\beta) = N - (B) = 1000 \text{-}600=400$$

$$(\alpha\beta) = (B) - (AB) =600\text{-}100=500$$

$$(\alpha\beta) = (B) - (AB) = 400\text{-}200=200$$

Thus the missing frequencies are:

$(A\beta) \quad = \quad 200, (\beta B) = 500, (\alpha\beta) = 200, (\beta) = 400, (\alpha) = 700.$

9.6 Consistency of Data

In order to find out whether the given data are consistent or not we have to apply a very simple test. The test is to find out whether any one or more of the ultimate class – frequencies is negative or not. If none of the class-frequencies is negative we can safely calculate that the given data are consistent (i.e., the frequencies do not conflict in away with each other). On the other hand, if any of the ultimate class frequencies comes out to be negative the given data are inconsistent. Thus the necessary and sufficient condition for the consistency of a set of independent class-frequencies is that no ultimate class frequency is negative.

Example

From the following two cases find out whether the data are consistent or not:

Case I. (A) = 100, (B) = 150, (AB) =60, N = 500

Case II. (A) = 100, (B) = 150, (AB) =140, N = 500

Solution

Case I : We are given (A) = 100 (B) = 150, (AB) = 60, N = 500

Substituting the values in the nine-square table;

	A	α	Total
B	(AB) 60	$(\alpha\beta)$ 90	(B) 150
β	$(A\beta)$ 40	$(\alpha\beta)$ 310	(β) 350
Total	(A) 100	(α) 400	N 500

From the table

$(A\beta) \quad = \quad (A) - (AB) = 100-60=40$

$(\alpha\beta) \quad = \quad (B) - (AB) = 150-60=90$

$(\alpha\beta) \quad = \quad (\alpha) - (\alpha\beta) = 400-90=310$

Since all the ultimate class frequencies are positive we conclude that the given data are consistent.

Case II : Given values are : (A) = 100, (B) = 150, (AB) =140, N = 500

By putting these values in the nine-square table we can determine the missing value:

	A	α	Total
B	(AB) 140	(αβ) 10	(B) 150
β	(Aβ) –40	(αβ) 390	(β) 350
Total	(A) 100	(α) 400	N 500

From the table

(AB) = (A) - (AB) =100-140=-40

(αβ) = (B)- (AB) =150-140=10

(αβ) = (α)- (αβ) =400-10=390

Thus one of the ultimate class frequencies, i.e., (Aβ) is negative and hence the given data are inconsistent.

9.7 Association and Disassociation

The word association as used in Statistics has a technical meaning different from the one in ordinary speech. In common language one speaks of A and B AS BEING 'associated' if they appear together in a number of cases. But in Statistics, A and B are associated only if they are independent. On the other hand, if this number (or proportion) is less than expected for independence, they are disassociated. Thus, in case iof second order frequencies, A and B are:

(i) associated if (AB) (αβ) > (Aβ) (αB); and

(ii) disassociated if (AB) (αβ) > (Aβ) (αB).

Hence, it should carefully be noted that association cannot be inferred from the mere fact that some A's are B's, however great the proportion.

9.8 Methods of Studying Association

In order to whether two attributes are associated or not the fo9llowing methods may be used.

I. Comparison of Observed and Expected Frequencies Method.

II. Proportion Method.

III. Yule's Coefficient of Association.

IV. Coefficient of Colligation.

V. Coefficient of Contingency.

I. Comparison of observed and expected frequencies method

When this method is applied, the actual observation is compared with the expectation*. If the actual observation is equal to the expectation, the attributes are said to be independent; if actual observation is more than the expectation the attributed are said to be positively associated and if the actual observation is less than the expectation, the attributes are said to be negatively associated.

Symbolically, attributes A and B are:

(i) Independent if $(AB) = \frac{(A) \times (B)}{N}$; (expectation) (actual observation)

(ii) Positively associated if $(AB) > \frac{(A) \times (B)}{N}$; (expectation) and (actual observation)

(iii) Negatively associated if $(AB) < \frac{(A) \times (B)}{N}$ (expectation) and (actual observation)

The same is true for attributes α and β; α and β and A and B; Thus, attributes α and β shall be called:

Expectation is the product of the probability i.e., chance of happening of an event and the number of observation. For example, when a coin is tossed, the probability of head or tail is equal. i.e., 50% or ½ . If the coin is tossed 100 times tossed, chance of two heads or tow tails coming up is reduced to ½ × ½ =1/4. When tow attributes A and are studied in a universe N and the class frequencies of these attributes are (A) and (B), then

$$\text{Probability of } (A) = \frac{(A)}{N} : \text{Probability of } (B) = \frac{(B)}{N}$$

$$\text{Probability of (A) and (B) combined} = \frac{(A)}{N} \times \frac{(B)}{N} :$$

$$\text{Expectation of (A) and (B) combined} = N \times \frac{(A)}{N} \times \frac{(B)}{N} = \frac{(A) \times (B)}{N}$$

(i) Independent, if $(\alpha\beta) = \frac{(\alpha) \times (\beta)}{N}$;

(ii) Positively association, if $(\alpha\beta) > \frac{(\alpha) \times (\beta)}{N}$; and

(iii) Negatively associated, if $(\alpha\beta) < \frac{(\alpha) \times (\beta)}{N}$.

Example

(a) As from the following data find out whether attributes

(i) (AB), (ii) (Aβ), (iii) (αB) and (iv) (αβ) are independent, associated or dissociated *N= 100, (A) =40, (B) =80, (AB) =30.*

Solution

(i) Apply the criterion of independence, i.e., attributes (AB) shall be called

independent if $(AB) = \frac{(A) \times (B)}{N}$;

Positively associated if $(AB) > \frac{(A) \times (B)}{N}$; and

Negatively associated or disassociated if $(AB) < \frac{(A) \times (B)}{N}$

Expectation of $(AB) = \frac{(A) \times (B)}{N}$, Here(A) = 40, (B) = 80, N = 100

Expectation of $(AB) = \frac{40 \times 80}{100} = 32.$

The actual observation [i.e., the given value of (AB), i.e., 30] is less than the expectation and hence the attributes are disassociated or negatively associated.

(ii) For finding out the nature of association between the attributes (AB), (αB) and αβ we shall have to determine the unknown values. This can be done bu preparing a nine-square table:

	A	α	Total
B	30	50	80
β	10	10	20
Total	40	60	100

From the table (AB) =10, (αB)=50, (αβ)=10, (α)=60, (β)=20,

Attributes A and β shall be independent if $(A\beta) = \frac{(A) \times (\beta)}{N}$

Expectation of $(A\beta) = \frac{(A) \times (\beta)}{N}$, where (A) =40, (β)=20, N=100

$\therefore$ Expectation of $(A\beta) = \frac{40 \times 20}{100} = 8$.

Thus the actual observation [i.e., (AB)=10] is more than expectation and hence the attributes A and β are positively associated.

(iii) Attributes α and B shall be called independent if $(\alpha B) = \frac{(\alpha) \times (B)}{N}$

Expectation of $(\alpha B) = \frac{(\alpha) \times (B)}{N}$, where (α)=60, (B)=80, N=100

$\therefore$ Expectation $(\alpha B) = \frac{60 \times 80}{100} = \square 8$.

Thus actual observation [i.e., (αβ)=50] is more than the expectation and hence the attributes are positively associated.

(iv) Attributes α and β shall be called independent if $(\alpha\beta) = \frac{(\alpha) \times (B)}{N}$

Expectation of $(\alpha B) = \frac{(\alpha) \times (B)}{N}$, where (α)=60, (β)=20, N=100

$\therefore$ Expectation of $(\alpha\beta) = \frac{60 \times 20}{100} = 12$.

Thus actual observation [(αβ)=10] is less than expectation (12). Hence the attributes are disassociated.

Example

(b) Find if A and B are independent, positively associated or negatively associated from the data given below:

(A) =470, (B)=620, (AB)=320, N=1000,

[(*M. com., Andhra Univ., 1987*)]

Solution. Attributes A and B shall be called independent if

$$(AB) = \frac{(A) \times (B)}{N}$$

(AB) =320, (A) =470, (B) =620, N=1000

$$\text{Expectation of (AB)} = \frac{470 \times 620}{1000} = 291.\square$$

Since (AB) actual observation (320) is more than the expectation (291.4) attributes A and B are positively associated.

Limitation Method : With the help of this method we can only determine the nature of association (i.e., whether there is positive or negative association or no association) and not the degree of association (i.e., where association is high or low). Yule's coefficient is superior because it provides information not only on the nature but also on the degree of association.

II. Proportion method

If there is no relationship of any kind between two attributes A and B we expect to find the same proportion of A's amongst the B's as amongst the β's. Thus, if a coin is tossed we expect the same proportion of heads irrespective of whether the coin is tossed but the right hand or the left hand.

Symbolically, two attributes may be termed :

(i) Independent if $\frac{(AB)}{(B)} = \frac{(AB)}{\alpha}$

(ii) Positively associated if $\frac{(AB)}{(B)} > \frac{(AB)}{\beta}$

(iii) Negatively associated if $\frac{(AB)}{(B)} > \frac{(AB)}{\beta}$

If the relation (i) holds good the corresponding relations

$$\frac{(\alpha B)}{(B)} = \frac{(\alpha\beta)}{(\beta)}; \frac{(AB)}{(A)} = \frac{(\alpha B)}{(\alpha)}; \frac{(AB)}{(A)} = \frac{(\alpha\beta)}{(\alpha)}$$

Must also hold true.

Example

In a population of 500 students the number of married is 200. Out of 150 students who failed 60 belonged to the married group. It is required to find out whether the attributes marriage and failure are independents, positively associated or negatively associated.

Solution

Let denote married students.

$\therefore \alpha$ Represents unmarried students.

Let B denote number of failures.

$\therefore$ b would denote non - failures.

We are given the total number of students i.e., *N=500*

(A)=200, (B)=150 and (AB), i.e., the number of married students two failed = 60

Applying the proportion method

Attributes A and B shall be called independent if $\frac{(AB)}{(A)} = \frac{(\alpha B)}{\alpha}$

In other words, if the proportion of married students who failed is the same as the proportion of unmarried students who failed we say that the attributes, marriage and failure, are independent.

Proportion of unmarried students who failed: i.e., $\frac{(AB)}{(A)} = \frac{(60)}{200} = 3$ or 30%

Proportion of unmarried students who failed: i.e.,

$$\frac{(\alpha B)}{(\alpha)} = \frac{(90)}{300} = 0.3 \text{ or } 30\% \begin{pmatrix} (\alpha B) = (B) - (AB), \text{ i.e., } 150 - 60 = 90 \\ (\alpha) \;=\; N = (A), \text{i.e.,} 500 - 200 = 300 \end{pmatrix}$$

Since the two proportions are the same we conclude that the attributes marriage and failure are independent.

Limitation of the Method : Just like the previous method, in this method also we can only determine the nature of association and not ht degree of association.

III. Yule's coefficient of association

The most popular method of studying association is the Yule's Coefficient because here not only we can determine the nature of association, i.e., whether the attributes are positively associated, negatively associated or independent, but also the degree or extent to which the two attributes is associated. The Yule's coefficient is denoted by the symbol Q and is obtained by applying the following formula:

$$Q = \frac{(AB)(\alpha\beta) - (A\beta)(\alpha B)}{(AB)(\alpha\beta) + (A\beta)(\alpha B)}$$

The value of this coefficient lies between ±1. When the value of Q is +1 there is perfect positive association between the attributes. When Q is -1 there is perfect negative association (or perfect dissociation*)

*By the word 'disassociation' we do not mean absence of association; rather it implies the presence of negative association. Between the attributes and when the value Q is zero the two attributes are independent.

The coefficient of association can be used to compare the intensity of association between two attributes with the intensity of association between two other attributes.

Example

Investigate the association between eye colour of husbands and eye colour of wives from the data given below:

Husbands with light eyes and wives with light eyes	=	309
Husbands with light eyes and wives with not-light eyes	=	214
Husbands with not-light eyes and wives with light eyes	=	132
Husbands with not-light eyes and wives with not-light eyes	=	119

(M.Com., Gorakhpur Univ., 1984)

Solution

Since we have to find out the association between eye colour of husband and that of wife one attribute we would take as A and another as B.

Let A denote husbands with light eyes.

$\therefore$ α would denote husbands with not - light eyes.

Let B denote wives with light eyes.

$\therefore$ β would denote wives with not- light eyes.

The given data in terms of these symbols is

$$(AB) = 309,\ (A\beta) = 214,\ (\alpha B) = 132,\ (\alpha\beta) = 119,$$

Applying Yule's method: $Q = \dfrac{(AB)(\alpha\beta) - (A\beta)(\alpha B)}{(AB)(\alpha\beta) + (A\beta)(\alpha B)}$

Substituting the above values in the formula

$$Q = \frac{(309 \times 119) - (214 \times 132)}{(309 \times 119) + (214 \times 132)} = \frac{8523}{65019} = 0.131$$

Thus there is a very little association between the eye colour or husband and wife.

Example

Eighty –eight residents of an Indian city, who were interviewed during a sample every, are classified below according to their smoking and tea drinking habits. Calculate Coefficient of Association and comment on its value.

	Smokers	**Non - smokers**
Tea Drinkers	40	33
Non-tea Drinkers	3	12

(M.Com., Gorakhpur Univ., 1984)

Solution. Let A denote smokers.

$\therefore$ α would denote non-smokers.

Let B denote tea drinkers.

$\therefore$ β would denote non-tea drinkers.

The given data in terms of these symbols are:

(AB), i.e., number of smokers and tea drinkers =40

(Ab), i.e., number of smokers and non-tea drinkers =3

(aB), i.e., number of smokers and non-smokers =33

(ab), i.e., number of smokers and non-tea drinkers =12

Applying Yule's method: $Q = \frac{(AB)(\alpha\beta) - (A\beta)(\alpha B)}{(AB)(\alpha\beta) + (A\beta)(\alpha B)}$

Substituting the values of (AB), $(A\beta)$, (αB), and $(\alpha\beta)$ in this formula

$$Q = \frac{(40 \times 12) - (3 \times 33)}{(40 \times 12) + (3 \times 33)} = \frac{(480 - 99)}{(480 + 99)} = \frac{318}{579} = 0.658$$

This shows that the attributes tea drinking and smoking are positively associated.

9.9 Association of Three Attributes

In case of three attributes, the frequencies are grouped as given below:

Order 0 $\quad N \qquad = 1$

$$\text{Order 1} \quad \left\{\begin{matrix} (A) & (B) & (C) \\ (\alpha) & (\beta) & (\lambda) \end{matrix}\right\} = 6$$

$$\text{Order 2} \quad \left\{\begin{matrix} (AB) & (AC) & (C) \\ (A\beta) & (A\gamma) & (B\gamma) \\ (\alpha B) & (\alpha C) & (BC) \\ (\alpha\beta) & (\alpha\gamma) & (\beta\gamma) \end{matrix}\right\} = 12$$

$$\text{Order 3} \quad \left\{\begin{matrix} (ABC) & (\alpha BC) \\ (AB\gamma) & (\alpha B\gamma) \\ (A\beta C) & (\alpha\beta C) \\ (AB\gamma) & (\alpha\beta\gamma) \end{matrix}\right\} = 8$$

$= 27$

Thus in case of three attributes there 27 distinct frequencies: 1 of order, 6 of the first order, 12 of the second order and 8 of the third order.

Any class frequency can always be expressed in terms of class frequencies of higher order. The total number of observations must clearly be equal to the number of A's added to the number of α's, i.e.,

$$N = (A) + (\alpha)$$

Similarly, the number of A's is equal to the number of A's which are B's added to the number of A's which are B's, i.e.,

$$(A) = (AB) = (A\beta)$$

Similarly $\qquad (AB) = (ABC) + (AB\gamma)$, and so on.

It follows the result that any class frequency can be expressed in terms of the frequencies of the highest order, i.e., of order n. For any frequency can be analysed into higher order frequencies, and the process need stop only when we have reached the frequencies of the higher order.

For example, with three attributes

$$A = (AB) + (A\beta) = (ABC) + (AB\gamma) + (A\beta C) + (A\beta\gamma)$$

The class specified by n attributes, i.e., those of the highest order, are termed the ultimate class frequencies.

Every class frequency can be expressed as the sum of certain of the ultimate class frequencies. Thus

$$(B) = (ABC) + (AB\gamma) + (\alpha BC) + (\alpha BC) + (\alpha B\gamma);$$

$$(C) = (ABC) + (\alpha BC) + (\alpha BC) + (A\beta C) + (\alpha\beta C)$$

In case of three attributes the following relationship need be remembered:

$(AB) = (ABC) + (AB\gamma)$ $(BC) = (ABC) + (\alpha BC)$ $(AC) = (ABC) + (A\beta C)$

$(AB) = (ABC) + (A\beta\gamma)$ $(B\gamma) = (AB\gamma) + (\alpha B\gamma)$ $(A\gamma) = (AB\gamma) + (A\beta\gamma)$

$(\alpha B) = (\alpha BC) + (\alpha B\gamma)$ $(\beta C) = (A\beta C) + (\alpha\beta C)$ $(\alpha C) = (\alpha BC) + (\alpha\beta C)$

$(\alpha\beta) = (\alpha\beta C) + (\alpha\beta\gamma)$ $(\beta\gamma) = (A\beta\gamma) + (\alpha\beta\gamma)$ $(\alpha\gamma) = (\alpha B\gamma) + (\alpha\beta\gamma)$

$(A) = (AB) + (A\beta)$ $(B) = (BC) + (B\gamma)$ $(C) = (AC) + (\alpha C)$ or

$(A) = (AC) + (A\gamma)$ or $(B) = (BC) + (B\gamma)$ or $(C) = (BC) + (\beta C)$

$N = (ABC) + (AB\gamma) + (A\beta C) + (A\beta\gamma) + (\alpha BC) + (\alpha B\gamma) + (\alpha BC) + (\alpha\beta\gamma)$

The following chart will clearly reveal the inter-relationship between frequencies of the different orders:

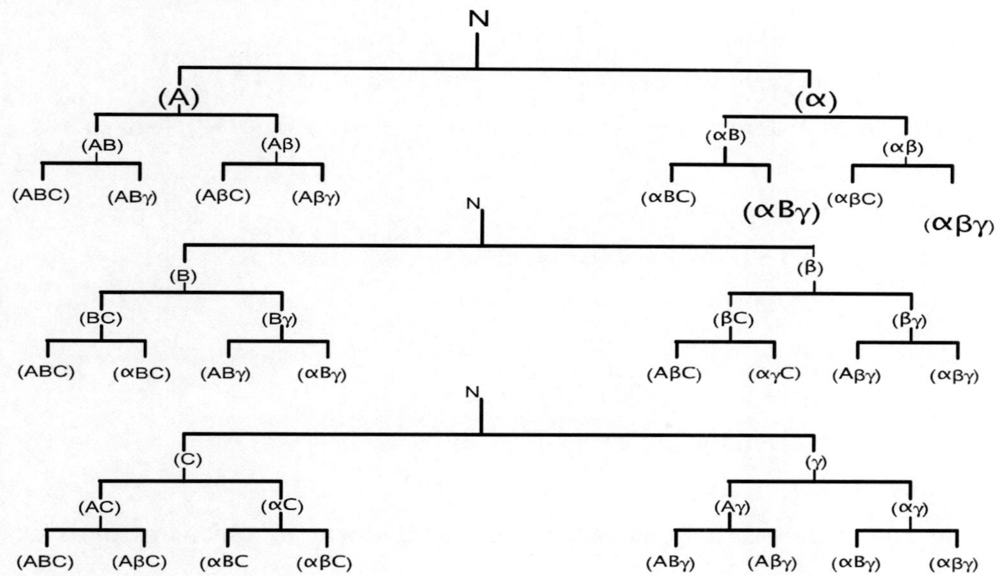

Example

Given the following frequencies of the positive class, find the frequencies of the rest of the classes:

(A) = 977; (AB) = 453; (ABC) = 127; (B) = 1.185; (AC) = 284; N = 12,000; (C) = 596; (BC) = 250.

Solution: In case of three attributes, we have 27 distinct frequencies of which only 8 are given – we have to find the remaining 19:

Second order frequencies

The following second order frequencies are to be ascertained:

(AB), (αB), ($\alpha\beta$), (Bγ), (BC), ($\beta\gamma$), (Aγ), (αc), ($\alpha\gamma$).

$(AB) = (A)-(AB) = 977 - 453 = 524$

$(\alpha B) = (B)- (AB) = 1185 - 453 = 732$

$(\alpha\beta) = (\alpha)-(\alpha B) = 11023 - 732 = 10291$

$[\because (\alpha) = N - (A)]$

$(B\gamma) = (B) - (BC) = 1185 - 250 = 935$

$(\beta C) = (C) - (BC) = 596 - 250 = 346$

$(\beta\gamma) = (\beta) - (\beta C) = 10815 - 336 = 10469$

$\because [(\beta) = N - (B)]$

$(A\gamma) = (A) - (AC) = 977 - 284 = 693$

$(\alpha C) = (C) - (AC) = 596 - 284 = 212$

Third order frequencies

The Third order frequencies to be obtained are (ABγ), (αBC), (αBγ), (AβC), (A$\beta\gamma$), ($\alpha\beta$C), ($\alpha\beta\gamma$).

$(AB\gamma) = (AB) - (ABC) = 453 - 127 = 326$

$(\alpha BC) = (BC) - (ABC) = 250 - 127 = 123$

$(\alpha B\gamma) = (\alpha B) - (\alpha BC) = 732 - 123 = 609$

$(A\beta C) = (AC) - (ABC) = 284 - 127 = 157$

$(A\beta\gamma) = (A\beta) - (A\beta C) = 524 - 157 = 367$

$(\alpha\beta C) = (\beta C) - (A\beta C) = 346 - 157 = 189$

$(\alpha\beta\gamma) = (\alpha\beta) - (\alpha\beta C) = 10291 - 189 = 10102$

It may be noted that there are more than one way in which any one class frequency can be obtained.

Example

Given the following data, find frequencies of (i) the remaining positive classes, and (ii) ultimate classes.

$N = 1800, (A) = 850, (B) = 780, (C) = 326$

$(AB\gamma) = 200, (A\beta C) = 94, (\alpha BC) = 72, (ABC) = 50$

Solution: We are to find out (i) (AB), (AC) and (BC) (ii) (Aβγ), (αBγ), (AβC), (αβγ)

(AB) = (ABC) – (ABγ) = 50 + 200 = 250

(BC) = (ABC) – (αBC) = 50 + 72 = 122

(AC) = (ABC) – (AβC) = 50 + 94 = 144

(Aβγ) = (Aβ) – (AβC) or (A) – (AB) – (AβC) = 850 – 250 – 84 = 506

(αβγ) = (αB) – (αβC) = (B) – (AB) = (αBC) = 780 – 250 – 71=458

(αβC) = (βC) – (AβC) = (C) – (BC) – (AβC) = 320 – 111 – 23 = 110

(αβγ) = N – (A) – (B) – (C) + (AB) + (BC) + (AC) – (ABC)

= 1100 – 820 – 780 – 326 +250 + 112 + 144 + 50 = 310

Example

100 children took three examinations. 40 passed the first, 39 passed the second and 48 passed the third. 19 passed all three, 9 passed first two and failed in third, 19 failed in the first two and passed the third. Find how many children passed at least two examinations. Show that for the question asked certain of the given frequencies are not necessary.

Solution

We are given

(A) = 40, (B) = –39, (C) = 48, (ABC) = 19, (ABγ) = 9, (αβC) = 19, N = 100

We have to find the number of children who passed at least two examinations.

i.e., (ABC) + (ABγ) + (AγC) + (αBC) + (AβC). Of these we are given (ABC) and (ABγ).

We have to find (AβC) and (αBC).

(C) = (AC) + (αC) = (ABC) + (AβC) + (αβC)

48 = (ABC) + (AβC) + (αBC) + 19

∴ (ABC) + (AβC) + (ABC) = 48 – 19 = 29

∴ (ABC) + (AβC) + (αBC) + (ABγ) = 29 + 9 = 38

It should be noted that we required only (C), (αβC); the other frequencies are not necessary.

Example

(a) In a very hotly fought battle,

70% at lest of combatants lost an eye.

75% at least an ear

80% at least a leg

85% at least a arm

what percentage at least lost all the four organs?

(M. Com., Rajasthan Univ., 1983)

Solution

Let A stand for combatants who lost eye, B for those who lost an ear, C for those who lost leg and D for those who lost an arm.

N stands for the total number of combatants

Then (A) = 0.70N, (B) = 0.75, (C) = 0.80N, (D) = 0.85N

We have to find the least value of (ABCD)

(ABCD) = (A) + (B) + (C) + (D) – 3N – 0.70N + 0.75N + 0.80N + 0.85N – 3N

= 0.10N

The least value of (ABCD) = 0.10N or 10%.

Hence 10% at least of combatants lost all the four organs.

(b) The following are the proportions per 5000 of workers observed for certain classes of defect among a number of factory workers:

A = Development defects; B = Nerve signs; C = Mental duliness.

N = 5000	(C) = 400	(A) = 440
(AB) = 170	(B) = 545	(BC) = 228.

Show that some full workers do not exhibit development defects and state how many at least do not do so.

Solution

It is required to find the least value of (αC),

By the condition of consistencies

$$(BC) - (AB) + (AC) \not> (C); \quad (AC) \not> -(BC) + (AB) + (C)$$

Now $-(BC) + (AB) + (C) = -228 + 170 + 400 = 342$

∴ $(AC) \not> 342$; $(C) - (\alpha C) \not> 342$ or $(\beta C) \not> 400 - 342 = 58$

∴ At least 58 dull workers do not exhibit development defects.

Example

At a competitive at which 600 graduates appeared boys out numbered girls by 96. Those qualifying for interview exceeded in number those failing to qualify by 310. The number of Science graduates boys interviewed was 300 while among art girls there were 25 who failed to qualify for interview. Altogether there were 135 Arts graduates and 33 among them failed to qualify. Boys who failed to qualify numbered 18.

Find (a) the number of boys who qualified for interview, (b) the total number of Science graduate boys appearing, and (c) the number of Science graduates girls who qualified.

$N = 600$	$(\alpha\beta\gamma) = 25$
$(A)\ (\alpha) = 96$	$(\gamma) = 135$
$(B)\ (\beta) = 310$	$(\beta\gamma) = 35$
$(ABC) = 300$	$(A\beta) = 18$

We are to find the value of (i) (AB), (ii) (AC), and (iii) (αBC)

$N = (A) + (\alpha) = 600; (A) - (\alpha) = 96$

$2(A) = 696$ or $(A) = 348$

$(B) + (\beta) = 600$ or $(A) = 348$

$2(B) = 910$ or $(B)\ 455$ and $(\beta) = 145$

$(C) = N - (\gamma) = 600 - 135 = 465$

Hence the number of boys who qualified for interview was 330:

$$(AC) = (ABC) + (A\beta C) = (ABC) + (A\beta) - (AB\gamma)$$

$$= (ABC) + (A\beta) - [(\beta\gamma) - (\alpha\beta\gamma)] = 300 + 18 - 33 + 25 = 310$$

Hence the total number of Science graduate boys appearing was 310.

$$(\alpha BC) = (BC) - (ABC) = (C) - (\beta C) - (ABC)$$

$$= (C) - [\beta - (\beta\gamma)] - (ABC) = 465 - 145 + 33 - 300 = 53$$

Hence the number of Science graduate girls who qualified was 53.

Consistency of data : For three attributes the following conditions should be satisfied otherwise the frequencies given on the right will be negative:

(a)	$(ABC) \nless 0$	otherwise (ABC) will be negative	
(b)	$(ABC) \nless (AB) + (AC) - (A)$	"	$(A\beta\gamma)$
(c)	$(ABC) \nless (AB) + (BC) - (B)$	"	$(\alpha B\gamma)$
(d)	$(ABC) \nless (AC) + (BC) - (C)$	"	$(\alpha\beta C)$
(e)	$(ABC) \ngtr (AB)$	"	$(AB\gamma)$
(f)	$(ABC) \ngtr (AC)$	"	$(A\beta C)$
(g)	$(ABC) \ngtr (BC)$	"	(αBC)
(h)	$(ABC) \ngtr (AB) + (AC) + (BC) - (A) - (B) - (C) + N$	"	$(\alpha\beta\gamma)$

Since all these comparison are not independent, we get the following four conditions: (i) is obtained by combining (a) and (h), (j) by (b) and (g) and so on.

(i) $(AB) + (AC) + (BC) \nless (A) + (B) + (C) - (N)$

(j) $(AB) + (AC) - (BC) \ngtr (A)$

(k) $(AB) - (AC) + (BC) \ngtr (B)$

(l) $(AC) + (BC)$ " $(AB) \ngtr (C)$

or

$(AB) + (AB) - (A) \ngtr (BC)$

$(AB) + (BC) - (B) \ngtr (AC)$

$(AC) + (BC) - (C) \ngtr (AB)$

Example

Do you find any inconsistency in the data given below:

$$N = 1000, (A\beta) = 483, (A\gamma) = 378, (B\gamma) = 226$$

$$(A) = 525, (B) = 312, (C) = 470 \text{ and } (ABC) = 25$$

Solution

This is a case of three attributes. The ultimate class frequencies are $2^3 = 8$ in number and are as follows:

$$(ABC), (AB\gamma), (A\beta C), (AB\gamma), (\alpha BC), (\alpha B\gamma), (\alpha\beta B)\ (\alpha\beta\gamma)$$

Before proceeding to evaluate them we find the value of

$(AB) = (A) - (A\beta) = 525 - 42$

$(AC) = (A) - (A\gamma) = 525 - 147$

$(BC) = (B) - (Bg) = 312 - 86$

Now the ultimate frequencies are:

$(ABC) = 25$ (given)

$(AB\gamma) = (AB) - (ABC) = 12 - 25 = 17$

$(A\beta C) = (AC) - (ABC) = 147 - 25 = 122$

$(A\beta\gamma) = (A\beta) - (A\beta C) = 86 - 25 = 61$

$(\alpha BC) = (BC) - (ABC) = 86 - 25 = 61$

$(\alpha B\gamma) = (\alpha B) - (\alpha BC) = (B) - (AB) - (\alpha BC) = 312 - 42 - 61 = 209$

$(\alpha\beta C) = (C) - (AC) - (BC) + (ABC) = 470 - 147 - 86 + 25 = 262$

$(\alpha\beta\gamma) = N - (A) - (B) - (C) + (AB) + (AC) + (BC) - (ABC)$

$= 1000 - 525 - 312 - 470 - 42 - 147 - 86 - 25 = -57$

As one of the ultimate class frequencies is negative, the given data are inconsistent.

Example

There were 400 students in B. Com. Hons, in a certain college. Their results in various terminal examination are given below:

180 passed in first terminal

140 passed in second terminal

180 passed in third terminal

60 passed in all terminals

80 failed in all terminals

40 passed in the first and second terminals but failed in the third terminal, 70 failed in the first and second terminals but passed in the third terminal.

Find out how many students passed at least two examinations.

Solution

Let Success in first terminal be denoted by A.

Success in second terminal by B

Success in third terminal by C

α, β and γ will denote failure in Ist, 2nd and 3rd terminals respectively.

We are given N = 400, (A) = 180, (B) = 140, (C) = 180, (ABC) = 60, $(\alpha\beta\gamma)$ = 80, $(AB\gamma)$ = 40, $(\alpha\beta C)$ = 70.

We have to calculate (ABC) + $(AB\gamma)$ + (αBC) + $(A\beta C)$ to get the required answer.

$(ABC) = 60, (AB\gamma) = 40$ (given)

$(C) = (ABC) + (\alpha\beta C) + (A\beta C) + (\alpha BC)$

$180 = 60 + 70 + (A\beta C) + (\alpha BC)$

$(\alpha BC) + (A\beta C) = 180 - 60 - 70 = 50$

$\therefore (ABC) + (AB\gamma) + (\alpha BC) + (A\beta C) = 60 + 40 + 50 = 150$

i.e., 150 students passed at least two examinations.

Example

Of 1000 people consulted, 811 liked chocolates, 752 liked toffee and 418 liked sweets, 570 liked chocolates and toffee; 356 liked chocolates and sweets and 348 liked toffee and sweets; 297 liked all three. Is this information correct?

Solution

Denoting liking of chocolates. Toffee and sweets by A, B and C respectively, the data would be:

N = 1000, (A) = 811, (B) = 752, (C) = 418

(AB) = 570, (AC) = 356, (BC) = 348, (ABC) = 297.

If one of the ultimate class frequencies is negative, the given data would be inconsistent.

$(\alpha BC) = (BC) - (ABC) = 348 - 297 = 51$

$(AB\gamma) = (AB) - (ABC) = 570 - 297 = 273$

$(A\beta C) = (AC) - (ABC) = 356 - 297 = 59$

$(A\beta\gamma) = (A) - (AB) - (A\beta C) = 811 - 570 - 59 = 132$

$(\alpha B\gamma) = (B) - (AB) - (\alpha BC) = 752 - 570 - 51 = 131$

$(\alpha\beta C) = (C) - (BC) - (A\beta C) = 418 - 348 - 59 = 11$

$(\alpha\beta\gamma) = N - (A) - (B) - (C) + (AB) + (AC) + (BC) - (ABC)$

$= 1000 - 811 - 752 - 418 + 570 + 356 + 348 + 297 = -4$

Since, $(\alpha\beta\gamma)$ is negative, the given information is not correct.

9.10 Partial Association

So far we have discussed the association of A and B in the universe as a whole without finding the other attributes in the universe. It is possible, however, that there is no direct relationship between A and B, i.e., the association between attributes A and B may be due to their association with a third attribute, say, C. Thus if A is positively associated with C and if B is associated with C, A may be found to be positively associated with B. But this type of association between A and B is not direct it is the effect of their association with a third attribute C. To find out whether the association between .14 and B is real, and not merely due to their association with a third attribute C, it would be necessary to study the association of A and B in the sub-populations C and γ. If A and B are associated in both the sub-population. of C and γ it would indicate that A and B arc really associated with each other.

The associations between A and B in sub-populations are called partial associations, to distinguish them from the total associations between A and B in the population at large. The following example will illustrate clearly the concept of partial association:

An association is observed between vaccination and prevention from attack by the small-pox. It means that vaccination prevents attack of smallpox. However, on a detailed analysis one may find that the attributes vaccination and attack of small-pox are not directly associated the & association between them is due to a third factor, namely, economic condition Those people who are economically well-off live in better conditions, open houses get better food and nutrition and can afford the cost of vaccination and as such the possibility of their getting an attack of small-pox is less. On the other hand those who are poor, live in filthy conditions, dirty surroundings, dirty houses and because of illiteracy do not believe in vaccination. They cannot afford the cost of vaccination also. As such they are liable to suffer more from diseases. If we denote A for vaccination, B for small-pox and C for economic conditions, we may find that there is positive association between A and C and also between Band C. Hence in order to arrive at correct conclusions it is necessary that on the basis of economic conditions the population is divided into two parts rich (C) and poor (γ) and in each sub-population association is ascertained between vaccination (A) and prevention from small-pox (B), If this third attribute is ignored it will give rise to misleading conclusions or technically illusory association.

The association found between the attributes A and B in the universe of C's and the universe of γ is termed as partial association to distinguish them from total association found between A and B in the universe at large.

The methods of finding out partial association are same as used in finding the total association. The only differences is that we have to find out separately the association of A and B in C and γ.

First method

Association between A and B for sub-population	Independent	Positive Association	Negative Association
C	$(ABC) = \frac{(AC) \times (BC)}{(C)}$	$(ABC) > \frac{(AC) \times (BC)}{(C)}$	$(ABC) < \frac{(AC) \times (BC)}{(C)}$
γ	$(AB\gamma) = \frac{(A\gamma) \times (B\gamma)}{(C)}$	$(AB\gamma) > \frac{(A\gamma) \times (B\gamma)}{(C)}$	$(AB\gamma) < \frac{(A\gamma) \times (B\gamma)}{(\gamma)}$

Second method

Association between A and B for sub-population	Independent	Positive Association	Negative Association
C	$\frac{(ABC)}{(AC)} = \frac{(\alpha BC)}{(\alpha C)}$	$\frac{(ABC)}{(AC)} > \frac{(\alpha BC)}{(\alpha C)}$	$\frac{(ABC)}{(AC)} < \frac{(\alpha BC)}{(\alpha C)}$
γ	$\frac{(AB\gamma)}{(A\gamma)} = \frac{(\alpha B\gamma)}{(\alpha\gamma)}$	$\frac{(AB\gamma)}{(A\gamma)} > \frac{(\alpha B\gamma)}{(\alpha\gamma)}$	$\frac{(ABC)}{(A\gamma)} < \frac{(\alpha BC)}{(\alpha\gamma)}$

Third method (Yule's coefficient)

$$Q_{AB.C} = \frac{(ABC)(\alpha\beta C) - (A\beta C)(\alpha BC)}{(ABC)(a\beta C) + (A\beta C)(\alpha BC)}$$

$Q_{AB.C}$ = Coefficient of partial association between A and B for sub-population C

$$Q_{AB.\gamma} = \frac{(AB\gamma)(\alpha\beta\gamma) - (AB\gamma)(\alpha B\gamma)}{(AB\gamma)(\alpha\beta\gamma) + (AB\gamma)(\alpha B\gamma)}$$

Association between A and C for sub-population B

$$Q_{AB.B} = \frac{(ABC)(\alpha B\gamma) - (AB\gamma)(\alpha BC)}{(ABC)(\alpha B\gamma) + (AB\gamma)(\alpha BC)}$$

$$Q_{AB.B} = \frac{(A\beta C)(\alpha\beta\gamma) - (A\beta\gamma)(\alpha\beta C)}{(A\beta C)(\alpha\beta\gamma) + (A\beta\gamma)(\alpha\beta C)}$$

Illustration : Calculate coefficient of partial association between A and B and A and C from the following data:

$(ABC) = 200, (AB\gamma) = 210, (A\beta C) = 208, (A\beta\gamma) = 190, (\alpha BC) = 209,$

$(\alpha B\gamma) = 105, (\alpha\beta C) = 170, (\alpha\beta\gamma) = 178.$

Solution : (i) Between A and B for sub-population C

$$Q_{AB.C} = \frac{(ABC)(\alpha\beta C)-(A\beta C)(\alpha BC)}{(ABC)(\alpha\beta C)+(A\beta C)(\alpha BC)}$$

$$= \frac{(200 \times 170)-(208 \times 209)}{(200 \times 170)+(208 \times 209)} = \frac{9472}{77472} = 0.122$$

(ii) Between A and B for sub-population γ

$$Q_{AB.\gamma} = \frac{(AB\gamma)(\alpha B\gamma)-(A\beta\gamma)(\alpha\beta\gamma)}{(AB\gamma)(\alpha\beta\gamma)+(A\beta\gamma)(\alpha\beta\gamma)} = \frac{(210 \times 178)-(190 \times 105)}{(210 \times 178)+(190 \times 105)}$$

$$= \frac{37380-19950}{37380+19950} = \frac{17430}{57330} = 0.304$$

(iii) Between A and C for sub-population B

$$Q_{AB.B} = \frac{(ABC)(\alpha B\gamma)-(AB\gamma)(\alpha BC)}{(ABC)(\alpha B\gamma)+(AB\gamma)(\gamma BC)} = \frac{(200 \times 105)-(210 \times 209)}{(200 \times 105)+(210 \times 209)}$$

$$= \frac{21000-43890}{21000+43890} = \frac{-22890}{64890} = -0.353$$

(iv) Between A and C for sub-population β

$$Q_{AB.\beta} = \frac{(A\beta C)(\alpha\beta\gamma)-(A\beta\gamma)(\alpha\beta C)}{(A\beta C)(\alpha\beta\gamma)+(A\beta\gamma)(\alpha\beta C)} = \frac{(208 \times 178)-(190 \times 170)}{(208 \times 178)+(190 \times 170)}$$

$$= \frac{37024 - 32300}{37024 + 32300} = \frac{4724}{69324} = +0.068$$

Illustration. A survey of 1000 companies gives the following data:

(i)	Companies with a capital of more than Rs.10 lakhs	510
(ii)	Companies making profits	490
(iii)	Companies under managing agents	427
(iv)	Companies with a capital of more than Rs.10 lakhs and making profits	189

(v) Companies with a capital of more than Rs.10 lakhs and under managing agents 140

(vi) Companies making profits and under managing agents 85

Show that the information as it stands must be incorrect.

Solution

Let A denote companies with a capital of more than Rs.10 lakhs

B denote companies making profits, and

C denote companies under managing agents

We are given

N = 1000, (A) = 510, (B) = 490, (C) = 427

(AB) = 189, (AC) = 150, (BC) = 85

The condition of consistency when positive class frequencies are given except (ABC) is:

$(AB) + (AC) + (BC) \nless (A) + (B) + (C) - (N)$

Submitting the given values

$189 + 140 + 85 \nless 510 + 490 + 427 \nless 1000 = 414 \nless$ which is not possible.

Hence the information as it stands must be incorrect.

Exercise

1. Explain the difference between the correlation and association.
2. Explain various methods of studing the association.
3. Explain coefficient of association.
4. Of 1000 people consulted, 511 liked chocolates, 552 liked toffee and 618 liked sweets, 700 liked chocolates and toffee; 350 liked chocolates and sweets and 340 liked toffee and sweets; 200 liked all three. Is this information correct?
5. Explain partial association and its Yule's coefficient.

❑❑❑

Chapter – 10

Correlation and Regression

10.1 Introduction

In previous lessons we have been dealing with problems connected with variation occurring in any one variable, say the income of a person, the height or weight of an individual, the wage of a worker in a factory, the sales of a shop, demand of a commodity etc. The values of a single variable were obtained from every member of the population and the different characteristics were described by certain descriptive constants after grouping into frequency distribution. In this lesson, we shall be dealing with problems wherein there are paired variables and every individual or member of the population exhibits two values, one for each of the variables under consideration. Example of the two variables which are to be studies together are (i) the income and expenditure of a household, (ii) the price and demand or supply of a commodity, (iii) the height and weight of a student, and (iv) the grain yield and straw yield of paddy, (v) Height of father and height of son, etc.

A population of this kind in which the individuals exhibit paired values is known as a bivariate population bivariate universe.

10.2 Meaning of Correlation

Let there be two variables, whenever there is a change in the value of a variable, correspondingly there is a change in the value of another variable either in the same direction or in the opposite direction, then two variables are said to be correlated. If the change is in such a way that an increase (or a decrease) in one is accompanied by an increase (or a decrease) in the other, the two variables are said to be positively correlated. For example (i) yield and rainfall, (ii) the price and supply of the commodity are positively correlated or the correlation between the two is defined as direct. If on the other hand an increase (or a decrease) in one is accompanied by a decrease (or a increase) in the other, the two variables are said to be negatively correlated. For example (i) the price and demand of a commodity, (ii) the price and the value of the money are negatively correlated. That is the correlation between the two is of the 'Inverse' type.

Further if the changes in both variables are in the same direction and also in the same proportion, the variables are said to be perfect positively correlated. On the other hand the changes in the variables are in the opposite direction but in the same proportion, he variables are said to be perfect negatively correlated. For some formal definitions of correlation are given below:

i. "If two or more quantities vary in sympathy so that movements in the one tend to be accompanied by corresponding movements in the other(s) then they are said to be correlated". **–L.R. Cornor,**

ii. "When the relationship is of a quantitative nature, the appropriate statistical tool for discovering and measuring the relationship and expressing it in a brief formation is known as correlation". **–Croxton & Cowden.**

iii. "Correlation analysis contributes to the understanding of economic behaviour, aids in locating the critically important variables on which others depend, may reveal to the economist the connections by which disturbances spread and suggest to him the paths through which stabilizing forces may become effective". **–W.A. Neiswanger.**

10.3 Linear and Non-linear Correlation

The correlation between two variables is said to be linear (or perfect) if corresponding to a unit change in one variable, there is constant change in the other variable over the complete range of the values. For example, observation following data in two variables X and Y.

X	1	2	3	4	5
Y	6	10	14	18	22

Thus for a unit change in the value of X, there is a constant change, 4 in the corresponding values of Y. Mathematically the above data can be expressed by the relation.

$$Y = 4X + 2$$

In general, two variables X and Y are said to be linearly related, if there exists a relationship of the form.

Y = A + BX between them. This relation when it is traced in the graph paper gives a straight line with slope B.

The relationship between two variables is said to be non- linear or curvilinear if corresponding to a unit change in one variable, the other variable does not change at constant rate but a fluctuating rate. In this case if the data are plotted on a graph paper, we do not get a straight line curve and the slope of the plotted curve is not constant. Such phenomena are common in the data relating to economics and social sciences.

10.4 Simple, Multiple and Partial Correlation

When only two variables are studied, it is a problem of simple correlation. That is a simple correlation measures the relation between a dependent and an independent variable.

When three or more variables are studied it is a problem of either multiple or partial correlation. A multiple correlation coefficient measures the combined relation between a dependent and a series of independent variables. For example, when we study the relationship between the yield of rice per acre (depended variable) and both the amount of rain fall (independent variable) and the amount of fertilizers used (independent variable) it is a problem of multiple correlation.

On the other hand, in partial correlation we recognize more than two variables, but consider only two variables to be influencing each other the effect of other influencing variables being kept constant. For example, in the above rice problem if we limit our correlation analysis of yield and rainfall to periods when the amount of fertilizers used is constant over periods, it becomes a problem of partial correlation.

10.5 Correlation and Causation

Correlation analysis helps us in determining the degree and direction of the relationship between the two variables understudy. But it does not tell us anything about cause and effect relationship, they are found to change in sympathy with each other and therefore there is bound to be a high degree of correlation between them. In other words causation always implies correlation, but even a high degree of correlation between them. In other words causation always implies correlation, but even a high degree of correlation between the two variables need not imply a cause and effect relationship between them. It establishes only covariation. The high degree of correlation between the variables may be due to the following reasons:

i. Both the variables may be mutually influencing each other so that neither can be designated as the cause and the other the effect.

ii. Both the correlated variables may be influenced by one or more other variables or external factors.

iii. The correlation may be due to pure chance.

10.6 Usefulness of Correlation

The study of correlation is of immense use both in physical and social sciences, but we shall confine ourselves to the latter and particularly to the fields of business and economics.

1. Most of the variables how some kind of relationship. For example, there is relationship between price and supply, price and demand, income and expenditure, etc. The correlation analysis helps in deriving precisely the degree and direction of such relationships.
2. Once we know that tow variables are closely related, we can estimate the value of one variable given the value of another. This is done with the help of regression analysis which is discussed in the next lesson.
3. In business, correlation analysis enables the executive to estimate costs, sales, prices and other variables on the basis of some other series with which these costs, sales or prices may be functionally related.
4. Progressive development in the methods of science and philosophy has been characterized by increase in the knowledge of relationship or correlations. In nature also one finds multiplicity of interrelated forces.
5. The effect of correlation is to reduce the range of uncertainty. The prediction based on correlation analysis is likely to be more reliable and nearer to reality.

10.7 Methods of Studying Correlation

We confine ourselves to simple linear correlation. The commonly used methods for studying the correlation between two variables are:

i. Scatter diagram method

ii. Karl Pearson's coefficient of correlation

iii. Rank method

iv. Concurrent deviation method.

i. Scatter diagram method

Scatter diagram is one of the graphical representation of a bivariate ungrouped data which is also known as dot diagram. In this representation, on variable normally, independent variable is represented on the horizontal axis or X-axis. The other variable known as the dependent variable is shown on the vertical axis or Y-axis. Suppose we are given N pairs of values (X_1, Y_1); (X_2, Y_2);...; (X_N, Y_N) of the two variables x and Y. For example if the variables X and Y denote the price and demand respectively, then the pairs (X_1, Y_1); (X_2, Y_2);...; (X_N, Y_N) may represent the prices and demands (in pairs) of N points of time of N places. These N points may be plotted as dots (.) on the X-axis in a graph. The diagram of dots so obtained is known as scatter diagram.

The following points may be borne in mind in interpreting the scatter diagram regarding the correlation between the two variables.

i. The greater the scatter of the plotted points on the graph, the lesser is the relationship between the two variables. This is the case of poor correlation. The more closely the points come to a straight line, the higher the degree of relationship. This indicates a fairly good amount of correlation between the variables.

ii. If the points on the scatter diagram reveal any trend (either upward or downward), the variables are said to be correlated and if no trend is revealed the variables are uncorrelated.

iii. If there is a strip or a band of points which rises from left hand bottom to the upper right hand top, the correlation is positive (Fig 10.1) since this reveals that the values of the two variables more in the same direction. If on the other hand the strip of points depicts a downward trend from the left hand top to the right hand bottom, the correlation is negative (Fig. 10.2) since in this case the values of this two variables move in the opposite direction.

iv. In particular, if all the plotted points lie on a straight line starting from the left bottom and going up towards the right top (Fig. 10.3) the correlation is perfect and positive, and if all the points lie on (Fig. 10.4) the correlation is perfect and negative.

v. If the plotted points have scattered in all direction and if there is no strip of points, showing any trend (Fig 10.5) it shows absence of any linear relationship between the variables. It is a case of no correlation.

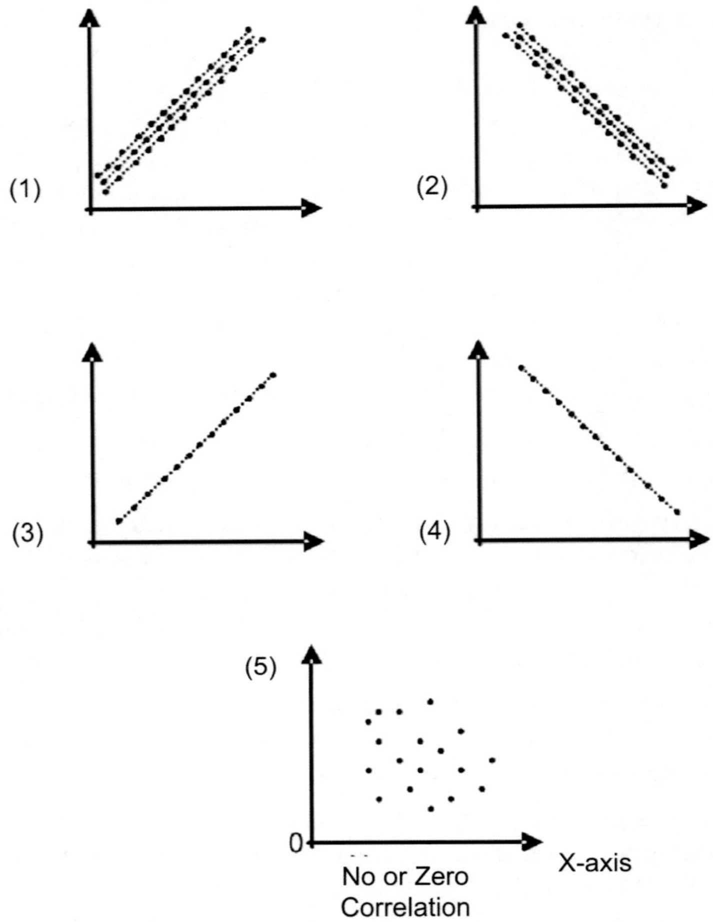

Figure : 10.1

Example

Following data represent the heights in inches and the weights in kilograms of 10 students of BBA class.

Table 10.1 :

Height	X	62	72	68	58	65	70	66	63	60	72
Weight	Y	50	65	63	50	54	60	61	55	54	63

Draw a scatter diagram and indicate whether the correlation is positive or negative solution.

For the above data the scatter diagram is shown below:

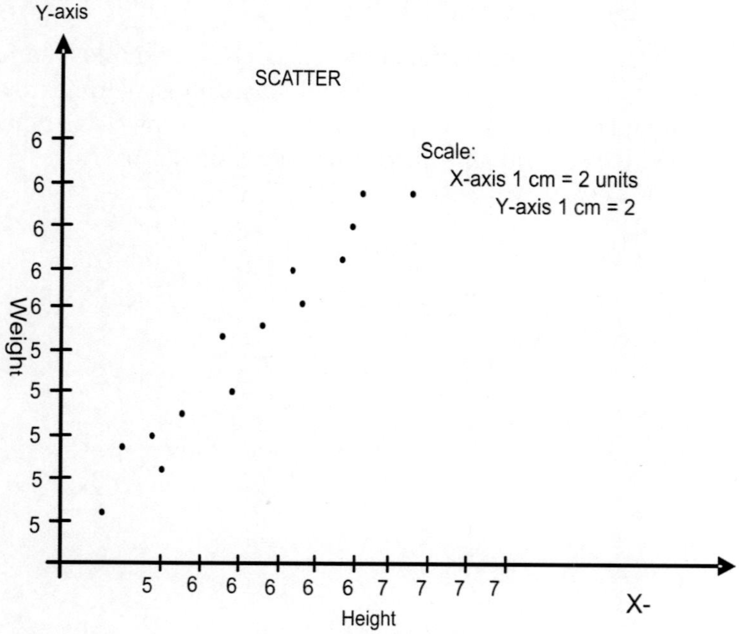

Figure : 10.2

Since the plotted points are close to each other, we may expect, a high degree of correlation between the series of heights and weights. Further, since the points show an upward trend starting from left hand bottom and going upward to right hand top, the correlation is positive. Hence we may expect a high degree of positive correlation between the series of heights and weights in the class of BBA students.

ii. Karl Pearson coefficient of correlation

An algebric device for measuring the intensity of or the magnitude of liner relationship between two variables was given by Karl Pearson (1867-1936).

Standard deviation indicates the amount of variability of the values from their arithmetic mean in the data set. Similarly the covariance between the two variables measures the joint or combined variation of values of the two variables from their arithmetic means in the bivariate data. The covariance between the variables X and Y is defined as follows:

Covariance between X and Y = Cov. (X,Y)

$$= \frac{\sum(X-\overline{X})(Y-\overline{Y})}{N}$$

where $\overline{X}$ and $\overline{Y}$ are means of X and Y respectively, and N denotes the total number of pairs of values of X and Y.

Karl Pearson Correlation coefficient between two variables X and Y, which is usually denoted by r (X,Y) or simply r is a numerical measure of linear relationship between them and is defined as the ratio of the covariance between X and Y to the product of the standard deviations of X and Y.

Symbolically,

$$r = \frac{\text{Cov.}(X, Y)}{(\text{S.D. of } X)(\text{S.D. of } Y)}$$

$$\text{Where Cov. }(X,Y) = \frac{\sum(X-\overline{X})(Y-\overline{Y})}{N}$$

OR

$$\text{Cov. }(X,Y) = \frac{\sum(XY)}{N} - \overline{X}\overline{Y}$$

$$\text{S.D.of } X = \sqrt{\left(\frac{\sum X^2}{N}\right) - \overline{X}^2}$$

$$\text{S.D.of } Y = \sqrt{\left(\frac{\sum X^2}{N}\right) - \overline{Y}^2}$$

Where $\overline{X}$ and $\overline{Y}$ are means of X and Y respectively and N denotes the total number of pairs of values of X and Y.

Properties of the correlation coefficient

i. The correlation coefficient r is a pure number and is independent of the units of measurement.

ii. It is independent of the choice of both the origin and the scale of observation, that is, if

$$V = \frac{X-A}{h} \text{ and } V = \frac{Y-B}{K}$$

Where A, B, h, K and arbitrary constants, then correlation coefficient between U and V is equal to the correlation coefficient between X and Y.

Symbolically,

$$r\,(U,V) = r\,(X,Y)$$

iii. The correlation coefficient, r lies between -1 and +1.

That is, $-1 \le r \le 1$.

The following descriptions enable us to interpret the correlation coefficient, r between the two variables X and Y.

a. If r = +1 implies that there is perfect positive correlation between the two variables.

b. If 0 < r < 1 implies that there is a positive correlation between the two variables.

c. If r = 0 implies that there is no correlation between the two variables.

d. If -1 < r < 0 indicates that there is a negative correlation between the two variables.

r = -0.9 and -0.8 shows a high degree of negative correlation.

r = -0.1 and -0.2 shows a low degree of negative correlations.

e. If r = -1 shows that there is a perfect negative correlation between the two variables.

Example

Compute Pearson's Coefficient of correlation between advertisement cost and sales as per the data given below:

Table 10.2 :

Advertisement cost in 1000Rs.	39	65	62	90	82	75	25	98	36	78
Sales in lakhs Rs.	47	53	58	86	62	68	60	91	51	84

Solution

The formula to find the Pearson's coefficient of correlation between the variables is:

$$r = \frac{\text{Cov.}(X,\ Y)}{(\text{S.D. of } X)(\text{S.D. of } Y)}$$

$$\text{Where Cov. }(X,Y) = \frac{\sum(XY)}{N} - \overline{XY}$$

$$\text{S.D.of X} = \sqrt{\left(\frac{\sum X^2}{N}\right) - \overline{X}^2}$$

$$\text{S.D.of Y} = \sqrt{\left(\frac{\sum X^2}{N}\right) - \overline{Y}^2}$$

The following table enables us to compute the standard deviations and covariance of the two variables X and Y.

Here X = Advertisement cost in 1000 Rs.

Y = Sales in lakhs Rs.

Table 10.3 :

	X	Y	X^2	Y^2	XY
	39	47	1521	2209	1833
	65	53	4225	2809	3445
	62	58	3844	3364	3596
	90	86	8100	7396	7740
	82	62	6724	3844	5084
	75	68	5625	4624	5100
	25	60	625	3600	1500
	98	91	9604	8281	8918
	36	51	1296	2601	1836
	78	84	6084	7056	6552
Total	650	660	47648	45784	45604

Here N = 10

$\Sigma X = 650$

$\Sigma Y = 650$

$\Sigma X^2 = 47648$

$\Sigma Y^2 = 45784$

$\Sigma XY = 45604$

Mean of X $= \overline{X} = \sum X / N$

$\overline{X} = 650/10 = 65$

Mean of Y $= \overline{Y}$ Y $= \sum Y / N$

$\overline{Y} = 660/10 = 66$

$$\text{S.D. of X} = \sqrt{(47648/10) - 65^2}$$

$$= \sqrt{(47648/10) - 65}$$

$$= \sqrt{536.8}$$

$$\text{S.D. of X} = 23.2336$$

$$\text{S.D. of X} = \sqrt{(45748.10) - 66^2}$$

$$= \sqrt{4578.4 - 4356}$$

$$= \sqrt{222.4}$$

$$\text{S.D. of Y} = 14.913$$

$$\text{Cov. (X.Y)} = (45604/10) - 65 \text{ X } 66$$

$$= 4560.4 - 4290.0$$

$$\text{Cov. (X,Y)} = 270.4$$

$$= \frac{\text{Cov.(X, Y)}}{\text{(S.D. of X)(S.D. of Y)}}$$

$$= \frac{270.4}{(23.2336)(14.9130)}$$

$$= \frac{270.4}{346.4827}$$

$$= 0.7804$$

Thus there is a high degree of positive correlation between advertisement cost and the sales.

Example

The following results are obtained between two series X and Y from their respective means. Compute the coefficient of correlation.

Number of items	**X-Series**	**Y-Series**
Arithmetic mean	7	7
Sum of squares of deviation	4	8
from the mean	28	76
Sum of products of deviations	46	
of X and Y series from their	7	7
respective means		
Solution:		
Here, N =7	4	8

Contd.

	28	76
$X = 4 \sum(X-\overline{X})^2 = 28$		
$Y = 8 \sum(Y-\overline{Y})^2 = 78$	46	

$$\sum(X-\overline{X})(Y-\overline{Y}) = 46$$

$$\text{S.D. of X} = \sqrt{\sum(X-\overline{X})^2 / N}$$

$$= \sqrt{28/7} = \sqrt{4=2}$$

$$\text{S.D. of X} = 2$$

$$\text{S.D. of Y} = \sqrt{\sum(Y-\overline{Y})^2 / N}$$

$$= \sqrt{76/7} = \sqrt{10.8571}$$

$$\text{S.D. of Y} = 3.2950$$

$$\text{Cov. (X,Y)} = \frac{\sum(X-\overline{X})(Y-\overline{Y})}{N}$$

$$= 46/7 = 6.5714$$

$$\text{Cov. (X,Y)} = 6.571$$

$$r = \frac{\text{Cov.(X, Y)}}{\text{(S.D. of X)(S.D. of Y)}}$$

$$= \frac{6.5714}{2 \times 3.295} = \frac{6.5714}{6.590}$$

$$r = 0.9972$$

The two variables X and Y and highly positively correlated (very near to perfect positive correlation)

iii. Rank correlation

In some problems of business and industry we come across statistical series in which the variables under consideration are not cashable of quantitative measurement but can be arranged in serial order. For example, it may be possible for the two judgers to rank (by preference) 10 different brands of cigarettes in terms of taste, where as it may be possible for two foremen to rank their ten employees for promotion, whereas it may be difficult to assign them a numerical grade. Thus the characteristics (attributes) such as honesty, beauty, morality, taste etc., cannot be measured quantitatively but can be arranged serially. Charles Edward Spearman developed a device which consists in obtaining the correlation coefficient between the ranks of N individuals in the two attributes under study.

Suppose we want to know if two characteristics. A, say intelligence and B, say beauty are related or not. Both the characteristics are not capable of quantitative measurements but we can arrange a group of N individuals in order of merit (ranks) with respect to proficiency in the two characteristics. Let the variables X and Y denote the ranks of the individuals in the characteristics A and B respectively.

Case - A

If we assume that there is no tie, that is of no two individuals get the same rank in a characteristic, then obviously X and Y assume numerical values n some order ranging from 1 to N.

The Pearson's correlation coefficient when the ranks X and Y is called the rank correlation coefficient between the characteristics A and B for that group of individuals. The rank correlation coefficient is denoted by the symbol 'ρ' (Rho).

Spearman's rank correlation coefficient when there is notice in the ranks of a characteristics and N is the total number of pairs.

$$= 1 - \left[\frac{6\sum d^2}{N(N^2-1)}\right]$$

Where d is the difference between the pair of ranks of the same individual in the two characteristics and N is the total number of pairs.

The ranks of the same 15 students in two subject A and B are given below; the two numbers within the brackets denoted the ranks of the same students in A and B respectively.

(1,10)	(2,7)	(3,2)	(4,6)	(5,4)
(6,8)	(7,3)	(8,1)	(9,11)	(10,15)
(11,9)	(12,5)	(13,14)	(14,12)	(15,13)

use Spearman's formula to find the rank correlation coefficient.

Solution

Spearman's rank correlation coefficient p is given by:

$$\rho = 1 - \left(\frac{6\sum d^2}{N\left(N^2 - 1\right)} \right)$$

Table 10.4 :

Rank in A X	Ranks in B Y	Difference d = X-Y	d^2
1	10	-9	81
2	7	-5	25
3	2	1	1
4	6	-2	4
5	4	1	1
6	8	-2	4
7	3	4	16
8	1	7	49
9	11	-2	4
10	15	-5	25
11	9	2	4
12	5	7	49
13	14	-1	1
14	12	2	4
15	13	2	4
-	-	Total	272

$$\rho = 1 - \left(\frac{6 \times 272}{15(15^2) - 2} \right)$$

$$= 1 - \frac{6 \times 272}{15 - 224}$$

$$= 1 - 0.4857$$

$$\rho = 0.5143$$

Note-1: The value of rank correlation coefficient also varies between -1 and +1. When the value of ρ is + 1, it implies complete agreement in the order of the rates in both the characteristics. The ranks will also be in the same direction. When ρ = -1, the ranks will be in opposite directions showing complete disagreement in the order of ranks. The value of r is interpreted in the same manner as the correlation coefficient r.

Note-2: Spearman's rank correlation formula, $\rho = 1 - \left[\frac{6\sum d^2}{N(N^2-1)}\right]$ can also be used even if we are dealing with variables which are measured quantitatively, that is when the actual data or values of the variables are given. In this case we shall have to convert the data into ranks. The highest (smallest) observation is given the rank 1. The next highest (next lowest) observation is given rank 2 and so on. It is immaterial in which way (ascending or descending) the ranks are assigned. But the same approach should be adopted for all the variables under consideration. This shall be clear from the following example.

Example

Find the rank correlation co-efficient between poverty and over crowding from the table below:

Table 10.5 :

Town	No. per 200 households below Minimum Standard of living	Over crowding
A	17	36
B	13	46
C	15	35
D	16	24
E	6	12
F	11	18
G	14	27
H	9	22
I	7	2
J	12	8

Solution

Formula to find the rank correlation coefficient ρ is:

$$\rho = 1 - \left[\frac{6\sum d^2}{N(N^2-1)}\right]$$

Calculations for Rank correlation coefficient

X - the rank of the poverty

Y- the rank of the over crowding.

Table 10.6 :

Town	Poverty		Poverty		D=X-Y	X2
	Value	Rank	Value	Rank		
A	17	1	36	2	–1	1
B	13	5	46	1	4	16
C	15	3	35	3	0	0
D	16	2	24	5	.3	9
E	6	10	12	8	2	4
F	11	7	18	7	0	0
G	14	4	27	4	0	0
H	9	8	22	6	2	4
I	7	9	2	10	–1	1
J	12	6	8	9	–3	9
Total	–	–	–	–	–	44

$$\rho = 1 - \left(\frac{6 \times 44}{10(10^2 - 1)} \right)$$

$$= 1\text{- } 264/990$$

$$= 1\text{-}0.266$$

$$\rho = 0.734$$

Case-B

If we assume that there is a tie, that is if any two or more individuals are placed together in any classification with respect to an attribute or if in case of variable data there is more than one item with the same value in either or both series then spearman's rank correlation coefficient formula will not be valid. Because the variables X (the ranks of the individuals in the characteristic A) and Y (the ranks of the individuals in the characteristic B) do not take the value from 1 to n and hence their means are different.

If this case, common ranks are given to the items repeated. This common rank is the mean of the ranks which these items would have assumed if they were slightly different from each other and the next item will get the rank next to the rank already assumed. For example if two individuals are ranked equal at fifth place, they are each given the rank (5+6)/2 that is 5.5 and the and the next item will be, assigned the rank 7. If three are ranked equal at fifth place, they are given rank (5 + 6 +7)/3 =6 and the next item will be assigned the mark 8.

As a result of this following adjustment or correction is made in the rank correlation formula.

In the formula we add the factor $\frac{m(m^2-1)}{12}$ to Σd^2, where m is the number of members in a tie. The correction factor is to be added for each repeated value in both the series. Hence when there is a tie, the rank correlation coefficient formula:

$$\rho = 1 - \left[\frac{6\sum d^2 - \sum_{tie} CF}{N(N^2-1)} \right]$$

Where CF denotes the correction factor.

The following illustration makes these points clear.

Example

Find the spearman's rank correlation coefficient from the following bivariate data.

Table 10.7 :

Roll Nos	1	2	3	4	5	6	7	8	9	10
Marks in Statistics	45	56	39	54	45	40	56	60	30	36
Marks in law	40	36	30	44	36	32	45	42	20	36

Solution

Since 45 and 56 are repeated values in the first series (Statistics marks) and since 36 is the repeated value in the second series (Law marks) the formula to find the rank correlation coefficient is given by:

$$\rho = 1 - \left[\frac{6\sum d^2 - \sum_{tie} CF}{N(N^2-1)} \right]$$

Table 10.8 : Calculation for Rank correlation coefficient in case of tie

Role No.	Statistics		Law		Difference d = X″Y	X^2
	Marks	Rank	Marks	Rank		
1	45	5.5	40	4	+1.5	2.25
2	56	2.5	36	6	3.5	12.25
3	39	8.0	30	9	-1.0	1.00
4	54	4.0	44	2	2.0	4.00
5	45	5.5	36	6	-0.5	0.25
6	40	7.0	32	8	-1.0	1.00
7	56	2.5	45	1	1.5	2.25
8	60	1.0	42	3	-2.0	4.00
9	30	10.0	20	10	0.0	0.00
10	36	9.0	36	6	3.0	9.00
Total	–	–	–	–	–	36.00

Formula to find correction factor is :

$$CF = \frac{m(m^2 - 1)}{12}$$

The item 45 repeated two times x in statistics marks. Hence,

i) $CF = \frac{2(2^2 - 1)}{12} = 2 \times 3/12$

$CF = 0.5$

The item 56 also repeated two times in statistics marks Hence,

ii) $CF = 2(2^2 - 1)/12$

$= 2 \times 3/12$

$= 0.5$

The item 36 repeated three times in the Law marks. Hence,

iii) $CF = 3(3^2 - 1)/12$

$= 3 \times 8/12$

$= 24/12 = 2$

$$\rho = 1 - \left[\frac{6(36 + 0.5 + 0.5 + 2)}{10(10^2 - 1)}\right] = 1 - \left[\frac{6 \times 39}{10 \times 99}\right]$$

$= 1 - 234/990 = 1.0.236$

$\rho = 0.764$

iv) Concurrent deviations method

This is very simple and casual method of determining the correlation between two variables. This method is based on the signs of the deviations (that is direction of change) of the values of the variable from its preceding value and does not take into account the exact magnitude of the values of the variables.

The deviations in the values of two variables are said to be concurrent if they have the same sign, that is either both deviations are positive or both are negative.

The formula to find the correlation coefficient by this method is given by:

$r_c = \pm\sqrt{\pm\left(\frac{2c-n}{n}\right)}$ where μ_2 is the coefficient to concurrent deviation c is the number of concurrent deviations and n is the number of pairs of deviations.

If (2c-n) is positive, we take positive size in and outside of the square root and if (2c-n) is negative, we taken negative sign in and outside the square root in the formula of the coefficient of concurrent deviation.

Example

Compute the coefficient of correlation by concurrent deviation method from the following data.

Price	Imports	Price	Imports
368	22	384	26
384	21	395	24
385	24	403	29
361	20	400	28
374	22	385	27

Table 10.9 : Calculation of coefficient of concurrent deviation

Price	Sign of deviation from the Preceding Price, X	Import	Sign of deviation from the preceding import, Y	Product of deviations XY
368		22		
384	-	21	-	-
385	+	24	+	+
361	-	20	-	+
347	-	22	+	-
384	+	26	+	+
395	-	24	-	-
403	+	29	+	+
400	-	28	-	+
385	-	27	-	+

Here, n = number of pairs of deviations = 9

c = number of positive signs in the product deviation column of the table = 6

Formula to find the correlation coefficient by concurrent method is:

$$r_c = \pm\sqrt{\pm\left(\frac{2_c - n}{n}\right)}$$

Here, $\frac{2_c - n}{n} = \frac{2 \times 6 - 9}{9} = \frac{2 - 9}{9}$

$= 3/9 = 0.3333$ which is positive.

$r_c = +\sqrt{+(0.333)}$

$r_c = 0.5777$

10.8 Coefficient of Determination

The coefficient of determination (μ^2) is the sqauare of the coefficient of correlation between the two variables. Coefficient of correlation between two variables is a measure of linear relationship between them and indicates the amount of variation of one variable which is associated with or is accounted for by another variable. The coefficient of determination gives the percentage variation in the dependent variable that is accounted for by the independent variable. In other words the coefficient of determination gives the ration of the explained variance to the total variance. Thus we have the formula for coefficient of determination as:

$$\text{Coefficient of domination} = r_c = \frac{\text{Explained variance}}{\text{Total variance}}$$

The coefficient of determination is a much useful and better measure for interpreting the value of coefficient of correlation between the variables, because it shows the degree of dependence. For example if the Coefficient of correlation between two variables, r = 0.8 we cannot conclude that 80% of the variation in the dependent variable is due to the variation in the independent Variable. But the coefficient of determination in this case is $r^2 = 0.64$ which implies that one 64% of the variation in the dependent variable has been explained by the independent variable and the remaining 36% of the variation is due to other factors.

10.9 Coefficieint of Non-determination

The coefficient of non-determination is the complement of coefficient of determination and it is usually denoted by k^2. The ratio of the unexplained variation to the total variation is called the coefficient of non-determination.

It is given by the formula:

$$K^2 = \frac{\text{unexplained variance}}{\text{Total variance}} = 1 - \frac{\text{Explained variance}}{\text{Total variance}} \qquad K^2 = 1 - r^2$$

10.10 Coefficient of Alienation

The coefficient of Alienation is given by square root of the coefficient of non-determination, that is

$$k = \pm\sqrt{1-r^2}$$

10.11 Probable Error

The probable error is used for ascertaining the reliability of the coefficient of correlation and it is usually denoted by S.E (r) is given by

$$\text{S.E (r)} = \frac{1-r^2}{\sqrt{n}}$$

probable error of the correlation correlations coefficient s given by

P.E. (r) = 0.6745 X S.E . S.E.(r)

$$= 0.6745\left[\frac{1-r^2}{\sqrt{n}}\right]$$

Interpretation and use of probable error

i. If the value of r is less than the probable error there is no evidence of correlation, that is the value of r is not all significantly different from zero.

ii. It the value of r is more than six times the probable error, the existence of correlation is practically certain, that is the value of r is significantly different from zero.

iii. By adding and subtracting the value of probable error from the coefficient of correlation we get respectively the upper and lower limits within which coefficient of correlation in the population can be expected to lie. Symbolically correlation in the population = r ± P.E. (r). For example with r =0.6 and n = 64, the P.E. (r) of the coefficient of correlation and the limits of the measure are:

$$\text{P.E. (r)} = 0.6745 \times \frac{1-r}{\sqrt{n}}$$

$$\text{P.E. (r)} = 0.6745 \times \left[\frac{1-(.6)^2}{\sqrt{64}}\right]$$

$$= \frac{0.6745 \times .64}{8}$$

$$\text{P.E. (r)} = 0.654$$

Limits population correlation coefficient are: = 0.6 ±0.054

t = 0.546 and 0.654

10.12 Regression Analaysis

10.12.1 Introduction and meaning

If two variables are correlated than there exists some relationship between them. Now we may be interested in estimating (predicting) the value of one variable given the value of another. For example, if we know that advertising and sales are correlated we may find out expected amount of sales for a given advertising expenditure or the required amount of expenditure for attaining a given amount of sales. This requires a functional relationship between variables. Regression analysis deals with the derivation of an appropriate functional relationship between variables. It is a mathematical measure expressing the average relationship between two or more variables in terms of the original units f the data. The variable predicated on the basis of other variables is called the 'dependent' or the 'explained' variable and the other (s). The estimation or prediction is based on average of relationship which is derived statistically by regression analysis. The equation, linear or otherwise is called the regression equation.

In dictionary the word regression mean "moving backward", "going back" or "the return to the mean value". Sir Francis Galton used it in the study of heredity. According to him, with a correlation coefficient of 0.8 between heights of fathers and children if the average height of a certain set of fathers is x cm above (below) the general average, the average height of children shall be 0.8 x cm above (below) the general average. Thus this supports the statement that the average height of son's of a group of tall fathers is less than that of the fathers and the average height of the sons of a group of short fathers is more than that of the fathers.

This type of relationships between the two variables can be seen in (i) rainfall and agricultural production, (ii) price of an input and the overall cost of product, (iii) consumer expenditure and disposable income, etc.

In general sense regression analysis means the estimation or prediction of the unknown value of an variable from the known value of the other variable.

Some definitions of regression are:

"Regression is the measure of the average relationship between two or more variables in terms of the original units of the data". **- M M Blair.**

"One of the most frequently used techniques in economics and business research, to find a relation between two or more variables that are related casually is regression analysis". **- Taro Yamane**.

"R egression analysis attempts to establish the nature of the relationship" between variables - that is, to study the functional relationship between the variables and thereby provide a mechanism for prediction or forecasting".

-Ya-lun Chon.

10.12.2 Types of regression

The regression analysis can be classified as follows:

a. Simple and multiple regression and

b. Linear and non-linear regression.

a. Simple and multiple regression

The regression analysis confined to the study of only two variables at a time is termed as simple regression. For example the cost of production and expenditure influences the price of a product. In correlation it did not matter which one is a dependent variable and which one is an independent variable. But in regression analysis obviously the price of a product is the dependent variable which derives impulse for change from cost of product and advertising. The converse is not possible. The cost of production and advertising would then be an independent variable. If Y denotes the price of a product and X denotes the cost of production and advertising, the functional relationship can b expressed as Y = f(X).

Most of the times the values of a particular phenomenon may be affected by multiplicity of factors. The regression analysis for studying more than two variables at a time in known as multiple regression. In this whole one variable is a dependent variable the remaining variables are independent ones. For example, the turnover of product (Z) may depend on advertising expenditure (x) and the income of the people (y). Then the functional relationship can be expressed as z = f (x, y). However, in this lesson we shall confine ourselves to simple regression only.

b. Linear and non-linear regression

If the given bivariate data are plotted on a graph, the dots or points so obtained on the scatter diagram will more or less concentrate round a curve which may be called the curve of regression. In this case the relationship is said to be expressed by means of curvilinear regression or non-linear regression.

In the particular case when the curve is a straight line, it is called the line of regression and the regression is said to be linear. The mathematical equation of the regression curve or straight line, usually called the regression equation, enables us to study the average change in the value of the dependent variable for any given value of the independent variable (s). However, in this lesson we shall confine our discussion to linear regression between two variables only.

10.12.3 Lines of regression

The line of regression is the straight line which gives the 'best' fit in the least square sense to the given bivariate data and it gives the best estimate f one variable for any given value of the other variable. In case of two variables x and y, we shall have two lines of regression; one of y depends on x (or simply y on x) and the other x depends on y (or simply x on y).

Principle of least squares

The term best fit is interpreted in accordance with the principle of least squares which consists in minimising the sum of the squares of the residuals or the errors of estimates, that is the deviations between the given observed values of the variable and their corresponding estimated or expected values as given by the line of best fit.

Let the mathematical relationship in linear form between the variables y (dependent) and x (independent) be y = a + b x where 'a' and 'b' are arbitrary constants. These constants may be determined using least square technique from the bivariate data of x and y. Let (Xi, Yi) be any observed pair of values of X and Y. The expected value of Y when X = Xi from the linear equation is a + b Xi.

The difference between the observed value, Yj of Y and the expected value a + Xi of y is called the residual corresponding to X =Xi that is Residual Corresponding to Xi = Yi - (a + Xi). According to principle of least squares the constant 'a' and 'b' are determined by minimising the sum of square the residuals, Σ (Yi-a Xi)^2, where the symbol Σ denotes the summation with respect to all the pairs of the values of X and Y.

In the figure 10.3, for any given point P (Xi, Yi) the observed values of X and Y in the scatter diagram, the error estimate or residue as given by the line of best fit y = a + bx is PH residue as given by the line of best fit y = a + bx is PH.

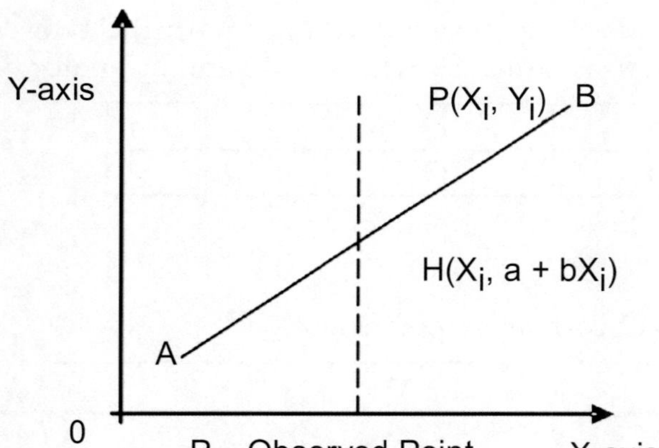

P – Observed Point
H – Point corresponding to P on the regression line AB

Figure 10.3

10.12.4 Equations of the regression lines

i. Line of regression of y on x is the line which gives the best estimates for the value of y for any specified value of x in least squares sense. Hence the equation of regression line of y on x is given by

$$\left(\frac{y-\bar{y}}{\sigma_y}\right)=r\left(\frac{x-\bar{x}}{\sigma_x}\right)$$

ii. Similarly line of regression of x on y is the line which gives the best estimate for the value of x for any given value of y is least squares sense. Hence the equation of regression line of x on y is given by

$$\left(\frac{x-\bar{x}}{\sigma_x}\right)=r\left(\frac{y-\bar{y}}{\sigma_y}\right)$$

Where in (i) and (ii) x and y are variables

$\bar{x}$ and $\bar{y}$ are respectively the means of x and y

σ_x and σ_y are respectively the

standard deviations of X and Y

and r is the correlation coefficient

between x and y.

Example

From the following bivariate data obtain the two equations of the regression lines. Also estimate y when x = 12 and estimate x when y = 12

X:	6	8	10	2	4
Y:	9	7	5	11	8

Solution

Calculation of correlation coefficient

X	Y	XY	X^2	Y^2
6	9	54	36	81
8	7	56	64	49
10	5	50	100	25
2	11	22	4	121
4	8	32	16	64
30	40	214	220	340

Total number of pairs (N) = 5

$\Sigma X = 30, \Sigma Y = 40, \Sigma XY = 214$

$\Sigma X^2 = 220, \Sigma Y^2 = 340$

Mean of X = $\overline{X} = \Sigma X/N = 30/5 = 6$

Mean of Y = $\overline{Y} = \Sigma Y/N = 40/5 = 8$

$$\text{S.D. of X} = \sigma x = \sqrt{\left(\frac{\sum X^2}{N}\right) - \overline{X}^2}$$

$$= \sqrt{22/5 - 6^2}$$

$$= \sqrt{44 - 36} = \sqrt{8}$$

$$\sigma x = 2.8284$$

$$\text{S.D. of Y } \sigma y = \sigma y = \sqrt{\left(\frac{\sum Y^2}{N}\right) - \overline{Y}^2}$$

$$= \sqrt{340/5 - 8^2} = \sqrt{68 - 64} = \sqrt{4}$$

$$\sigma y = 2$$

Covariance between X and Y = Cov. (X,Y)

$= \Sigma XY/N - XY$

$= 214/5 - 6 \times 8$

$= 42.8 - 48$

Cov. (X, Y) $= -5.2$

Correlation coefficient between X and Y is given by

$$r = \frac{\text{Cov.}(X,Y)}{\sigma x \sigma y} = \frac{-5.2}{(2.8284)(2)}$$

$$r = \frac{-5.2}{5.6568} = -0.9192$$

The equation of the regression line of Y on X is given by

$$\left(\frac{Y - Y}{\sigma_y}\right) = r\left(\frac{X - X}{\sigma_x}\right)$$

$$\frac{Y - 8}{2} = -0.9192 \frac{X - 6}{2.8284} \times$$

$$Y-8=\frac{0.9192\times 2}{2.8284}(X-6)$$

$$Y-8=\frac{-1.8384}{2.8284}(X-6)$$

$$Y = -0.65\ X + 0.65 \times 6 + 8$$

$$Y = -0.65\ X + 11.8999$$

The estimate of Y where X = 12 is obtained from the equation of the regression line Y on X.

$$Y = -0.65\ X\ 12 + 11.8999$$

$$Y = -7.80 + 11.8999$$

$$Y = 4.0999$$

The equation of the regression line of x on y is give by

$$\left(\frac{x-\bar{x}}{\sigma_x}\right)=r\left(\frac{y-\bar{y}}{\sigma_y}\right)$$

$$\frac{X-6}{2.8284}=-0.9192\left(\frac{Y-8}{2}\right)$$

$$X-6=\frac{(-0.9192)(2.8284)}{2}(Y-8)$$

$$X - 6 = -1.2999\ (y - 8)$$

$$X = -\ 1.2999y + (1.2999) \times 8 + 6$$

$$= -1.2999y + 10.3992 + 6$$

$$\underline{X = -1.2999y + 16.3992}$$

The estimate of X where Y = 12 is computed from the equation of the regression line of x on y.

$$X = -\ 1.2999 \times 12 + 16.3992$$

$$= -\ 15.5988 + 16.3992$$

$$\underline{X = 0.8004}$$

Example

Form the following results, obtain the two regression equations and estimate the yield of crops when the rainfall is 22 cms and the rainfall when the yield is 600 kgs.

	Yield in kgs	Rainfall in cms
Mean	508.4	26.7
S.D	36.8	4.6

Correlation coefficient between yield and rainfall is 0.52.

Solution

Let the yield of crops and the rainfall be respectively denoted by Y and X.

Then $\overline{X} = 26.7$ $\qquad \overline{Y} = 508.4$

$\sigma_x = 4.6$ $\qquad \sigma_y = 36.8$

$r = 0.52$

Equation of the line of regression yield (y) on rainfall (x) is

$$\left(\frac{Y-Y}{\sigma_y}\right) = r\left(\frac{X-X}{\sigma_x}\right)$$

$$\frac{Y-508.4}{36.8} = 0.52\left(\frac{X-26.7}{4.6}\right)$$

$$Y-508.4 = \frac{36.8 \times 0.52}{4.6} = (X-26.7)$$

$$= 4.16\ (X - 26.7)$$

$$= 4.15x - 111.072$$

$$Y = 4.16x - 111.072 + 508.4$$

$$Y = 4.16x + 397.328$$

The most likely yield of crop (y) when the rainfall x = 22 cms is given by

$$Y = 4.16 \times 22 + 397.328$$

$$= 91.520 + 397.328$$

$$= 488.848$$

$$= 488.85 \text{ kgs}$$

Equation of the line of regression of x on y is:

$$\left(\frac{Y-Y}{\sigma_y}\right) = r\left(\frac{X-X}{\sigma_x}\right)$$

$$\frac{X-26.7}{4.6}=0.52\left(\frac{Y-508.4}{36.8}\right)$$

$X - 26.7 = 0.065\ (Y - 508.4)$

$= 0.065y - 0.065 \times 508.4$

$= 0.065y - 33.046$

$X = 0.065y - 33.046 + 26.7$

$X = 0.65\ y - 6.346$

The most likely estimate of rainfall (x) corresponding to the yield

y = 600 kgs is given by

$X = 0.065 \times 600 - 6.346$

$= 39.000 - 6.346$

$X = 32.654$ cms

Regression coefficients

Let us consider the equation of regression line of y on x.

$$\left(\frac{Y-\overline{Y}}{\sigma_y}\right)=r\left(\frac{X-\overline{X}}{\sigma_x}\right)$$

This equation may be rewritten as follows:

$$(Y-\overline{Y})=r.\frac{\sigma_Y}{\sigma_X}(X-\overline{X})$$

$Y - \overline{Y} =$ by x $(X - \overline{X})$ where the symbol byx $= r.\frac{\sigma_Y}{\sigma_X}$ is called the regression coefficient y on x. The quantity b_{yx} is the slope of the line of regression of y on x. It represents the increment in the value of the dependent variable y for a unit change in the value of the independent variable x. In other words b_{yx} represents the rate of change of y with respect to x. The regression coefficient y on x may also be calculated from the bivariate data using the following formula.

$$b_{yx}=r.\frac{\sigma_Y}{\sigma_X}$$

But $r = \frac{Cov.(x,y)}{\sigma_x\sigma_y}$

$$b_{yx} = \frac{\text{Cov.}(x,y)}{\sigma_x \sigma_y} \times \frac{\sigma_y}{\sigma_x}$$

$$b_{yx} = \frac{\text{Cov.}(x,y)}{\sigma_{x^2}}$$

$$b_{yx} = \frac{\text{Cov.}(x,y)}{\text{Var. of } x}$$

Similarly the equation of the regression line x on y

$$\left(\frac{X-\overline{X}}{\sigma_x}\right) = r\left(\frac{Y-\overline{Y}}{\sigma_y}\right)$$

Rewriting as before, we have

$$(x-\overline{x}) = r\frac{\sigma_x}{\sigma_y}(y-\overline{y})$$

$(x-\overline{x}) = b_{xy}(y-\overline{y})$ where the symbol b_{xy} is called the regression coefficient x on y. The N Quantity b_{xy} is the slope of the line of regression x on y. It represents the increment in the value of the dependent variable x for a unit change in the value of the independent variable y. That is b_{xy} is also calculated using the following formula.

$$b_{xy} = \frac{\text{Cov.}(x,y)}{\text{Variance of } y}$$

OR

$$b_{xy} = \frac{\text{Cov.}(x,y)}{\sigma_{y^2}}$$

Properties of regression coefficients

Let b_{xy} and b_{xy} be respectively the regression coefficients of y on x and x on y.

i. Both the regression coefficients have the same sign. They cannot have different signs.

ii. If one of the regression coefficients is greater than unit 'y' (one), the other must be less than unit 'y'.

iii. The product of the two regression coefficients of y on x and x on y is equal to the square of the correlation coefficient, (r^2)

That is $b_{xy}\ b_{xy} = r^2$

We have $r = \pm\sqrt{b_{yx} \times b_{xy}}$ where the sign of correlation coefficient (r) is the same as the signs of the regression coefficients.

iv. The average of the regression coefficients is greater than the correlation coefficient.

v. Regression coefficients are independent of change of origin but not of scale.

Some important results of regression equations

The equations of the regression lines y on x and x on y are respectively:

$$\left(\frac{Y-\overline{Y}}{\sigma_y}\right)=r\left(\frac{X-\overline{X}}{\sigma_x}\right)$$

and

$$\left(\frac{X-\overline{X}}{\sigma_x}\right)=r\left(\frac{Y-\overline{Y}}{\sigma_y}\right)$$

The two regression lines coincide when $r = \pm 1$. That is in the case of perfect correlation (positive or negative) the two regression lines coincide and we get only one line of regression.

i. The two regression lines intersect each other when the correlation coefficient, r lies in between - 1 and +1.

   That is $-1 < r < +1$.

ii. The point of intersection of two regression lines is (X,Y). That is both regression lines pass through the point (X,Y) in the scatter diagram.

The by plotting the lines of regression on a graph paper, we can have an approximate idea about the degree of correlation between the two variables under study. The following scatter diagrams or graphs help us to study the degree of correlation between the variable, through the lines of regression.

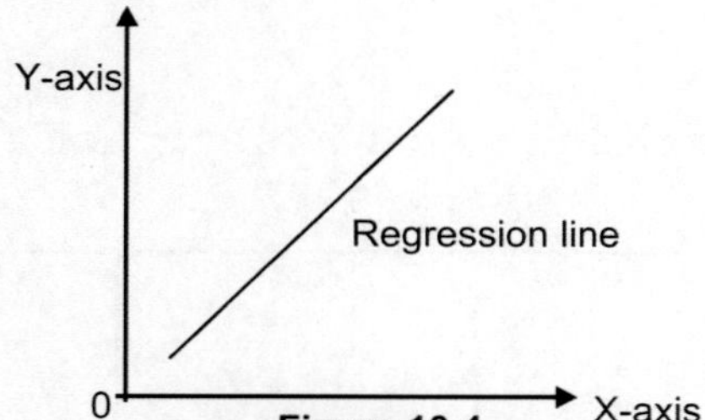

Figure 10.4
Two regression lines coincide

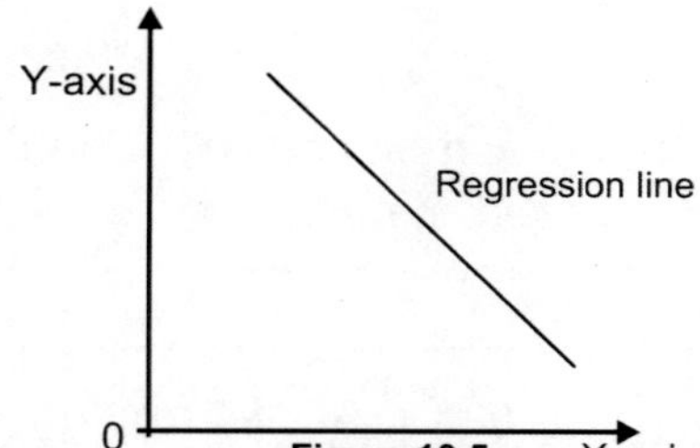

Figure 10.5
Two regression lines coincide

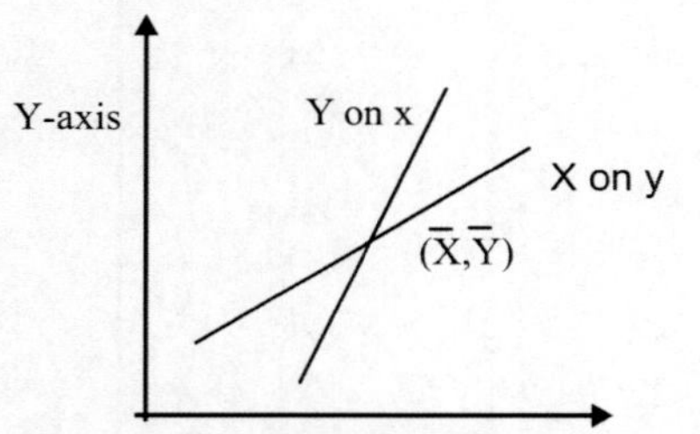

Figure 10.6
Two regression lines intersect And closer high degree of correlation

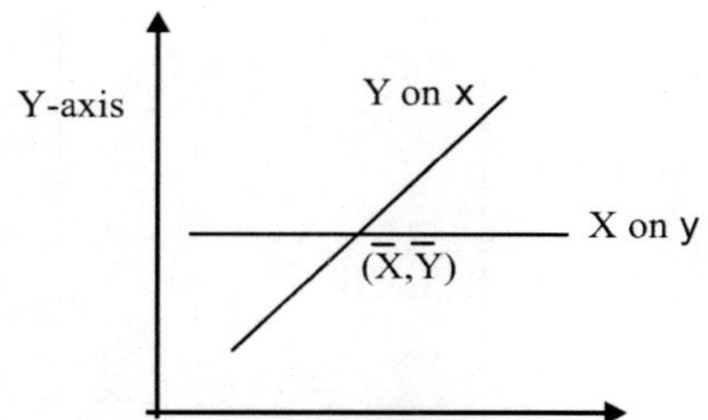

Figure 10.7
Two regression lines intersect And apart low degree of correlation

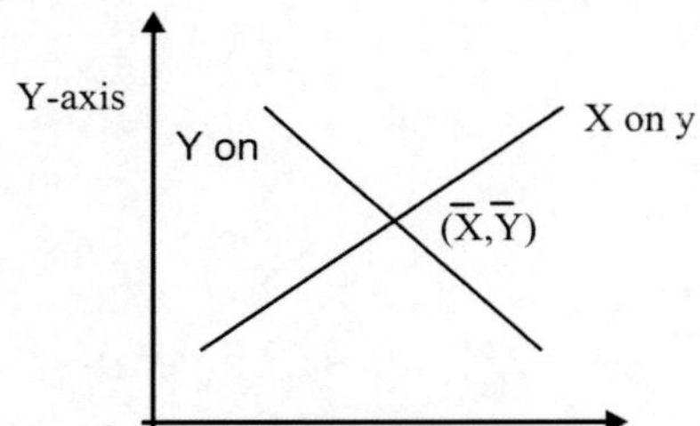

Figure 10.8
Two regression lines intersect Perpendicularly. No correlation

Example

The following bivariate data represent the age of husband and the age of wife in years.

Husband's age:	18	19	26	20	22	21	27	23	25	24
Wife's age	17	17	21	18	19	18	22	19	20	19

a. Compute the coefficients of regression.

b. Form two regression lines and

c. Calculate the husband's age when the wife's age is 16.

Solution

Let the age of husbands be denoted by X and age of wives by Y. Calculation of regression coefficients.

Age of		X^2	Y^2	XY
Husband's X	Wives Y			
18	17	324	289	306
19	17	361	289	323
26	21	676	441	546
20	18	400	324	360
22	19	484	361	418
21	18	441	324	378
27	22	729	484	594
23	19	529	361	437
25	20	625	400	500
24	19	576	316	456
225	190	5145	3634	4318

Here N = 10 $\Sigma X = 225$ $\Sigma Y = 190$

$\Sigma X^2 = 225$ $\Sigma Y^2 = 3634$

$\Sigma XY = 4318$

$$\text{Mean of X} = \overline{X} = \frac{\sum X}{N} = 225/10 = 22.5 \text{ years}$$

$$\text{Mean of Y} = \overline{Y} = \frac{\sum X}{N} = 190/10 = 19 \text{ years}$$

$$\text{S.D. of X} = \sigma_x = \sqrt{\frac{\sum X^2}{N} - \overline{X}^2}$$

$$= \sqrt{5145/10 - (22.5)^2}$$

$$= \sqrt{5145 - (506.25)}$$

$$= \sqrt{8.25}\ \sigma_x = 2.8723$$

$$\text{S.D. of Y} = \sigma_y = \sqrt{\frac{\sum Y^2}{N} - Y^2}$$

$$= \sqrt{3634/10-(19)^2}$$

$$= \sqrt{363.4-361} = \sqrt{2.4}$$

$$\sigma_y = 1.5492$$

$$\text{Cov. (X,Y)} = \left(\frac{\sum XY}{N}\right) - \overline{X}\overline{Y}$$

$$= 4318/10 - 22.5 \times 19$$

$$= 431.8 - 427.5$$

$$\text{Cov.(X,Y)} = 4.3$$

a. The regression coefficient Y on X is

$$b_{xy} = \frac{\text{Cov.(X,Y)}}{\text{Variance of X}}$$

$$= \frac{4.3}{(1.5492)^2}$$

$$= 4.3/8.25$$

$$b_{yx} = 0.5212$$

The regression coefficient of X on Y is

$$b_{xy} = \frac{\text{Cov.(X,Y)}}{\text{Variance of Y}}$$

$$= \frac{4.3}{(2.8723)^2}$$

$$b_{yx} = 1.7917$$

b. The equation of the regression line y on x is

$$Y - Y = b_{yx}(X - Y)$$

$$Y - 19 = 0.5212\,(X - 22.5)$$

$$= 05212\,X - 0.5212 \times 22.5$$

$$= 0.51212X - 11.727$$

$$Y = 0.5212X - 11.727 + 19$$
$$Y = 0.5212\,X + 7.273$$

The equation of the regression line x on y is:

$$X - X = b_{xy}\,(Y\text{-}Y)$$
$$X - 22.5 = 1.7917\,(Y - 19)$$
$$= 1.7917Y - 1.917 \times 19$$
$$= 1.7917Y - 34.0423$$
$$X = 1.7917Y - 34.0423 + 22.5$$
$$X = 1.791Y - 11.5423$$

c. The husband's age when the wife's age is 16 is estimated from the regression equation X on Y.

The regression equation X on Y is

$$X = 1.7917\,Y - 11.5423$$
$$= 1.7917 \times 16 - 11.5423$$
$$= 28.6672 - 11.5423$$
$$X = 17.1249$$

The husband's age is 17.1249 years.

Example

The lines of regression of a bivariate population are:

$$8X - 10Y + 66 = 0$$
$$40X - 18Y = 214$$

The variance of X is 9. Find (the mean values of X and Y, (i) the correlation coefficient between X and Y; and (ii) standard deviation of Y.

Solution

Since both regression lines pass through the mean values (X,Y) of X and Y, the point (X,Y) must satisfy the equation of the regression lines.

The mean value of X and Y are thus obtained by solving the given regression equations with respect to X and Y.

$$8X - 10Y = -66 \quad \dots (1)$$
$$40X - 18Y = 214 \quad \dots (2)$$

Subtracting (2) from (1) after multiplying (1) by 5 we get

$$40X - 50Y = -330 \quad \ldots (1)$$

$$40X - 18Y = 214 \quad \ldots (2)$$

$$-32Y = -544$$

$$Y = \frac{-544}{-32} = 17$$

$$Y = 17$$

Substituting Y = 17 in (1) we find

8X = -66 + 170

8X = 104

X = 104/8 = 13

Hence the mean values of X and Y are given by x = 13, Y = 17

ii. Let us assume that the equation of the regression line x on Y be

8X – 10Y +66 = 0

Expressing it in standard form we get:

8X = 10Y + 66

$$X = \frac{10}{8}Y + \frac{66}{8}$$

The regression coefficient of X on Y

= the coefficient of Y in the regression equation.

= 10/8

That is b_{xy} = 10/8 = 1.25

The equation of the regression line y on x be

40X – 18Y = 214

18Y = 40X – 214

$$Y = \frac{40}{18}X - \frac{214}{18}$$

The regression coefficient y on x = the coefficient of x in the regression equation = 40/18.

That is b_{yx} = 40/8 = 2.22

Since both the regression coefficients are greater than one and since the correlation coefficient

$$r = \pm\sqrt{b_{yx} X b_{XY}}$$

the assumption of the regression lines is wrong. Now we can assume that the equation (1) is the regression equation of y on x and the equation (2) as the regression of x on y.

That is the equation of the line of regression of y on x is

$8X - 10Y + 66 = 0$

$10Y = 8X + 66$

$$Y = \frac{8}{10}X + \frac{66}{10}$$

$b_{yx} = 8/10 = 0.8$

The equation of the line of regression of x on y is

$40X - 18Y = 214$

$40X = 18Y + 214$

$$X = \frac{18}{40}Y + \frac{214}{40}$$

$X = 0.45\ Y + 5.35$

$b_{yx} = 0.45$

since both regression coefficients are the same sign and less than one, our assumption regarding regression equation is correct.

But $r^2 = b_{yx}\ X\ b_{xy}$

$r = \pm\ 0.8\ X\ 0.45 = \pm\ .360$

$r = \pm\ 0.6$

Since both regression coefficients are + ve, r must be positive

$r = 0.6$

iii. We are given

$X^2 = 9 \qquad X = \pm\ 3$

But since standard deviation is always non – negative, we take

$X = 3$

$$\text{We have } b_{yx} = \frac{r\sigma Y}{\sigma X}$$

$$0.8 = \frac{6X\sigma Y}{3}$$

$$\frac{2.4}{6} = \sigma Y$$

$$\therefore \quad \sigma y = 4$$

Example

If two regression coefficients are 0.8 and 1.2, what would be the value of the coefficient of correlation?

Solution

$r = \pm\sqrt{b_{yx} X b_{xy}}$ where b_{yx} and b_{yx} are regression coefficients.

$$r = \pm\sqrt{0.8 X 1.2} \pm \sqrt{.96}$$

$$= \pm 0.9798$$

Since regression coefficients are + ve, r must be positive.

$$R = 0.9798$$

Example

Comment on the following:

For a bivariate distribution, the coefficient of regression of y on x is 4.2 and coefficient of regression of x on y is 0.5.

Solution

$$b_{yx} = 4.2$$

$$b_{xy} = 0.5$$

$$r^2 = b_{yx} X b_{xy}$$

$$+ \quad = 4.2 X .5$$

$$= 2.10 > 1$$

Since r^2 cannot be greater than 1, the given statement is wrong.

Difference between Correlation and Regression Analysis

The following are the points of difference between the two:

1. Correlation literally means the relationship between two or more variables which vary in sympathy so that movements in one tend to be accompanied by the corresponding movements in the other(s).

On the other hand regression means returning to the average relationship between the two variables.

2. Correlation coefficient between two variables x and y is a measure of the direction and degree of the linear relationship between the two variables which is mutual. It is immaterial which of x and y is dependent variable and which is independent variable.

   Regression analysis gives the functional relationship between the two variables under study and then using this relationship we predict or estimate the value of the dependent variable for any given value of the independent variable. It also reflects upon the nature of the variable, that is which is dependent variable and which is independent variable. The regression co – efficient are not symmetric in x and y. that is $b_{yx} \neq b_{xy}$ except when they are equal to one.

3. Correlation need not imply cause and effect relationship between the variable understudy. However regression analysis clearly indicates the cause and effect relationship between the variables. The variable corresponding to cause is taken as independent variable and the variable corresponding to effect is taken as dependent variable.

4. Correction coefficient is a relative measure of the linear relationship between x and y and is independent of the units of measurement. That is it is pure number lying between – 1 and +1.

   The regression coefficients are absolute measures representing the change in the value of the variable y (or x), for a unit change in the value of the another variable x (or y).

5. Correlation analysis is confined only to the study of linear relationship between the variables and therefore has limited applications. Regression analysis has limited much wider applications as it studies linear as well as non- linear relationship between the variables.

6. There may be non- sense correlation between two variables which is purely due to change and has no practical relevance such as increase in income and increase in weight of a group of people. However, there is nothing like non – sense regression.

Uses of Regression Analysis

1. Regression analysis is widely used in almost all the scientific disciplines. In economics it is the basic technique for measuring or estimating the relationship among economic variables that constitute the essence of economic theory and economic life.

2. Regression analysis help in establishing a functional relationship between two or more variables.
3. Regression analysis provides estimates of value of the dependent variable form the values of the independent variable. That is it is very useful of prediction purposes.
4. It also gives a measure of the error involved in using the regression lines as a basis for estimation.
5. With the help of regression coefficients we can calculate the correlation coefficients.

Exercise

1. What is meant by correlation? Distinguish between positive, negative and zero correlation.
2. What are the various methods of studying correlation?
3. Define Kearl Pearson's coefficient of correlation What is it intended to measure? How would you interpret the sign and magnitude of a correlation coefficient?
4. What is scatter diagram? Indicate by means of suitable scatter diagrams different types of correlation that may exist between the variables in bivariate data.
5. What is rank correlation? Explain the method of finding rank correlation coefficient when (i) then is a tie and (ii) then is no tie.
6. Explain coefficient of concurrent deviation method of finding coefficient of correlation.
7. Define
   (i) Co-efficient of determination
   (ii) Probable error
   (iii) Co-efficient of alienation
8. The following data represent the test scores of skill and achievement of nineteen workers in a factory.

	Scores of			Scores of	
Workers	**Skill**	**Achievement**	**Workers**	**Skill**	**Achievement**
A	41	32	J	69	50
B	53	29	K	41	25
C	64	47	L	32	21
D	43	35	M	38	19
E	44	29	N	62	34
F	51	41	O	68	41
G	68	46	P	58	43
H	52	39	Q	45	44
I	53	37	R	59	49

Draw a scatter diagram and indicate the type of correlation between the two scores.

9. Find the Pearson's coefficient of correlation between price and demand from the following data:

Price:	11	13	15	17	18	19	20
Demand	30	29	24	24	21	18	15

10. Ten competitors in a beauty contest are ranked by three judges in the following order:

I Judge:	1	5	4	8	9	10	7	3	2	6
II Judge:	4	8	7	6	5	9	10	3	2	1
III Judge:	6	7	8	1	5	10	9	2	3	4

use the rank correlation coefficient to discuss which pair of judges have the nearest approach to common tastes in beauty.

11. Calculate the coefficient of concurrent deviation from the data given below:

Year:	1963	1964	1965	1966	1967	1968	1969	1970
Supply:	160	164	172	182	166	170	178	192
Price:	292	280	160	234	266	254	230	190

12. The coefficient of correlation between consumption expenditure (c)and disposable income (y) in a study was found to be + 0.8 What percentage of variation in c are explained by variation in Y. Find the probable error. Also calculate the limits of the population correlation coefficient.

13. What do you understand by regression? Point out the significance of its study.

14. What is regression line? Why are there in general two regression lines? When do they coincide?

15. Write the equations of the regression lines. Explain the use of regression in an economic theory.

16. Distinguish clearly between correlation and regression

17. Explain the meaning of the regression coefficients and state their properties.

18. A student obtained the two regression lines as

$2x - 5y - 7 = 0$

$3x + 2y - 8 = 0$

Do you agree with him?

19. The following figures relate to advertising expenditure and sales:

Advertising expenditure (Rs.Lakhs)	60	62	65	70	73	75	71
Sales (Rs. Crores)	10	11	13	15	16	19	14

Estimate (i) the sales for advertising expenditure of Rs.90/- lakhs and (ii) the advertising expenditure for a sales target of Rs.25/- crores.

20. In a partially destroyed record the following data are available:

Variance of $x = 25$

Regression equations are

i. $5x\text{-}Y = 22$

ii. $64x\text{-}45y = 2$

Find (a) mean values of x and y

(b) correlation coefficient between x and y.

(c) Standard deviation of y.

21. Data relating to prices of wheat in two markets are given below:

	Market A	Market B
Mean Price	39.5	47.6
Standard deviation	10.8	16.9

Correlation coefficient between two prices is equal to 0.42.

Find the two regression equations. Estimate the price in Market A when price in the market B is 50.

22. In a correlation study on the prices of shares A and B, the following regression equations were obtained:

$$4y - 15x + 530 = 0$$

$$20x - 3y - 975 = 0$$

Find the mean prices of shares A and B. Also estimate the price of share B when the price of share A is Rs.70/-.

❑❑❑

Chapter – 11

Analysis of Variance

11.1 Introduction

The analysis of variance is a powerful statistical tool for tests of significance. The test of significance based on t-distribution is an adequate procedure only for testing the significance of the difference between two sample means. In a situation when we have three or more samples to consider at a time an alternative procedure is needed for testing the hypothesis that all the samples are drawn from the same population, i.e., they have the same mean. For example five fertilizers are applied of four plots each of wheat and yield of wheat on each of the plot is given we may be interested in finding out whether the effect of these fertilizers on the yields is significantly different or in other words, whether the samples have come from the same normal population. The answer to this problem is provided by the technique of analysis of variance. Thus basic purpose of the analysis of variance is to test the homogeneity of several means.

The term *'Analysis of Variance'* was introduced by Prof.R.A.Fisher in 1920's to deal with problem in the analysis of agronomic data. Variation is inherent in nature. The total variation in any set of numerical data is due to a number of causes which may be classified as:

(i) Assignable causes, and (ii) Chance causes.

The variation due to assignable causes can be detected and measured whereas the variation due to chance causes is beyond the control of human hand and cannot be traced separately.

Definition: According to Prof.R.A.Fisher, Analysis of Variance (ANOVA) is the "*Separation of variance ascribable to one group of causes from the variance ascribable to other group.* By this technique the total variation in the sample data is expressed as the sum of its non-negative components where each of these components is a measures of the variation due to some specific independent source of factor of cause. The ANOVA consists in the estimation of the amount of variation duet o each of the independent factors (causes) separately and then comparing these estimates due to assignable factors (causes) with the estimate due to chance factor (causes), the latter being known as experimental error or simply error.

Remark: In addition to testing the homogeneity of several means the ANOVA technique is now frequently applied in testing the linearity of the fitted regression line or the significance of the correlation ratio.

Assumption For the validity of the F-test in ANOVA, the following assumptions are made:

(i) The observations are independent.

(ii) Parent population from which observations are taken is normal, and

(iii) Various treatment and environmental effects are additive in nature.

In the following sequences we will discuss the analysis of variance for (a) one way classification, and (b) two-way classification. Before that we state below (without proof) Cochran's theorem, which is of fundamental importance in Analysis of Variance.

Cochran's Theorem

Let $X_1, X_2, \ldots, X_n$ denote a random sample from normal population $N(0, \sigma^2)$. Let the sum of the squares of these values be written in the form.

$$\sum_{i=1}^{n} Xi^2 = Q_1 + Q_2 + \ldots\ldots + Q_k$$

Where Q_i is a quadratic form in $X_1, X_2, \ldots, X_n$, with rank (degrees of freedom) r_j, j= 1,2 ..., k. Then the random variables $Q_1, Q_2, \ldots, Q_k$ are mutually independent and Q_j/σ^2 is Ψ^2 variate with r_j degress of freedom

$$\text{If and only if } \sum_{j=1}^{k} r_j = n$$

11.2 One-way Classification

Let us suppose that N observations x_{i_j}, (i = 1,2, ..., k ; j = 1, 2, ... n_i) of a random variable X are grouped, on some basis, into k classes of sizes $n_1, n_2 \ldots n_k$ respectively, $\left(N = \sum_{i=1}^{k} n_i\right)$ as exhibited below:

		Means	Total
x_{11}	x_{12} ..... x_{1n1}	$\overline{x}_{1.}$	$T_{1.}$
x_{21}	x_{23}.....x_{2n2}	$\overline{x}_{2.}$	$T_{2.}$
⋮	⋮	⋮	⋮
x_{i1}	x_{i2}..... x_{in}		$T_{i.}$
⋮	⋮	⋮	⋮
x_{k1}	x_{k2} ...... x_{knk}	$\overline{xk.}$	$T_{k.}$
			G

The total variation in the observations xij can be split into the following two components:

(i) The variation *between the classes* or the variation due to different bases of classification, commonly known as treatments.

(ii) The variation *within the classes,* i.e., the inherent variation of the random variable within the observations of a class.

The first type of variation is due to *assignable causes* which can be detected and controlled by human endeavour and the second type of variation is due to *chance causes* which are beyond the control of human hand.

The main object of analysis of variances technique is to examine if there is significant difference between the class means is view of the inherent variability within the separate classes.

In particular, let us consider the effect of k different rations on the yield in milk of N cows (of the same breed and stock) divided into k classes of sizes n_1, n_2, ..., n_k respectively, $N = \sum_{i=1}^{k} n_i$. Here the sources of variation are

(i) Effect of the ration (treatment) t_i ; i = 1, 2, …, k.

(ii) Error ε produced by numerous causes of such magnitude that they are not detected and identified with the knowledge that we have and they together produce a variation of random nature obeying Gaussian (Normal) law of errors.

Statistical Model: In this case the *linear* Statistical model will be

$$x_{ij} = \mu_i + \varepsilon_{ij}$$
$$= \mu + (\mu_i - \mu) + \varepsilon_{ij}$$
$$= \mu + \alpha_i + \varepsilon_{ij} \text{ ; where } (i = 1,2, \ldots k \text{ ; } j=1,2,\ldots,n_i)$$

(i) x_{ij} is the yield from the jth cow, (j=1,2,…n_i) fed on the ith ration (i = 1, 2,…,k),

(ii) μ is the general mean effect given by

$$\mu = \sum_{i=1}^{k} n_i \mu_i / N$$

Where μ_I is the fixed effect due to the ith ration, i.e., if there were no treatment differences and no chance causes then the yield of each cow will be μ

(iii) α_I is the effect of the ith ration given by

$\alpha_I = \mu_i - \mu$, (i=1,2,…,k)

i.e., the ith ration increases or decreases the yield by an amount α_I. then we get

$$\sum_{i=1}^{k} n_i \alpha_i = \sum_i n_i (\mu_i - \mu) = \sum_i n_i \mu_i - \mu \sum n_t$$

$$= N . \mu - \mu . N = 0$$

(iv) ε_{ij} is the error effect due to chance.

Assumptions in the Model

(i) All the observations x_{ij} are independent.

(ii) Different effects are additive in nature.

(iii) ε_{ij} are i.i.d N(O, σs^2)

Under the third assumption, the model (5.1) becomes:

$$E(xij) = \mu i = \mu + \alpha_i; \begin{pmatrix} i = 1, \ 2\ldots..,k \\ j = 1, \ 2,\ldots..n_i \end{pmatrix}$$

Hence the 'est statistic for H_0 is the provided by the variance ratio

$$F = \frac{S_t^2}{S_E^2}$$

If H_0 is true then F should take the value 1, otherwise it should be greater than unity. In order to find out if an observed value of F is significantly greater than unity, we have to obtain the sampling distribution of the statistic F.

Under H_0, by Cochran's theorem, $\frac{S_t^2}{\sigma_e^2}$ and $\frac{S_{E^2}}{\sigma_e^2}$ are independely distributed as χ^2 – variates with (k-1) and (N-k) d.f. respectively.

Hence the statistic

$$F = \left[\frac{St^2}{\sigma_e^2}\cdot\frac{1}{(k-1)}\right] \div \left[\frac{S_E^2}{\sigma_e^2}\cdot\frac{1}{(N-K)}\right] = \frac{s_{t^2}}{s_{E^2}}$$

Follows Snedecor's F (central) distribution with (k-1, N-k) d.f.

Thus, if an observed value of F obtained is greater than the tabulated value of F for (k-1, N-k) d.f. at specified level of significance, (usually 5% of 1%), then H_0 is refuted at that level otherwise it may be retained.

The above statistical analysis is very elegantly presented in the following table, known as the analysis of variance (ANOVA) table.

Anova Table for One Way Classified Data

Source of variation	*Sum of squares*	*d.f.*	*Mean Sum of Squares*	*Variance Ratio*
Treatment (Ration)	s_t^2	k - 1	$S_t^2 \quad \frac{S_t^2}{(k-1)}$	$\frac{S_{t^2}}{S_{E^2}} = F_{k-1, N-k}$
Error	s_E^2	N-k	$S_E^2 \quad \frac{S_E^2}{(N \quad k)}$	
Total	s_T^2	N-1		

Remark

1. We have seen above that although S_t^2 and S_E^2 add up to S_T^2 and the corresponding d.f. are also additive, their mean squares (i.e., variances), viz., s_t^2 and s_E^2 do not add up to total M.S.S. The technique, though known as ANOVA, is in fact the Analysis of the sum of squares.

2. For practical problems, the arithmetic for calculation of the various sum of squares is reduced to a great extent by using the following simplified formulae:

$$\text{Total S.S.} = \sum_i \sum_j \left(x_{ij} - \bar{x}..\right)^2 \frac{\left(\sum\sum x_{ij}\right)^2}{N}$$

$$= \sum_i \sum_j x_{ij^2} - \frac{G^2}{N}$$

where G is the grand total of all the observations and $N = n_1 + n_2 + \ldots + n_{k.}$ The expression $\Sigma\Sigma x_{ij}^2$ i.e., the sum of the squares of all the observations is known as Raw Sum of squares (R.S.S.) and the expression G^2/N is called the Correction Factor (C.F.)

$\therefore$ Total S.S = R.S.S – C.F.

Where T_i, is the total yield from the units receiving the ith treatment.

$$\text{Treatment S.S.} = \text{T.S.S} - \text{S.S.E} = \sum_i \left(\frac{T_i^2}{n_t}\right) - \frac{G^2}{N}$$

$$= \sum_i \left(\frac{T_i^2}{n_t}\right) - \text{C.E}$$

In numerical problems we calculate total sum of squares and treatment sum of squares by using (5.13) and (5.14) respectively and then within or error sum of squares is obtained by subtraction.

3. If the error mean sum of squares (SE^2) is greater than the M.S.S. of any factor of classification, then F is calculated by keeping SE^2 in the numerator.

4. In the ANOVA table, the values of the variance ratio F which are significant at the level significance, will be marked with one asterisk (*). Double star (**) will represent highly significant value.

5. Since variance is independent of change of origin, the shifting of origin to some arbitrary point, if necessary, also reduces arithmetic to a great extent. Finally, since e are to calculate variance ratio which is independent of change of scale also, the scale may be changed if possible. Hence the change of origin and scale facilitates calculations to a very great extent.

6. Critical Difference (C.D). If the treatment show significant effect then we would be interested to find out which pair (s) of treatments differ significantly. For this, instead of calculating Student's t for different pairs of treatment means, we calculate the Least significant difference at the given level of significance. This least difference is known as the critical difference (C.D.) and C.D at $\alpha\%$ level of significance is given by C.D.=S.E. of difference between two treatment means X$t_{\alpha}\%$ level of significance is given by C.D.= S.E. of difference between two treatment means X $t_{\alpha}\%$ for error d.f. we have:

$$\text{Var}\ \left(\overline{x}_i - \overline{x}_j\right) = \frac{\sigma_0^2}{n_i} + \frac{\sigma_0^2}{n_j} = \sigma_0^2\left(\frac{1}{n_i} + \frac{1}{n_j}\right)$$

$$\therefore\ \ \text{S.E}\left(\overline{x}_i - \overline{x}_j\right) = \sigma_e\left(\frac{1}{n_i} + \frac{1}{n_j}\right)^{1/2}$$

Hence

$$\text{C.D. for } (\left(\overline{x}_i - \overline{x}_j\right) = t_{\alpha\%} \text{ for error d.f. } S_E\left(\frac{1}{n_i} + \frac{1}{n_j}\right)^{\frac{1}{2}}$$

Since $S_E{}^2$ provides an unbiased estimate of σ_e^2.

11.3 Two – way Classification

Let us consider the case when there are two factors which may affect the variate values x_{ij}, e.g, the yield of milk may be affected by differences *in treatments, i.e., rations* as well as the differences is *variety, i.e.* breed and stock of the cows. Let us now suppose that the *N* cows are divided into *h different* groups containing *k* cows and then let us consider the effect of *k* treatments (i.e., rations given at random to cows in each group) on the yield of milk.

Let the suffix *i* refer to the treatments (rations) and suffix *j* refer to the varieties (breed of the cow). Then the yields of milk x_{ij}, (i = 1, 2, ... K; j = 1, 2, ..., h) of $N = h \times k$ cows furnish the data for the comparison of the treatments. The yields may be expressed as variate values in the

							Means	Totals
	x_{11}	x_{12}		x_{1j}	......	x_1k	$\bar{x}_{1.}$	$T_{1.}$
	x_{21}	x_{22}	......	x_{2j}	......	x_2k	$\bar{x}_{2.}$	$T_{2.}$
	⋮	⋮	......	⋮	......	⋮	⋮	⋮
	x_{i1}	x_{i2}	......	x_{ij}	......	x_ik	$\bar{x}_{i.}$	$T_{i.}$
	⋮	⋮	......	⋮	......	⋮	⋮	⋮
	x_{k1}	x_{k2}	......	x_{kj}	......	x_kk	$\bar{x}_{k.}$	$T_{k.}$
Means	$\bar{x}_{\cdot 1}$	$\bar{x}_{\cdot 2}$		$\bar{x}_{\cdot i}$		$\bar{x}_{\cdot k}$	$\bar{x}_{..}$	↓
Totals	$\bar{T}_{\cdot 1}$	$T_{\cdot 2}$		$T_{\cdot i}$		$T_{\cdot k}$		G

Statistical model : Let x_{ij} be the yield from the cow of j_{th} variety fed on the i_{th} ration (i = 1, 2,…, k; j = 1, 2, …h).

Let us suppose that x_{ij} (i = 1, 2, …., k; j = 1, 2, …, h) are independent, normally distributed as N (□$_{ij}$, □$^{□}$).

The linear mathematical model becomes

E(x_{ij}) = □$_{ij}$

x_{ij} = □$_{ij}$ + ε_{ij}

or x_{ij} = □$_{ij}$ + ε_{ij}

where ε_{ij} are i.i.d. $N(0, \sigma^2)$.

□$_{ij}$ is further split into the following parts:

(i) The general mean effect given by

$$\mu = \sum_i \sum_j \mu_{ij}/N$$

(ii) The effect (i – 1, 2, …., k) due to the ith ration given by

$$\alpha_i = \mu_i - \mu$$

Where $$\mu_i = \frac{1}{h}\sum_{j=1}^{h}\mu_{ij};\ (i = 1, 2, \ldots, k)$$

Obviously, $$\sum_{j=1}^{k}\alpha_i = 0$$

(iii) The effect β_i, (j = 1, 2, …., h) due to the jth variety (breed of cow) given by $\beta_i = \mu._j - \mu$

Where $$\mu_j = \frac{1}{k}\sum_{j=1}^{h} \mu_{ij};\ (j = 1, 2, \ldots, h)$$

Obviously, $$\sum_{i=1}^{h} \beta_i = 0$$

(iv) The interaction effect γ_{ij} when the ith level of first factor (rations) and j[th] level of second factor (breed of cow) occur simultaneously and given by

$$\gamma_{ij} = \mu_{ij} - \mu_{i}. - \mu._j + \mu$$

where $\sum_j \gamma_{ij} = 0,\ \forall\ i = 1, 2, \ldots, k$

and $\sum_i \gamma_{ij} = 0,\ \forall\ j = 1, 2, \ldots, h$

Thus we have

$$\mu_{ij} = \mu + (\mu._i - \mu) + (\mu._j - \mu) + (\mu_{ii} - \mu_i. - \mu_{.j} + \mu)$$

and consequently the model (5.16) becomes

$$x_{ij} = \mu + \alpha_i + \beta_i + \gamma_{ij} + \varepsilon_{ij}$$

where is the error effect due to chance and

$$\sum_{i=1}^{k} \alpha_i = 0 = \sum_{j=1}^{h} \beta_i$$

and $\sum_i \gamma_{ij} = \sum_j \gamma_{ij} = 0$

for all i for all j

As there is only one observation in each cell, the observation corresponding to the ith level of ration and j[th] level of breed of cow is only one i.e., x_{ij}. But we cannot estimate by one value alone. Hence in this case (one observation per cell), the interaction effect $\gamma_{ij} = 0$ and the model reduces to

$$x_{ij} = \mu + \alpha_i + \beta_i + \gamma_{ij} + \varepsilon_{ij}$$

The statistical analysis is very elegantly presented in the following ANOVA Table:

Anova Table For Two-way Classified Data

Sources of variation	Sum of squares (S.S)	d.f.	M.S.S	Variance Ratio
Treatments	$S_T^2 = \sum_i h(\bar{x}_i - \bar{x}.,)^2$	k–1	$S_{i^2} = \frac{Sv^2}{(h-1)}$	$Ft = \frac{St^2}{S_{E^2}}$ $\sim F_{(k\text{-}1,\ (n\text{-}1)\ (k\text{-}1)}$
Varieties	$S_V^2 = \sum_i h(\bar{x}_i - \bar{x}.,)^2$	h–1	$S_{v^2} = \frac{S_{v^2}}{(h-1)}$	$F_v = \frac{Sv^2}{SE^2}$ $\sim F_{(k\text{-}1,\ (n\text{-}1)\ (k\text{-}1)}$
Residual (or Error)	$SE^2 = \sum_{ij}\left(x_{ij} - \bar{x}.ij - \bar{x}._j + \bar{x}.\right)$	k–1		

Remark : For numerical computation f the various sums of squares the following formulae are used.

$$\text{Total sum of Squares (T.S.S.)} = \text{R.S.S. - C.F.} = \sum_i \sum_j x_{ij}^2 - \frac{G^2}{n}$$

$$\text{Treatment sum of squares} = \frac{1}{h}\sum_{i=1}^{k} T_i.^2 - \text{C.F.}$$

$$\text{Varieties sum of squares} = \frac{1}{k}\sum_{j=1}^{h} T._j^2 - \text{C.F.}$$

Error sum of squares, is then calculated by subtracting the total of treatment sum of squares and varieties sum of squares from the total sum of squares.

Exercise

1. What is "analysis of variance" and where it is used?
2. State the basic assumptions made in ANOVA.
3. Describe the techinique of the analysis of variance.
4. State the model used in in analysis of variance in a two-way classification. Discuss the advantages of this method over one-way classification, if any?

❑❑❑

Chapter – 12

Design of Experiments

12.1 Introduction

The design of the experiment includes (i) planning of the experiment (ii) obtaining the relevant information from it regarding the statistical hypothesis under study and (iii) making a statistical analysis of the data. Design of experiment may be defined as the logical construction of the experiment in which the degree of the uncertainty with which the inference is drawn may be well defined. It may also be redefined as the choice of treatments, the method of assigning treatments to experimental units and arrangement of experimental units in varies patterns to suit the requirement of particular problems, are combined known as the design of experiment.

12.2 Basic Concepts

Experiment : An experiment is a device of drawing information to the problem under consideration. Experiment may be classified into two categories as follows: (a) Absolute and (b) Comparative.

Absolute experiment consists in determining the absolute value of the characteristics under consideration. e.g., finding the correlation coefficient between two variables, where as comparative experiments are designed to compare the effect of two or more objects on some population characteristic. e.g., comparison of different varieties of crop, different cultivation processes different types of fertilizers.

Treatments : Various objects of comparisons in a comparative experiment are termed as treatments, e.g., in field experimentation different fertilizers or different varieties of crop.

Experimental Unit : The smallest division of the experimental material to which we apply the treatments. e.g., in the field experiment the plot of land is the termed as experimental unit.

Blocks : In agricultural experiments, most of the times we divide the whole experimental units in to relatively homogeneous sub-groups or strata. The strata which are uniform among themselves are known as blocks.

Yield : The measurement of the variable under study on different experimental units are termed as yields.

Experimental error : Let us suppose that a large homogeneous field is dived in to different plots (of equal size and shape) and different treatments are applied to these plots. If the yields from some of the treatments are more than those of others, the experimenter is faced with the problem of deciding if the observed differences are due to treatment effects or due to chance factors. The variations due to (i) the inherent variability in the experimental material to which treatments are applied, (ii) failure to standardise the experimental technique , and (iii) lack of representativeness of the sample to the population under study.

Uniformity trials enable to have an idea about the fertility variation of the field. By uniformity trial we mean a trial in which the field is divided into plots and same treatment is applied on each of the plots and their yields are recorded. From these yields, we can draw a fertility contour map accordingly the field can be divided into relatively homogeneous sub-groups to control the experimental error. Incidentally, uniformity trials also give us some idea about the shape and size of the plots

12.3 Basic Principles of Experimental Designs

The purpose of designing an experiment is to increase the precision of the experiment by reducing the experimental error. For reducing the experimental error one may adopt certain standard statistical techniques and these techniques are called the principles of experimental designs. According to Prof. Ronald A Fisher, the basic principles of the experimental designs are (i) Replication, (ii) Randomization and (iii) Local control or error control.

12.3.1 Replication

The repeated application of the treatments under investigation is known as *replication*. Thus, the repetition of treatments results in more reliable estimate than is possible with a single observation by estimating and minimizing experimental error.

Only with the help of experimental error one can determine whether observed differences between treatment means are real or not. We know that standard error of the mean is given by,

$$SE(Y) = \frac{s}{\sqrt{r}}$$

Where, s is the standard deviation and r is the number of observations (replication). That is, the standard error of the mean is proportional to the square root of the number of replications. Therefore, the number of replications is increased the experimental error will be reduced but, it can't be increased indefinitely. The number of replications required in an experiment depends on the factors cost, variability of the test material, the size of mean differences, the level of desired accuracy, and the error variance. Consequently replication has an important but limited role in increasing the efficiency of the design. Thus, functions of the replication are, (i) to provide an estimate of experimental error, and (ii) to reduce the experimental error. One can get the required number of replications by substituting this information in the formula,

$$t = \frac{d}{\sqrt{\frac{2s^2}{r}}}$$

Where,

t = table value of t for a given level of significance and degrees freedom,

d = the difference between the means of two treatments,

s^2 = error variance, and

r = number of replications (to be computed).

Then we have, $r = \frac{2t^2.s^2}{d^2}$

In practice it may not be possible to know s^2. Hence some approximate rules may be followed to fix the number of replications. A satisfactory precision can be obtained by taking the number of replications in such a way that the error degree of freedom is not less than 12.

12.3.2 Randomization

Replication will provide an estimate of estimate of experimental error. For valid conclusions about our experimental results, we should have not merely an estimate of experimental error but it should be an unbiased estimate. Also, if our conclusions are to be valid, the treatment means and also difference among treatment means should be estimated without any bias. For this purpose we use the technique of randomization. Randomization is the process of assigning the treatments to various plots in a purely random manner. More over the validity of the statistical tests of significance of the difference of two means depends on the fact that the statistic under consideration obeys some statistical distribution. Randomization provides a logical basis for that and makes it theory based on probability theory. Randomization eliminates bias in any form and it equalises even factors of variation over which we have no control. The actual procedure of randomization will vary from design to the design.

12.3.3 Error control

An estimate of the experimental error is based on the variations from experimental unit to experimental unit and is a measure of "within block" variation. This suggests that if we group the homogeneous experimental units into blocks, the experimental error into blocks is known as control of error.

Local control can be accomplished by uniformity trial, or by examination of the results of actual experiments. From the experimental results; it is possible to estimate through analysis of variance what the error variance would have been if any particular grouping had been done. Uniformity trials are costly and time consuming. Hence the second method is preferred over the uniformity trial. In order to have valid estimate of experimental error, the principles of replication and randomization are used. In order to reduce the experimental error, the principles of replication and local control are used.

There are another methods reducing error variance; one such method is called analysis of covariance for which observations on another variate called concomitant variate from each of the experimental units are used. It is, however, necessary that there is a linear relationship connecting the variate under study(Y) and the concomitant variate (X). By this method the portion of variability in Y which is due to the variation in X, is eliminated from the error variance. This method will also be discussed.

12.4 Size and Shape of Experimental Units

The size and shape of the experimental units will affect the accuracy of experimental results. The size of the plot depends on a number of factors such as the total experimental area available, the number of treatments, number of replication of each treatment, the crop and so on. If the total experimental area is fixed, then an increase in the size of the plot will results in decrease in the number of plots and consequently results in an increase in the size of the block and decrease in the number of blocks. While deciding about the number of plots it should also be kept in mind that an increase in the number of plots increases the non-experimental error. Therefore, we have to select a plot with optimum size for this purpose. The minimum size of an experiment plot for a given degree of precision is known as optimum plot size.

12.5 Completely Randomized Design

There are many types of experimental designs. They can be broadly classified as *single-factor experiments* and *multi-factor (factorial) experiments*. The single-factor experiments can be grouped as *complete block designs*. The treatments consists different levels of a single variable factor and all other factors are kept at a single prescribed level, it is known as a single factor experiment. For example, in fertilizer trials several rates of single fertilizer element, say nitrogen, may be tested. All other factors like agronomic practices, water management, insect and pest control, etc., are kept at a same level.

The completely randomized design is the simplest of all the designs , based on principles of randomization and replication.

12.5.1 Description of completely randomized design

In this design treatments are allocated at random to the experimental units over the entire experimental material. Thus the randomization gives every experimental unit in the experimental material an equal probability of receiving the treatment.

The CRD is appropriate only when the experimental material is homogenous. In field experiments there is generally large variation among experimental plots due to soil heterogeneity. Hence CRD is not preferred in field experiments. In laboratory experiments and greenhouse studies, it is easy to achieve homogeneity of experimental materials. Therefore, CRD is most useful in such experiments.

12.5.2 Advantages and disadvantages

CRD results in the maximum use of the experimental units since all the experimental material can be used without any wastage. The design is very flexible. It provides the maximum number of degrees of freedom for the estimation of experimental error. The statistical analysis of data from CRD is very simple. In some experiments it is possible that some units are likely to be destroyed or likely to fail to respond. Even when results are missing like this or rejected due to suspected quality, the analysis remains simple.

The disadvantage of CRD is that it is less accurate than other designs. When large numbers of treatments are included, a relatively large amount of experimental material must be used. Hence, the heterogeneity of experimental material will be increased. This will result in increased experimental error and reduced precision.

12.5.3 Layout of CRD

The arrangement of the treatments on the experimental units along with the arrangement of experimental units is known as the layout of an experiment.

Suppose that there are t treatments, namely, T_1, T_2,........,T_t. Further suppose that the treatments are replicated r times each. The entire experimental material is divided into n number of experimental units. The units are numbered serially starting with one end and proceeding in the same manner. For example, suppose that there are five treatments each with four replications. We need 20 experimental units. The 20 units are numbered as follows:

1	2	3	4	5
10	9	8	7	6
11	12	13	14	15
20	19	18	17	16

Then n distinct three-digit random numbers are selected from random number tables. Since the number of units will not be greater than two digits we take three-digit random numbers to avoid repetition of the same number.

The random numbers are written in order and are ranked. The lowest random number given rank 1, and the highest rank is alloted to the largest random number. These ranks correspond to the unit number. The first set of r units are allocated to treatment T_1, the next r units are allocated to treatment T_2, the next r units to treatment T_3, and so on. This procedure is continued until all treatments have been applied. For our example, the selected random numbers and their ranks are as follows:

Random number	Rank	Treatment to be applied
807	18	
186	4	T_1
410	10	
345	9	
626	14	
340	7	
883	19	T_2
569	13	
341	8	
094	2	
322	6	T_3
252	5	

Contd.

047	1	
469	12	
632	15	T_4
183	3	
417	11	
782	17	
969	20	T_5
697	16	

That is treatment 1 is applied to units 18,4,10 and 9; treatment 2 is applied to units 14,7,19 and 13 and so on. The final layout will be as follows:

1 T_4	2 T_3	3 T_4	4 T_1	5 T_3
10 T_1	9 T_1	8 T_3	7 T_2	6 T_3
11 T_5	12 T_4	13 T_2	14 T_2	15 T_4
20 T_5	19 T_2	18 T_1	17 T_5	16 T_5

12.5.4 Analysis and interpretation of results

The ANOVA model for CRD is given by

$$Y_{ij} = \mu + t_i + e_{ij}$$

The symbols have been explained in earlier sections. The sources of variation are, therefore, between treatments and within treatments' or 'experimental error'. The computational procedure is given below.

First, the observed results from a CRD are arranged as in Table 12.1

Table 12.1 : Arrangement of results for CRD

		Treatment			
1	2	3	...	T	
Y_{11}	Y_{21}	Y_{31}	...	Y_{t1}	
Y_{12}	Y_{22}	Y_{32}	...	Y_{t2}	
Y_{13}	Y_{23}	Y_{33}	...	Y_{t3}	
-	-	-	-	-	
-	-	-	-	-	
-	-	-	-	-	
-	-	-	-	-	
Total: T_1	T_2	T_3		T_t	GT
No. of replications: r_1	r_2	r_3		r_1	n

Then the homogeneity of variances is tested. If the variances are homogeneous proceed with the analysis. In case of heterogeneous variances, the data transformation has to be done and then only the analysis should be continued. Next, the required sums of squares are computed.

$$\text{Correction factor (CF)} = \frac{(GT)^2}{n}$$

$$\text{Total sum of squares (TSS)} = \left(Y_{11}^2 + Y_{12}^2 + \ldots\ldots + Y_{tr}^2\right) - CF$$

$$\text{Treatment sum of squares (TrSS)} = \left[\frac{T_1^2}{r_1} + \frac{T_2^2}{r_2} + \ldots + \frac{T_t^2}{r_t}\right] - CF$$

Error sum of squares (ESS) = TSS – TrSS

These results are summarised in the analysis of variance (ANOVA) table, and mean squares and F are computed, as given in table below.

Table 12.2 : Analysis of variance for CRD with *t* treatments

Sources of variation	*df*	*SS*	*MS*	*F*
Treatments	t-1	TrSS	$TMS = \frac{TSS}{t-1}$	$\frac{TMS}{EMS}$
Error	n-t	ESS	$EMS = \frac{ESS}{n-t}$	
Total	n-l	TSS		

For pair comparisons the CD value is computed as

CD = t. SE(d)

Where,

$$SE(d) = \sqrt{EMS\left(\frac{1}{r_i} + \frac{1}{r_j}\right)}$$

The treatment means are then calculated and arranged according to their ranks. Using the CD value, the bar chart is completed. The interpretation is written using this bar chart.

Example

An experiment was conducted on black gram using CRD with five varieties, V_1, V_2, V_3, V_4 and V_5 and 3, 4, 5, 4 and 4 replications, respectively. The results are presented in Table 12.3. The net plot size was 5.0 × 3.5 square metres.

Table 12.3 : Black gram yield, Kg per plot

v1	v2	v3	v4	v5
1.6	2.5	1.3	2.0	1.6
1.2	2.2	0.9	1.5	1.0
1.5	2.4	0.8	1.6	0.8
	1.9	1.1	1.4	0.9
		1.0		
Total:43	9.0	5.1	6.5	4.3
Mean:1.43	2.25	1.02	1.62	1.08
Variance:0.0433	0.0700	0.0370	0.0692	0.1292

$$\text{CF} = \frac{(29.2)^2}{20} = 42.6320.$$

$$\begin{aligned}\text{TSS} &= (1.6)^2 + (1.2)^2 + \ldots + (0.9)^2 - \text{CF} \\ &= 47.8400 - 42.6320 \\ &= 5.2080\end{aligned}$$

$$\begin{aligned}\text{Variety SS} &= \left[\frac{(4.3)^2}{3} + \frac{(9.0)^2}{4} + \frac{(5.1)^2}{4} + \frac{(6.5)^2}{4} + \frac{(4.3)^2}{4}\right] - \text{CF} \\ &= 46.8003 - 42.6320 = 4.1683\end{aligned}$$

$$\text{Error SS} = \text{TSS} - \text{Variety SS} = 5.2080 - 4.1683 = 1.0397$$

Table 12.4 : ANOVA for the data presented in Table 12.3

Sources of Variation	df	SS	MS	F
Variety	4	4.1683	1.0421	15.037**
Error	15	1.0397	0.0693	
Total	19	5.2080		

The standard error for the difference between the means of variety 1 and variety 2 is

$$\begin{aligned}\text{SE(d)} &= \sqrt{\text{EMS}\left(\frac{1}{r_1} + \frac{1}{r_2}\right)} \\ &= \sqrt{0.0693\left(\frac{1}{3} + \frac{1}{4}\right)} \\ &= \sqrt{0.040423} = 0.2011\end{aligned}$$

The table value of t for $\alpha = 0.05$ and 15 d.f. is 2.131. Hence,

CD = (2.131) (0.2011) = 0.4285.

Similarly, for other comparisons we have the following results:

Comparison between	SE(d)	CD
V_1 and V_3	$\sqrt{0.0693\left(\frac{1}{3}+\frac{1}{3}\right)} = 0.1992$	0.1096
V_1 and V_4 V_1 and V_5	$\sqrt{0.0693\left(\frac{1}{3}+\frac{1}{4}\right)} = 0.2011$	0.4285
V_2 and V_3 V_3 and V_4 V_3 and V_5	$\sqrt{0.0693\left(\frac{1}{4}+\frac{1}{5}\right)} = 0.1766$	0.3763
V_2 and V_4 V_2 and V_5	$\sqrt{0.0693\left(\frac{1}{4}+\frac{1}{4}\right)} = 0.1861$	0.3966

Comparison of the difference between the mean yields of the varieties with the corresponding CD values will result in the following bar chart:

V_2 $\quad$ $\overline{V_4 \quad V_1}$ $\quad$ $\underline{V_5 \quad V_3}$

Variety 2 gives significantly higher yield compared to all other varieties; variety 4 and variety 1 are on par and both of them give significantly higher yields than varieties 5 and 3; variety 5 and 3 are also on par.

12.5.5 Analysis of covariance for completely randomized design

There are another methods reducing error variance; one such method is called analysis of covariance for which observations on another variate called concomitant variate from each of the experimental units are used. It is, however, necessary that there is a linear relationship connecting the variate under study(Y) and the concomitant variate (X). By this method the portion of variability in Y which is due to the variation in X, is eliminated from the error variance. The following is the ANCOVA for CRD with one concomitant variable.

The completely randomized design consists of t treatments, the ith treatment having r_i replications. There will be $\Sigma ri = n$ observations in total. The data arrangement is given in the below.

Data Arrangement for CRD

	Treatment							
	1		2			t		
	Y	X	Y	X	……	Y	X	
	Y_{11}	X_{11}	Y_{21}	X_{21}	……	Yt_1	Xt_1	
	Y_{12}	X_{12}	Y_{22}	X_{21}	……	Yt_2	Xt_2	
	Y_{13}	X_{13}	Y_{23}	X_{23}	……	Yt_3	Xt_3	
	-	-	-	-		-	-	
	-	-	-	-		-	-	
	-	-	-	-		-	-	Grand
	-	-	-	-		-	-	Total
Total	T_{y1}	T_{x1}	T_{x2}	T_{x2}	…..	T_{y1}	T_{x1}	GT_yGT_x

The linear model of covariance for CRD is

$$Y_{ij} = \mu + t_i + b\left(X_{ij} - \overline{X}\right) - e_{ij}$$

Where, the symbols have the usual meaning.

The first step in the analysis of covariance is to compute the sum of squares for the variance (Y) and the covariate (X) as well as the sum of products for Y and X. The sum of squares for both Y and X are computed in the usual manner for a CRD. The sum of products (SP) of Y and X is computed as follows:

$$CF = \frac{(GT_Y)\ (GT_x)}{n}$$

$$\text{Total SP} = G_{yx} = \Sigma\Sigma Y_{ij}.X_{ij} - CF$$

$$\text{Treatment SP} = T_{yx} = \Sigma \frac{T_{yi} \cdot T_{xi}}{r_i} - CF$$

$$\text{Error SP} = E_{yx} = G_{yx} - T_{yx}$$

The next step is to verify whether the covariate is affected by the treatments. If X is not affected by the treatments there should not be significant difference between treatments with reference to X.

Then the regression co-efficient within treatments is computed as

$$b = \frac{E_{yx}}{E_{xx}}$$

The significance of b is tested using the F-test. The test statistic F is given by

$$F = \frac{\text{Mean square of b}}{\text{Adjusted error mean square}}$$

$$= \frac{\left[\frac{E_{yx}^2}{E_{xx}} / 1\right]}{\left[\left\{E_{yy} - \frac{E_{yx}^2}{E_{xx}}\right\} / (n-t-1)\right]}$$

The F follows a F-distribution with a and(n - t - 1)df.

If the regression co-efficient is significant we proceed to make adjustments for the variate. If it is not significant, it is not worthwhile to make the adjustments.

The adjusted values for the variable Y are then computed as follows.

$$G_{yy}^t = G_{yy} - \frac{(G_{yx})^2}{G_{xx}}$$

$$E_{yy}^t = E_{yy} - \frac{(E_{yx})^2}{E_{xx}}$$

$$T_{yy}^t = G_{yy}^t - E_{yy}^i$$

One degree of freedom is lost in error due to fitting a regression line.

Conventionally the above results are combined and given in a single table as in Table 12.6.

Sources of Variation	**df**	**Sum of Products**		**Adjusted Values for Y**				
		YY	**XX**	**YX**	*df*	**SS**	**MS**	**F**
Total	n - 1	G_{yy}	G_{xx}	G_{yx}	n - 2	G_{yy}^1	-	-
Treatments	t - 1	T_{yy}	T_{xx}	T_{yx}	-	-	-	-
Error	n - 1	E_{yy}	E_{xx}	E_{yx}	n - t - 1	E_{yy}^1	EMS	-
Treatment adjusted for the average regression within treatments					t - 1	T_{yy}^1	TMS	$\frac{TMS}{EMS}$

The adjusted treatment means are obtained from the formula,

$$\overline{Y}_i^1 = \overline{Y}_i - b\left(\overline{X}_i - \overline{X}\right)$$

The standard error for the difference between two adjusted means is given by:

$$SE(d) = \sqrt{EMS\left[\frac{1}{r_i} + \frac{1}{r_j} + \frac{\left(\overline{X}_i - \overline{X}_j\right)^2}{E_{xx}}\right]}$$

Where, the symbols have the usual meanings.

The SE(d) depends upon the magnitude overall values of $\left(\overline{X}_i - \overline{X}_j\right)^2$. When the number of replications is same for all the treatments and when averaged over all values of $\left(\overline{X}_i - \overline{X}_j\right)^2$ we get

$$SE(d) = \sqrt{\frac{2EMS}{r}\left[1 + \frac{T_{xx}}{(t-1)E_{xx}}\right]}$$

12.6. Randomized Block Design

In field experimentation, if the whole of the experimental area is not homogeneous and fertility gradient is only in one direction, then a simple method of controlling the variability of the experimental material consists in grouping the whole area into relatively homogeneous sub-group or blocks perpendicular to the direction of the fertility gradient. Now if the treatments are applied at random to the relatively homogeneous units within each block and replicated over all the blocks, the design is a Randomised Block design (RBD).

In some experiments certain operations like spraying of insecticides may not be completed for the whole experiment in one day. Further, climatic factors like rainfall may influence the effects of the insecticide. Hence a set of treatment may be applied on the same day. In such cases a day forms a block. In animal experiments animals of same age or litter or weight may form blocks.

12.6.1 Description of randomized block design

Suppose the experimental material is divided into *r* block. Let there be t treatments. Each block is then divided into t units and the treatments are allocated within a block at random. The resulting design is called randomized block design.

12.6.2 Advantages and disadvantages

The advantage of RBD is that it increases the precision of the experiment. This is due to the reduction of experimental error by adoption of local control.

The amount of information got in RBD is more as compared to CRD. Hence, RBD is more efficient than CRD.

Flexibility is another advantage of RBD. Any number of replications can be included in RBD.

The statistical analysis is simple and easy. Even when some observations are missing for certain treatments, the data can be analysed by the use of missing-plot technique.

When the number of treatments is increased, the block size will increase. If the block size is large it may be difficult to maintain homogeneity within blocks. Consequently, the experimental error will be increased. Hence, RBD may not be suitable for large number of treatments. It is the most frequently used design in agricultural experiments.

12.6.3 Layout of RBD

The entire experimental material is divided into number of homogeneous blocks. If there are t treatments each block is divided into t units. The units in each block are numbered from 1 to t. The treatments are also numbered conveniently.

By using random number tables, we select t distinct random numbers from 1 to t. These random numbers correspond to the treatment numbers. The first selected treatment is allotted to the first unit of a block, the second selected treatment to the second units, and so on. The randomization is done afresh for each block in the same way.

12.6.4 Analysis and Interpretation of RBD Results

The results from RBD experiment can be arranged in two-way tables according to the replications (blocks) and treatments. There will be *rt* observations and the arrangements are given in Table12.5.

Table 12.5 : Arrangement of data from RBD

Treatment	**Replication**					**Total**
	1	**2**	**3**	**.......**	**r**	
1.	Y_{11}	Y_{12}	Y_{13}	....	Y_{1r}	T_1
2.	Y_{21}	Y_{22}	Y_{23}	....	Y_{2r}	T_2
3.	Y_{31}	Y_{32}	Y_{33}	....	Y_{3r}	T_3
-	-	-	-	....	-	-
t	Y_{t1}	Y_{t2}	Y_{t3}	....	Y_{tr}	T_t
Total	R_1	R_2	R_3	......	R_r	G.T.

The analysis of variance model for RBD is given by

$$Y_{ij} = \mu + t_i + r_j + e_{ij}$$

where, μ = the overall mean,

t = the ith treatment effect,

rj = the jth replication effect, and

e_{ij} = the error term.

The total variance is thus divided into three sources of variation, viz., between replications, between treatments and error. The required sums of squares are obtained as follows:

$$CF = \frac{(GT)^2}{rt}$$

$$TSS = \sum Y_{ij}^2 - CF$$

$$\text{Replication SS} = \frac{1}{t}\sum R_j^2 - CF$$

$$\text{Treatment SS} = \frac{1}{r}\sum T_j^2 - CF$$

Error SS = TSS - Replication SS - treatment SS

With these results the analysis of variance table is completed. The form of ANOVA table for RBD with t treatments and r replications each is given in Table 12.6.

Table 12.6 : Analysis of variance for RBD

Sources of Variation	Df	SS	MS	F
Replication	r-1	RSS	RMS	RMS/EMS
Treatment	t -1	TrSS	TMS	TMS/EMS
Error	(r-1) (t-1)	ESS	EMS	
Total	rt-1	TSS		

If by F-test we find significant difference between treatments, than we can use critical difference (CD) for comparing pairs of treatments. Such differences can also be tested by Duncan's multiple range test. The CD is given by

$$CD = t \,.\, E(d)$$

Where, t = table value of t for a specified level of significance and error degrees of freedom.

$$SE\ (d) = \sqrt{\frac{2EMS}{r}}$$

Based on the CD value the bar chart can be drawn. Using the bar chart conclusions can be written.

Example

An experiment was conducted in RBD to study the comparative performance of five varieties. The rearranged data are given in Table 12.7.

Table 12.7 :

Variety	Replication				Total	Mean
	I	II	III	IV		
V1	22.9	25.9	39.1	33.9	121.8	30.4
V2	29.5	30.4	35.3	29.6	124.8	31.2
V3	28.8	24.4	32.1	28.6	113.9	28.5
V4	47.0	40.9	42.8	32.1	162.8	40.7
V5	28.9	20.4	21.1	31.8	102.2	25.6
Total	157.1	142.0	170.4	156.0	625.5	31.3

$$CF = \frac{(625.5)^2}{20} = 19562.5125$$

$$TSS = [(22.9)^2 + (29.5)^2 + \ldots\ldots + (31.8)^2] - CF$$

$$= 20514.95 - 19562.5125 = 952.4375$$

$$\text{Replication SS} = \frac{1}{5}\,(157.1)^2 + (156.0)^2$$

$$= 19643.3140 - \text{CF} = 80.8015$$

$$\text{Variety SS} = \frac{1}{4}\,[(121.8)^2 + (102.2)^2] - \text{CF}$$

$$= 20083.0425 - \text{CF} = 520.5300$$

Error SS = Total SS – Rep. SS – Variety SS = 351.1060

Table 12.8 : Analysis of variance for the data

Sources of Variation	*Df*	SS	MS	F
Replication	3	80.8015	26.9338	<1
Variety	4	520.5300	130.1325	4.448*
Error	12	351.1060	29.2588	
Total	19	952.4375		

$$\text{SE (d)} = \sqrt{\frac{2\text{EMS}}{r}} = \sqrt{\frac{2(29.2588)}{4}}$$

$$= \sqrt{14.6294} = 3.8248$$

$$\text{CD} = t.\text{SE(d)}$$

$$= (2.179)\,(3.8248) = 8.33$$

$$\text{CV} = \frac{s}{\mu} \times 100 = \frac{5.41}{31.28} \times 100 = 17.3\%$$

V_4 $\quad$ $\overline{V_2 \quad V_1 \quad V_3 \quad V_5}$

From the bar chart it can be concluded that sorghum variety V_4 produces significantly higher green matter than all other varieties. The remaining varieties are all on par.

12.6.5 Missing plot technique in RBD

With a single missing value in RBD with t treatments and r replications each, the first step is to estimate the missing value by using the formula.

$$X = \frac{rR' + tT' - G'}{(r-1)(t-1)}$$

where,

X = estimate of the missing value

R^i = total of available values of the replication that contains the missing value

T^i = total of available values of the treatment that contains the missing value

G^i = grand total of all available values

The degree of freedom for error is corrected by subtracting 1 from the actual d.f.

For comparing the mean of the treatment with a missing value and the mean of any other treatment, the standard error formula is given by

$$SE(d) = \sqrt{\frac{2EMS}{r}\left[1 + \frac{t_{xx}}{(r-1)(t-1)}\right]}$$

When there are two or more missing values all but one missing value is estimated roughly as the average of the replication mean and treatment mean corresponding to the missing value. The left out missing value is estimated by using the formula for one missing value. After inserting this value, the other values are estimated one by one using the formula. The completion of estimates for all the missing value constitutes one cycle. A second approximation is then found for all the missing value in succession. After the completion of the second cycle, the estimates from the first and the second cycles are compared. If they are equal or approximately equal the iteration process of estimation is stopped, otherwise, the process is continued.

The analysis is then carried out as usual. A separate analysis is done as RBD with the available data and with estimated values of the missing values. The error *df* is corrected by subtracting the number of missing values from the actual one.

In case of two or more missing values one more SE(d) has to be computed for comparing the means of the treatments involving missing values. It is given by

$$SE(d) = \sqrt{EMS\left[\frac{1}{r_i} + \frac{1}{r_j}\right]}$$

Example

Consider the data in Table 12.9 suppose that the value for treatment 2 is missing in replication III. The data will then be as presented in the table below.

Table 12.9 : RBD data with one missing value

Variety	Replication				Total
	I	II	III	IV	
1	22.9	25.9	39.1	33.9	121.8
2	29.5	30.4	X	29.6	89.5
3	28.8	24.4	32.1	28.6	113.9
4	47.0	40.9	42.8	32.1	162.8
5	28.9	20.4	21.1	31.8	102.2
Total	157.1	142.0	135.1	156.0	590.2

The estimate of missing value,

$$X = \frac{rR^1 + tT^1 - G^1}{(r-1)(t-1)}$$

$$= \frac{4(135.1) + 5(89.5) - 590.2}{(3)(4)}$$

$$= \frac{397.7}{12} = 33.1$$

After substituting the estimated missing value, we get

Treatment 2 total = 89.5 + 33.1 = 122.6,

Replication 3 total = 135.1 + 33.1 = 168.2, and

The grand total = 590.2 + 33.1 = 623.3.

Treatment SS =

$$\frac{1}{4}\left[(121.8)^2 + (122.6)^2 + (113.9)^2 + (162.8)^2 + (102.2)^2\right] - \frac{(623.3)^2}{20}$$

$$= 19946.9725 - 19425.1445 = 521.8280$$

Corrected treatment SS = 521.8280 – 0.3645 = 521.4635

Table 12.10 : Analysis of Variance

Sources of Variation	*df*	SS	MS	F
Replication	3	69.1855	23.0618	< 1
Treatment	4	521.4635	130.3659	4.117*
Error	11	348.3120	31.6647	
Total	18	938.9610		

SE(d) for comparing means of treatment not involving missing values

$$= \sqrt{\frac{2(31.6647)}{4}} = 3.9790$$

SE(d) for comparing means of the treatment involving missing value with any other treatment

$$= \sqrt{\frac{31.6647}{4}\left[2 + \frac{5}{3 \times 4}\right]}$$

$$= \sqrt{19.1310} = 4.3739$$

Example

An experiment was conducted in RBD to compare the yield of seven varieties with two missing observations and is given in the following table. Analysis the data and comment the result.

Tabel 12.11 :

Variety	Replication			Total
	I	II	III	
1	14.5	14.0	14.0	42.5
2	16.5	16.9	16.7	50.1
3	X	16.7	17.4	34.1
4	17.6	16.9	17.5	52.0
5	18.5	17.9	17.6	54.0
6	19.3	18.3	18.8	56.4
7	19.5	19.0	X	38.5
Total	105.9	119.7	102.0	327.6

In the above data the value for variety 3 in replication I and for variety 7 in replication III are missing. Let them be denoted by X_{31} and X_{73}, respectively.

They are estimated as follows:

First Cycle estimates:

$$X_{31} = \left[\frac{105.9}{6} + \frac{34.1}{2}\right] / 2$$

$$= \frac{17.65 + 17.05}{2} = 17.4$$

$$G^{l} = 327.6 + 17.4 = 345.0$$

$$X_{73} = \frac{rR^{l} + tT^{l} - G^{l}}{(r-1)(t-1)} = \left[\frac{rR^{l} + tT^{l}}{(r-1)(t-1)} - \frac{G^{l}}{(r-1)(t-1)}\right]$$

$$= \left[= \frac{3(102.0) + 7(38.5)}{2\times 6} - \frac{345.0}{2\times 6}\right]$$

$$= \left[= \frac{575.5}{12} - \frac{345.0}{12}\right]$$

$$= 47.96 - 28.75 = 19.2$$

Second cycle estimates:

Substituting the value of X, we get

$$G^{l} = 327.6 + 19.2 = 346.8$$

$$X_{31} = \frac{3(105.9) + 7(34.1)}{12} - \frac{346.8}{12}$$

$$= 46.37 - 28.90 - 17.5$$

$$G^{l} = 327.6 + 17.5 = 345.8$$

$$X_{31} = 47.96 - \frac{345.1}{12}$$

$$= 19.2$$

The values in the two cycles are nearly same. Hence, we take the estimates $X_{31} = 17.5$, and $X_{73} = 19.2$ for further analysis. The replication, treatment and grand totals are then corrected with these values.

$T_3 = 34.1 + 17.5 = 51.6$

$T_7 = 38.5 + 19.5 = 57.7$

Replication I = 105.9 + 17.5 = 123.4

Replication II = 102.5 + 19.2 = 121.2

Grand Total = 327.6 + 17.5 + 19.2 = 364.3

With these values we get,

CF = 6319.7376

Total SS = 6371.65 – CF = 51.9124

Replication SS = 6320.7271 – CF = 0.9895

Treatment SS = 6369.69 – CF = 49.9524

Error SS = 0.9705

Ignoring the treatment classification and analyzing the results in Table 12.12 as CRD, we get

CF = 5648.5137

Total SS = 48.2463

Replication SS = 5650.005 – CF

= 1.4913

Error SS = 46.755

The corrected treatment sum of squares is given as

TSS = ESS for CRD – ESS for RBD

= 46.7550 – 0.9705 = 45.7845

Corrected error d.*f.* = 12 – 2 = 10.

These results are presented in the following table.

Table 12.12 : Analysis of Variance

Sources of Variation	*df*	SS	MS	F
Replication	2	0.9895	0.4948	5.101
Treatment	6	45.7845	7.6308	78.668**
Error	10	0.9705	0.0970	
Total	18	47.7445		

SE(d) for comparing means of treatment not involving missing values is given by

$$= \sqrt{\frac{2\text{EMS}}{r}} = \sqrt{\frac{2(0.0970)}{3}} = 0.2543$$

SE(d) for comparing means of the treatment involving missing value with any other treatment is given by

$$-\sqrt{\frac{EMS}{r}\left[2+\frac{t}{(r-1)(t-1)}\right]}$$

$$-\sqrt{\frac{0.0970}{3}\left[2+\frac{7}{12}\right]}$$

$= 0.2890$

CD = (2.228) (0.2890) = 0.6439

For comparing the means of treatment 3 and 7

$$SE(d) = \sqrt{EMS\left[\frac{1}{r_3}+\frac{1}{r_7}\right]}$$

where, r_3 = effective number of replications for treatment 3

= 0 + 1 + 5/6 = 11/6

r_7 = effective number of replications for treatment 7.

= 5/6 + 1 + 0 = 11/6

Hence,

$$SE(d) = \sqrt{(0.0970)(6/11+6/11)}$$

= 0.3253

CD = (2.228) (0.3253) = 0.7248

The Mean values are

T_1 = 14.2, T_2 = 16.7, T_3 = 17.2, T_4 = 17.3, T_5 = 18.0, T_6 = 18.8 and T_7 = 19.2

on the basis of the above result, we conclude that the varieties T7 and T6 are the best and on par. Then T5 is next whereas the other treatments T1, T2 and T3 are on par and low yield varieties.

12.6.6 Analysis of covariance for RBD

The linear model for the analysis of covariance analysis for RBD is

$$Y_{ij} = \mu + t_i + r_j + b\left(X_{ij} - \overline{X}\right) + e_{ij}$$

where, the symbols have the usual meaning.

The procedure of covariance analysis for RBD is similar to that for CRD. The analysis of covariance for RBD is given in Table 12.13.

Table 12.13 : Analysis of Covariance for RBD

Sources of Variation	*df*	Sum of Products			Adjusted values for Y		
		YY	XX	YX	*df*	SS	MS
Total	n - 1	G_{yy}	G_{xx}	G_{yx}			
Replication	r - 1	R_{yy}	R_{xx}	R_{yx}			
Treatment	t - 1	T_{yy}	T_{xx}	T_{yx}			
Error	(r - 1) (t - 1)	E_{yy}	E_{xx}	E_{yx}	(r - 1) (t - 1) - 1	E^1_{yy}	EMS
Treatment + Error	r (t - 1)	T_{yy} E_{yy}	T_{xx} E_{xx}	T_{yx} E_{yx}	r (t - 1) - 1	$(T_{yy} + E_{yy})^1$	-
Treatment adjusted for the average regression within treatments.					t - 1	T^1_{yy}	TMS

$$E^1_{yy} = E_{yy} - \frac{(E_{yx})^2}{E_{xx}}$$

$$(T_{yy} + E_{yy})^1 = (T_{yy} + E_{yy}) - \frac{(T_{yx} + E_{yx})^2}{(T_{xx} + E_{xx})}$$

$$T^1_{yy} = (T_{yy} + E_{yy})^1 E^1_{yy}$$

The adjusted treatment means and SE(d) are found by using the formulae given for analysis of covariance for CRD.

An experiment of fertilizer on paddy was conducted in RBD. The yield was the primary variable, Y. The height of the crop was the covariate, X. The results are presented in Table 12.14.

Table 12.14 : Yield, kg per plot and number of productive

Treatment	Replication								Total	
	I		II		III		IV			
	Y	X	Y	X	Y	X	Y	X	Y	X
Control	7.0	5.1	6.4	5.5	8.0	5.0	6.9	5.5	28.3	21.1
AN_1	10.8	6.5	9.0	6.3	10.5	6.7	9.6	6.5	39.9	26.0
AN_2	13.0	7.6	12.6	7.6	12.0	7.3	13.0	8.6	50.6	31.1
AN_3	15.0	8.5	14.8	8.9	14.0	9.5	14.0	9.5	57.8	36.4
AN_4	14.8	10.4	15.0	9.5	13.0	9.7	14.1	10.1	56.9	39.7
UN_1	9.9	6.3	10.5	6.4	9.0	6.3	9.6	6.2	39.0	25.2
UN_2	13.1	7.5	11.9	7.1	12.9	7.8	12.5	7.9	50.4	30.3
UN_3	14.4	8.1	14.2	9.5	13.5	9.5	14.1	8.8	56.2	35.9
UN_4	15.0	9.2	14.8	10.1	13.8	10.4	12.8	9.9	56.4	39.6
Total	113.0	69.2	109.2	70.9	106.7	72.2	106.6	73.0	435.5	285.3

Analysis for Y:

$$CF = \frac{(435.5)^2}{36} = 5268.3403$$

$$TSS = G_{yy} = (7.0)^2 + (100.8)^2 + \ldots + (12.8)^2 - CF = 227.6097$$

$$\text{Replication SS} = R_{yy} = \frac{1}{9}\left[(113.0)^2 + (109.2)^2 + (106.6)^2 + (106.6)^2\right] - CF$$

$$= 3.0030$$

$$\text{Treatment SS} = T_{yy} = \frac{1}{4}\left[(28.3)^2 + (39.9)^2 + \ldots.. + (56.4)^2\right] - CF$$

$$= 214.7272$$

$$\text{Error SS} = E_{yy} = 9.8795$$

Analysis for X:

$$CF = \frac{(285.3)^2}{36} = 2261.0025$$

$$\text{Total SS} = Gxx = [(5.2)^2 + (6.5)^2 + \ldots + (9.9)^2] - CF$$

$$= 93.8875$$

$$\text{Replication SS} = R_{xx} = \frac{1}{9}\left[(113.0)^2 + (109.2)^2 + (106.7)^2 + (106.6)^2\right] - CF$$

$$= 0.9186$$

$$\text{Treatment SS} = T_{xx} = \frac{1}{4}\left[(21.1)^2 + (26.0)^2 + \cdots + (39.6)^2\right] - CF$$

$$= 88.8900$$

$$\text{Error SS} = E_{xx} = 4.0789$$

Analysis for Y and X:

$$CF = \frac{(435.5)(285.3)}{36} = 3451.3375$$

Total sum of products = Total SP = G_{yx}

$$= [(7.0)(5.1)+(10.8)(6.5)+\ldots++(12.8)(9.9)] - CF$$

$$= 3582.1000 - 3451.3374 = 130.7625$$

$$\text{Replication SP} = R_{YX} = \frac{1}{9}\left[(7.0)(5.1) + (10.0)(6.5)+\ldots.+(12.8)(9.9)\right] - CF$$

$$= 3449.7133 - CF = 1.6242$$

$$\text{Treatment SP} = T_{YX}\frac{1}{4}[(113.0)(69.2) + (109.2)(70.9)+\ldots.+(106.6)(73.0)] - CF$$

$$= 3582.9950 - CF = 1.6242$$

$$\text{Error SP} = E_{yx} = 0.7292$$

For the covariance X,

$$TMS = 88.8900/8 = 11.1112$$

$$EMS = 4.0789/24 = 0.1700$$

$$F = \frac{11.1112}{0.1700} = 65.36$$

Since F is significant at 1% level of significance, we conclude that the covariate is also affected by the treatments. The final conclusion has to be drawn keeping this in view.

$$b = \frac{E_{yx}}{E_{xx}} = \frac{0.7292}{4.0789} = 0.1788$$

$$F\ (\text{for } b) = \left[\frac{E_{yx}^{x}}{E_{xx}} / 1\right] + \left[\left\{E_{yy} - \frac{E_{yx}^{x}}{E_{xx}}\right\} / (r-1)(t-1) - 1\right]$$

$$\frac{E_{yx}^{x}}{E_{xx}} = \frac{(0.7292)^2}{4.0789} = 1.3036$$

$$E_{yy} - \frac{E_{yx}^{x}}{E_{xx}} = 9.8795 - 1.3036 = 8.5759$$

$(r - 1)(t - 1) - 1 = 24 - 1 = 23$

Hence,

$F = (1.3036/1) + (8.5759/23) = 1.3036/0.3729 = 3.496$

For 1 and 23 *df* and $\alpha = 0.05$, the table value of F is 4.28. In this case F is not significant and hence b is not significant. Since b is not significant, the effect covariate in reducing the error will not be significant.

Table 12.15 : Analysis of covariance

Sources of Variation	Sum of Products				Adjusted values for Y			
	df	YY	XX	YX	df	SS	MS	F
Total	35	227.6097	93.8875	130.7625	-			
Replication	3	3..0030	0.9186	-1.6242	-			
Treatment	8	214.7272	88.8900	.131.6575	-			
Error	24	9.8795	4.0789	0.7292	23	8.5759	0.3729	
Treatment + Error	32	224.6067	92.9689	132.3867	-	-	-	
Treatment adjusted for the average regression within treatments.					8	27.5136	3.4392	9.223**

Treatment	$\overline{Y}_i$	$\overline{X}_i$	$b(\overline{X}_i - \overline{X}) = 0.17$	$\overline{Y}_i = \left[\overline{Y}_i - b(\overline{X}_i - \overline{X})\right]$
1	7.08	5.28	-0.4738	7.55
2	9.98	6.50	-0.2557	10.24
3	12.65	7.78	-0.0268	12.68
4	14.45	9.10	0.2092	14.24
5	14.42	9.92	0.3558	14.06
6	9.75	6.30	-0.2914	10.04
7	12.60	7.58	-0.0626	12.66
8	14.05	8.98	0.1877	13.86
9	14.10	9.90	0.3522	13.75

$$E_{yy}^{1} = E_{yy} - \frac{E_{yx}^{x}}{E_{xx}} = 9.8795 - \frac{(0.7292)^2}{4.0789} = 8.5759$$

$$\left(T_{yy}+E_{yy}\right)^{1}=\left(T_{yy}+E_{yy}\right)-\left[\left(T_{yx}+E_{yx}^{2}\right)/\left(T_{xx}+E_{xx}\right)\right]$$

$$= \quad 224.6067-\frac{(132.3867)^{2}}{92.9689}$$

$$= \quad 36.0895$$

$$T_{yy}^{1}\left(T_{yy}+E_{yy}\right)^{1}-E_{yy}^{1}$$

$$= \quad 36.0895 - 8.5759 = 27.5136$$

Computation of adjusted treatment means :

$$SE(d) \quad = \quad \sqrt{\frac{2EMS}{r}\left[1+\frac{T_{xx}}{(-1)E_{xx}}\right]}$$

$$= \quad \sqrt{\frac{2.(0.3729)}{4}\left[1+\frac{88.8900}{8(4.0789)}\right]}$$

$$= \quad \sqrt{(0.18645)(3.7241)}$$

$$= \quad 0.8333$$

$$CD \quad = \quad (2.069)\ (0.8333) = 1.724$$

12.7 Latin Square Design

Randomized block design is an improvement over completely randomized design because it provides error control measures for the elimination of block variation. In some experiments there may be two sources of variation. For example, in agricultural fields the fertility gradient may run in two directions – north to south and east to west directions. In such cases blocking in one direction as done in RBD will not be sufficient to achieve error control. The field has to be divided into rows and columns to have two-directional blocking. This will reduce the experimental error considerably. The opportunity for such reduction in experimental error is provided by the Latin square design. Thus the Latin square design is an improvement over RBD.

The usage of the terms rows and columns is only customary. In practice rows may represent the levels of one factor and the columns the levels of another factor that contribute to the variation in the responses of experimental units.

12.7.1 Description of latin square design

In this design the number of treatments is equal to the number of replications. The whole experimental area is divided into squared number of plots arranged in a square so that each row and each column contains equal number of plots. When the experimental material is divided into rows and columns, and the treatments are allocated such that each treatment occurs only once in a row and once in a column, the design is known as *latin square design* (LSD). Hence the arrangement will form a square. It is identified as 5x5 latin squares, 6x6 latin squares, etc., according to the number of rows and columns. In LSD each row and each column is a complete block or replication.

12.7.2 Advantages and disadvantages of LSD

With two-way grouping, the experimental error is small for LSD compared to that of CRD and RBD. Hence LSD is more efficient than CRD and RBD. Missing observations can be analysed by using missing plot technique as in RBD.

The disadvantage of LSD is that it is not flexible as RBD. In LSD, the number of treatments is limited to the number of rows and columns. With the increase in size of square the experimental error is likely to increase. Hence LSD is seldom used more than 12 treatments since in that case the square becomes too large and does not remain homogeneous.

12.7.3 Layout of LSD

In LSD the treatments are usually denoted by alphabets like A,B,C, etc. For a latin square with five treatments the arrangement may be as follows:

A	B	C	D	E
B	A	E	C	D
C	D	A	E	B
D	E	B	A	C
E	C	D	B	A

Square 1

A	B	C	D	E
B	A	D	E	C
C	E	A	B	D
D	C	E	A	B
E	D	B	C	A

Square 2

A	B	C	D	E
B	C	D	E	A
C	D	E	A	B
D	E	A	B	C
E	A	B	C	D

Square 3

These squares are said to be standard squares. A standard square is one in which the first row and first column are ordered alphabetically. Two standard squares are said to be conjugate squares when the rows of one square are the columns of the other square. It can be seen that the squares 1 and 2 are conjugate squares. A standard square is said to be self-conjugate if its arrangement remains same when its rows and columns are interchanged. Square 3 given above is a self conjugate square.

The layout of LSD starts with dividing the experimental material into number of rows and columns depending on the number of treatments. A t ´ t standard square is then selected. The standard squares may be selected from Fisher and Yates (1953) statistical tables. The columns of the selected standard square are rearranged randomly by using random number tables. Then, keeping the first row of the rearranged square as such, the remaining rows are randomized. The treatments are then allocated as in the final arrangement.

An example of layout of 5x5 Latin square will help in understanding the layout of LSD. For 5 x 5 latin square, there are 56 possible standard squares. In Fisher and Yates tables they are given as 25 pairs of standard squares plus 6 separate standard squares. The first 25 squares are assigned pairs of numbers like (1,2), (3,4) and so on. The first number indicates the standard square and the second number indicates the conjugate of the square. Thus we can get 50 standard squares from the given 25 squares.

As a first step a random number between 1 and 56 (both numbers inclusive) is selected using random number tables. If the selected random number is 50 or below see whether it is odd or even. If it is odd, the standard square with that number is taken as such. If the number is even, the conjugate of the standard square with that number is written. If the number is between 51 and 56 the corresponding standard square is selected.

Suppose the selected random number is 48. The standard square corresponding to this number is.

A	B	C	D	E
B	E	A	C	D
C	D	B	E	A
D	C	E	A	B
E	A	D	B	C

The conjugate of this square is,

A	B	C	D	E
B	E	D	C	A
C	A	B	E	D
D	C	E	A	B
E	D	A	B	C

In the second step the columns of the square are randomized, for this purpose a set of five single digit random numbers from 1 to 5 are selected. The random numbers may be 5,1,3,2,4. They represent the column numbers and their random order. That is, the original column 5 will be column 1 in the rearrangement; column 1 will be column 2 and so on. Thus the randomization will result in the square;

E	A	C	B	D
A	B	D	E	C
D	C	B	A	E
B	D	E	C	A
C	E	A	D	B

In the next step the rows of the square got in the second step are randomized, keeping the first row as such, for this, select a set of four single digit random numbers from 2 to 5. The random numbers may be 4,2,5,3. This indicates that row 4 should be placed after row 1, row 2 next, and so on. Thus, we have the square

E	A	C	B	D
B	D	E	C	A
A	B	D	E	C
C	E	A	D	B
D	C	B	A	E

This is the final layout of 5 × 5 LSD. The treatments are allocated as given in the layout.

12.7.4 Analysis and interpretation of LSD results

The analysis of variance model for LSD is

$$Y_{ijk} = \mu + r_i + c_j + t_k + e_{ijk}$$

Where, r_i = i^{th} row effect

C_j = j^{th} column effect

t_k = k^{th} treatment effect.

And other notations have usual meaning.

The results of LSD will be in the form of two-way tables according to rows and columns. The results have to be arranged according to treatments also. Let R_i be the ith row total, C_j be the jth column total, T_k be the kth treatment total, and G.T. be the grand total. The different sums of squares for t x t LSD can be obtained as follows:

$$CF = \frac{(G.T)^2}{t^2}$$

$$\text{Total SS} = \sum y_{ijk}^2 - CF$$

$$\text{Row SS} = \frac{1}{t}\sum R_i^2 - CF$$

$$\text{Column SS} = \frac{1}{t}\sum C_j^2 - CF$$

$$\text{Treatment SS} = \frac{1}{t}\sum T_k^2 - CF$$

Error SS = Total SS - Row SS - Column SS - Treatment SS these results can be summarized in the form of analysis of variance table (12.16).

Table 12.16 : Analysis of variance for t x t LSD

Sources of variation	df	ss	MS	F
Rows	t-1	RSS	RMS	RMS /EMS
Columns	t-1	CSS	CMS	CMS/EMS
Treatments	t-1	TSS	TMS	TMS/EMS
Error	(t-1) (t-2)	ESS	EMS	
Total	R^2-1	Total SS		

If F is not significant for treatments, we can conclude that the treatment effects do not differ significantly among themselves. If F is significant, the significance of any treatment contrast can be tested by using the CD value in the same way as discussed for RRD. The CD is given by

$$CD = t \,.\, SE(d)$$

Where, t – table value of t for a specified level of significance and error d.f.

$$SE(d) = \sqrt{\frac{2EMS}{r}}$$

Where, r = number of rows.

Example

An experiment was conducted on five paddy varieties (A,B,C, D and E), an experiment was laid out in a 5 x 5 latin square design. The results are given in Table 12.17. Analysis the data and comment the result.

Table 12.17 : Yield of paddy, kg/plot

D 39.0	A 24.1	E 26.1	B 37.0	C 42.2	Total 168.4
E 21.2	B 33.5	A 24.0	C 39.3	D 33.1	155.7
C 35.6	E 33.5	B 38.1	D 40.8	A 24.2	172.2
A 30.8	C 31.1	D 46.7	E 28.7	B 44.9	182.2
B 44.3	D 29.6	C 41.1	A 26.3	E 24.4	165.7
Total 170.9	156.4	176.0	172.1	168.8	844.2

The treatment wise arrangement of the result is as follows:

	A	B	C	D	E
	24.1	37.0	42.2	39.0	26.1
	24.0	38.1	39.3	33.1	21.2
	24.2	38.1	35.6	40.8	33.5
	30.8	44.9	31.1	46.7	28.7
	26.3	44.3	41.1	29.6	24.4
Total	129.4	202.4	189.3	189.2	133.9
Mean	25.88	40.48	37.86	37.84	26.78

$$CF = \frac{(844.2)^2}{25} = 28506.95$$

$$\text{Total SS} = \left[(39.0)^2 + (24.1)^2 + ... + (24.4)^2\right] - CF$$

$$= 29892.86 - 28506.95 = 1385.91$$

$$\text{Row SS} = \left(\frac{1}{5}(168.4)^2 + (155.7)^2 + ...(165.7)^2\right) - CF$$

$= 28581.44 - 285\text{-}6.95 = 74.49$

$$\text{Column SS} = \left(\frac{1}{5}(170.9)^2 + (156.4)^2 + ...(168.8)^2\right) - \text{CF}$$

$= 28551.12 - 28506.95 = 44.17$

$$\text{Variety SS} = \left(\frac{1}{5}(129.4)^2 + (202.4)^2 + ...(133.9)^2\right) - \text{CF}$$

$= 29454.09 - 28506.96 = 947.14$

Error SS = 1385.91 – 74.49 – 44.17 – 947.14 = 320.09

Table 12.18 : Analysis of variance

Sources of variation	df	SS	MS	F
Rows	4	74.49	18.62	<1
Columns	4	44.17	11.04	<1
Varieties	4	947.14	236.78	8.87**
Error	12	320.09	26.66	
Total	24	1385.91		

The treatments differ significantly

$$SE(d) = \sqrt{\frac{2(26.66)}{5}} = 3.263$$

The table value of t for $\alpha = 0.05$ and 12 d.f. is 2.179, Hence

CD = (2.179) (3.263) = 7.11

12.7.5 Missing plot technique in LSD

The method of analysis of data from LSD with missing value is similar to that for missing data analysis in RBD. In case of LSD a single missing value is estimated by using the formula.

$$X = \frac{t.(R^1 + C^1 + T^1) - 2G^1}{(t-1)(t-2)}$$

where,

R′ = total of available values of the row containing the missing value,

C′ = total of available values of the column containing the missing value,

T′ = total of available values of the treatment containing the missing value,

t = number of treatments, and

G′ = grand total of all available values

The upward bias in the treatment sum of squares is computed by using the formula.

$$SE(d) = \sqrt{\frac{EMS}{r}\left[2 + \frac{t}{(t-1)(t-2)}\right]}$$

In case of two or more missing values of estimation is done similar to that of missing plot technique in RBD.

For correcting the treatment sum of squares, the missing values are estimated as in the case of RBD ignoring the treatment classification. The error sum of squares for RBD is then obtained from the completed data. The corrected treatment sum of squares is obtained as

TSS (Corrected) = ESS(RBD) – ESS (LSD)

The standard error for comparing the means of treatments with missing values is given by

$$SE(d) = \sqrt{EMS\left[\frac{1}{r_i} + \frac{1}{r_j}\right]}$$

where, r_i = the effective number of replications for treatment i with missing value,

r_j = the effective number of replications for treatment j with missing value,

Example

The data in Table 12.19 is the yield of paddy from a varietals trail in 5 × 5 latin square design with five varieties of paddy. The yield of variety C is missing and is given by (X). Estimate the missing value and carryout the analysis.

Table 12.19 : Yield of paddy, kg/plot.

E 26	C 42	D 39	B 37	A 24	Total 168
A 24	D 33	E 21	C (X)	B 38	116
D 47	B 45	A 31	E 29	C 31	183
B 38	A 24	C 36	D 41	E 34	173
C 41	E 24	B 44	A 26	D 30	165
Total 176	168	171	133	157	805

The estimate of missing value is

$$X = \frac{t.\left(R^1 + C^1 + T^1\right) - 2G^1}{(t-1)(t-2)}$$

$$= \frac{5(116 + 133 + 150) - 2(805)}{(5-1)(5-2)}$$

$$= \frac{385}{12} = 32$$

On substitution of the estimated value we get the corrected total as follows:

Total of second row = 148

Total of fourth column = 165

Total of treatment C = 182

Grand total = 837

CF = 28022.76

Total SS	= 29399.00 – CF = 1376.24
Row SS	= 28154.00 – CF = 131.44
Column SS	= 28063.00 – CF = 40.24
Treatment SS	= 28925.00 – CF = 902.24
Error SS	= 302.32.

Table 12.20 : Analysis of Variance

Sources of Variation	D*f*	SS	MS	F
Row	4	131.44	32.8600	1.196
Column	4	40.24	10.0600	<1
Treatment	4	888.80	222.2000	8.085
Error	11	302.32	27.4836	
Total	23	1362.80		

SE(d) for comparing means of treatments without involving missing value is

$$SE(d) = \sqrt{\frac{2(27.4836)}{5}} = 3.3156$$

CD = (2.201) (3.3156) = 7.2976

SE(d) for comparing the mean of treatment C with other treatments not involving missing value is

$$SE(d) = \sqrt{\frac{EMS}{r}\left[2 + \frac{1}{(t-1)(t-2)}\right]}$$

$$= \sqrt{\frac{27.4836}{5}\left[2 + \frac{5}{(5-1)(5-2)}\right]}$$

$$= \sqrt{5.49672(2+0.4167)}$$

$$= \sqrt{13.2839} = 3.6447$$

CD = (2.201) (3.6447) = 8.0220

The bar chart is given as

$\overline{\text{B D C}}$ $\quad$ $\underline{\text{E A}}$

Example

Consider the data given in Table 12.21 with two missing observations and they are denoted by (X), one in treatment B and another in treatment C.

Table 12.21 : Yield of paddy, kg/plot.

E 26	C 42	D 39	B 37	A 24	Total 168
A 24	D 33	E 21	C (X)	B 38	116
D 47	B 45	A 31	E 29	C 31	183
B 38	A 24	C 36	D 41	E 34	173
C 41	E 24	B (X)	A 26	D 30	121
Total 176	168	127	133	157	761

The treatment totals are

A = 129, B=158, C= 150, D= 190, E= 134

The means for second row and fourth column in which C is missing are $\frac{116}{4} = 29.0$ and $\frac{133}{4} = 33.25$ respectively. Hence the first estimate for C is

$$C_1 = \frac{29.00 + 33.25}{2} = 31.12$$

$$G^1 = 761 + 31.12 = 792.12$$

$$B_1 = \frac{t.\left(R^1 + C^1 + T^1\right) - 2G^1}{(t-1)(t-2)}$$

$$= \frac{5(121 + 127 + 158) - 2(792.12)}{(5-1)(5-2)}$$

$$= \frac{2030}{12} - \frac{1584.24}{12}$$

$$= 169.17 - 132.02 = 37.15$$

$$G^1 = 761 + 37.15 = 798.15$$

$$C_1 = \frac{5(116 + 133 + 150) - 2(798.15)}{12}$$

$$= \frac{1995}{12} - \frac{1596.3}{12}$$

$$= 166.25 - 133.03 = 33.22$$

$$G^l = 761 + 33.22 = 794.22$$

$$B_2 = 169.17 - \frac{2(794.22)}{12}$$

$$= 36{,}8$$

For the third cycle, we have

$$G^l = 761 + 36.8 = 797.8$$

$$C_3 = 166.25 - \frac{2(797.8)}{12}$$

$$= 33.3$$

$$G^i = 761 + 33.22 = 794.3$$

$$B_3 = 169.17 - \frac{2(794.3)}{12}$$

$$= 36{,}8$$

It can be seen that the estimated values for B are same and that for C are very close. Hence we stop the iteration process at third cycle. The final estimates for B and C for the missing plots are 36.8 and 33.3, respectively.

The column total, row, total, etc., with respect to the missing plots are modified by adding the estimated values. Thus we have,

Treatment B total	=	158 + 36.8 = 194.8
Treatment C total	=	150 + 33.3 = 183.3
Second row total	=	116 + 33.3 = 149.3
First row total	=	121 + 36.8 = 157.8
Third column total	=	127 + 36.8 = 163.8
Fourth column total	=	133 + 33.3 = 166.3
Grand Total	=	761 + 36.8 + 33.3 = 831.1

The data is then analysed in the usual manner.

$$CF = \frac{(831.1)^2}{25} = 27629.0884$$

Total SS = 28902.130 – CF = 1273.0416

Row SS = 27766.666 – CF = 137.5776

Column SS = 27667.026 – CF = 37.9376

Treatment SS = 28448.586 – CF = 819.4976

Error SS = 278.0288

The final results are presented in the following table.

Table 12.22 Analysis of Variance

Sources of Variation	Df	SS	MS	F
Row	4	137.5776	34.3944	1.237
Column	4	37.9376	9.4844	<1
Treatment	4	753.5568	188.3892	6.776
Error	10	278.0288	27.8029	
Total	22	1273.0416		

SE(d) for comparison of the means of treatments not involving missing value is

$$SE(d) = \sqrt{\frac{2(27.8029)}{5}} = 3.3348$$

$$CD = (2.228)\ (3.3348) = 7.4299$$

SE(d) for the comparison of the mean of treatments with missing values and that of other treatment is

$$SE(d) = \sqrt{\frac{27.8029}{5}\left[2+\frac{5}{(5-1)(5-2)}\right]}$$

$$= \sqrt{13.4371} = 3.6657$$

$$CD = (2.228)\ (3.6657) = 8.1672$$

The effective number of replications for treatment B and C are $3\frac{1}{3}$ and 3 1/3 respectively. Hence the SE(d) for comparing the means of B and C is

$$SE(d) = \sqrt{EMS\left[\frac{1}{r_i}+\frac{1}{r_j}\right]}$$

$$= \sqrt{27.8029\left[\frac{3}{10}+\frac{3}{10}\right]} = 4.0843$$

$$CD = (2.228)\ (4.0843) = 9.0998$$

Inferences can be drawn as usual.

12.7.6 Analysis of covariance for LSD

The linear model for the covariance analysis for Latin square design is given by

$$Y_{ijk} = \mu + r_i + C_j + t_k + b(X_{ijk} - \overline{X}) + e_{ijk}$$

Where, the symbols have the usual meaning. The analysis of covariance for a t × t latin square design is given in Table 12.23.

Table 12.23 : Analysis of covariance for LSD

Sources of Variation	*df*	Sum of Products			Adjusted values for Y		
		YY	XX	YX	D*f*	SS	MS
Total	t – 1	R_{yy}	R_{xx}	R_{yx}	-	-	-
Replication	t – 1	C_{yy}	C_{xx}	C_{yx}	-	-	-
Treatment	t – 1	T_{yy}	T_{xx}	T_{yx}	-	-	-
Error	(r – 1) (t – 1)	E_{yy}	E_{xx}	E_{yx}	(r - 1) (t - 1) - 1	E^1_{yy}	EMS
Treatment + Error	(r – 1) + (t – 1) (r – 1)	T_{yy} + E_{yy} E_{yy}	T_{xx} + E_{xx}	T_{yx} + E_{yx}-			
Treatment adjusted for the average regression within treatments.					t - 1	T^1_{yy}	TMS

$$E^1_{yy} = E_{yy} - \frac{(E_{yx})^2}{E_{xx}}$$

$$(T_{yy} + E_{yy})^1 = (T_{yy} + E_{yy}) - \frac{(T_{yx} + E_{yx})^2}{(T_{xx} + E_{xx})}$$

$$T^1_{yy} = (T_{yy} + E_{yy})^1 E^1_{yy}$$

The adjusted treatment means and SE(d) are computed by using the formulae given for CRD.

Exercise

1. What do you understand by "Design of Experiment" and explain the need of the design of the experiment.
2. Explain the principles of the Design of Experiment.
3. Discuss how the efficiency of an experiment can be increased by increased replication and local control.
4. Give the complete statistical analysis of CRD.
5. What is meant by a randomised block design?
6. Discuss the advantages and disadvantages of RBD.
7. Explain the method of analysing the results of a RBD.
8. Explain the procedure of obtaining the estimate of one missing observation in RBD.
9. What is LSD? Under what conditions can this design be used?
10. Discusses briefly the advantages and disadvantages of LDS.
11. Give the layout and analysis of LSD.
12. Explain why the number of treatments tested in a LSD should not be less than 3.

❑❑❑

Chapter – 13

Multiple Comparison Tests

In many situations, experiments may not known in advance which contrasts they wish to compare, or they may be interested in more than (m – 1) possible comparisons. In many exploratory experiments, the comparisons of interest are fixed only after preliminary examinations of the data.

13.1 Scheffe's Method for Comparing All Contrasts

Scheffe (1953) has proposed a method for comparing any all possible contrasts between treatment means. In the Scheffe method, the type I error is at most α for any of the possible comparisons.

Suppose that a set of m contrasts in the treatment means

$$\Gamma_u = c_{1u}\mu_1 + c_{2u}\mu_2 + \cdots + c_{au}\mu_a \quad u = 1,2,\cdots,m$$

of interest have been determined. The corresponding contrast in the treatment averages $\overline{y}_i$, is,

$$C_u = c_{1u}\overline{y}_1 + c_{2u}\overline{y}_2 + \ldots\ldots\ldots + c_{au}\overline{y}_a \quad u = 1, 2, \ldots\ldots\ldots, m$$

and the standard error of this contrast is

$$S_{C_u} = \sqrt{MS_E \sum_{i=1}^{a} \left(c_{iu}^2 / n_i\right)}$$

Where n_i is the number of observations in the ith treatment. The critical value against which C_u should be compared is

$$S_{\alpha,u} = S_{C_u}\sqrt{(a-1)F_{\alpha,a-1,M-a}}$$

To test the hypothesis that the contrast Γ_u differs significantly from zero, refer C_u to the critical value. If $|Cu| > S_{a,u}$, the hypothesis that the contrast Γ_u equals zero is rejected.

The Scheffe procedure can also be used to form confidence intervals for all possible contrasts among treatment means. The resulting intervals, say $C_u - S_{\alpha,u} \leq \Gamma_u \leq C_u + S_{\alpha,u,}$ are simultaneous confidence intervals in that the probability is at least $1 - \alpha$ that all of them are simultaneously true.

The illustrate the procedure, consider the contrast of interest are

$\Gamma_1 = \mu_1 + \mu_3 - \mu_4 - \mu_5$ and $\Gamma_2 = \mu_1 - \mu_4$

The numerical values of these contrasts are

$$C_1 = \bar{y}_1 + \bar{y}_3 - \bar{y}_4 - \bar{y}_5$$

$$= 9.80 + 17.60 - 21.60 - 10.80$$

$$= 5.00 \text{ and}$$

$$C_2 = \bar{y}_1 - \bar{y}_4$$

$$= 9.80 - 21.60 \qquad = -11.80$$

and the standard errors are

$$S_{C_u} = \sqrt{MS_E \sum_{i=1}^{a} \left(C_{i1}^2 / n_i\right)} = \sqrt{8.06((1+1+1+1)/5)} = 2.54$$

and

$$S_{C_u} = \sqrt{MS_E \sum_{i=1}^{a} \left(C_{i2}^2 / n_i\right)} = \sqrt{8.06(1+1)/5} = 2.54$$

Therefore the 1 percent critical values are

$$S_{0,\,01.1} = S_{C_1}\sqrt{(a-1)F_{0.01,,a-1,N-a}} = 2.54\sqrt{4(4.43)} = 10.69$$

and

$$S_{0,\,01.2} = S_{C_2}\sqrt{(a-1)F_{0.01,,a-1,N-a}} = 1.80\sqrt{4(4.43)} = 7.58$$

Because $|C_1| < S_{0,01.1}$, we conclude that the contrast $\Gamma_1 = \mu_1 + \mu_3 - \mu_4 - \mu_5$ equals zero that is, there is no strong evidence to conclude that the means of treatments 1 and 3 as a group differ from the means of treatments 4 and 5 as a group. However, because $|C_2| < S_{0,01.2}$, we conclude that the contrast $\Gamma_2 = \mu_1 - \mu_4$ does not equal zero; that is, the mean strengths of treatments 1 and 4 differ significantly.

In many practical situations, we wish to compare only pairs of means. Frequently, we can determine which means differ by testing the differences between all pairs of treatment means. Thus, we are interested in contrasts of the form $\Gamma = \mu_i - \mu_j$ for all $i \neq j$. Although the Scheffe method could be easily applied to this problem, it is not the most sensitive procedure for such comparisons.

Comparing Pairs of Treatment Means

Suppose that we are interested in comparing all pairs of a treatment means and the null hypotheses that we wish to test are H_0:: $\mu_i = \mu_j$ for all $i \neq j$. We now present four methods for making such comparisons.

13.2 Tukey's Test

Suppose that, following an analysis of variance in which we have rejected the null hypothesis of equal treatment means, we wish to test all pair wise mean comparisons.

H_0: $\mu_i = \mu_j$

H1: $\mu_i \neq \mu_j$

for all $i \neq j$. Tukey (1953) proposed a procedure for testing hypothesis for which the overall significance level is exactly α when the sample sizes are equal and at most α when the sample sizes are unequal. His procedure can also be used to contrast confidence intervals on the differences in all pairs of means. For these intervals, the simultaneous confidence level is 100 $(1 - \alpha)$ percent when the sample sizes are unequal. This is an excellent data snooping procedure when interest focuses on pairs of means.

Tukey's procedure makes use of the distribution of the studentized range statistic.

$$q = \frac{\overline{y}_{max} - \overline{y}_{min}}{\sqrt{MS_E / n}}$$

Where $\overline{y}_{max} - \overline{y}_{min}$ are the largest and smallest sample means, respectively, out of a group of p sample means. For equal sample sizes, Tukey's test declares two means significantly different it the absolute value of their sample differences exceeds

$$T_{\alpha} = q_{\alpha}(a,f)\sqrt{\frac{MS_E}{n}}$$

Equivalently, we could construct a set of 100(1 – α) percent confidence intervals for all pairs of means as follows:

$$\overline{y}_i - \overline{y}_j = q_{\alpha}(a,f)\sqrt{\frac{MS_E}{n}} \le \mu_i - \mu_j$$

$$\le \overline{y}_i - \overline{y}_j = q_{\alpha}(a,f)\sqrt{\frac{MS_E}{n}} \le i \ne j$$

When sample sizes are not equal, Equations 1.5 and 1.6 become

$$T_{\alpha} = \frac{q_{\alpha}(a,f)}{\sqrt{2}}\sqrt{MS_E\left(\frac{1}{n_i}+\frac{1}{n_j}\right)}$$

and

$$\overline{y}_i - \overline{y}_j - \frac{q_{\alpha}(a,f)}{\sqrt{2}}\sqrt{MS_E\left(\frac{1}{n_i}+\frac{1}{n_j}\right)} \le \mu_i - \mu_j$$

$$\le \overline{y}_i - \overline{y}_j - \frac{q_{\alpha}(a,f)}{\sqrt{2}}\sqrt{MS_E\left(\frac{1}{n_i}+\frac{1}{n_j}\right)} i \ne j$$

respectively. The unequal sample size version is sometimes called the Tukey – Kramer procedure.

Example

To illustrate Tukey's test, we use the old results. With a = 0.05 and $f = 20$ degrees of freedom for error, table gives $q_{0.05}(5,20) = 4.23$. Therefore,

$$T_{0.05} = q_{0.05}(5.20)\sqrt{\frac{MS_E}{n}} = 4.23\sqrt{\frac{8.06}{5}} = 5.37$$

$\overline{y}_1$	$\overline{y}_5$	$\overline{y}_2$	$\overline{y}_3$	$\overline{y}_4$
9.8	10.8	15.4	17.6	21.6

Results of Tukey's test

Thus, any pair of treatment averages that differ in absolute value by more than 5.37 would imply that the corresponding pair of population means is significantly different. The five treatment averages are

$\bar{y}_1 = 9.8 \quad \bar{y}_2 = 15.4 \quad \bar{y}_3 = 17.6 \quad \bar{y}_4 = 21.6 \quad \bar{y}_5 = 10.8$

and the differences in averages are

$\bar{y}_1 - \bar{y}_2 = 9.8 - 15.4 = -5.6^*$
$\bar{y}_1 - \bar{y}_3 = 9.8 - 17.6 = -7.8^*$
$\bar{y}_1 - \bar{y}_4 = 9.8 - 21.6 = -11.8^*$
$\bar{y}_1 - \bar{y}_5 = 9.8 - 10.8 = -1.0$
$\bar{y}_2 - \bar{y}_3 = 15.4 - 17.6 = -2.2$
$\bar{y}_2 - \bar{y}_4 = 15.4 - 21.6 = -6.2^*$
$\bar{y}_2 - \bar{y}_5 = 15.4 - 10.8 = 4.6$
$\bar{y}_3 - \bar{y}_4 = 17.6 - 21.6 = -4.0$
$\bar{y}_3 - \bar{y}_5 = 17.6 - 10.8 = 6.8^*$
$\bar{y}_4 - \bar{y}_5 = 21.6 - 10.8 = 10.8^*$

The starred values indicate pairs of means that are significantly different. Underlining pairs of means that do not differ significantly. When using any procedure for pair wise testing of means we occasionally find that the overall F test from the analysis of variance is significant, but the pair wise comparison of means fails to reveal any significant differences. The situation occurs because the F test is simultaneously considering all possible contrasts involving the treatment means, not just pair wise comparisons. That is, in the data at hand, the significant contrasts may not be of the form $\mu_i - \mu_j$.

For the student zed range statistic q we have

$$P\left(\frac{\max(\bar{y} - \mu_i) - \min(\bar{y}_i - \mu_i)}{\sqrt{MS_E} / n} \le q_\alpha(a, f)\right) = 1 - \alpha$$

If is max $(\bar{y}_i - \mu_i) -$ min $(\bar{y}_i - \mu_i)$ less than or equal to q_α (a, *f*) $\sqrt{MS_E / n}$, it must be true that $\left|(\bar{y}_i - \mu_i) - (\bar{y}_i - \mu_i)\right| \le q_\alpha$ (a, *f*) $\sqrt{MS_E / n}$, for every pair of means. Therefore

$$P\ P\left(-q_\alpha(a,f)\sqrt{\frac{MS_E}{n}} \leq (\bar{y}_i - \bar{y}_j) - (\mu_i - \mu_j) \leq q_\alpha(a,f)\sqrt{\frac{MS_E}{n}}\right) = 1 - \alpha$$

Rearranging this expression to isolate $\mu_i - \mu_j$ between the inequalities will lead to the set of 100 (1 – α) percent simultaneous confidence intervals.

13.3 The Fisher Least Significant Difference (LSD) Method

This procedure uses the F statistic for testing H_0: $\mu_i - \mu_j$

$$t_0 = \frac{\bar{y}_i - \bar{y}_i}{\sqrt{MS_E\left(\frac{1}{n_i} + \frac{1}{n_j}\right)}}$$

Assuming a two – sided alternative, the pair of means μ_i and μ_j would be declared significantly different if $|\bar{y}_i - \bar{y}_j| > t_{a/2,N-a}\sqrt{MS_E(1/n_i + 1/n_j)}$. The quantity

$$LSD = t_{\alpha/2,N-a}\sqrt{MS_E\left(\frac{1}{n_i} + \frac{1}{n_j}\right)}$$

is called the least significant difference. If the design is balanced then $n_1 = n_2 = \ldots = n_a = n$, and

$$LSD = t_{\alpha/2,N-a}\sqrt{\frac{2MS_E}{n}}$$

To use the Fisher LSD procedure, we simply compare the observed difference between each pair of averages to the corresponding LSD.

To illustrate the procedure, if we use the pervious data from the experiment in the LSD at α = 0.005 is

$$LSD = t_{.025.20}\sqrt{\frac{2MS_E}{n}} = 2.086\sqrt{\frac{2(8.06)}{5}} = 3.75$$

Thus, any pair of treatment averages that differ in absolute value by more than 3.75 would imply that the corresponding pair of population means are significantly different. The differences in averages are

$\overline{y}_1 - \overline{y}_2 = 9.8 - 15.4 = -5.6*$
$\overline{y}_1 - \overline{y}_3 = 9.8 - 17.6 = -7.8*$
$\overline{y}_1 - \overline{y}_4 = 9.8 - 21.6 = -11.8*$
$\overline{y}_1 - \overline{y}_5 = 9.8 - 10.8 = -1.0$
$\overline{y}_2 - \overline{y}_3 = 15.4 - 17.6 = -2.2$
$\overline{y}_2 - \overline{y}_4 = 15.4 - 21.6 = -6.2*$
$\overline{y}_2 - \overline{y}_5 = 15.4 - 10.8 = 4.6$
$\overline{y}_3 - \overline{y}_4 = 17.6 - 21.6 = -4.0$
$\overline{y}_3 - \overline{y}_5 = 17.6 - 10.8 = 6.8*$
$\overline{y}_4 - \overline{y}_5 = 21.6 - 10.8 = 10.8*$

$\overline{y}_1$	$\overline{y}_5$	$\overline{y}_2$	$\overline{y}_3$	$\overline{y}_4$
9.8	10.8	15.4	17.6	21.6

Results of the LSD procedure

The starred values indicate pairs of means that are significantly different. Clearly, the only pairs of means that do not differ significantly are 1 and 5 and 2 and 3, and treatment 4 produces a significantly greater than the other treatments.

13.4 Duncan's Multiple Range Test (DMRT)

A widely used procedure for comparing all pairs of means is the multiple range test developed by Duncan (1955). To apply Duncan's multiple range test for equal sample sizes, the a treatment averages are arranged in ascending order, and the standard error of each average is determined as

$$S_{\overline{y}_i} = \sqrt{\frac{MS_E}{n}}$$

For unequal sample sizes, replace n by the harmonic mean n_h of the (n_i), where

$$n_h = \frac{a}{\sum_{i=1}^{a}(1/n_i)}$$

if $n_1 = n_2 = \ldots = n_a$, $n_h = n$. From Duncan's table of significant ranges, obtain the values $r_\alpha(p, f)S_{\overline{y}_i}$ p = 2, 3, ..., a where α is the significance level and f is the number of degrees of freedom for error. Convert these ranges into a set of (a – 1) least significant ranges (e.g. R_p) for p = 2,3,…, a by calculating

$$R_p = r_\alpha(p, f)S_{\bar{y}_i} \quad p = 2, 3, \ldots\ldots, a$$

Then, the observed differences between means are tested, beginning with largest versus smallest, which would be compared with the least significant range R. Next, the difference of the largest and the second-smallest is computed and compared with the least significant range $R_{\alpha-1}$. These comparisons are continued until all means have been compared with the largest mean. Finally, the difference between the second-largest mean and the smallest is computed and compared against the least significant range $R_{\alpha-1}$. This process is continued until the differences between all possible a(a – 1)/2 pairs of means have been considered. If an observed difference is greater than the corresponding least significant range, we conclude that the pair of means in question is significantly different. To prevent contradictions, no differences between a pair of means are considered significant if the two means involved fall between two other mean that do not differ- significantly.

We can apply Duncan's multiple range test. If $MS_E = 8.06$, N = 25, n = 5, and there are 20 error degrees of freedom. Ranking the treatment averages is ascending order, we have

$\bar{y}_1 = 9.8$

$\bar{y}_2 = 10.8$

$\bar{y}_3 = 15.4$

$\bar{y}_4 = 21.6$

$\bar{y}_5 = 10.8$

The standard error of each average is $S_{\bar{y}_i} = \sqrt{8.06/5} = 1.27$. From the table of significant for 20 degrees of freedom and α = 0.05, we obtain $r_{0.05}(2, 20)$ = 2.25, $r_{0.05}(3, 20)$ = 3.10, $r_{0.05}(4, 20)$ = 3.18, and $r_{0.05}(5, 20)$ = 3.25. Thus the least significant ranges are

$$R_2 = r_{0.05}(2,\ 20)\ S_{\bar{y}_i} = (2.95)(1.27) = 3.75$$
$$R_3 = r_{0.05}(3,\ 20)\ S_{\bar{y}_i} = (3.10)(1.27) = 3.94$$
$$R_4 = r_{0.05}(2,\ 20)\ S_{\bar{y}_i} = (3.18)(1.27) = 4.14$$
$$R_5 = r_{0.05}(5,\ 20)\ S_{\bar{y}_i} = (3.25)(1.27) = 4.13$$

The comparisons would yield

4 vs. 1: 21.6 – 9.8 = 11.8 > 4.13(R_5)

4 vs. 5: 21.6 – 10.8 = 10.8 > 4.04(R_4)

4 vs. 2: 21.6 – 15.4 = 6.2 > 3.94(R_3)

$$4 \text{ vs. } 3: 21.6 - 17.6 = 4.0 > 3.75(R_2)$$
$$3 \text{ vs. } 1: 17.6 - 9.8 = 7.8 > 4.04(R_4)$$
$$3 \text{ vs. } 5: 17.6 - 10.8 = 6.8 > 3.95(R_4)$$
$$3 \text{ vs. } 2: 17.6 - 15.4 = 2.2 > 3.75(R_3)$$
$$2 \text{ vs. } 1: 15.4 - 9.8 = 5.6 > 3.94(R_2)$$
$$2 \text{ vs. } 5: 15.4 - 10.8 = 4.6 > 3.75(R_4)$$
$$5 \text{ vs. } 1: 10.8 - 9.8 = 1.0 > 3.75(R_4)$$

Duncan's test requires a greater observed difference to detect significantly different pairs of means as the number of means included in the group increases. For instance, in the above example $R_2 = 3.75$(two means) whereas $R_3 = 3.94$(three means). For two means, the critical value R_2 will always exactly equal the LSD value from the t test. The values $r_\alpha(p,f)$ are chosen so that a specified protection level is obtained. That is, when two means that are p steps apart are compared, the projection level is $(1 - \alpha)^{p-1}$, where a is the level of significance specified for two adjacent means. Thus, the error rate is $1 - (1 - \alpha)^{p-1}$ of reporting at least one incorrect significant difference between two means when the group size is p. For example, if $\alpha = 0.05$, then $1 - (1 - 0.05)^1 = 0.05$ is the significance level for comparing the adjacent pair of means, $1 - (1 - 0.05)^2 = .10$ is the significance level for means that are one step apart, and so forth.

Duncan's procedure is quite powerful; that is, it is very effective at detecting differences between means when real differences exist. For this reason, Duncan's multiple range test is very popular.

13.5 The Newman – Keuls Test

This test was devised by Newman (1939). Because new interest in Newman's test was generated by Keuls (1952), the procedure is usually called the Newman-Keuls test. Operationally, the procedure is similar to Duncan's multiple range test, except that the critical differences between means are calculated somewhat differently. Specifically, we compute a set of critical values

$$K_p = q_\alpha(p,f)S_{\bar{y}_i} \quad p = 2, 3, \ldots\ldots, a$$

Where $q_\alpha(a,f)$ is the upper α percentage point of the studentized range for groups of means of size p and f error degrees of freedom. Once the value K_p are computed, extreme pairs of means in groups of size p are compared with K_p exactly as in Duncan's multiple range test.

The Newman–Keuls test is more conservative than Duncan's test in that the type I error rate is smaller. Specifically, the type I error of the experiment is α for all tests involving the same number of means. Consequently, because

α is generally lower, the power of the Newman–Keuls test is generally less the Duncan's test. To demonstrate that the Newman–Keuls procedure leads to a less powerful test than Duncan's multiple range test, we note from a comparison of Tables VII and VIII of the Appendix that for p > 2 we have $q_\alpha(p, f) > r_\alpha(p, f)$. That is, it is "harder", to declare a pair of means significantly different using the Newman–Keuls test than it is using Duncan's procedure. This is illustrated below for the case $\alpha = 0.01$, a = 8, and $f = 20$:

p	2	3	4	5	6	7	8
$r_{0.01}(p,20)$	4.02	4.22	4.33	4.40	4.47	4.53	4.58
$q_{0.01}(p,20)$	4.02	4.64	5.02	5.29	5.51	5.69	5.84

As indicated above, there are several other multiple comparison procedures

In many experiments one of the treatments is a control and the analyst is interest in comparing each of the other a – 1 treatment means with the control. Thus, there are only a – 1 comparisons to be made. A procedure for making these comparisons has been developed by Dunnett (1964). Suppose that treatment is the control and we wish to test the hypothesis

H_0: $\mu_i = \mu_a$

H1: $\mu_i \neq \mu_a$

for i = 1,2,..., a – 1. Dunnett's procedure is a modification of the usual t-test. For each hypothesis, we compute the observed differences in the sample means

$$|\bar{y}_i - \bar{y}_a| \qquad i = 1, 2, \ldots\ldots, a - 1$$

The null hypothesis H_0: : $\mu_i = \mu_a$ is rejected using a type I error rate α if

$$|\bar{y}_i - \bar{y}_a| > d_\alpha(a-1, f)\sqrt{MS_E\left(\frac{1}{n_i} + \frac{1}{n_a}\right)}$$

Where the constant $d_{\alpha.}(a-1, f)$ and α is the joint significance level associated with all a – 1 tests.

Example

To illustrate Dunnett's test, consider the experiment with treatment 5 considered the control. In this example, a = 5, a – 1 = 4, $f = 20$, and $n_i = n = 5$. At the 5 percent level, we find from Table and $d_{0.05}(4.20) = 2.65$. Thus, the critical differences becomes,

$$d_{0.05}(4.20)\sqrt{\frac{2MS_E}{n}} = 2.65\sqrt{\frac{2(8.06)}{5}} = 4.76$$

Thus, any treatment mean that differs from the control by more than 4.76 would be declared significantly different. The observed differences are

1 vs. 5: $\overline{y}_1 - \overline{y}_5 = 9.8 - 10.8 = -1.0$
2 vs. 5: $\overline{y}_2 - \overline{y}_5 = 15.4 - 10.8 = 4.6$
3 vs. 3: $\overline{y}_3 - \overline{y}_5 = 17.6 - 10.8 = 6.8$
24 vs. 5: $\overline{y}_4 - \overline{y}_5 = 21.6 - 10.8 = 10.8$

Only the differences indicate any significant difference when compared to the control; thus, we conclude that $\mu_3 \neq \mu_5$ and $\mu_4 \neq \mu_5$.

When comparing treatments with a control, it is good idea to use more observations for the control treatment (say n_a) than for the other treatments (say n), assuming equal numbers of observations for the remaining a - 1 treatments. The ratio n_a/n should be chosen to be approximately equal to the square root of the total number of treatments. That is, choose $n_a/n = \sqrt{a}$.

Exercise

1. Explain the concept of multiple comparison test.
2. Explain LSD method with an example.
3. Explain Duncan's Multiple Range Test and interpretation of the results.
4. Explain the method of Newman - Keuls Test procedure for comparisons.

❑❑❑

Chapter – 14

Factorial Experiments

In the foregoing experiments performed either in CRD or RBD or LSD. We were primarily concerned with the comparison and estimation of the effects of a single set of treatments like varieties of paddy, different methods of cultivation etc., and such experiments which deal with one factor only may be called simple experiments. In factorial experiment the effects of several factors of variation are studied and investigated simultaneously in a single experiment, such experiments are known as factorial experiments. In these experiments an attempt is made to estimate the effects of each factors and also the interaction effects i.e. the variation in the effect of one factor as a result to different levels of other factors. These experiments provide an opportunity to study not only the individual effects of each factor but also interactions. In many biological and clinical trials factors are likely to have interaction. Therefore, factorial experiments are more informative in such investigations.

14.1 Advantages and Disadvantages of Factorial Experiments

The following are the advantages of a factorial experiment over single factor experiment.

In factorial experiments we can evaluate the combined effect of two or more factors when they are used simultaneously.

In factorial experiments we can study the individual effects of each factor as well as their interactions.

In single factor experiments the effect of interactions cannot be studied. Hence the information obtained from factorial experiments is much more than that obtained from a series of single factor experiments. That is, we can obtain a considerable increase in efficiency.

In factorial experiments a wide range of factor combinations are used. It helps us to predict what will happen when two or more factors are used in combination.

The factorial approach will result in a considerable saving of the experimental resources.

Further the time required for the combined experiment is less than that required for the separate experiments. Thus the experimental material and time are saved in factorial experiments.

When we have several related factors, single factor experiments might be unsatisfactory because of changes in environmental conditions. But, if several factors are investigated simultaneously in a single experiment such difficulties will not arise.

The following are the disadvantages of a factorial experiment over single factor experiment.

When the number of factors or levels of factors or both are increased, the number of treatment combinations will increase. Consequently, the block size will increase. If block size increases it may be difficult to ensure homogeneity of experimental material. This will lead to increased experimental error and loss of precision in the experiment.

In some cases we may not be interested in certain treatment combinations. However, we are forced to incorporate them in the experiment. This leads to wastage of the experimental material as well as time.

When several treatment combinations are involved, the execution of the experiment and statistical analysis become more complex.

14.2 Basic Concepts

In order to define the factorial experiment it is necessary to know the meanings of different terminologies and notations used in factorial experiments.

Factor

The term factor refers to a set of related treatments. For example, we may apply different dosages of nitrogen to a crop. Here 'nitrogen', irrespective of the doses is a factor. Similarly, crop variety, spacing, date of sowing, etc., are also known as factors.

Levels of a factor

The different states making up a factor are known as the levels of that factor. The rates of nitrogen application, seed rates, spacing, concentrations of insecticides, etc., are examples for quantitative levels. The varieties of a crop, different insecticides, sources of nitrogen, etc., are some examples for qualitative levels. The levels are usually indicated by codes by codes such as 0, 1, 2, etc.

Types of Factorial Experiment

A factorial experiment is named based on the number of factors and the level of each factor. For example, if there are four factors each at two level of experiment is known as 2^4 factorial experiments. If there are the factors each with three levels, the experiment is known as 3^2 factorial experiments. In general if there are n factors each with p levels, then it is known as p^n factorial experiment. If all the factors have the same levels, the experiment is called symmetrical factorial experiment; otherwise it is called asymmetrical factorial or mixed factorial.

Notations

In factorial experiment, the factors and the numerical measures of their effects are presented by capital letters. The treatment combinations are usually represented by small letters. Consider, for example, an experiment in which two varieties of paddy (v_0 and v_1) are tried with two dates of sowing (d_0 and d_1), and two levels of nitrogen (n_0 and n_1). There will be eight treatment combinations in this case. They are $n_0d_0v_0$, $n_0d_1v_0$, $n_1d_1v_0$, $n_0d_0v_1$, $n_1d_0v_1$, and $n_1d_1v_1$. The treatment combinations can be written as, (1) n, d, nd, v, nv, dv and ndv. The symbol (1) indicates the combination of the first or basal level of all factors. In other combinations, the first level of factor is signified by the absence of the corresponding letter. The corresponding capital letters G, N, D, V, ND, NV, DV and NDV denote the numerical measures of the mean response of the respective treatment combinations. It may be noted that the treatment combinations are written in a specified order. This is the standard order and is useful for many purposes. In factorial our main objective is to carry out separate tests for the main effects and interaction effects, splitting the treatment SS each with 1d.f.

Simple and Main Effects

The effects of a factor are usually termed either as simple effect or main effect. The simple effect of a factor is the difference between its responses for a fixed level of other factors. The mean of the simple effects of a factor is called the main effect of that factor.

Interaction

The effect of one factor changes as the level of the other factors changes. This means that the factors are not independent. The dependence of factors in their responses is known as interaction. The interaction is measured as the mean of the differences between simple effects of the factors. The interaction can be negative or positive.

The interaction between two factors is known as a two factor interaction or first order interaction. The interaction between n factors is known as n factor interaction or $(n - 1)^{th}$ order interaction. The interaction between the factors is denoted by the product of the factors. For example if the factors are A, B and C then the three factor interaction is ABC. With a factors, there will be $\binom{n}{1}$ = n main effects, $\binom{n}{2}$ two factor interactions, $\binom{n}{3}$ three factor interactions, and so on.

14.3 Computation of Main Effects and Interactions

The main effects and interaction effects in factorial experiments can be computed by many methods. They are described below.

14.3.1 Fisher's algebraic method

Let us consider an experiment with two factors A and B each at two levels 0 and 1. The four treatments combinations may be represented as a_0, b_0, a_0b_1 and a_1b_1 or (1), a, b and ab.

The simple effect of A at level $b_0 = a_1b_0 - a_0b_0 = a - (1)$

The simple effect of A at level $b_1 = a_1b_1 - a_0b_1 = ab - b$

The simple effect of B at level $a_0 = a_0b_1 - a_0b_0 = b - (1)$

The simple effect of B at level $a_1 = a_1b_1 - a_1b_0 = ab - a$

The main effect of A = average of the simple effects of A

$$= \frac{1}{2}[a - (1) + ab - b]$$

$$= \frac{1}{2}[ab + a - b - (1)]$$

The main effect of B $= \frac{1}{2}[b - (1) + ab - a]$

$$= \frac{1}{2}[ab + b - a - (1)]$$

The interaction effect of AB is given by

$$AB = \frac{1}{2}[\text{simple effect of A at } b_1 - \text{simple effect of A at } b_0]$$

$$= \frac{1}{2}[(ab - b) - (a - (1))]$$

$$= \frac{1}{2}[ab - a - b + (1)]$$

It can also be written as

$$AB = \frac{1}{2}[\text{simple effect of B at } a_1 - \text{simple effect of B at } a_0]$$

$$= \frac{1}{2}[(ab - a) - (b - (1))]$$

$$= \frac{1}{2}[ab - a - b + (1)]$$

This method of computation of main effects and interactions can be extended to more than two factors. If we have three factors A, B and C each at two levels 0 and 1. There are four simple effects of each of factors A, B and C. They are as follows:

Tabel 14.1 :

(1) Level of		Simple effect of A
B	C	
b_0	c_0	$a_1b_0c_0 - a_0b_0c_0 = a - (1)$
b_0	c_1	$a_1b_0c_1 - a_0b_0c_1 = ac - c$
b_1	c_0	$a_1b_1c_0 - a_0b_1c_0 = ab - b$
b_1	c_1	$a_1b_1c_1 - a_0b_1c_1 = abc - bc$
(2) Level of		Simple effect of B
A	C	
a_0	c_0	$b_1a_0c_0 - b_0a_0c_0 = b - (1)$
a_0	c_1	$b_1a_0c_1 - b_0a_0c_1 = bc - c$
a_1	c_0	$b_1a_1c_0 - b_0a_1c_0 = ba - a$
a_1	c_1	$b_1a_1c_1 - b_0a_1c_1 = bac - ac$

Contd.

(3) Level of		Simple effect of C
A	B	
a_0	b_0	$c_1a_0b_0 - c_0a_0b_0 = c - (1)$
a_0	b_0	$c_1a_0b_1 - c_0a_0b_1 = cb - b$
a_1	b_1	$c_1a_1b_0 - c_0a_1b_0 = ca - a$
a_1	b_1	$c_1a_1b_1 - c_0a_1b_1 = abc - bc$

The main effects and interaction effects can be computed using these simple effects.

$$A = \frac{1}{4}[a-(1)+ac-c+ab-b+abc-bc]$$

$$= \frac{1}{4}[abc-ab+ac+a-bc-b-c-(1)]$$

Similarly,

$$B = \frac{1}{4}[abc + ab + bc + b - ac - a - c - (1)]$$

$$C = \frac{1}{4}[abc + ac + bc + c - ab - a - b - (1)]$$

$$AB = \frac{1}{2}\text{[simple effect of A at } b_1 \text{ (mean of } c_0 \text{ and } c_1)$$

$$\text{- simple effect of A at } b_0 \text{ (mean of } c_0 \text{ and } c_1)]$$

$$= \left[\frac{1}{2}\{abc-bc+ab-b\}-\frac{1}{2}\{a-(1)+ac-c\}\right]$$

$$= \frac{1}{4}[abc+ab+c+(1)-ac-bc-a-b]$$

Similarly,

$$AC = \frac{1}{4}[abc+ac+b+(1)-ab-bc-a-c]$$

$$BC = \frac{1}{4}[abc+bc+a+(1)-ab-ac-b-c]$$

The above method of computation of main effects and interaction effects is known as Fisher's algebraic method. This method can be used any experiments involving several factors at two levels.

The Fisher's algebraic method of computation of main effects and interactions is laborious. For three factors A, B and C, each with two levels, the main effects and interaction are summarised in term of the treatment combinations in the following table.

Table 14.2 : Algebraic method of computing effect totals.

Factorial effect	Treatment (1)	a	b	ab	Combinations c	ac	bc	abc	Divisor
G	+	+	+	+	+	+	+	+	8
A	-	+	-	+	-	+	-	+	4
B	-	-	+	+	-	-	+	+	4
AB	+	-	-	+	+	-	-	+	4
C	-	-	-	-	+	+	+	+	4
AC	+	-	+	-	-	+	-	+	4
BC	+	+	-	-	-	-	+	+	4
ABC	-	+	+	-	+	-	-	+	4

It may be noted that the treatment combinations are arranged in the standard order. The sign + is given an effect if the corresponding small letter is present and – if it is absent. The sign for interactions is the product of the corresponding signs of the individual letters. For example, the sign for AB is the product of the signs for A and B.

From the above table, the main effects and interactions effects can be computed. For Example,

$$A = \frac{1}{4}\left[-(1) + a - b + ab - c + ac - bc + abc\right]$$

$$= \frac{1}{4}\left[abc + ab + ac + a - bc - b - c - (1)\right]$$

14.4 Layout Factorial Experiments

When the factorial experiment has been chosen, we know the total number of treatment combinations that must be tested. For this number of treatments any basic design such as CRD, RBD or LSD may be adopted. For example, for a 3^2 factorial experiment there will be 9 treatment combinations. We can arrange the 9 treatments in RBD or in 9×9 LSD. Depending upon the basic design the randomization is carried out.

Thus, we can have factorial CRD, factorial RBD or factorial LSD. The relative advantages of these designs are the same as that of simple CRD, RBD and LSD.

14.5 Analysis and Interpretation Factorial Experiments

Factorial experiments are conducted either in CRD or RBD or LSD and thus they can be analysed in the usual manner except that in the case the treatment SS is split into main effects and interactions. However, the treatment degrees of freedom will be split up according to the components.

Suppose that we have a factorial RBD with three factors, A, B and C having p, q and s levels, respectively then there will be pqs treatment combinations. The analysis of variance model for this experiment is given by

$$Y_{ijkd} = \mu + r_i + a_j + b_k + ab_{jk} + c_t + ac_{jt} + bc_{kt} + abc_{jkt} + e_{ijkt}$$

The terms, ab, ac, bc and abc are the interaction effects. The order terms have the usual meanings. The sums of squares can be computed using the effect totals arrived at by the methods, for example, in case 2^n experiment with r replications,

$$SS(X) = \frac{(\text{effect total of } X)^2}{2^n . r}$$

Where, X represents a main effect or interaction. Alternatively, one may use Yates algorithm or tabular method.

The degrees of freedom associated with a factor are equal to its level minus one. For interactions the degree of freedom will be the product of the d.*f*. of the individual factors of that interaction. In case of three factors A, B and C with p, q and s levels respectively, the degrees of freedom are as follows:

Factorial effect	d.*f*
A	p – 1
B	q – 1
C	s – 1
AB	(p – 1) (q – 1)
AC	(p – 1) (s – 1)
BC	(q – 1) (s – 1)
ABC	(p – 1) (q – 1) (s – 1)

The analysis of variance table can be completed with these results. Once the analysis of variance is completed, the computation of critical difference and other steps are completed as with single factor experiments. The general formula for SE (d) is,

$$SE(d) \text{ for } X = \sqrt{\frac{2EMS}{r.\ D}}$$

where,

X = the main factors or interactions,

D = the product of the levels of the left out factors in X, and

r = number of replications.

For example, consider a factorial RBD with factors A, B and C with levels p, q and s, respectively. Then

$$\text{SE(d) for A} = \sqrt{\frac{2\text{EMS}}{\text{rqs}}}$$

$$\text{SE(d) for B} = \sqrt{\frac{2\text{EMS}}{\text{rps}}}$$

$$\text{SE(d) for C} = \sqrt{\frac{2\text{EMS}}{\text{rpq}}}$$

$$\text{SE(d) for AB} = \sqrt{\frac{2\text{EMS}}{\text{rs}}}$$

$$\text{SE(d) for AC} = \sqrt{\frac{2\text{EMS}}{\text{rp}}}$$

$$\text{SE(d) for BC} = \sqrt{\frac{2\text{EMS}}{\text{rp}}}$$

$$\text{SE(d) for ABC} = \sqrt{\frac{2\text{EMS}}{\text{r}}}$$

The bar charts for the main factors are then drawn as usual. From significant interactions the bar charts for each factor is drawn at each level of the other factors. For example, for AB interaction the bar chart may be as follows:

At level a_0: b1 b3 <u>b2 b0</u>

At level a1: b3 b2 <u>b1 b0</u>

and so on. ____________

Example

An experiment was conducted in RBD on paddy crop with three factors each at two levels. The factors were,

Paddy variety: v_0 and v_1

Plant production schedule : p_0 and p_1

Irrigation Schedule : w_0 and w_1

The order of treatment combination is vpw. They are represented by the levels of the factors. Thus, 101 indicate the treatment combination v1pow1. The results are given in the following table.

Table 14.3 : Yield paddy, kg/plot

Rep I	110 108.2	001 128.9	111 116.8	101 112.4	110 115.8	000 122.8	011 119.8	010 114.6
Rep. II	110 108.6	111 125.3	011 122.8	001 129.1	101 123.8	010 113.3	000 127.8	100 117.6
Rep. III	000 126.0	010 119.5	001 134.6	011 120.4	100 107.1	111 116.5	110 124.0	101 115.8

The statistical analysis is carried out in two stages. In the first stage the analysis is done in the case of RBD with eight treatments. In the second stage the treatment sum of squares is split into components. The first stage analysis starts with arrangement of data as tabulated below:

Table 14.4 : Re-arrangement of data given in Table 14.3

Treatment Combinations	Replication			Total
	I	II	III	
000 : (1)	122.8	127.8	126.0	376.6
100 : v	108.2	117.6	107.1	332.9
010 : p	114.6	113.3	119.5	347.4
110 : vp	115.8	108.6	124.0	348.4
001 : (1)	128.9	129.1	134.6	392.6
101 : v(1)	112.4	123.8	115.8	352.0
011 : p(0)	119.8	122.8	120.4	363.0
111 : vp(1)	116.8	125.3	116.5	358.6
Total	939.3	968.3	963.9	2871.5

Analysis at first stage:

$$\text{CF} = \frac{(2871.5)^2}{24} = 343563.0104$$

$$\text{Total SS} = [(122.8)^2 + (108.2)^2 + \ldots + (116.5)^2] - \text{CF}$$

$$= 344737.63 - \text{CF} = 1174.6196$$

Replication SS = $1/8[(939.3)^2 + \ldots + (963.9)^2] - CF$

= 343624.0737 – CF = 61.0634

Treatment SS = $1/3[(376.6)^2 + \ldots + (358.6)^2] - CF$

= 344373.67 – CF = 810.6596

Error SS = 302.8966

Analysis at second stage :

The sum of squares for the main effects and interactions are calculated using the factorial effect total which can be obtained by the algebraic method. In case of 2^n system, Yates algorithm method can also be used to find out the effect totals. For the use of algebraic method, we form the following table:

Table 14.5 : Algebraic method of computing effect totals.

Factorial effect	**Treatments Combinations and their totals**								**Effect total**
	(1) 376.6	**v 332.9**	**p 347.4**	**vp 348.4**	**w 392.6**	**vw 352.0**	**pw 363.0**	**vpw 358.6**	
G	+	+	+	+	+	+	+	+	2871.5
V	-	+	-	+	-	+	-	+	- 87.3
P	-	-	+	+	-	-	+	+	- 36.7
VP	+	-	-	+	+	-	-	+	80.9
W	-	-	-	-	+	+	+	+	60.9
VW	+	-	+	-	-	+	-	+	= 2.3
PW	+	+	-	-	-	-	+	+	- 9.3
VPW	-	+	+	-	+	-	-	+	- 8.5

The effect total for factor V is give

V = – (1) + v – p + vp – w + vw – pw + vps

= – 376.6 + 332.9 – 347.4 + 348.4 – 392.6 + 352.0 – 363.0 + 358.6

= – 87.7

Similarly, all other effect totals are computed and are given in the following table.

The steps in computing the factorial effect totals by Yates algorithm are as follows:

Step 1: Write down the treatment combinations in the systematic order as given in Table 14.5. In the next column write down the corresponding treatment totals.

Step 2: Add the treatment totals in pairs. These results will form the first half of column (1) in Table 14.5. Then subtract the first number of each pair from the second. These results from the second half of column (1).

Step 3: To obtain column (2), apply the same process are in step (2) to column (1).

Step 4: Continue the process until we reach column n, where n is the number of factors. The values in the last column are the effect totals.

Table 14.6 : Computation of effect totals of data in Table 14.3. Using Yates algorithm

Treatment Combinations	Total	Effect totals		
		1	2	3
(1)	376.6	709.5	1405.3	2981.5
v	332.9	695.8	1466.2	- 87.7
p	347.4	744.6	- 42.7	- 36.7
vp	348.4	721.6	- 45.0	80.9
Sub total	-	2871.5	2783.8	2828.0
w	392.6	- 43.7	- 13.7	60.9
vw	352.0	1.0	- 23.0	- 2.3
pw	363.0	- 40.6	44.7	- 9.3
vpw	358.6	- 4.4	36.2	- 8.5
Grand Total	2871.5	2783.8	2828.0	

The computations in Table 14.6 can be checked in two ways. The first check is that the total of upper half of a column should be equal to the total of the previous column. The second check is that the first value in the last column should be equal to the grand total.

The effect totals in Table 14.5 and Table 14.6 can be compared. The sums of squares are computed as follows:

$$X\ SS = \frac{(\text{effect total of } X)^2}{r.2^n}$$

where, X represents a factorial effect. In our example r. $2^n = 3.2^3 = 24$.

$$V\ SS = \frac{(-87.7)^2}{24} = 320.4704$$

$$P\ SS = \frac{(-36.7)^2}{24} = 56.1204$$

$$\text{W SS} = \frac{(60.9)^2}{24} = 154.5338$$

$$\text{VP SS} = \frac{(80.9)^2}{24} = 272.7004$$

$$\text{VW SS} = \frac{(-2.3)^2}{24} = 0.2204$$

$$\text{PW SS} = \frac{(-9.3)^2}{24} = 3.6038$$

$$\text{VPW SS} = \frac{(-8.5)^2}{24} = 3.0104$$

It can be verified that the sum of all these SS values is equal to the overall treatment SS.

We can also calculate the SS using tabular method and is easier than any other method. In tabular method first we form two–way table for all possible treatment combinations. Then this analyzed similar to RBD analysis. The divisor for computing the factorial effect sum of squares is worked out as

D = the product of the left out factors on the left hand side of SS formula.

For our example the possible two–way tables are given below.

Table 14.7 : Two – way tables for the data given in Table 14.3

	(a) $V \times P$ table				**(b) $V \times W$ table**		
	v_0	v_1	**Total**		v_0	v_1	**Total**
p_0	769.2	684.9	1454.1	w_0	724.0	681.3	1405.3
p_1	710.4	707.0	1417.4	w_1	755.6	710.6	1466.2
Total	1479.6	1391.9	2871.5	Total	1479.6	1391.9	2871.5

	(c) $P \times W$ table		
	p_0	p_1	**Total**
w_0	709.0	695.8	1405.3
w_1	744.6	721.6	1466.4
Total	1479.6	1391.9	2871.5

(d) $V \times PW$ table

	p_0w_0	p_0w_1	p_1w_0	P_1w_1	Total
v_0	376.6	392.6	347.4	363.0	1479.6
v_1	332.9	352.0	348.4	358.6	1391.9
Total	709.5	744.6	695.8	721.6	2871.5

The value 769.2 against v_0p_0 in Table 14.7(a) is the sum of the values for $v_0p_0w_0$ and $v_0p_0w_1$ from all the three replications. Thus, it is the sum of six observations. The other values are computed in the same manner.

CF = 343563.0104

V SS = 1/12[$(1479.6)^2 + (1391.9)^2$ – CF

= 320.4704

On the left hand side, we have only one factor. The factors P and W are left out. Hence the divisor is,

D = r × levels of P × levels of W

= 3 × 2 × 2 = 12

P SS = 1/12 [$1454.1)^2 + (1417.4)^2$]

= 56.1204

V × P Table SS = 1/6[$(769.2)^2 + (710.4)^2 + (684.9)^2 + (707)^2$] – CF

= 649.2912

VP SS = V × P Tables SS – VSS – PSS

= 649.2912 – 320.4704 – 56.1204

= 272.7004

Similarly, from Table 14.7(b)

W SS = 1/12 [$1405.3)^2 + (1466.2)^2$] – CF

= 154.5338

V × W Table SS = 1/6[$(724.0)^2 + \ldots + (710.6)^2$] – CF

= 475.2246

VW SS = V × W Tables SS – VSS – WSS

= 475.2246 – 320.4704 – 154.5338

= 0.2204

From Table 14.7(c),

$$P \times W \text{ Table SS} = 1/6[(709.5)^2 + \ldots + (721.6)^2] - CF$$
$$= 214.2578$$

$$PW\ SS = P \times W \text{ Tables SS} - PSS - WSS$$
$$= 214.2578 - 56.1204 - 154.5338$$
$$= 3.6038$$

From Table 14.7(d)

$$V \times PW \text{ Table SS} = 1/3[(376.6)^2 + \ldots + (358.6)^2] - CF = 810.6596$$

This is nothing but the overall treatment SS.

$$VPW\ SS = \text{Overall treatment SS} - VSS - PSS - WSS - VPSS - VWSS - PWSS$$
$$= 810.6596 - 320.4704 - 56.1204 - 154.5338$$
$$- 272.7004 - 0.2204 - 3.6038 = 3.0104$$

The results are summarized in the following ANOVA table.

Table 14.8 : Analysis of variance

Sources of variation	*df*	SS	MS	F
Replication	2	61.0634	30.5317	
V	1	320.4704	320.4704	14.812**
P	1	56.1204	56.1204	2.594
W	1	154.5338	154.5338	7.143*
VP	1	272.7004	272.7004	12.604**
VW	1	0.2204	0.2204	<1
PW	1	3.6038	3.6038	<1
VPW	1	3.0104	3.0104	<1
Error	14	302.8966	21.6355	
Total	23	1174.6196		

Since F is significant for the treatment combinations V, W and VPy, and therefore we need to calculate CD for V, W and VP only.

We have,

$$SE(d) \text{ for } V = \sqrt{\frac{2(21.6335)}{3 \times 2 \times 2}}$$

$$= \sqrt{\frac{43.2710}{12}} = 1.8989$$

$$CD = (2.365)\ (1.8989) = 4.4909$$

The CD value for W is the same as for V.

$$\text{SE(d) for VP} = \sqrt{\frac{2(21.6335)}{3 \times 2}}$$

$$= 2.6855$$

$$CD = (2.365(2.6855) = 6.3512$$

In case of 2^n experiments, there is no need for CD values for comparing the levels of main factors. If F is significant for a factor, we can write the conclusion directly based on the comparison of the mean values. However, to explain the method of calculation of CD for factorial experiments, they have been computed.

The mean values for each level of the factors are given below:

v_0 : 123.3	p_0 : 121.2	w_0	: 117.1
v_0 : 116.0	p_0 : 118.1	w_0	: 122.2
v_0 at p_0 : 128.2		v_0 at p_0	: 118.4
v_1 at p_0 : 114.3		v_1 at p_1	: 117.8

Based on the above results, we can conclude that v0 gives significantly higher yield than v1. both old and new plant protection schedules are similar in their effect; the w1 irrigation schedule increases paddy yield significantly compared to the local practice; v0 gives significantly yield than v1 under p0 plant protection schedule but their performance is similar under p1 plant protection schedule.

14.6 Confounding in Factorial Experiments

In factorial experiments as the number of factors and the levels at which they are employed increase, the total number of treatment combinations increases rapidly and consequently the block size has to be enlarged. In many experiments even s single replication of each treatment combination may require far too many experimental units. As a result the experimental error is inflated and the precision of treatment comparisons is reduced. Thus the advantage of factorial experiments is lost. In order to keep the advantages of the factorial experiments and at the same time reduce the experimental error to a minimum, a device known as confounding is introduced. By this technique we can reducing the size of a replication over a number of blocks at the cost of losing some information on some effects which is not much practical importance.

14.6.1 Confounding

Confounding is the device of reducing the block size by making one or more interaction contrasts identical with block contrasts, is known as confounding. Preferably, only higher order interactions, that is, interactions with three or more factors are confounded, because their loss is immaterial. As an experimenter is more interested in main effects and two factor interactions, these should not be confounded as far as possible. The designs for such confounded factorials can be called incomplete RBD. The treatment groups are first allotted at random to the different blocks. The treatments allotted to a block are then distributed at random to its different experimental units.

Complete and Partial Confounding : When there are two more replications, a question arises whether the same interactions are confounded in each replication or different sets of interactions are confounded in different replications. Both the procedure are practised in all agricultural experiments. If the same set of interaction effect is confounded in all replications, confounding is called complete confounding. If different sets of interactions are confounded in different replications the confounding is called partial confounding. In complete confounding all the confounded interactions are lost. But in partial confounding, the confounded interaction effects can be recovered from those replications in which they are not confounded.

Consider, for example, a factorial experiment with two factors A and B each at two levels 0 and 1. The treatment comparisons will be a_0b_0, a_1b_0, a_0b_1, a_1b_1, or (1), a, b, ab. The replication can be divided into two blocks. Then the four treatment combinations have to be divided into two sets. There are three possible ways of having such sets, viz., (i) set a: a ab; set 2; (1), b (ii) set 1: b, ab; set: 1, a (iii) set 1: a,b; set 2: (1), ab. In this case, each block a replication should have to plots. One set of treatment combinations can be allotted at random to these plots. For the three groups of treatment combinations, the arrangements may be as follows:

Replication

Block I	**II**
a	(1)
ab	b

Group I

Replication

Block I	**II**
b	(1)
ab	a

Group II

Replication

Block I	**II**
(1)	a
ab	b

Group III

Suppose that the first group has been taken. It can be seen from the layout that 1 levels of factor A are allotted to block I and 0 levels of factor A to block II. The comparison (a + ab – b – (1)), representing the main effect of A is the same as the comparison between the two blocks. Thus, the main effect of A is inseparably mixed up or completely confounded with block effects. Likewise, the main effect of B is confounded in the second group and the interaction AB in the third group.

For example, consider a 2^3 experiment with three replications. The arrangement of the treatment combinations may be as follows:

Replication I

Block I	II
abc	a
c	ac
ab	b
(1)	bc

Replication II

Block I	II
(1)	bc
b	c
abc	a
ac	ab

Replication III

Block I	II
ac	c
(1)	Abc
ab	b
bc	a

In replication I, interaction AB is confounded with block effects; in replication II interaction AC is confounded and in replication III interaction ABC is confounded. This last interaction is called generalized interaction of the previous two independent interactions. The generalized interaction can also be obtained from the product of the independent interactions. In partial confounding, it is possible to confound effects of a certain order, say, all two-factor interactions, an equal number of times, so that a balance is maintained in the amount of information available from the different treatment effects. This type of confounding is termed as balanced partial confounding.

In confounded experiments, the degrees of freedom of those treatment effects which are confounded do not contribute to the error. Thus, the error degrees of freedom are less by the confounded number of degrees of freedom. Hence, to obtain greater efficiency of the experiment with confounding the loss of degrees of freedom for error due to confounding has to be compensated by the reduction in the error sum of squares.

The technique confounding leads to reduction in error degrees of freedom, but the computational procedure is more difficult. Further, considerable difficulties are encountered if the treatments interact with blocks.

14.6.2 Methods of Confounding

The methods of confounding depend on the number of factors and the number of levels of each factor under trail. Usually, confounding is adopted only when the number of treatment combinations is more.

When any two interactions are completely confounded, their generalized interaction will also be confounded. For example, in 2^4 experiment if AB and BC are confounded, their generalized interaction ABC is also confounded. For a particular system of confounding, first the intra block subgroup or key block should be constructed. The block containing the control, viz., (1), is called the key block. In order to determine the treatment combinations in the key block, all the treatment combinations indicating their levels should be written first. Then those treatment combinations which satisfy the equations

$$x_i + x_j + x_k + \ldots\ldots = 0 \text{ (mod P)}$$

The resultant treatment combinations will form the key block. The above equation is known as defining equation.

For example, consider a 2^4 factorial experiment with AB, ACD and BCD confounded. The treatment combinations are,

abcd	abcd
0000	0001
1000	1001
0100	0101
1100	1101
0010	0011
1010	1011
0110	0111
1110	1111

The treatment combinations satisfying the defining equating for AB are selected first. The defining equation for AB is

$$x_1 + x_2 = 0 \pmod 2$$

The treatment combinations satisfying this equation are

0000	0001
1000	1101
0100	0011
1100	1111

From the selected ones, the treatment combinations satisfying the defining equation for ACD, i.e.,

$$x_1 + x_3 + x_4 = 0 \pmod 2)$$

are selected. They are

0000

0100

1101

0011

Note that these treatment combinations satisfy the defining equation for BCD, i.e.,

$$x_2 + x_3 + x_4 = 0 \pmod 2),$$

also. Thus, the key block is one that contains the treatment combinations(1), abc, abd and cd.

The treatment combinations in other blocks may be obtained by multiplying the treatment combinations in the key block by any remaining treatment combinations. In our example, the treatment combinations in the key block are multiplying by a, b and c. The four blocks will be as follows.

Confounding in Factorial Experiments

Block I (Key block)	Block II (Block I × a)	Block III (Block I × b)	Block IV (Block I × c)
(1)	a	b	c
abc	bc	ac	ab
abd	bd	ad	abcd
cd	acd	bcd	d

It may be noted that Block IV can also be obtained by multiplying the key block by d.

14.6.3 Confounding in 2^n Series

In 2^n series, the size of blocks has to be decided first. Then by dividing the number of treatment combinations by the size of the blocks, the number of blocks is obtained. The number of treatment combinations of effects to be confounded will then be equal to the degrees of freedom for blocks. Suppose that in a 2^n series we want to have blocks of size k in a replication. The number of blocks will be $\frac{2^n}{k}$. We have to confound $\frac{2^n}{k}-1$ effects. For example, in case 24 experiments, if block size is 4 there will be $\frac{2^n}{4}=\frac{16}{4}=4$ blocks. We have to confound 4 – 1 = 3 effects. If the block size is 8, there will be $\frac{2^n}{8}=2.$ blocks and we have to confound 2 -1 = 1 effect.

Once the number of effects to be confounded is decided, the effects that are to be confounded independently have to be determined. This can be done based on the number of blocks. In 2n series, the number of blocks will be in powers of 2, say 2p. If the number of blocks is 8, p = 2; if it is 16, p = 4 and so on. We can select any p effects to be confounded in such a way that any of their generalized interactions in neither the main effect nor the other selected effect. The remaining effects to be confounded are their generalized interactions. If p = 1 only, one effect is to be confounded. In such cases usually the highest order interaction is confounded. Analysis of the confounded factorial design can be carried out as in the case of factorial experiment by eliminating the confounded interaction from the AV table or adjusted in treatment sum of square if complete confounding or partial confounding respectively.

Exercise

1. Define "Factorial experiment". Why these are considered better than the experiments in which the factors are studied one by one?
2. State the advantages of factorial experiments.
3. Explain what is meant by main effects and interactions in factorial experiment.
4. What is a treatment contrast?
5. What is meant by "confounding "in a factorial experiment?
6. Explain Yates method for the factorial experiment with an example.
7. Distinguish between complete confounding and partial confounding in factorial experiment.
8. Discusses the advantages and disadvantages of confounding and state how the disadvantages can be partially overcome.

❑❑❑

Chapter – 15

Split Plot Design

In factorial experiment it may sometime happen that certain factors require bigger plots than other for convenience of operation of the experiment. For example, in an agricultural experiment involving two factors, say, irrigation and fertilizer, it is organizationally very inconvenient to apply different levels of irrigation to small neighbouring plots. But there is no such difficulty for the application of different levels of fertilizer. To meet such situations it is desirable to have different sizes of the experimental units in the same experiment.

For this purpose first a design with bigger plots to accommodate the factors which require bigger plots. Next, each of the bigger plots is split into as many parts as the number of treatments coming from the other factor. The bigger plots are called main plots and the treatments allotted to them are called main treatments. The constituent parts of the main plots are called subplots and the treatments allotted to them are subplot treatments. The different types of treatments are allotted at random to their respective plots. Such designs are called split-plot design.

The split-plot designs are thus a combination of two or more randomized block designs such that the plots of design form the block of another design. It is possible to have three or more plot sizes to accommodate different types of treatments.

15.1 Advantages and Disadvantages of Split Plot Design

The following are the advantages of the split-plot design.

The split- plot design will have more precision in the estimates of sub-plot treatments and interaction compared to a factorial RBD with two factors.

The split plot design helps in reducing the number of plots. In many cases, it would suffice to have wide border between main plots only. These results in the saving of experimental area and resources devoted to the provision of border rows.

The disadvantages of the split plot design are that the effects of main plot treatments are estimated with less precision than they are in factorial RBD with two factors. The other disadvantage of this design is that the analysis becomes more complex when missing data occur.

The main plots are larger in size than the sub - plots therefore the heterogeneity wills more within main plots than within sub - plots. Hence the experimental error for the main plot treatments will be more than that for the sub - plot treatments.

15.2 Layout and Analysis

First, the replication is then divided into number of main plots equivalent to the main plot treatments. Each main plot is divided into sub - plots depending on the number of sub-plots treatments. The main plot treatments are allocated to the main plots at random as in the case of RBD. Within each main plot the sub-plot treatments are allocated at random as in the case of RBD. This procedure is followed for all replications.

The model for the split- plot experiment in RBD is

$$Y_{ijk} = \mu + r_i + m_j + m_{ij} + s_k + (ms)_{jk} + e_{ijk}$$

where

Y_{ijk} = the observes of ith replication, j^{th} main plot and k^{th} sub-plot.

μ = overall mean

r_i = i^{th} replication effect

m_i = j^{th} main plot treatment effect

m_{ij} = main plot error or error (a)

s_k = k^{th} sub-plot treatment effect

$(ms)_{jk}$ = interaction effect

e_{ijk} = error component for sub-plot and interaction or error (b)

The analysis of variance will have two parts which correspond to the main plots and sub-plots. For the main plots analysis, replication X main plot treatments table is formed. From this two-way table sums of squares for replication, main plot treatments and error (a) are computed.

For the analysis of sub-plot treatments, main plot sub-plot treatments table is formed. From this table the sums of squares for sub-plot treatments and interaction between main plot and sub-plot treatments are computed. Error(a) sum of squares is found out by residual method.

The analysis of variance table for a split plot design in randomized blocks with m main plot treatments and s sub-plot treatments is given in the following table.

Table 15.1 : Analysis of variance for split plot experiment in randomized blocks with factor A in main plots and factor B in sub-plots

Sources of Variation	*df*	SS	MS	F
Replication	r – 1	R SS	R MS	R MS/E MS(a)
A	m – 1	A SS	A MS	A MS/E MS(a)
Error (a)	(r – 1) (m – 1)	E SS(a)	EMS(a)	
B	s– 1	B SS	B MS	B MS/E MS(b)
AB	(m – 1) (s – 1)	AB SS	AB MS	AB MS/E MS(b)
Error (b)	m(r – 1)(s – 1)	E SS(b)	EMS(b)	
Total	rms – 1	TSS		

If F's for the main plot treatments and sub-plot treatments are significant, the SE(d) and CD values are computed for the treatment comparisons.

For comparing two main plot treatments the formula for SE (d) is

$$SE(d) = \sqrt{\frac{2EMS(a)}{rs}}$$

CD = t.SE(d)

Where, t is the table value of t for a specified level of significance, and the error(a) degrees of freedom.

For comparing two sub-plot treatment means we have

$$SE(d) = \sqrt{\frac{2EMS(b)}{rm}}$$

CD = t. SE(d)

Where, t corresponds to error (b) degrees of freedom.

In case of interaction, there are two formulae. For comparing two sub-plot treatments means at a given main plot treatment, the formula for SE(d) is

$$SE(d) = \sqrt{\frac{2EMS(b)}{r}}$$

For computing the CD value, the t value is taken against error (b) degrees of freedom. The other SE(d) formula for comparing two main plot treatment means, either a given sub-plot treatment or at different sub-plot treatment is

$$SE(d) = \sqrt{\frac{2[EMS(a) + (s-1)EMS(b)]}{rs}}$$

The CD is given by

$$CD = t_w \, SE(d)$$

where,

$$t_w = \frac{t(a)EMS(a) + t(b)[(s-1)EMS(b)]}{EMS(a) + (s-1)EMS(b)}$$

where

t(a) = table t value for error (a) df and a given level of significance, and

t(b) = table t value for error (b) df and a given level of significance as for t(a).

Example

An experiment was conducted in split - plot design to study the effect of fertilizer (F) and seed rate (S) on the yield of paddy. The main plot treatments were the seed rate 75, 100 and 125 kg/ha denoted by s_1, s_2 and s_3, respectively. The sub-plot treatments were the fertilizer rates at N:P:K.

75:15:20 = f_1; 75:30:20 = f_4; 75:45:20 = f_7

75:15:40 = f_2 75:30:40 = $f_{5;}$ 75:45:40 = f_8

75:15:60 = f_3; 75:30:60 = f_6 75:45:60 = f_9

and, 50:15:40 = f_{10};

The results are given in the following table.

Table 15.2 : Layout plan and grain yield of paddy in kg/plot

Replication I		
s_2	s_1	s_3
f_5 13.82	f_7 11.05	f_{10} 11.80
f_2 13.21	f_1 9.75	f_7 14.01
f_{10} 11.50	f_6 10.79	f_2 13.58
f_8 14.46	f_9 11.83	f_9 14.31
f_3 13.22	f_2 10.21	f_1 13.16
f_1 12.98	f_3 10.27	f_8 14.22
f_6 13.80	f_{10} 8.06	f_4 13.70
f_4 13.34	f_5 10.66	f_3 13.62
f_7 14.10	f_4 10.53	f_6 13.88
f_9 14.12	f_8 11.96	f_5 13.89

Replication II			Replication III		
s_1	s_3	s_2	s_2	s_3	s_1
f_9 12.31	f_4 13.72	f_{10} 11.30	f_2 13.36	f_8 14.26	f_6 10.48
f_4 10.92	f_7 14.02	f_8 14.06	f_8 14.22	f_6 13.81	f_8 11.82
f_2 10.67	f_1 13.26	f_1 13.12	f_7 14.16	f_{10} 11.96	f_4 10.40
f_1 10.14	f_9 14.18	f_9 14.20	f_4 13.69	f_7 14.04	f_{10} 7.80
f_3 10.79	f_3 13.65	f_7 13.78	f_9 14.01	f_5 13.54	f_1 10.01
f_6 11.31	f_5 13.84	f_2 13.26	f_6 13.92	f_4 13.68	f_9 11.70
f_{10} 8.45	F_8 14.19	f_5 13.65	f_{10} 11.60	f_1 13.31	f_3 10.46
f_8 12.22	f_6 13.91	f_6 13.70	f_1 13.29	f_9 14.40	f_2 10.23
f_5 11.28	f_{10} 12.48	f_4 13.43	f_3 13.48	f_2 13.49	f_7 10.79
f_7 11.44	f_2 13.56	f_3 13.31	f_5 13.81	f_5 13.74	f_3 10.17

From Table 15.2, we compute CF and total sum of squares

CF = 14228.2355

Total SS = 235.9742

From Table 15.2 replication X seed rates table is formed.

R × S Table

	I	II	III	Total
s_1	105.11	109.53	103.86	318.50
s_2	134.55	133.81	135.54	403.90
s3	136.17	136.81	136.23	409.21
Total	375.83	380.15	375.63	1131.61

From Table 15.2 we have

$$\text{R} \times \text{S Table SS} = \frac{1}{10}\left[(105.11)^2 + \ldots\ldots\ldots + (136.23)^2\right] - \text{CF}$$

$$= 14402.9601 - \text{CF} = 174.7246$$

$$\text{Replication SS} = \frac{1}{30}\left[(375.83)^2 + \ldots\ldots\ldots + (375.630)^2\right] - \text{CF}$$

$$= 14428.6703 - \text{CF} = 0.4348$$

$$\text{S SS} = \frac{1}{30}\left[(318.50)^2 + \ldots\ldots\ldots + (409.21)^2\right] - \text{CF}$$

$$= 14428.6703 - \text{CF} = 0.4348$$

$$\text{Error (a) SS} = \text{R} \times \text{S Table SS - Replication SS - SSS}$$

$$= 174.7246 - 0.4348 - 172.7740 = 1.5158$$

From Table 15.2 seed rate × fertilizer rate table is formed

S × F Table

	s1	s2	s3	Total/Mean
f_1	29.90(9.97)	39.39.(13.13)	39.75(13.24)	109.02(12.11)
f_2	31.11(10.37)	39.83(13.28)	40.63(13.54)	111.57(12.40)
f_3	31.23(10.41)	40.01(13.34)	40.81(13.60)	112.05(12.45)
f_4	31.85(10.62)	40.46(13.49)	41.10(13.70)	113.41(12.60)
f_5	32.40(10.80)	41.28(13.76)	41.47(13.82)	115.15(12.79)
f_6	32.58(10.86)	41.42(13.81)	41.60(13.87)	115.60(12.84)
f_7	33.28(11.09)	42.04(14.01)	42.07(14.02)	117.39(13.04)
f_8	36.00(12.00)	42.74(14.25)	42.67(14.22)	121.41(13.49)
f_9	35.84(11.95)	42.33(14.11)	42.89(14.30)	121.06(13.45)
f_{10}	24.31(8.10)	34.40(11.47)	36.24(12.08)	94.95(10.55)
Total	318.50	403.90	409.21	
Mean	(10.62)	(13.46)	(13.64)	

(The values is the parentheses are mean values)

From Table 15.2, we have

$$\text{S} \times \text{F Table SS} = \frac{1}{3}\left[(29.90)^2 + \ldots\ldots\ldots + (36.24)^2\right] - \text{CF}$$

$$= 14461.4401 - \text{CF} = 233.2045$$

$$\text{F SS} = \frac{1}{9}\left[(109.02)^2 + \ldots\ldots\ldots + (94.95)^2\right] - \text{CF}$$

$$= 14284.9961 - \text{CF} = 56.7606$$

$$\text{SF SS} = \text{S} \times \text{F Table SS} - \text{SSS} - \text{FSS}$$

$$= 233.2045 - 172.7740 - 56.7606$$

$$= 3.6699$$

$$\text{Error (b)SS} = \text{Table SS - all other SS}$$

$$= 0.8191$$

Table 15.3 : Analysis of variance

Sources of Variation	*df*	SS	MS	F
Replication	2	0.4348	0.2174	
S	2	172.7740	86.3870	227.934**
Error (a)	4	1.5158	0.3790	
F	9	56.7606	6.3067	414.914**
SF	18	3.6699	0.2039	13.414**
Error (b)	54	0.8191	0.0152	
Total	89	235.9742		

$$\text{SE(d) for S} = \sqrt{\frac{2(0.3790)}{3(10)}}$$

$$= \sqrt{0.025267} = 0.1590$$

$$t(0.05.4) = 2.776$$

$$\text{CD} = (2.776)\ (0.1590) = 0.4414$$

$$\text{SE(d) for S} = \sqrt{\frac{2(0.0152)}{3}}$$

$$= 0.1007$$

$$\text{CD} = (2.005)\ (0.1007) = 0.2014$$

$$\text{SE(d) for S at F} = \sqrt{\frac{2(0.03790) + 9(0.0152)}{3 \times 10}}$$

$$= \sqrt{0.034387} = 0.1854$$

$$t_w = \frac{(0.3790)(2.776)+[9(0.0152)(2.005)]}{(0.3790)+[9(0.0152)]}$$

$$= \frac{1.052104+0.274284}{0.5158}$$

$$= 2.572$$

$$CD = (2572)\ (0.1854) = 0.4768$$

The bar charts for the main plot treatments, sub-plot treatments and the interaction are as follows:

Tabel 15.4 :

		S_3		S_2		S_1			
f_8	f_9	f_7	f_6	f_5	f_4	f_3	f_2	f_1	f_{10}
F at s_1:									
f_8	f_9	f_7	f_6	f_5	f_4	f_3	f_2	f_1	f_{10}
F at s_2:									
f_8	f_9	f_7	f_6	f_5	f_4	f_3	f_2	f_1	f_{10}
F at s_3:									
f_8	f_9	f_7	f_6	f_5	f_4	f_3	f_2	f_1	f_{10}

S at f_1:	s_3	s_2	s_1
S at f_2:	s_3	s_2	s_1
S at f_3:	s_3	s_2	s_1
S at f_4:	s_3	s_2	s_1
S at f_5:	s_3	s_2	s_1
S at f_6:	s_3	s_2	s_1
S at f_7:	s_3	s_2	s_1
S at f_8:	s_3	s_2	s_1
S at f_9:	s_3	s_2	s_1
S at f_{10}:	s_3	s_2	s_1

The conclusions are written on the basis of these bar charts.

15.3 Some Variations in the Split Design

It is also possible to have some variations in the split-plot designs and they are described in the following sections.

More than One Factor in Main Plots or Sub-plots or Both

It is also possible to have more than one factor for main plot and more than one factor for sub-plot also. There may be combinations of two or more factors either in main plots or in sub-plots or in both. In such cases the main plot analysis and sub-plot analysis are carried out as in the case of factorial experiment. For example, let the combination of factors A and B be the main plot treatments; and the combination of factors C and D be the sub-plot treatments. If the levels of the factors A, B, C and D are, a, b, c and d, respectively and if r is the number of replications, the structure of analysis of variance will be as in Table 15.5

Table 15.5 : Analysis of variance for split plot experiment in randomized blocks with two factors each in main plots and sub-plots

Sources of variation	*df*
Replication	r – 1
A	a – 1
B	b – 1
AB	(a – 1) (b – 1)
Error (a)	(r – 1) (ab – 1)
C	(c – 1)
D	(d – 1)
CD	(c – 1) (d – 1)
AC	(a – 1) (c – 1)
BC	(b – 1) (c – 1)
ABC	(a – 1) (b – 1) (c – 1)
AD	(a – 1) (d – 1)
BD	(b – 1) (d – 1)
ABD	(a – 1) (b – 1) (c – 1)
ACD	(a – 1) (c – 1) (d – 1)
BCD	(b – 1) (c – 1) (d – 1)
ABCD	(a – 1) (b – 1) (c – 1) (d – 1)
Error (b)	(ab) (r – 1) (cd – 1)
Total	rabcd – 1

Dummy Plots

Another variation in split plot design is with dummy comparisons among some split plots. Consider, for example, an experiment with different pesticides as main plot treatments and different methods of application of pesticides as sub-plot treatments. In this type of experiment, it is impossible to compare methods of application of pesticides in the main plot representing no application of pesticide (control). Any variation between the sub-plots within the main plot representing control is only due to chance. Therefore, it is assignable to experimental error. Consequently, the error (b) degrees of freedom are altered.

15.4 Split-Split Plot Design

The split-split plot design may be considered as extension of split plot design. The design is used when there are three factors each requiring a different level of precision.

The layout of split- split plot design is similar to split plot design. Each replication is divided into number of main plots. The main plots are divided into sub-plots. The sub-plots are further divided into sub- sub-plots. The less important factor is allocated at random to the main plots; somewhat more important factor to the sub-plots, and the most important factor to the sub-sub-plots. Of course, the requirements of plot sizes for different factors are also taken into account. As in the case of split plot design combination of factors may be accommodated in different plots. Dummy plots are also possible in split-split plot design.

The analysis of split-split plot design is done in three stages, viz., main plots analysis, sub-plot analysis and sub-sub-plot analysis. The breakdown of degree of freedom for split-split plot design will be as shown in the following table 15.6.

The required sums of squares are obtained from appropriate two-way tables. For F tests the respective error mean squares are used.

Table 15.6 : Analysis of variance for strip-split plot design

Sources of variation	***df***
Replication	r – 1
A	a – 1
Error (a)	(r – 1) (a – 1)
B	b – 1
AB	(a – 1) (b – 1)
Error (b)	(r – 1) (b – 1)
C	(c – 1)
AC	(a – 1) (c – 1)
BC	(b – 1) (c – 1)
ABC	(a – 1) (b – 1) (c – 1)
Error (c)	ab (r – 1) (c – 1)
Total	rabc – 1

For a split-split plot design twelve types of pair comparisons can be made, each requiring its own CD value. The required SE(d) values are obtained using the principle applied for factorial experiments and appropriate error mean squares. For interaction the SE(d) formulae are given below:

Comparison between	**SE(d)**
Two A means at the same or different level of B	$\sqrt{\frac{2[E(a)+(b-1)E(b)]}{rbc}}$
Two B means at the same or different level of C	$\sqrt{\frac{2[E(b)+(c-1)E(c)]}{rac}}$
Two B means at the same combination of A and C	$\sqrt{\frac{2[E(b)+(c-1)E(c)]}{rc}}$
Two A means at the same or different level of C	
Two A means at the combination of B and C	$\sqrt{\frac{2[E(a)+(b-1)E\ (b)\ +b\,(c-1)E(c)]}{rbc}}$

In the formulae,

A = main plot treatment

a = number of main plot treatments

B = Sub-plot treatments

b = number of sub-plot treatments

C = Sub-sub-plot treatment

c = number of sub-split plot design sub-plot treatments

E(a) = E MS(a)

E(b) = E MS(b)

E(c) = E MS(c)

Further, it is also possible to consider missing plots in the split-plot design and strip-plot design. But the analyses of the data obtained from these designs are very complex.

Exercise

1. Define "Split plot".
2. State the advantages of split plot design.
3. Explain what is meant by main plot treatment and sub-plot treatment in a split plot design.
4. Explain the concept of dummy plots.
5. Explain the split-split plot design.
6. Show that the split plot design is a special case of a factorial experiment in which all main effects are confounded.

❑❑❑

References

DAS, M.N and N.C.GIRI (1997). '*Design and Analysis of Experiments*', New Age International (P) Limited Publishers, New Delhi.

FEDERER,W.T(1955). '*Experimental design, Theory and Applications*', MacMillan and Co.

KEMPTHORNE, O (1952). ' *The Design and Analysis of Experiments*'. Wiley, New York.

❑❑❑

FSC
www.fsc.org
MIX
Papier | Fördert gute Waldnutzung
FSC® C083411

Kolibri 360 GmbH
Ferdinand-Jühlke-Straße 7
99095 Erfurt, Deutschland
produktsicherheit@kolibri360.de